Joe Weinman's masterful book looks past the hype to offer new insights into the impact of cloud computing. *Cloudonomics* is must-reading for anyone interested in a more analytically based understanding of the cloud's transformative potential.

—Christopher S. Yoo, John H. Chestnut Professor of Law, Communication, and Computer & Information Science and founding director of the Center of Technology, Innovation and Competition, University of Pennsylvania

The cloud is redefining how technology is being used for businesses. *Cloudonomics* is a book that will help you understand the economics and importance of this change and what it means for your industry.

—Om Malik, founder, GigaOM & Structure: the Cloud Computing conference

Cloudonomics

The Business Value of Cloud Computing

JOE WEINMAN

WILEY

John Wiley & Sons, Inc.

Published by John Wiley & Sons, Inc., Hoboken, New Jersey.
Published simultaneously in Canada.

For general information on our other products and services or for technical support, please contact our Customer Care Department within the United States at (800) 762-2974, outside the United States at (317) 572-3993 or fax (317) 572-4002.

Wiley also publishes its books in a variety of electronic formats. Some content that appears in print may not be available in electronic books. For more information about Wiley products, visit our web site at www.wiley.com.

Library of Congress Cataloging-in-Publication Data:

Weinman, Joe, -
    Cloudonomics: the business value of cloud computing / Joe Weinman.
      p.   cm.
    Includes index.
    ISBN 978-1-118-22996-5 (cloth); 978-1-118-28696-8 (ebk); 978-1-118-28402-5 (ebk); 978-1-118-28288-5 (ebk);
      1. Cloud computing—Economic aspects.   2. Information technology—Management.   I. Title.
QA76.585.W45 2012
004.6782—dc23

2012012399

Printed in the United States of America

10 9 8 7 6 5 4 3 2 1

To Paige, Ali, and Sierra

Contents

Preface

In the course of human history, there have been a number of bona fide revolutions in the interdependent arenas of technology, society, religion, economics, and politics: flint tools, money, writing, agriculture, democracy, printing, steam power, capitalism, mass production, telephony, and electricity, to name a few. We are 65 or 70 years into one such revolution—the *information age*—which has permeated every corner of the earth and beyond—from video games to war games to baseball games, and from first-world stock markets to third-world fish markets, to out-of-this-world interstellar probes.[1] Oh yes, and musical greeting cards, talking dolls, and intelligent thermostats too.[2]

Does the advanced age of this advanced age signal impending retirement? Some argue that "the opportunities for gaining IT-based advantages are already dwindling,"[3]; however, this sounds suspiciously similar to alleged pronouncements, such as "everything that can be invented has been invented" or "there is a world market for maybe five computers."[4]

The revolution is accelerating, not slowing.

Technologies such as quantum computing, digital electro-holographic displays, brain-computer interfaces, natural-language interaction via speech-to-text and semantic processing, homomorphic encryption, and new electronic components such as HP's nanoscale memristor, Intel's

---

[1] Michael Lewis, *Moneyball: The Art of Winning an Unfair Game* (Norton, 2003). Robert Jensen, "The Digital Provide: Information (Technology), Market Performance, and Welfare in the South Indian Fisheries Sector," *Quarterly Journal of Economics* 122, No. (2007): 879–924.

[2] www.nest.com/living-with-nest/.

[3] Nicholas Carr, "IT Doesn't Matter," *Harvard Business Review* (May 2003). 81(5) 41–49.

[4] These quotes are of questionable authenticity. See Kevin Maney, "Tech Titans Wish We Wouldn't Quote Them on This Baloney," *USA Today*, July 5, 2005. www.usatoday.com/tech/columnist/kevinmaney/2005-07-05-famous-quotes_x.htm.

three-dimensional chips, and on-chip optical interconnects are still in their infancy. Innovative cognitive computers are now being designed by IBM to use "brainlike" neurosynaptic chips. Other disturbing anomalies, from quantum entanglement to apparently faster-than-light neutrinos, may form the foundation for future disruption.[5]

In this ocean of innovation, *cloud computing* is the latest of successive waves that have eroded the shoreline of prior paradigms, such as the mainframe, the minicomputer, and the personal computer.

Cloud computing is a tsunami of transformation exemplifying Schumpeterian creative destruction: amassing immense wealth for companies that didn't exist a few years ago—such as Google, Facebook, Amazon, Salesforce.com, and Zynga; disrupting long-standing business models and ecosystems including publishing, advertising, television, the recording industry, telecommunications, and retailing; and reordering relationships within the computing industry: among hardware vendors, licensed software vendors, distributors, value-added resellers, and systems integrators, to name a few.

The cloud is both an existential threat and an irresistible opportunity. Virtually any summary of key trends or chief information officer (CIO) focus areas ranks cloud computing at or near the top of the list. A recent Gartner survey of 2,000 CIOs places cloud computing as the number-one technology priority.[6] Most if not all of the rest of the top priorities—virtualization, mobility, collaboration, business intelligence—enable, are enabled by, or otherwise relate to the cloud.

Wharton fellow and author Jeremy Rifkin would consider this to be a natural consequence of "the Age of Access."[7] He has argued that the market economy—in which people own and trade goods—is being replaced by the network economy—where people pay to access them. Why bother owning something if you can access it anytime, anywhere? People don't want drills but the holes that they make; people don't want CDs or applications but the music or functionality that they provide.

Although Rifkin has positioned this trend as something new, in many respects it represents a return to a prior age. After all, the idea of content ownership is relatively new: Before *owning* records, CDs, or MP3s, people *accessed* audio content via the concert hall or radio; before VHS, Beta, or

---

[5] Adrian Cho, "From Geneva to Italy Faster than a Speeding Photon?" *Science*, September 30, 2011, Vol. 333, No. 6051, p. 1809.

[6] Gartner, "Gartner Executive Programs Worldwide Survey of More than 2,000 CIOs Identifies Cloud Computing as Top Technology Priority for CIOs in 2011," *Gartner Newsroom*, January 21, 2011. http://www.gartner.com/it/page.jsp?id=1526414.

[7] Jeremy Rifkin, *The Age of Access: The New Culture of Hypercapitalism, Where All of Life Is a Paid-For Experience* (Tarcher, 2001).

DVDs, there was broadcast and cable television, movie theaters, and, even earlier, plays and operas. In the Age of Access 2.0, however, the logic, characteristics, and payment models are certainly changing. Rather than traveling to theaters and opera halls, the content comes to you; unlike broadcast, it is personalized, contextualized, and on demand.

So the cloud is the *new*, new thing, but what it actually *is*, is a matter of disagreement. Cloud computing, so named by Ram Chellappa of Emory University, is, at a high level, computing that is done *somewhere* out there in an undisclosed location away from your own laptop, smartphone, tablet, or data center.[8] The cloud model applies to the discovery and acquisition of applications, services, and content, such as eBooks from ebookstores; tablet and smartphone apps from app stores; songs from Lady Gaga on Vevo or blockbuster movies on demand; and customer relationship management software executed far from your device. The cloud is at the heart of social networks such as Facebook and LinkedIn, social games such as Zynga's FarmVille, microblogs such as Twitter, and texting, messaging, and mail such as AOL Instant Messenger, RIM's BlackBerry Messenger, Microsoft Hotmail, and Google Gmail. But it also applies to the core infrastructure (computer servers and data storage), the utility software (middleware and databases), and the currency of the digital economy, "big data" (petabytes of information), that together enable those applications to run at the scale of millions or hundreds of millions of users.

Like the parable of the blind men describing an elephant—one feels the legs and says the elephant is like a pillar, the other the tail and says it is like a rope—or perhaps like real cloud gazers—one sees a rabbit, one his Aunt Martha—everyone has a different perspective on the cloud. Some see a new technology, say, virtualization; others, a new silo-busting integrated development and operations model; others, a means of delivering software functionality; still others, an ecosystem that enables applications spanning mobile devices, networks, and cloud-based resources and services. They are all correct in their own way.

For the purposes of this book, however, we consider cloud computing primarily from the business, financial, and economic perspective: *Cloudonomics*, to use the term I coined in the summer of 2008 for Cloudonomics.com and a blog post for the popular technology site GigaOM.com, syndicated to *BusinessWeek*.[9] As such, we consider core characteristics of

---

[8] www.bus.emory.edu/ram/.

[9] Joe Weinman, "The 10 Laws of Cloudonomics," *GigaOM.com*, September 7, 2008, http://gigaom.com/2008/09/07/the-10-laws-of-cloudonomics/. Joe Weinman, "The 10 Laws of Cloudonomics," *BusinessWeek*, September 6, 2008, www.businessweek.com/technology/content/sep2008/tc2008095_942690.htm.

the cloud—on-demand resources, usage-based charging, resource sharing, geographic dispersion, and the like—and how they map to and drive business—and even societal—value.

I would claim that such a perspective is one of the most important ways to evaluate and exploit the cloud, since *unless a technology drives compelling value, it will end up in the dustbin of history*. Remember the CueCat barcode reader?[10]

The value of the core characteristics of the cloud has been proven time and again in domain after domain: hotel chains, airlines, electric utilities, taxi services, manufacturing service providers, and others. Taxis offer transportation capacity on an on-demand, pay-per-use basis. Banks rent resources as well—principal—on a pay-per-use basis—interest. Companies can buy workers' services from what could be called the "labor cloud" either on a flat-rate basis—a salary—or a pay-per-use basis—hourly wages.

Ubiquitous access and location independence are key. When you order a *physical* book from Amazon.com or DVD from Netflix, you don't really need to know what distribution center it was sent from as long as it arrives on time, and when you order an eBook from Amazon.com or stream a video from Netflix, you don't really need to know what data center it came from. Either way, you trust that the provider has figured out the appropriate locations to get you what you want within the time frame that you would like and to which you agree via the terms of service.

In the pay-per-use model of the cloud, we see the same charging model used by hotels and barber shops. In on-demand provisioning, we see the same resource allocation strategy used in accessing energy resources by turning on an electric switch, or financial resources by tapping into a home equity line of credit. Geographically dispersed data centers and content-delivery networks echo the approach used by coffee shops and fast food chains to distribute their wares globally. Resource sharing of computer servers in a cloud data center is not that different from sharing servers—waiters and waitresses—in a restaurant.

These are more than casual analogies; the point is that the same immutable principles—say, resource utilization improvements from demand aggregation or diminishing returns from investments in geographic dispersion for latency reduction—apply *regardless* of domain. I call these the *Laws of Cloudonomics*. The Laws of Cloudonomics are not restricted to cloud computing any more than the Law of Gravity is restricted to apples.

From these parallels—and an analysis of underlying, abstract models—we can determine that there are quite a few characteristics and behaviors

---

[10] Dan Tynan, "The 25 Worst Tech Products of All Time," *PCWorld*, May 26, 2006. www.pcworld.com/article/125772-8/the_25_worst_tech_products_of_all_time.html.

that contravene simplistic thinking, a sort of freakonomics of the cloud. For example, branch expansion is doomed to fail eventually. Rational customers often should be *delighted* to pay *more* for cloud services—really—even when there are *no differences* in characteristics such as performance or security. It can cost nothing to accelerate performance. Even after both heavy and light users switch rate plans from flat rate to pay-per-use or vice versa to save money, a firm or industry can maintain revenues. As the cost of IT plummets, IT spend will stay the same—or increase.

This book doesn't focus on industry market projections or vendor offerings but rather on strategy, business models, customer value, and their relationships. The intent of this book is to be multidisciplinary, seminal, evergreen, rigorous, forward-looking, and irreverent and to appeal to a broad range of customers, prospects, strategists, venture capitalists, investors, technologists, executives, service providers, and academics, both within the field of cloud computing and beyond.

This book is first and foremost *multidisciplinary*, drawing on illustrative industry examples but also a broad range of fields: strategy, economics, psychology, system dynamics, calculus, statistics, computing technology, and theoretical computer science, with forays into botany, biology, and physics. Most readers should find most of the book quite readable, and experts in a variety of fields should find the breadth of *Cloudonomics* of interest.

Second, I hope that much of this book is *seminal*. I believe I've been first to explore a number of areas as they relate to the cloud, such as the architectural implications of cost optimization, analysis of latency for interactive applications using packing of spherical caps, and computational intractability of networked resource allocation.

Third, rather than conducting a *Consumer Reports*–style analysis of ratings of the different vendors and service providers that would be out-of-date before the book is even published, the intent is for the book to be *evergreen* (i.e., usable for a long time to come) in assessing architectural and business alternatives, developing new business models, and incorporating cloud into your own business strategy.

The suffix "-nomics" has been used for important insights into business trends and strategy—Eric Qualman's *Socialnomics* on social media, Ken Doctor's *Newsono*mics regarding the digitalization of news, and Don Tapscott and Anthony Williams' *Wikinomics* covering IT-based collaboration—to the more quantitative *Freakonomics*, presidential economic policies such as Reaganomics, Clintonomics, and Obamanomics, and humorous insurance advertising—Geckonomics. However, *Cloudonomics* is quantitatively rigorous. I've skimmed the surface of much of the math for this volume. However, it is worth noting that most claims are supported by detailed proofs. My research has taken me far afield of "the cloud" and uncovered unusual connections. For example, cell site or content delivery network node placement is related to cannonball stacking, the Tammes problem—solved by evolution—of designing pollen spores, and the Thomson problem of minimum energy electron configurations, which in turn relates to baryon density isosurfaces of Skyrmions, whatever they are.[11]

References are provided to more detailed papers and to my simulation Web site: ComplexModels.com, which provides easy-to-use Monte Carlo simulations illustrating the Laws of Cloudonomics.

Of course, being overly quantitative can lead to precise yet *incorrect* conclusions due to quirks, biases, and anomalies in human behavior, which I will touch on. These experiments have led to more than one Nobel Prize in economics[12] and provide fascinating insights into what Duke University professor Dan Ariely calls "predictable irrationality."[13]

Cloudonomics posits forward-looking scenarios for cloud computing and industry ecosystem evolution and revolution. For example, braking at high speed through a turn on a wet road used to be the domain of professional stunt drivers; now any driver can perform at the same level using standard antilock braking systems (ABS), electronic stability control, and traction control. Similarly, proprietary virtual server provisioning tools, for example, are not likely to offer sustainable competitive advantage to a cloud service provider. This technology is diffusing just like ABS.

Finally, the book is *irreverent*, challenging conventional wisdom. The truth in cloud is often counterintuitive and nuanced; better mental models mean better business and technology strategies and investments.

I hope to provide a lens to view the world of cloud computing economics, so that you can consider my questions and evaluate my arguments but draw your own conclusions. I do not necessarily provide all the answers but present models with which you can perceive, comprehend, and thereby exploit the cloud for your own uses, whether as a customer, service provider, equipment manufacturer, software vendor, venture capitalist, or investor. This is not the end of the dialogue, but the beginning.

---

[11] Gerald Edward Brown and Mannque Rho, *The Multifaceted Skyrmion* (World Scientific Publishing, 2010).

[12] Technically, the Sveriges Riksbank Prize in Economic Sciences in Memory of Alfred Nobel, nobelprize.org.

[13] Dan Ariely, *Predictably Irrational: The Hidden Forces that Shape Our Decisions* (HarperCollins, 2008).

Acknowledgments

A book like this owes so much to so many that it is impossible to fully trace the directed causal graph. First and foremost, however, I'd like to thank the wonderful team at John Wiley & Sons, Inc. Sheck Cho, executive editor at Wiley, immediately saw the potential of this book and has been extremely professional, flexible, insightful, transparent, collaborative, and patient. I'd also like to thank the rest of the terrific Wiley team, especially Natasha Andrews-Noel, Stacey Rivera, and Helen Cho, who helped make this book a reality. Thanks to Bennett Ruiz of AT&T, Barrie Sosinsky, and Hunter Muller of HMG Strategy for helping make the connection with Wiley. And thanks to Zick Rubin and Brenda Ulrich at the Law Office of Zick Rubin, who were both knowledgeable and responsive.

I believe that a book such as this is immeasurably enriched by data. Beyond the extensive references, thanks are particularly due Greg Orelind of Alexa, who kindly permitted the use of the Alexa pageview data illustrating demand variability; Marty Kagan and Greg Unrein of Cedexis for HTTP response time data; Ali Kafel and Dave Connolly of Sonus Networks; Stephan Beckert and Olivia Vandenbussche of TeleGeography; and James Miller of the FCC.

The usual disclaimers apply; I take full responsibility for any errors, which, sadly, have a nonzero probability of existing in a book of this scope.

Any delineation of the main causal path of events leading to my involvement in the cloud would have to include Eric Shepcaro, Allan Leinwand, Om Malik, and Alistair Croll. I worked for Eric beginning at the turn of the millennium when he was AT&T's senior vice president of application networking. We were pioneers in introducing new hosting services—called utility computing at the time—and, thanks to Eric, I was an active participant in Don Tapscott's IT & Competitive Advantage program—the syndicated research effort that led to *Wikinomics* and included in-depth collaboration with a host of thought leaders: Don himself, David Ticoll, Joe Pine, Anthony Williams, Rena Granofsky, Paul Strassmann, Erik Brynjolfsson, Charlie Fine, Mike Dover, and others.

Eric also introduced me to Chris Albinson and Allan Leinwand of Panorama Capital, who invited me to join their Technology Advisory Board. Allan also introduced me to Om Malik. My first official cloud event was Om's Structure, in June 2008, where I was on a panel moderated by Alistair, who asked a number of thought-provoking questions, which in turn led to my first blog posts for GigaOM.com, including "The 10 Laws of Cloudonomics." This book is a 100,000-word-plus expansion of the "Laws" post and a number of others I've done for GigaOM.com.

Om is the epicenter of the cloud, between his own social and professional network, the focus GigaOM.com and GigaOM Pro put on it, and the Structure event, which I've had the pleasure of participating in as MC, moderator, and panelist since its inception. At Giga Omni Media, I've had the good fortune to work with Paul Walborsky, Stacey Higginbotham, Surj Patel, Derrick Harris, Carolyn Pritchard, Celeste LeCompte, Mike Sly, a host of cloud innovators and executives, and the magnificent Magnify Communications team: Stacey Tomlinson, Erin McMahon Lyman, and Jill Short Milne.

Extra-special thanks to Carl Brooks (now at The 451 Group) and Jo Maitland (now at GigaOM) of TechTarget, who were overly kind in naming me to their prestigious list of Cloud Computing Leaders.

I'd also like to thank UBM TechWeb, which owns and operates Interop, Cloud Connect, Light Reading, Heavy Reading, *Information Week*, and the former *Business Communications Review* (*BCR*, now moved online as No Jitter). Particular thanks go to Alistair Croll of Bitcurrent, Eric Krapf of *No Jitter*, and Blair Klein of AT&T. Alistair is always thinking several steps ahead of everyone else, and has been organizing both the Interop cloud summits as well as TechWeb's Cloud Connect, where I've served as track chair of the cloud economics track and had the opportunity to learn from many cloud thought leaders and to work with the TechWeb events leadership and crew: Lenny Heymann, Steve Wylie, Manuela Farrell, Andy Saldana, Paige Finkelman, Amy Jones, and Emily Johnson. Blair is AT&T's social media expert and also PR lead; it was she who originally asked me "Have you ever considered writing anything for external publication?" and suggested *BCR*; Eric Krapf was then editor in chief and published my first cloud article—"The Evolution of Networked Computing Utilities"—before cloud was cool. At Light Reading, special thanks to Ray Le Maistre and Carol Wilson, at *Information Week*, John Foley and Charlie Babcock.

At AT&T Labs, I was also fortunate to work with Ralph Wyndrum, Norm Shaer, Rick Kent, Rudy Alexander, Bernie McElroy, Stan Quintana, Steve Fisher, Sam Glazer, Clayton Lockhart, Tom Siracusa, Dave Belanger, Chuck Kalmanek, Ed Amoroso, Rick Schlichting, and dozens of other technical experts and executives and to interact with literally thousands of AT&T customer executives and their teams—in groups ranging from 1 to 1,000—thanks to executive/sales senior leaders Ron Spears, Donna

Henderson, John Finnegan, Bennett Ruiz, Andrea Messineo, Norihiko Minato, Gopi Gopinath, Bernard Yee, and Andrew Edison; countless excellent country managers; regional sales vice presidents; sales teams; and PR, marketing, events, and legal leads Greg Brutus, Peter J. Butler, June Chan, Fenny Fang, Karen Ko, Mary Beth Asher, Dagmar Hettler-Gentil, Niall Hickey, Donna Cobb, Eileen Whelan, Andrea Montesano, Christine O'Leary, Linda Plesnick, Don Parente, Joanne Murphy, Wendy Weinstein, Janet Wyles, Sara Vincent, and Karen Wentworth. I enjoyed working with AT&T strategy, hosting, and cloud product management executives Bill Archer, Steve Sobolevitch, Steve Mucchetti, Steve Caniano, Chris Costello, Tim Connors, Amy Anderson, Toby Ford, and others. I was fortunate to work with the team at Fleishman Hillard, including Morri Berman, Patrick Yu, Gioconda Beekman, Winnie Leung, and Brad Mays.

At HP, I had the pleasure of working with great colleagues: Erwan Menard, Sandeep Johri, Dave Shirk, Rick Halton, Russ Daniels, Dave Collins, Sybille Schieg-Heimann, Reem El-Tonsy, Julia Ochinero, Andrea Nicole Garcia, Paul Battaglia, Blaithin Underhill, Rebecca Lawson, and Emil Sayegh, as well as my global team and business and technical colleagues. Special thanks to Jujhar Singh for his support in permitting me to work on the book in my spare time and to Jan Tarantino for her critical role. As at AT&T, at HP I also had the pleasure of working with a large group of excellent regional sales VPs, country managers, account teams, and cloud experts too numerous to name. And I also had the superb support of IVORY Europe: Andrea Lee, Kristina Dalborg, Robbie Crittall, and Harry Whitbread.

I've been involved in dozens of cloud initiatives, events, planning committees, and conferences that have helped introduce me to customers with unique problems and insights and cloud thought leaders and innovators. In addition to GigaOM Structure and Techweb/UBM events, I've been fortunate to participate in numerous events and initiatives. Some highlights: Debbie Landa and her team at Dealmaker Media/Under the Radar; George Gilder and Telecosm; Sharon Nakama, Gary Kim, Anamarcia Lacayo, and the rest of the team at the Pacific Telecommunications Council; Frank Gens at IDC and John Gallant at IDG Enterprise; Karen Tucker and the Churchill Club; Stuart Sharrock and Katz Kiely of ICIN and ITU; Tier 1/The 451 Group; CDM Media; TM Forum; IIR/Informa; Cloud Expo; Milken Global Institute; Mobile World Congress; BSS/OSS World; SIIA/All About the Cloud; GDS International; Argyle Executive Forum; Simon Torrance and STL Partners/ Telco 2.0; Capacity Media; SWIFT/Sibos, and IEEE Technology Time Machine conference planners including Rico Malvar, Gerhard Fettweis, Maurizio Decina, and Roberto DeMarco.

I've also learned immensely from the academic/technical community: Special thanks to Ravi Rajagopal, a VP at CA Technologies but also an adjunct professor at NYU Polytechnic and the first to use my Cloudonomics papers in academia; Christopher Yoo, polymath professor of law at the University of Pennsylvania; Michael Lightner, past president of the IEEE and a professor at University of Colorado, Boulder, who gave selflessly of his time in ensuring the rigor and breadth of axiomatic cloud theory; Rico Malvar of Microsoft Research and the IEEE Technology Time Machine team including faculty of the Hong Kong University of Science and Technology; and Lucy Hood of the University of Southern California Marshall School.

The home of cloud computing, via both the invitation-only @Clouderati group and as an extended community is primarily on Twitter, where I am @joeweinman. Most of these individuals are also bloggers, executives, research analysts, CTOs, CIOs, and consultants. A special glue holds this group together, and I consider these leading cloud experts to be not only colleagues but friends and thought-leaders. Literally from A to Z, they are: Vanessa Alvarez, Dave Asprey, David Berlind, Linda Bernardi, Randy Bias, Benjamin Black, Simone Brunozzi, Rachel Chalmers, Sam Charrington, Jean-Luc Chatelain, Adrian Cockcroft, Peter Coffee, Reuven Cohen, Tim Crawford, Simon Crosby, Ellen Daley, William Fellows, Rodrigo Flores, Will Forrest, Mike Fratto, Jay Fry, Vijay Gill, Barton George, Bernard Golden, Charles Golvin, Christofer Hoff, Jason Hoffman, Sam Johnston, Ton Kalker, Jeff Kaplan, John Keagy, Ben Kepes, Michael Krigsman, Maribel Lopez, Bob Lozano, Tom Lounibos, William Louth, Barry Lynn, Lori Mac Vittie, Dave McCrory, Dave McCandless, Brenda Michelson, Marten Mickos, Rich Miller (Data Center Knowledge), Rich Miller (Telematica), Lew Moorman, Ofir Nachmani, Greg Ness, Vinay Nichani, Deb Osswald, Geva Perry, Antonio Piraino, Justin Pirie, Eric Pulier, Elizabeth Rainge, Surendra Reddy, Christian Reilly, Dave Roberts, Guy Rosen, Scott Sanchez, Steve Shah, James Staten, Krishnan Subramanian, Shlomo Swidler, Mark Thiele, Lew Tucker, James Urquhart, Jinesh Varia, Werner Vogels, Simon Wardley, James Watters, John Willis, Dan Young, Jian Zhen, Joe Ziskin.

Thanks to the cloud itself for helping research and connect, not just Twitter, but Google, Google Books, Google Scholar, Alexa, JSTOR, Wikipedia, and hundreds of other online resources such as newspaper and magazine articles.

Final thanks go to my family. To my wife, Carolyn, for helpful editorial comments and for her patience as I spent every night, weekend, and vacation day for six months typing away from behind a wall of books, in the presence of a monotonically increasing list of delayed household projects. To my mother, Elisa, and late father, Joe, for being two wonderful, loving, dedicated parents. Finally, to my daughters, Paige, Ali, and Sierra, for their love and support.

About the cover: The cover illustrates the three perspectives of the book: the real world, shrouded in actual meteorological clouds, symbolizing objectives such as optimized customer experience and issues such as cognitive biases; the world of IT, symbolized by a circuit board; and the abstract mathematics underlying both of them, symbolized by the grid.

CHAPTER 1

A Cloudy Forecast

The cloud—shorthand for "cloud computing"[1]—is transforming all spheres of our world: commerce, entertainment, culture, society, education, politics, and religion. Cloud start-ups are forming on a daily basis, and billions of dollars in wealth are being created as companies craft innovative strategies to exploit this opportunity. Conversely, long-standing corporate icons that have failed to do so are becoming history instead of making it.

The concept of a public cloud—shared, on-demand, pay-per-use resources, accessible over a wide-area network, available to a broad range of customers—might appear to be a recent breakthrough, but there is nothing new under the sun, not even the cloud. The ancient Romans implemented the information superhighway of their time, constructing an unprecedented wide-area network with thousands of route miles of roads, called *viae*, using state-of-the-art engineering, following documented standards.[2] The public network, made of public roads, or *viae publicae*, was complemented by and interoperable with metro networks, the *viae vicinales*, and private networks, the *viae privatae*, creating an Internet of sorts. The roads of the Romans carried people, goods, and soldiers, but, perhaps most important, they also served as a communications network, enabling information, coordination, and control of the far-flung republic and then empire.

These *viae* were multiprotocol networks—carrying pedestrians, animals, carts, military chariots, horses, and their riders—with class of service—military and chariots in the center lane, pedestrians and slower vehicles to the side.[3] Net neutrality was assumed: Any citizen could traverse the *viae publicae* and even had certain rights of passage on the *viae privatae*.[4] By order of Caesar, the core of the network had congestion management: Transport carts were banned from the network core—the narrow, winding streets at the heart of Rome—from dawn until dusk.[5] A complementary architecture was used for streaming content delivery: the aqueducts.

1

A variety of service providers—inns, taverns, posthouses, and the like—became embedded in the fabric of this network, offering value-added services. Each inn—called a *caupona*—offered lodging to travelers on an on-demand, pay-per-use basis: The traveler merely showed up, stayed, and paid. The inns serviced different classes of customers, from peasants to citizens and free men, and there were laws concerning security and limitations of liability. According to an edict issued by the *praetor*, a senior regulatory official of the time, the proprietor, or *caupo*—the cloud service provider of the age—was responsible for ensuring that the traveler's belongings were neither stolen nor damaged while resident at the service provider's facility.[6] Acts of the gods, such as fires, were excluded. Authentication, via the presentation of credentials or tokens, *tesserae hospitalitatis*, was required before service could be rendered.[7] Advertising and branding were important even then. In ancient Pompeii, the Elephant Inn had a logo: a painting of a pygmy defending an elephant entrapped by a snake. The signage also offered capacity status updates: *hospitium hic locatur* (i.e., "inn to let").[8]

Even before Rome, the Greeks had inns, the Persians had public roads, the Assyrians had aqueducts,[9] the Babylonians extended credit, and over 4,000 years ago, during the dawn of Western civilization in Sumeria, the advanced production, facilities, and power technologies of the time—farm implements, water rights, and oxen—were offered for access under a pay-per-use model: leasing. Thousands of years later, in the Middle Ages, knights' armor—the intrusion-prevention hardware of the time—was also leased.[10] It can even be argued that key elements of today's cloud computing environments have been anticipated by early biological systems: ant colonies will determine the shortest path to "content," such as sources of food, and exhibit behavioral plasticity, that is, will dynamically allocate resources—worker ants—to foraging, patrolling, nest maintenance, and midden work, that is, refuse pile maintenance.[11]

Clouds Everywhere

This proven architectural and business model, since applied to modern hotels, electricity, coffee shops, taxi fleets, rental car services, and others, has now come to computing, and in computing—as in meteorology—the cloud these days is covering a lot of ground. Now, as never before, information technology (IT) and cloud computing are having a broad impact.

The cloud is pervading the prosaic patterns of everyday existence. Teens, tweens, and even toddlers are tapping on touch screens or thumb-typing text messages. Even untethered applications, or "apps," need to be purchased and downloaded via a cloud-based app store, but, more important, many applications require additional cloud-based services to function. Natural-language interfaces are enabled by cloud-based speech processing and semantic analysis; search requires the near-infinite processing and storage power of the cloud; social gaming is mediated via the cloud; high scores are uploaded to the cloud; apps and content are updated from the cloud; and status updates, files, photos, videos, reviews, and check-ins are shared via the cloud.

The cloud complements the consumerization of IT, and broadens and deepens its democratization. Businesses used to dictate the desktop, laptop, and software used by employees. But if applications in the cloud process data in the cloud, "bring your own device" is a viable strategy—if not without security and interoperability concerns—potentially reducing corporate expenditures while enabling consumer-employees to make fashion and status statements as well as live a blended work-family lifestyle. Democratization of IT means that not only device access but the creation and modification of applications can expand beyond the IT shop, unleashing a torrent of innovation and motivation through empowerment.

Gaming is moving to the cloud as well. Traditionally, you bought a console and cartridges or discs at a physical store. Then you could order over the Web. Then you could take delivery over the Web, via game downloads from an app store. Then you could use your console over the Internet, with up to four-fifths of gamers using connected consoles to play online, download games, or chat.[12] Now, with "cloud gaming," even high-performance games—formerly requiring advanced consoles built to exploit state-of-the-art computing engines—are being played in real time *on* the net *over* even 3G networks, with polygons and video generated remotely but displayed on relatively low-performance endpoints, such as smartphones.[13] It would be a mistake to consider gaming merely to be the province of, say, 14- to 24-year-old males. Gaming is not only popular across many demographics, but represents the state of the art in everything from interfaces to performance that will trickle down into more mundane business applications. Moreover, "games" can represent a new era in collaboration: A long-standing problem in HIV research—the protein structure of the Mason-Pfizer monkey virus retroviral protease—was recently solved by global players of the online game Foldit, illustrating "the power of online games to channel human intuition and three-dimensional pattern-matching skills to solve challenging scientific problems."[14]

The conduct of commerce is undergoing a revolution, with new players in online retailing, group coupons, video distribution, and blogging—to name a few—dramatically disrupting market ecosystems and driving long-established players out of business, while creating fortunes for some in the process. Behind the scenes, cloud-based collaboration, innovation markets, and contests are enabling companies to tap into the smartest and most creative minds in any field, regardless of geographic location. Procter & Gamble explained the straightforward math[15]: Fewer than 10,000 researchers *within* the firm, 1.5 million *outside*. Or let's go beyond blue-chips: Sites like Mom Invented, which let moms go to market with mechanisms to prevent kids from unrolling toilet paper, are, well, on a roll.[16]

   In short, the cloud is disrupting every dimension of business, whether it is the research, engineering, or design of new products and services; their manufacturing, operations, and delivery; or any point along the customer interface and its myriad moments of truth[17]—branding, awareness, catalog, trial, customization, order processing, delivery, installation, support, maintenance, or returns.

   Consider the customer engagement life cycle and how IT and the cloud can play a role. Positioning, branding, and advertising today often require social media, and product positioning and customer awareness require trials, demos, and virtual tours. In developing solutions to meet customer requirements, cloud-mediated collaboration such as telepresence, 3-D models, electronic whiteboards, and contests can be vital. For product delivery, mobile tracking and installation support are needed. For service delivery, content delivery networks and continuous online connections can be essential. Billing and payment have gone online and mobile. Support and repair can be handled by user-driven knowledge bases, frequently asked questions (FAQs), and online chat. And the returns and recycling processes are being augmented by collaborative consumption, which is creating a cloud-enabled means of recycling, well, everything.[18] This includes eBay but also a plethora of niche sites.

   The cloud can be used to cut costs and to create value. *The New York Times* digitized archival copies of the paper from 1851 to 1980 for customer Web retrieval and was able to convert 11 million articles in less than a day for less than $1,000.[19] *The Washington Post* managed to process 17,481 pages of Hilary Clinton's daily schedule as First Lady in nine hours, for a cost of $144.62.[20] The cost reduction is useful, but these cases are more interestingly viewed in terms of unlocking hidden value and creating a time advantage for reporters to search for scoops. Moreover, the fact that IT was bypassed is both a threat to legacy organizations and an example of the empowerment created by the democratization of IT.

   The cloud is also radically reshaping the relationship among governments, the governed, and nongovernmental organizations, impacting regional balances of power and global stability. Arguably the most powerful man on earth—the President of the United States—has had to enlist Twitter to achieve his political objectives. Meanwhile, other world leaders are in prison, or worse, due to movements initiated and coordinated through cloud-based social networks. Throughout history, there has been an asymmetry between governments—organized megaliths with hierarchical, sometimes autocratic control structures—and their citizens—disorganized, incoherent, Brownian agglomerations with severely limited ability to exert influence, restricted to opinion polls, letter writing, and the occasional election of representatives. And that's in the best case. But increasingly, social media are enabling disparate individuals to behave as a coordinated population, the way that a single action potential—a neuronal voltage spike—can organize individuated muscle cells to throw a knockout punch.

These same trends are rewriting the rules for waging warfare: Why launch missiles when a government—or its agents—can accomplish the same result via an anonymous cyberattack and walk off scot-free? The *entire country* of Estonia—called the "most wired" in Europe—was taken off the net for days, apparently in response to its removal of a commemorative statue from a square a few days earlier.[21] As a result, cyberspace has now become the fifth domain of military operations: after land, sea, air, and space.[22]

U.S. Army General Keith Alexander, head of the U.S. Cyber Command, recently warned that in the future, we can expect cyberattacks to cause power outages and physical destruction.[23] We may not need to wait until the future: The Stuxnet computer worm appears to have been specifically engineered to wreak havoc in Iran's Bushehr nuclear complex, targeting the programmable logic controllers that run advanced machinery.[24] By rapidly speeding up and slowing down nuclear centrifuges, it may have caused thousands of them to blow apart.[25]

The United States has unequivocally stated its policy regarding such cyberattacks: According to the International Strategy for Cyberspace, "the United States will respond to hostile acts in cyberspace as we would to any other threat to our country. We reserve the right to use all necessary means—diplomatic, informational, military, and economic—as appropriate and consistent with applicable international law, in order to defend our Nation, our allies, our partners, and our interests."[26] In other words, a war beginning in the computing cloud might end in a mushroom cloud.

Education is evolving. The Massachusetts Institute of Technology (MIT) was a pioneer in offering Open Course Ware a decade ago, by posting lecture notes on the Web and permitting professors' lectures to be posted as videos. Recently, MIT found a way to leverage the cloud further, by launching MITx, an approach that includes self-paced learning but also interactive online labs and student collaboration and interaction.[27] In an example of MIT deep thinking, it is planning not only to gather research data from the initiative but also to market the underlying platform.

Religion is reforming. By leveraging the social media and information technology of the day—printing—Martin Luther's message, the "95 Theses," was, in effect, retweeted, ultimately driving the Protestant Reformation. Then, as now, short was sweet: Pamphlets could be read and reproduced more quickly than books, causing his message to spread like wildfire.[28]

Today, religion is relocating online: Various sites let users search for prayers by topic, submit prayer requests by e-mail, or meet like-minded singles.

The cloud is impacting and challenging privacy, regulation, and law. How exactly does the USA PATRIOT Act impact a German company hosting Canadian data on U.S. soil? Did any U.S. senators influence Amazon's decision to stop hosting WikiLeaks?[29] Is broadband access a basic human right, as the United Nations International Telecommunications Union Broadband Commission argues?[30] Finland thinks so, mandating 1 megabit-per-second (mbps) access for all 5 million plus citizens, with a 100-mbps minimum soon to follow.[31] Who exactly will pay for these "rights," which account for a substantial fraction of the $300 to $400 *billion* dollars of capital that telecommunications firms invest *annually?* According to Christopher Yoo, a professor of law and director of the Center for Technology, Innovation & Competition at the University of Pennsylvania, the rapid emergence of the cloud is rapidly outpacing a legal and regulatory system designed for an earlier age.[32]

Author and Wharton lecturer Jeremy Rifkin has argued that there are deep cultural trends at work here, as we transition from a capitalist age of ownership and thus markets to an Age of Access. Why waste money and space on owning goods if you can access the benefit that the goods offer? You don't want to own a DVD, you want access to the emotion, engagement, and entertainment that watching a movie can bring. Authors and innovators Rachel Botsman and Roo Rogers have proposed that the dissolution of ownership and the possibilities engendered by the cloud can give rise to an era of collaborative consumption, where goods may be recycled from one "owner" to the next, with such transactions managed via the cloud. I'll trade you my used DVD for your used book. At BookMooch.com—"Give books away. Get books you want."[33]—you type in the title of a book that you have but no longer want, someone else requests it, and you send it to them to earn points, which can then be used to "purchase" other books. Meanwhile, BookMooch uses Twitter as a book status broadcasting medium, indicating, for example, that "The Client: John Grisham" is now available.[34] Services such as SnapGoods—"Want It. Get It. Give It Back"— SwapStyle— the "number 1 fashion swap site" and Airbnb—which lets people "rent from real people in 19,732 cities in 192 countries"—are enabling peer groups of individuals to collectively behave as large service providers or even retailers.[35]

Cashing In on the Cloud

These trends, issues, and opportunities are universal: Is there *anyone* left on the *planet* who doesn't use either Google or Groupon; Facebook or

Foursquare; Yahoo! or YouTube; AOL or Amazon; Twitter or Tencent; or their equivalents? Who doesn't use at least one of e-mail, text messaging, music downloads, music streaming, video streaming, file backup, file sharing, voicemail, telephony, Voice over Internet Protocol (VoIP), instant messenger, video chat, Web meetings, wireless photo frames, netcams, online games, video telepresence, or similar technologies for communications, search, news, weather, gaming, entertainment, shopping, package tracking, hurricane tracking, price comparisons, daily deals, navigation based on real-time congestion, hot bar and restaurant check-ins, or just to launch irate fowls on parabolic arcs to destroy the dwellings of swine or whatever else it is that the hundreds of thousands of apps available from cloud-based online stores do?

Such widespread adoption, in the latest example of Schumpeterian creative destruction, has created immense wealth for vendors, service providers, and other market participants across the cloud ecosystem. This ecosystem comprises endpoints, such as smartphones and tablets but also televisions, sensors, and digital signs; the broadband mobile and fixed networks that carry traffic to and from the cloud; the cloud services and infrastructure required to deliver them; and vendors products and services embedded inside this infrastructure.

For a variety of companies, the cloud is not just *strategic* but *existential*. Some firms owe their very existence to the cloud, whether they call it that or not. Others can blame their demise to a failure to formulate effective cloud strategies. As Amazon accelerated to a market capitalization of over $80 billion, Borders Books became bankrupt. While Google searched for—and found—growth, rapidly returning results that include nearly $20 billion in gross profits on just over $35 billion in revenue annually, leading to a $200 billion market cap, numerous newspapers folded. As Apple's iTunes became a juicy hit, Tower Records tumbled. And as Salesforce.com sold customers on its approach, Siebel sagged.[36]

Companies that didn't even exist a few years ago now have market capitalizations of tens or hundreds of billions of dollars. Although some of this value may be a replay of the irrational exuberance of the dot-bomb era, much of it represents a rational valuation of irreversible secular trends: from atoms to bits, from the age of capitalism to the age of access, and from IT as a topic for academics and engineers to a main focus in the boardroom.

It seems that everyone is exploiting, or at least examining, the cloud. Amazon, BMC, CA Technologies, Cisco, Citrix, Dell, EMC, Facebook, Google, HP, IBM, Juniper, Microsoft, NetApp, Oracle, VMware, and Yahoo!, of course. But you don't need to be a traditional IT player: Walmart is increasingly complementing its Supercenters with Walmart.com. Global telcos—AT&T, Verizon, and BT—and smaller regional ones—Turkcell and Ibermatica, for example—are pursuing their cloud strategies. Barnes &

Noble is designing and distributing computing devices: the NOOK eReaders. Con Edison is becoming a smart-grid utility. Pfizer has moved half its workloads to the cloud. Eli Lilly recently ran a complex 64-processor bioinformatics task at a cost of just over $6, not much more than a burger and a soda.[37]

Beyond Business

If you are reading this book, you probably already know that such applications must be delivered out of enormous data centers, the size of one or more football fields, specially sited based on low power and cooling costs, leveraging state-of-the art broadband fiber and fourth-generation networks that connect such data centers to advanced technology endpoints such as high-definition smartphones and tablets. Or must they?

In fact, while you may think of these as advanced applications only for use in the developed world, emerging affordable mobile technologies, hardened, containerized data centers, and new middle earth orbit satellites will enable cloud-based applications *just about anywhere in the world*. It's not just smartphones that can sit in the palm of your hand; new technologies can place a wireless base station—formerly the size of a closet, if not a car—into that same palm. Alcatel-Lucent, for example, recently announced its lightRadio device, which looks like a bronze Rubik's cube but can process thousands of simultaneous cell phone calls over a multisquare-mile area and fit in your pocket.[38]

Solar-powered data centers in power-efficient containerized pods coupled with these mobile technologies mean that cloud services can be dropped into the middle of nowhere and provide end-to-end services: endpoint, network, and cloud, *even if there is a complete lack of power and network infrastructure*. Even without these advances, cloud-based services are already driving a dramatic transformation of all aspects of economy and society globally.

Examples from India, Japan, and Kenya show the breadth of applicability of a wide variety of services using a variety of cloud-based technologies.

In India, the fishermen of Kerala would arrive at various coastal markets at dawn with their catch, only to find that there was a glut—other fishermen had already arrived at those markets with *their* catch, and customers had already bought their desired quantity. Due to the lack of refrigeration, they would have to sell their fish at well-below-market prices or throw it away.

The advent of mobile telephony and short message service (SMS), that is, texting, which broadly speaking are cloud services, transformed this situation.[39] Once fishermen could determine which coastal markets would offer the best price and assess price differentials in light of fuel costs, shortages and surpluses were dramatically reduced. In short, the cloud can enable the proper and efficient functioning of even the simplest markets.

In Miyakonojo, in Miyazaki Prefecture, Japan, Shinpuku Seika is a "farm," actually comprising 300 individual plots across almost 250 acres. Using several cloud-based and mobile/wireless technologies, a variety of capabilities have been implemented that have increased crop yields and therefore revenues and profitability.[40] Wireless temperature and humidity sensors deployed throughout the acreage determine which plants need more irrigation. Mobile cameras are used to capture videos of potentially diseased crops for review by horticultural experts. Mobile tracking technology ensures that farmhands do not fall asleep in the fields.

Joe Pine and James Gilmore, authors of *The Experience Economy*, have posited that there is an evolution of business value under way: from commodities, to products, to services, to experiences, and ultimately to transformations.[41] For example, coffee beans are a commodity, priced lower than a product such as packaged coffee, which is priced lower than a service from a coffee shop, which is priced lower than an "experience," such as dining in a chic café. Each of these drives higher value and thus revenue and margin. The price of the coffee in a cup might be pennies as beans, a dime or two packaged and branded on your store shelf, a few dollars at a coffee shop, and $10 or more consumed on the Champs-Elyseés. Pine and Gilmore suggested that commodities are extracted, products are manufactured, and services are delivered, but experiences are *staged*.

At the top of their hierarchy are customized experiences leading to individual transformations, where "the customer is the product." These are experiences offering not only ephemeral enjoyment and entertainment but a transformation of the individual: a fitness membership, a graduate education, or life-saving surgery.

Cloud services are offering increasingly engaging experiences, ranging from immersive games exploiting motion sensing, video compositing, and virtual and augmented reality, to telepresence and even virtual worlds. But perhaps we can extend Pine and Gilmore's "transformations" even further, beyond individuals into societies. Such social transformation may be viewed as good business—"doing well by doing good"—supporting communities through sustainability, charity, and educational efforts. However, beyond the realm of business, there is no doubt that "social transformation" encompasses more than mere commercial experiences and sets the context for the society in which business must operate and individuals must live.

In Kenya, Ushahidi was cofounded by Juliana Rotich, currently executive director of the organization, to enable anyone with a basic mobile phone to easily report geo-tagged information and in turn get alerted to the status of a given area.[42] Originally deployed after contested elections and official government reporting of questionable accuracy, Ushahidi has allowed ordinary citizens in dozens of countries to become better informed and thus better protected from political unrest, crime, or natural disaster.

Ushahidi originally required a software install but has since evolved to a fully cloud-based solution called Crowdmap. As a result, ease of use has been enhanced, and Crowdmap can be—and has been—rapidly deployed for emergencies such as the Haitian earthquake relief effort.

According to Rotich, several principles are at the core of Ushahidi/ Crowdmap:

- A nonhierarchical *community* forming around an issue, such as crimes or election results
- *Sharing*, via not just the Web but SMS and e-mail and coupled with routing and analysis
- *Collaboration*, such as matching those who need assistance with those who can offer it
- *Context*, for example, acquiring, filtering, and presenting information based on location

It's not just nongovernmental agencies that are creating societal value. The City of Miami has built a similar system using cloud technologies, enabling residents to view nonemergency requests graphically on a map. Instead of a multi-month development and implementation time, the city was able to prototype the system in a week.[43]

And, according to John Dillon, chief executive officer of Engine Yard, cloud-based platform as a service offers not just a cost and time reduction benefit for IT operations but has real social impact as well.[44] For example, Case Commons used Engine Yard to deploy an innovative application called Casebook to provide cutting-edge, Web-based technology to replace public, state-level, child welfare enterprise systems. Such systems have the potential to help thousands of children in the U.S. foster care system.

Some governments are finding that the cloud can be essential to achieving social transformation via political means. At just after 4 P.M. on the afternoon of Tuesday, December 20, 2011, with most of Congress already home or headed that way for the holidays, in an attempt to force a divided Congress to pass a two-month extension to payroll tax cut legislation, U.S. President Barack Obama (@BarackObama) and the White House (@White-House) tweeted "What does #40dollars mean to you?" accompanied by a photo of two twenty dollar bills.[45]

Less than 72 hours later, the president signed the extension into law, after gaining the "unanimous consent" of Congress.[46] Seventy-two hours! Who has ever heard of any organization, much less government, moving that quickly? Forget e-government, we have entered the age of c-government: government of the people, by the people, for the people, via the cloud.

Conversely, other leaders are finding that the cloud has not been their friend, enabling populations with long-simmering issues to amplify their anger and coordinate their actions.

Facebook and Twitter have been credited with enabling the Arab Spring of peaceful—and not-so-peaceful—regime change from autocratic leadership toward greater freedom and democracy. According to the *Arab Social Media Report* from the Dubai School of Government, 90% of "Egyptians and Tunisians . . . were using Facebook to organize protests or spread awareness about them."[47]

There is also a more sinister side: the BlackBerry Messenger—enabled London flash mobs during the summer 2011 riots.[48] In any case, there is no doubting the power of today's technology. Cloud-based social networks, microblogs, and messaging services are having an impact as great as Paul Revere's midnight ride or the invention of gunpowder.

These megatrends and specific examples—India, Japan, and Kenya; Washington, D.C., London, and Cairo; Facebook, Twitter, and Angry Birds— all have the cloud in common. Given the importance of such services, you might think that all the kinks have been worked out, especially since issues in IT delivery are no longer just IT problems but corporate brand problems, leading to immediate loss of revenue, negative publicity and thus loss of brand equity, and customer churn. Well-publicized outages occasionally occur, however, these are likely to be growing pains, not insurmountable barriers, and an increasing number of customers and users are using the cloud in some fashion.

Clarifying the Cloud

What in the world is the cloud? Although there is perhaps no term with as many definitions, for this book we define the cloud with a helpful mnemonic, C.L.O.U.D., reflecting five salient characteristics:

> **C**ommon infrastructure
> **L**ocation independence
> **O**nline accessibility
> **U**tility pricing
> on-**D**emand resources

It is *common*, in that it uses pooled resources and dynamically shared infrastructure; *location-independent*, in that the service should be ubiquitous and responsive; *online*, that is, accessed over a network; a *utility*, creating value and with usage-sensitive pricing; and *on-demand*, that is, with the right quantity of the right resources available exactly and only when needed.

Some of the behind-the-scenes technologies supporting cloud computing are relatively new—for example, virtualization and automated bare-metal provisioning. This book does *not* delve into these assorted technologies. What we do investigate is the universal principles that have applied since the Roman Republic and are applicable to today's businesses.

These principles are applicable to the ancient *cauponae* and today's hotel chains, taxi fleets, airlines, electric utilities, and lenders. Hotels offer "utility," "pay-per-use," or "usage-sensitive" pricing: More rooms for more nights cost more. Electric utilities and taxi companies offer "on-demand" service—flick a switch or raise your hand and service magically appears. Whether data networks, the electric grid, or highways including the Appian Way, online networks make resource sharing and thus pay-per-use possible. And global dispersion—whether content delivery networks or thousands of corner coffee shops—ensures that location does not matter in meeting user experience targets.

Farther On

This book is written somewhat sequentially, but there is no reason not to jump straight to a chapter that is of interest as chapters are largely self-contained.

In the next few chapters, we look at IT and cloud computing in the context of competitive strategy and explore different use cases for which the cloud is particularly well suited—and those for which it is not. A review of the conventional wisdom regarding the cloud should help puncture some common myths—or at least make you think twice.

We look at the properties of pay-per-use pricing and on-demand resources, the conditions under which such charging and provisioning drive value—various combinations of unpredictability and variability—and architectural implications.

We examine the increasing importance of proximity, and the economics of dispersion in enhancing the user experience, then delve into the trade-offs between consolidation and dispersion and thus between processing time reduction and latency reduction.

We touch on behavioral economic concerns for and against cloud adoption, skimming the surface of the rich and often surprising field at the intersection of psychology, neuroscience, and economics.

We delve more deeply into advanced valuation of cloud patterns such as communications and markets, considering not just cost but topics such as the expected marginal value of an additional participant in a market.

Finally, we wrap our discussion up and draw conclusions regarding the evolution of cloud technology and the cloud ecosystem. The next decade is likely to bring untold innovation: as Don Tapscott, consultant, best-selling author, and an adjunct professor at the University of Toronto's Rotman School of Management, has claimed, "The cloud is becoming a global computation platform—a computer of sorts—and every time we use it we program it."[49]

Summary

The core ideas behind the cloud business model may be thousands of years old, but cloud *computing* is new and transforming all aspects of personal life, business, and society. The most exciting thing about the cloud is in how it can create value and transform traditional economic assumptions. For example, companies have challenges in managing variable and unpredictable demand. Traditional approaches shifted the locus of the problem without addressing it in any way, much like blowing your fallen leaves onto your neighbor's lawn. However, the cloud creates genuine economic value in unique ways. The interplay between multiple customers and one or more cloud service providers ameliorates many challenges facing companies today. We explore everything from strategy to statistics in the coming chapters.

Notes

1. Some differentiate between "cloud computing" and "cloud services." These distinctions are largely unnecessary for the purposes of this book.
2. Roads were to be 8 feet wide if straight, 16 feet if curved. Gregory Aldrete, *Daily Life in the Roman City: Rome, Pompeii and Ostia* (Greenwood, 2004), p. 36.
3. William Kaszynksi, *The American Highway: The History and Culture of Roads in the United States* (McFarland & Company, 2000).
4. Adolf Berger, "Encyclopedic Dictionary of Roman Law," *Transactions of the American Philosophical Society* 32, Part 2 (1953): 763.
5. Jerome Carcopino, *Daily Life in Ancient Rome* (Yale University Press, 1940), p. 49.
6. Sir William Smith, ed., *Dictionary of Greek and Roman Antiquities*, 2nd ed. (Taylor and Walton, 1848), p. 258.
7. W. C. Firebaugh, *Inns of Greece and Rome* (Benjamin Blom, 1928), p. 41.
8. August Lau, *Pompeii: Its Life and Art* (Macmillan, 1899), p. 392.
9. Peter J. Aicher, *Guide to the Aqueducts of Ancient Rome* (Bolchazy-Carducci, 1995).

10. Richard Dorf, ed., *The Technology Management Handbook* (CRC Press in conjunction with IEEE Press, 1999).

11. Deborah M. Gordon, "The Regulation of Foraging Activity in Red Harvester Ant Colonies," *The American Naturalist*, Vol. 159, No. 5, May 2002, pp. 509–518, www.stanford.edu/~dmgordon/gordon2002.pdf.

12. Eira Hayward, "Game Changing," *Capacity* (April 2011).

13. Nick Wingfield, "Phones Get Game Power in the Cloud," *New York Times*, December 8, 2011. www.nytimes.com/2011/12/08/technology/phones-and-tablets-getting-game-power-in-the-cloud.html.

14. Firas Khatib, "Crystal Structure of a Monomeric Retroviral Protease Solved by Protein Folding Game Players," *Nature*, Structural & Molecular Biology Advance Online Publication, September 18, 2011. www.cs.washington.edu/homes/zoran/NSMBfoldit-2011.pdf.

15. Henry Chesbrough, *Open Innovation: The New Imperative for Creating and Profiting from Technology* (Harvard Business School Press, 2003).

16. Nicole Laporte, "If These Moms Can't Find It They Invent It," *New York Times*, December 25, 2011. www.nytimes.com/2011/12/25/business/if-moms-cant-find-it-they-invent-it.html.

17. Jan Carlzon, *Moments of Truth* (HarperBusiness, 1989).

18. Rachel Botsman and Roo Rogers, *What's Mine Is Yours: The Rise of Collaborative Consumption* (HarperBusiness, 2010).

19. Derek Gottfrid, "Self-Service, Prorated, Supercomputing Fun," *New York Times*, November 1, 2007. http://open.blogs.nytimes.com/2007/11/01/self-service-prorated-super-computing-fun/; David Hilley, "Cloud Computing: A Taxonomy of Platform and Infrastructure-Level Offerings," College of Computing, Georgia Institute of Technology (April 2009).

20. Amazon Web Services, "AWS Case Study: Washington Post." http://aws.amazon.com/solutions/case-studies/washington-post/. Accessed April 6th, 2012.

21. Joshua Davis, "Hackers Take Down the Most Wired Country in Europe," *Wired*, August 21, 2007. www.wired.com/politics/security/magazine/15-09/ff_estonia?currentPage=all.

22. United States Department of Defense, "Department of Defense Strategy for Operating in Cyberspace" (July 2011). www.defense.gov/news/d20110714cyber.pdf.

23. Bill Gertz, "Computer-Based Attacks Emerge as Threat of Future, General Says," *Washington Times*, September 13, 2011. www.washingtontimes.com/news/2011/sep/13/computer-based-attacks-emerge-as-threat-of-future-/.

24. Robert McMillan, "Was Stuxnet Built to Attack Iran's Nuclear Program?" *PCWorld*, September 21, 2010. www.pcworld.com/businesscenter/article/205827/was_stuxnet_built_to_attack_irans_nuclear_program.html.

25. William J. Broad and David E. Sanger, "Worm Was Perfect for Sabotaging Centrifuges," *New York Times*, November 18, 2010. www.nytimes.com/2010/11/19/world/middleeast/19stuxnet.html.

26. The White House, "International Strategy for Cyberspace: Prosperity, Security, and Openness in a Networked World." www.whitehouse.gov/sites/default/files/rss_viewer/international_strategy_for_cyberspace.pdf. Accessed May, 2011.

27. "MIT Launches Online Learning Initiative," MITnews, December 19, 2011. http://web.mit.edu/newsoffice/2011/mitx-education-initiative-1219.html.

28. "Social Media in the 16th Century: How Luther Went Viral," *The Economist*, December 17, 2011. www.economist.com/node/21541719.

29. Geoffrey A. Fowler, "Amazon Says WikiLeaks Violated Terms of Service," *Wall Street Journal*, December 3, 2010. http://online.wsj.com/article/SB100014240 52748703377504575651321402763304.html.

30. Randall Lane, "The United Nations Says Broadband Is Basic Human Right," *Forbes*, November 15, 2011. www.forbes.com/sites/randalllane/2011/11/15/the-united-nations-says-broadband-is-basic-human-right/.

31. Saeed Ahmed, "Fast Internet Access Becomes a Legal Right In Finland," *CNN*, October 15, 2009.

32. Christopher Yoo, conversation with the author, December 30, 2011.

33. http://bookmooch.com/.

34. http://twitter.com/#!/bookmooch/.

35. http://snapgoods.com/. www.swapstyle.com/. The Green Samaritan, "Consume Less/Share More = Access Economy: Takeaway from Sustainable Brands '11." http://thegreensamaritan.com/2011/06/consume-lessshare-more-access-economy-takeaway-from-sustainable-brands-11/. www.airbnb.com/.

36. Alorie Gilbert, "Rivals Vie for Siebel's Customer Spoils," *CNET News*, September 27, 2002. http://news.cnet.com/Rivals-vie-for-Siebels-customer-spoils/2100-1017_3-959878.html.

37. "Take a Load Off: The Age of Cloud Computing," DrugDevelopment-Technology .com, November 21, 2011. www.drugdevelopment-technology.com/features/featuretake-a-load-off-the-age-of-cloud-computing//.

38. "[Full version] LightRadio News Conference [London, February 7, 2011]." www .youtube.com/watch?v=m0BDL61dYVQ&feature=relmfu.

39. Robert Jensen, "The Digital Provide: Information (Technology), Market Performance, and Welfare in the South Indian Fisheries Sector," *Quarterly Journal of Economics* 122, no. 3 (2007): 879–924.

40. Daisuke Wakabayashi, "Japanese Farms Look to the 'Cloud,'" *Wall Street Journal*, January 18, 2011. online.wsj.com/article/SB1000142405274870402970457608 7910899748444.html.

41. B. Joseph Pine II and James H. Gilmore, *The Experience Economy: Work Is Theatre and Every Business a Stage* (Harvard Business School Press, 1999).

42. Juliana Rotich, conversation with the author, November 22, 2011.

43. Ashlee Vance, "The Cloud: Battle of the Tech Titans," *Bloomberg Businessweek*, March 3, 2011. www.businessweek.com/magazine/content/11_11/b42190525 99182.htm?chan=magazine+channel_top+stories.

44. John Dillon, conversation with the author, January 29, 2012.

45. http://twitter.com/#!/whitehouse/status/149237000522825729/photo/1/large.

46. Colleen Curtis, "President Obama: Extending Payroll Tax Cut Is a 'Boost We Need Right Now,'" *The White House Blog*, December 23, 2011. www .whitehouse.gov/blog/2011/12/23/president-obama-extending-payroll-tax-cut-boost-we-need-right-now.

47. Carol Huang, "Facebook and Twitter Key to Arab Spring Uprisings: Report," *The National*, June 6, 2011. www.thenational.ae/news/uae-news/facebook-and-twitter-key-to-arab-spring-uprisings-report.

48. Josh Halliday, "London Riots: How BlackBerry Messenger Played a Key Role," *Guardian*, August 9, 2011. www.guardian.co.uk/media/2011/aug/08/london-riots-facebook-twitter-blackberry.

49. Don Tapscott, conversation with the author, November 9, 2011.

CHAPTER 2

Does the Cloud Matter?

Does IT generally, and the cloud in particular, really matter? A majority of respondents to a recent survey have the cloud on their radar, but apparently only 7% consider it critical.[1] Is that prioritization appropriate? Is the cloud strategic, or just a way to purchase and finance mere plumbing? To some the answer is obvious, but as much as those of us active in the cloud space might wish to respond with an unqualified "yes," the answer requires some thought and due diligence. Moreover, there may not be a single answer: The role and value of the cloud ultimately depend on a variety of firm-dependent factors, such as strategy, the competitive environment, and organizational design and processes.

IT investments by companies now appear to have been definitively linked with productivity increases. However, productivity increases may not necessarily result in profitability or market share increases: If every competitor in an industry is 20% more productive, each could retain those gains—increasing the so-called producer surplus and profitability—or may pass the gains on to consumers—increasing the consumer surplus—as lower prices, in an attempt to undercut the competition and gain share. If all market players execute similar strategies, market share may remain static; this is the Red Queen hypothesis, which has been proposed to explain how, even when different species evolve, they maintain the same relative fitness.[2] As Lewis Carroll wrote, "It takes all the running *you* can do, to keep in the same place. If you want to get somewhere else, you must run at least twice as fast as that!"[3] This has led some to question whether IT—via the cloud or otherwise—can deliver strategic competitive advantage.

Before we can assess whether cloud computing is strategic, we need to consider several things. First, what is "strategy," and what does being "strategic" mean? Second, "cloud computing" is both "cloud" and "computing." Before we can determine whether the "cloud" variation of IT is

17

strategic, we need to determine whether IT itself is strategic or, to be even more properly objective and skeptical in the pursuit of truth, ask whether there is *any* return whatsoever from IT investments. We then need to assess the marginal value created from *cloud* implementations of IT above and beyond the value from *traditional* implementations of IT and show not just a *correlation* between competitive success and basic IT plus cloud value-add but also *causality*.

We also must ask what "competitive success" is. Is it comparative revenue growth? Market share growth? Relative customer satisfaction? Customer churn reduction? Relative market capitalization? Cost reduction? Short or long term? And what do we consider "investment in IT"? Is it capital expenditures? Payrolls for training of systems engineers, enterprise architects, developers, and testers? Training of other users? The cost of process changes that accompany system implementations? Expenses for leases and public cloud services? Time spent in IT-related vendor selection and business development? All of the above?

Suppose we define success as profitability and contrast firms in terms of their IT capital expenditures. The first question we might ask is whether there is any correlation: Are firms that tend to invest more in IT more profitable? This simple question immediately presents a challenge, because simple investment does not imply use: Many people invest in treadmills and gym memberships but are still out of shape. Even if used, there may be a time delay between investment and payoff. After all, an investment in a home gym does not lead to abs of steel immediately after unpacking, but only after months or perhaps years of use. There may be complicating factors: The nicest set of weights won't do much without the right *process*: sets, reps, schedule, form, recovery, nutrition. Likewise, an investment in IT hardware may not compensate for poor systems engineering or development processes or a lack of alignment between business and IT.

Moreover, profitability is partly a function of the intensity of competitive rivalry. A monopoly with terrible processes and systems may be much more profitable than a role model of managerial excellence and IT deployment in a perfectly competitive market achieving razor-thin margins.

Even if there *is* a correlation between investment and competitive success, it does not necessarily signify a causal relationship. It *could* be that exploiting a strategic investment in IT was the foundation of successful companies' market dominance. Or it might just be that those firms that are more profitable—for reasons having nothing to do with IT—end up throwing away substantial money on unproductive investments, including IT. Many profitable firms have shiny office towers with extensive investments in lovely polished marble lobbies, but the marble is probably a result—rather than the root cause—of their success.

Productivity Paradox

The empirical data concerning whether IT generates any return has been a challenge to analyze. Robert Solow, a winner of the Nobel Prize in economics who has made a specialty out of studying the relationships of inputs to outputs in national economies, humorously remarked in 1987 that "you can see the computer age everywhere except in the productivity statistics."[4] In other words, mainframes, minis, and even PCs were increasingly being deployed, but it wasn't clear that they were having any impact on business results. In fact, some posited that IT was having a negative effect on productivity improvements, due to the time spent learning and transitioning over to new systems and applications. For example, Jeremy Greenwood and Boyan Jovanovic, professors of economics at the University of Rochester and NYU respectively, argued that "implementation is not free" and that IT projects require investment not only in capital equipment but human capital as well.[5]

In attempts to resolve the productivity paradox, studies were conducted on the impact of IT on economies, industries, and individual firms, and have looked at dozens of variables and metrics, IT capital, non-IT capital, sales growth, market share, labor costs, inventory holding costs, chief information officer (CIO) experience, percentage of IT budget spent on new products and services, and the like.[6] Sometimes use of IT led to no benefits, sometimes it led to significant gains in productivity but not profitability, sometimes it needed to be combined with process improvement such as reengineering, and so forth, with every study suggesting a different set of benefits or the lack thereof.

Several factors were proposed to account for those situations in which no benefits appeared to correlate with IT investment and for conflicting results. The sample size in some studies may have been too small to be statistically significant. Or the payoff from investments might take years to realize, the same way that a correlation between unhealthful behaviors and life expectancy may take a longitudinal study to demonstrate causality. Or IT investment may have been misplaced; it's not just investment per se that is required, but investment in specific areas aligned with business strategy. Or mere investment might be too coarse a metric: Perhaps we should consider actual usage and adoption. And, although accounting records may accurately define investment, how do we accurately capture usage? Event logs may capture that a user was logged in to a corporate system, but was he actively reviewing information or on a conference call during that time? Or it may be too difficult to control for noise or other issues: Enron may have made excellent use of IT to implement sophisticated trading algorithms, but that didn't overcome other corporate governance issues.

By the nineties, studies concluding that there were productivity gains attributable to IT began to appear. For example, two economists from the Federal Reserve Board, Stephen Oliner and Daniel Sichel, had rigorously examined the data and explained away the earlier productivity paradox: IT investment had not made much impact because "computing equipment still represented a small fraction of the total capital stock."[7] Oliner and Sichel, using U.S. Bureau of Labor Statistics and Bureau of Economic Analysis data including hedonic price indexes—"quality" adjustments that incorporate effects such as Moore's Law—argued that the then-recent productivity gains were attributable to both the *use* and *manufacture* of IT, including software and communications gear. In other words, a substantial portion of the significant gains in the U.S. economy were partly due to the purchase, implementation, and use of IT and also partly due to gains in production efficiencies in the IT sector of the economy: say, using fewer people to manufacture more computer chips or PCs. Only the former is relevant to our discussion here, of course. Oliner and Sichel showed that computer hardware, software, and communications equipment were responsible for well over a third of the productivity gains.

Erik Brynjolfsson, a professor at the Massachusetts Institute of Technology's Sloan School of Management and also director of the MIT Center for Digital Business, together with colleagues, such as Lorin Hitt of the Wharton School, University of Pennsylvania, also conducted a substantial amount of research in this area. Even with the plethora of data available, Brynjolfsson and Hitt warned that "productivity in the information economy has proven harder to measure than it ever was in the industrial economy."[8] However, after substantial research, they have arrived at a number of insights.

Most important, they identified a statistically significant correlation between IT investment and productivity improvement. Yes, Virginia, there *is* a meaningful return to IT. In fact, after looking at the data as well as a variety of other studies, they concluded that "IT has a positive and significant impact [that is] quite high."

However, they also noted that the average conceals a wide disparity in results: Some firms have little to show for their investment; others are wildly successful. Your mileage may vary. Merely having millions of dollars of computing equipment delivered to your loading dock accomplishes nothing; it is how this investment is convolved with business processes and reengineering, business strategy, and organizational redesign that matters: Brynjolfsson and Hitt attributed about half of the gains from IT to linkages with the unique attributes of each firm. Finally, they observed that gains don't happen overnight: Long-term benefits with IT investments were two to eight times larger than the short-term benefits.

One other point: "Productivity" may not measure a variety of intangibles. The fact that someone playing solitaire on a tablet might be "happier" than he would be staring at the wall—or seatback in front of him—or that someone using a graphical Web interface might experience less job stress or eye strain than when using a green screen is not something easily measured by productivity statistics.

Competitiveness Confrontation

So, based on the latest data, the productivity paradox appears to have been resolved: IT can be a good investment and has helped the economy and individual firms. But, to paraphrase the Red Queen Hypothesis, *even though a rising tide may lift all boats, that doesn't help any of them win the race.* IT may be a good thing, but is it strategic? Can it help firms successfully compete over the long haul?

Nicholas Carr didn't think so. In a much-discussed article in the *Harvard Business Review* that later led to a full-length book, he argued that "IT Doesn't Matter."[9] To oversimplify his argument—which is well worth a read, whether you agree or perhaps specifically if you *do* disagree—he claimed that "[a]s information technology's power and ubiquity have grown, its strategic importance has diminished."[10] In other words, IT can't be strategic, because it is a ubiquitous commodity, like pork bellies and frozen orange juice. Cloud computing itself wasn't around when he wrote the article, but he did anticipate "utility" models in his piece and lumped electricity together with IT. Electricity is certainly useful and no doubt enhances productivity. However, he essentially argued, it would be hard to find a company that had developed a strategic competitive advantage due to its mastery of electricity. Certainly, ensuring an uninterrupted supply is valuable, and cost-effective supply contracts are important to the degree to which they are a fraction of the cost structure of the business, but, Carr argued, these are just not *strategic*.

The lineup of distinguished academics, CIOs, researchers, analysts, commentators, and practitioners who disagreed with Carr drove the *Harvard Business Review* to publish a collection of rebuttals online.[11] It included John Seely Brown, the former chief scientist of Xerox, now at Deloitte and the University of Southern California, and John Hagel, also now at Deloitte. They called the article "dangerous." F. Warren McFarlan and Richard Nolan, both professors at the Harvard Business School, castigated Carr, saying "couple not knowing that you don't know with fuzzy logic, and you have the makings of Nicholas Carr's article." Paul Strassmann, known for his research into the business value of IT and former CIO of Kraft, Xerox, General Foods, NASA, and the Department of Defense, called Carr's recommendations "mistimed" and "abortive," summarizing a lengthy point-by-point rebuttal by observing that "information technologies are too important to be pronounced irrelevant." Steven Alter, a professor at the University of California, San Francisco, argued that "'IT Doesn't Matter' conveys a fallacy."

The original article and the lengthy rebuttals are well worth a read. Carr has done the entire community a service by asking the question and fostering debate.

However, there are numerous issues with the Carr piece, such as his claim that "IT is, first of all, a transport mechanism—it carries digital information just as railroads carry goods and power grids carry electricity." Perhaps that is true of data communications; it is not necessarily true that such is the main focus of IT in general. He also argues that "IT is also highly replicable. Indeed, it is hard to imagine a more perfect commodity than a byte of data," confusing the replicability of *data* with the lack of replicability of proprietary trade secret or patent-protected *algorithms* implemented in *software*—one-click ordering, for example—not to mention the challenge of successful implementation and operations.

Ignoring those details, however, at its heart such an argument is somewhat akin to the calculations proving that bumblebees can't fly.[12] The calculations are no doubt sophisticated, leveraging deep insights of very intelligent people, yet such positions are difficult to maintain in the light of empirical evidence and specific examples. Arguing that companies can't develop strategic competitive advantage using IT—and the cloud—is like arguing that, since steel and gunpowder are commodities, no army can possibly win a war. Since weapons and soldiers are available to all, and most armies are not dominant, this logic would suggest that weapons and soldiers "don't matter" in winning wars.

Using a similar argument, we could posit that no firm can achieve competitive advantage through *any* means: After all, every firm has access to people, plant, equipment, processes, and capital. Trade secrets, patents, and other intellectual property wouldn't matter, because one could argue that every firm has equal access to inventors and serendipity. This logic misses the point that firms have unique cultures, develop proprietary processes, have uneven access to capital, talent, and markets. Different firms have different market positions and growth prospects because of the way that they *uniquely* leverage the same things that are available to everyone and thus impact their own destiny. To put commodities in context, pork bellies may be a commodity, but a Michelin three-star restaurant extracts more value out of them than the average corner diner does.

In war, those with access to the same technologies, whether spears or stealth bombers, can win or lose based on how they employ those technologies on the battlefield. When the battleground is business, those with access to the same IT infrastructure technologies, including cloud delivery, can win or lose based on how they deploy IT in the context of resources, strategy, shifting customer requirements, technology evolution, and the competitive and regulatory environment.

The argument that IT doesn't matter misses the forest for the trees: The trees are individual servers and storage systems and load balancers and wide-area network acceleration gear and sensors and microchips; the forest is how these components are creatively combined and defined by software to support the implementation of strategy. The greater part of what makes a business differentiated today is its products/services and processes. It is hard to find a product or service that has not been digitalized and "informatio- nalized"[13] (i.e., enriched via information), and a process that is not embodied in some way through automation and IT. Cars have OnStar; greeting cards have recording and playback mechanisms; light bulbs incorporate Wi-Fi; dryers sense humidity; thermometers calculate digitally; thermostats adapt to preferences and sense occupancy. In services, enter- tainment companies generate movie recommendations, games incorporate artificial intelligence, posted videos foster additional text and video responses, smartphones converse via natural language. Outside of a few markets, say, that for pet rocks, how in the world could IT possibly be any *more* essential—and strategic—than it is today?

As Brynjolfsson and Hitt observed a decade ago, "As computers become cheaper and more powerful, the business value of computers is limited less by computational capability and more by the ability of managers to invent new processes, procedures and organizational structures that leverage this capability."[14] Or, as John Seely Brown and John Hagel put it, while "IT may be ubiquitous . . . the insight and ability required for it to create economic value are in very short supply."[15]

Consider a number of iconic examples over the past decades: Inditex, AMR, Goldcorp, Harrah's, Google, and Facebook.

IT certainly mattered to Amancio Ortega, founder of Inditex, one of the world's largest fashion design, manufacturing, and retail houses. He is cur- rently the seventh richest person in the world, with a personal fortune valued at $31 billion. Inditex has 5,000 stores, across several brands, including Zara. Zara is synonymous with "fast fashion," an approach to retailing that treats retail not as a one-way means of distribution but a rapid, information-intensive closed-loop feedback cycle where customer needs and market trends are rapidly responded to, leading to the right inventory of the right fashion at the right place, eliminating or minimizing "fashion risk." IT is what makes it work, as frequent store feedback on inventories and customer requests is rapidly aggregated and fed to production scheduling systems. Zara's cycle time from design to sale is a few weeks; that of its competitors, nearly a year.[16]

Another classic example: American Airlines, when it introduced the first airline reservation system: SABRE. When it spun off the technology as a business the reservations system was already worth several billion more than the airline's operations.[17] Today, Sabre Holdings—popularly known for its Travelocity brand—is vibrant; AMR—the parent company of American—has declared bankruptcy and been rated last in customer service.[18]

IT also mattered to Rob McEwen, chief executive officer (CEO) of Goldcorp, who leveraged IT generally—geological software, three-dimensional visualization, and data mining—and cloud-based co-opetition specifically—via an Internet-enabled contest called the GoldCorp Challenge—to enable a partnership of two Australian companies to win just over $100,000. Oh, and it also enabled GoldCorp, at the time with deeply serious cost and revenue issues, to increase gold production from barely over 50,000 ounces annually to over *500,000* ounces annually, at a *sixfold* reduction in cost.[19] In the past decade, production at the original Red Lake mine has grown another 200,000 ounces, and GoldCorp has plowed its profits and acumen—and algorithms—into acquisitions of other proper-ties.[20] IT, coupled with gold prices recently crossing $1,500 an ounce, led a once-ailing company to help reach its current market capitalization of nearly $40 billion, with earnings now surpassing $1 billion annually. Is this a sus-tainable competitive advantage? Perhaps not forever. Was it strategic? How could it not be?

IT mattered to Gary Loveman, CEO of Harrah's, who used sophisticated data mining, analytics, and experimentation to tune promotions and maxi-mize revenue per gamer, increasing revenues dramatically even in flat markets. As Loveman put it, "[I]nformation in our database, coupled with decision-science tools that enabled us to predict individual customers' the-oretical value to us, [allowed us] to create marketing interventions that profitably addressed players' unique preferences. The more we appealed to these preferences, the more money the customers would spend with us."[21]

IT mattered to Larry Page and Sergei Brin, founders, billionaires, and executives at Google. With nothing more than an algorithm—PageRank, some lines of code for a research project called "BackRub," and some bor-rowed servers—no capital, no brand, no advertising, no factories, no dis-tributor relationships, not even a nugget of an idea for monetization—they took over a market with entrenched competitors and created a global powerhouse out of, well, thin air.[22]

IT certainly mattered to Mark Zuckerberg, who founded Facebook with not much more than a laptop and a few lines of code and a prototype called Facemash coded as a lark in an evening.[23] The initial public offering valued the company at roughly $100 billion.[24]

Did or might competitors catch up with some of these firms eventually? Sure, but that is not a criticism of IT; it is a comment on the nature of competition and the impermanence of advantage in fast-moving markets. Strategy does not equate to eternity. Arguments such as Carr's confuse "strategic" with "sustainable" and incorrectly conflate IT commodity infrastructure with the innovative uses to which such a general-purpose technology can be put. In today's world, even strategic advantages may be ephemeral: The duration of advantage is a combination of technology evolution, barriers to entry, legal and regulatory protection, and much more. As Joseph Clark, Omar El Sawy, and Francis Pereira of the University of Southern California's Marshall School of Business have observed, in the current environment of Internet speed, global turbulence, and accelerating technological development, "competitive advantage is short-lived. Strategies are perishable, whether attained by first-mover advantage, advantageous positioning vis-à-vis the marketplace, or unique capabilities."[25]

However, to the extent that a company can significantly differentiate itself—even for only a short while—it can be argued to have developed a strategic advantage: literally, an advantage—over its competitors—based on its strategy—its approach to organizing assets and competencies to achieve a goal in the face of adversaries. Such an advantage can then lead to first-mover advantage, learning curve effects, and network effects that enhance sustainability.

Moreover, the fact that the same computer processors, memory chips, servers, and storage may be available to all is irrelevant. Even Carr acknowledged that there is a difference between what he calls "infrastructural technologies" and "proprietary technologies." IT generally and cloud computing specifically are a mix of both. At the software level, proprietary algorithms and designs for everything from book and movie recommendations, to angry bird characters, to oilfield drilling, to drug discovery can confer advantage. And today, even the hardware is not a commodity: Leading companies are tweaking components ranging from motherboard designs to cooling systems.

In addition, while IT does not inexorably lead to sustainable competitive advantage, it is surely true that—as the Red Queen observes—lack of IT to maintain parity can lead to decline, bankruptcy, or extinction. Can you imagine a global airline today being successful that didn't allow ticket purchases over the Web or didn't use automated flight and crew scheduling algorithms? An overnight package delivery company that didn't track packages, optimally plan routes, or extract efficiencies by optimally loading delivery trucks? A pharmaceutical company that didn't evaluate a molecule's potential efficacy or have automated record keeping on lots and suppliers? A brokerage firm that went up against program traders with pencil and paper?

For a time in the history of physics, the most eminent practitioners used analogies such as waves of water in the ocean and waves of sound in the air to develop a theory that light traveled through a medium as well: the luminiferous ether. They used sophisticated arguments that were all plausible, until Albert Michelson and Edward Morley conducted elegant experiments showing empirically that no such ether could be detected.

The argument that IT doesn't matter is a theoretical and philosophical argument—if all firms have access to the same things, none can be different—that, like the ether theory of light, flies in the face of empirical data and is thus meaningless in the face of today's competitive battlefield and the reality of examples such as Google's $200 billion IT-based, cloud-exploiting market cap, market dominance, and exceptional profitability. The logic is of little consolation to the former executives, employees, investors, and customers of the now-bankrupt and liquidated Borders Group, whose strategy failed in the context of Amazon.com's (retail operations) superior use of IT and the cloud.

Summary

In a world of hypercomplexity, hypercompetition, and hyperconnectivity, and one in which the economy is increasingly virtual and services based, information is the key to data-driven decision making, simplification, con-textualization, personalization, and differentiation. Information technology is the embodiment of a firm's ability to exploit information, and the cloud can offer unique implementations of such technology that otherwise would be difficult, if not impossible.

However, the important lesson for CIOs is that IT, or the cloud, by itself, may not accomplish very much. It is important to determine how cloud adoption aligns with the strategy of the business and its Web of relationships and complements other changes to products, processes, people, and part-ners. In the next chapter, we focus on the strategic value of the cloud, not just IT.

Notes

1. "Cisco CloudWatch Summer 2011," *Loudhouse*, www.cisco.com/cisco/Web/UK/pdfs/Cisco_CloudWatch_Summer2011_V3.pdf.
2. Leigh van Valen, "A New Evolutionary Law," *Evolutionary Theory* 1 (1973): 1–30.
3. Lewis Carroll, *Alice in Wonderland, and Through the Looking Glass* (Lothrop, 1898).
4. Louis Uchitelle, "Economics View; Productivity Finally Shows The Impact of Computers," *New York Times*, March 12, 2000. www.nytimes.com/2000/03/12/

business/economic-view-productivity-finally-shows-the-impact-of-computers
.html.

5. Jeremy Greenwood and Boyan Jovanovic, "Accounting for Growth," University
   of Rochester Working Paper No. 475, July 2000. http://rcer.econ.rochester.edu/
   RCERPAPERS/rcer_475.pdf.

6. Sarv Devaraj and Rajiv Kohli, "Performance Impacts of Information Technology:
   Is Actual Usage the Missing Link?" *Management Science* 49, No. 3 (March 2003):
   273–289.

7. Stephen D. Oliner and Daniel E. Sichel, "The Resurgence of Growth in the Late
   1990s: Is Information Technology the Story?" May 2000. www.federalreserve
   .gov/pubs/feds/2000/200020/200020pap.pdf.

8. Erik Brynjolfsson and Lorin Hitt, "Beyond the Productivity Paradox: Computers
   Are the Catalyst for Bigger Changes," *Communications of the ACM*, August,
   1998, (41)8, pp. 49–55.

9. Nicholas Carr, "IT Doesn't Matter," *Harvard Business Review* (May 2003), (81)5,
   pp. 41–49, and Nicholas Carr, *Does IT Matter? Information Technology and the
   Corrosion of Competitive Advantage* (Harvard Business School Press, 2004).

10. Ibid.

11. Thomas Stewart, John Seely Brown, John Hagel III, F. Warren McFarlan, Richard
    Nolan, Jason Hittleman, Paul Strassmann, Marianne Broadbent, Mark McDonald,
    Richard Hunter, Bruce Skaistis, Vladimir Zwass, Mark S. Lewis, Tom Pisello, Roy
    L. Pike, Vijay Gurbaxani, Steven Alter, Cathy Hyatt, Chris Schlueter Langdon, and
    Nicholas G. Carr, "Does IT Matter? An HBR Debate," *Harvard Business Review*
    Web Exclusive, June 2003. www.johnseelybrown.com/Web_Letters.pdf.

12. David E. Alexander and Steven Vogel, *Nature's Flyers: Birds, Insects, and the
    Biomechanics of Flight* (Johns Hopkins University Press, 2004).

13. To "digitalize" can denote "to administer digitalis," but I am using it to mean the
    embedding of digital technologies, and "informationalize" to mean the embed-
    ding and exploitation of information. "Digitize" connotes the conversion of data
    to digital form.

14. Erik Brynjolfsson and Lorin M. Hitt, "Beyond Computation: Information Tech-
    nology, Organizational Transformation and Business Performance," *Journal of
    Economic Perspectives* 14, No. 4 (Fall 2000): 23–48.

15. Stewart et al., "Does IT Matter?"

16. John A. Dawson, Roy Larke, and Masao Mukoyama, *Strategic Issues in Inter-
    national Retailing* (Routledge, 2006).

17. www.spinoffadvisors.com/articles/barrons041299.htm.

18. Scott McCartney, "The Airline That Loses Bags, Cancels Flights," *Wall Street
    Journal*, January 5, 2012. online.wsj.com/article/SB10001424052970204331304
    5771407403891945901.html.

19. Linda Tischler, "He Struck Gold on the Net (Really)," *Fast Company*, May 31,
    2002. www.fastcompany.com/magazine/59/mcewen.html?page=0%2C1.

20. http://goldcorp.com/.

21. Gary Loveman, "Diamonds in the Data Mine," *Harvard Business Review* (May
    2003): 109–113.

22. David A. Vise and Mark Malseed, *The Google Story: Inside the Hottest Business, Media and Technology Success of Our Time* (Bantam Dell, 2005).

23. Ben Mezrich, *The Accidental Billionaires: The Founding of Facebook, A Tale of Sex, Money, Genius, and Betrayal* (Doubleday, 2009).

24. Shayndi Raice, "Facebook Sets Historic IPO," *Wall Street Journal*, February 2, 2012, http://online.wsj.com/article/SB1000142405297020487900457711078007833 10366.html.

25. Joseph W. Clark, Omar A. El Sawy, and Francis Pereira, "Capabilities, Configurations and Customer-Contexts: A Business Model Framework for the Process of Digital Service Innovation," *Pacific Telecommunications Council Conference Proceedings*, January 2012. www.ptc.org/ptc12/images/papers/upload/PTC12_Telco%20WS_Sawy_Pereira%20(Paper).pdf.

CHAPTER 3

Cloud Strategy

As we discussed in the last chapter, one school of thought argues that IT—and thus the cloud—is a commoditized utility: Like running water or electricity, it's nice to have but hardly strategic. This argument fails to explain the runaway success—in market capitalization, revenues, and profits—of the leading cloud service providers such as Google and Facebook. However, the popularity of the cloud and rebranding of everything as "cloud" has generated its own backlash; chief information officers (CIOs) can be forgiven for a note of caution in pursuing the cloud. But paralysis by analysis can be dangerous, because the world is accelerating to warp speed, and the cloud can play a vital role in supporting competitive strategy.

Hunter Muller is an author and the founder and chief executive officer (CEO) of HMG Strategy. He runs exclusive workshops for CIOs around the country that provide a forum for peer-to-peer best-practice sharing and executive dialog on CIO issues. According to Muller, the cloud continues to be a priority topic for this community:[1] CIOs are grappling with the issues and implications of the cloud as well as defining and refining their cloud strategies.

Moreover, according to Ravi Rajagopal, adjunct professor at New York University and vice president of cloud strategy and solutions and advisor to senior client executives at CA Technologies, CIOs today have deep interest in cloud yet are wrestling with defining, deriving, and measuring accurate quantitative benefits that scale and evolve with changing business requirements. Rajagopal observes that getting basic unit cost components for infrastructure and applications that are necessary to baseline the current environment, streamline business processes, and evaluate economic feasibility of commercial cloud services can be daunting.[2]

Insanity or Inevitability?

Larry Ellison, the founder and CEO of Oracle, claimed at one point that the cloud was "gibberish," "insane," and "idiocy."[3] It's difficult to dismiss out of hand the perspective of the fifth richest person in the world, with a fortune recently valued at about $40 billion.[4]

And, after evaluating nearly 2,000 technologies, Gartner, one of the most respected IT research and analyst groups, recently singled out cloud computing as a technology at the "Peak of Inflated Expectations" using its "Hype Cycle" assessment methodology, which has been used "since 1995 to highlight the common pattern of overenthusiasm, disillusionment and eventual realism that accompanies" new technologies.[5]

Nicholas Carr, former executive editor of the *Harvard Business Review*, who, perhaps because he has claimed that *IT Doesn't Matter* and thus is an easily outsourced commodity, nevertheless projected a *Big Switch* to ubiquitous cloud computing.[6]

A CIO can be forgiven for some degree of confusion, given the articulate spokespersons for opposing points of view. And there is truth to these different perspectives: Cloud may well be overhyped, but it is demonstrably creating value. Some computing may be a commodity and thus shift to the cloud, but perhaps the cloud can also be wielded strategically. Cloud computing can be a ubiquitous, democratizing commodity; a tactical necessity; a strategic differentiator; or even of *existential* import.

As a number of companies found out during the dot-bomb explosion, it can be dangerous to dismiss traditional business principles and metrics such as revenues and profits. And yet there are tantalizing hints that digital businesses, such as the cloud, are challenging some of those assumptions.

As Dr. Francis Pereira, an adjunct professor at the University of Southern California Marshall School of Business, and his colleagues observed, firms are eliminating some traditional means of developing competitive advantage—such as unique capabilities, exclusive partnerships, or protected intellectual property—in favor of new models, where partnerships are dynamic and based on platforms; services aren't "delivered" but co-created with customers and partners; these services don't have value until the customer applies them in context; and the way to make money can be by giving things away, as hardware vendors do with open source software.[7]

Pereira also observed that in today's world, business and technology can't be strategized separately; they are irrevocably intertwined. To merely staple on the term "digital" to prior businesses leads to what he and his colleagues call the "horseless carriage fallacy," in which the strictures of prior paradigms constrain innovation.[8]

Democratization of IT

Cloud further democratizes IT. Computing used to be restricted to a few disciples granted admission to the inner sanctum of the glass house data center. Along came the PC, and anyone in the company could use *standard* applications, such as word processing, graphics, and spreadsheet tools. Now the cloud has unleashed creativity, innovation, and experimentation. YouTube enables you to "Broadcast Yourself,"[9] and Flickr lets you "Share your life in photos."[10] Moreover, cloud-based platform as a service (PaaS) enables virtually anyone to break through the limitations of a handful of packaged software programs and write their own: This is not just the democratization of the *use* of IT enabled by the PC and desktop software but the democratization of the *creation* of IT, something akin to the way the television democratized the use of moving pictures but the video camera democratized their creation.

Chris Anderson, serial author and editor-in-chief of *Wired* magazine, popularized the phrase "the long tail," referring to shifts in consumption—particularly relevant to information goods—associated with stockless and thus costless inventorying and frictionless distribution via web-based ordering and recommendation engines.[11] John Dillon, the CEO of Engine Yard, a cloud PaaS company, called this democratization the *long tail of IT*, noting the wide variation in use cases—and users—of Engine Yard's platform. Moreover, as with Zara's "fast fashion," in which new styles are rapidly designed, tested, sold, and retired, Dillon observed that this can lead to "fast failure"—a good thing—as innovation cycles are accelerated; the faster the failures, the sooner the successes.[12] Conversely, a failure to keep pace means that you're out of the race. Early.

Strategists, consultants, and authors John Hagel III, John Seely Brown, and Lang Davison have argued that overall competitive success can arise from many small things done well, using the example of skilled Maui surfers who made many small improvements to their technique to excel at their sport.[13] This perspective mirrors the Japanese spirit of *kaizen*: continuous improvement. The breadth of the long tail of IT can support this type of approach.

However, beyond many small improvements that may add up over time to an edge, isn't there anything more that the cloud can do? After all, there's more to competition than letting 100 flowers blossom; some firms owe their success to the cloud; others their demise to a failure to embrace it. Cloud may be important in the long tail, but it also may be strategic, and although some firms may benefit from a pull approach, it would be nice to know whether the cloud could support strategy in a more profound and coherent way.

Industrialization of IT

Author and technology prognosticator George Gilder has called today's cloud data centers "information factories."[14] This is a wonderful parallel, since the cloud can be viewed in part as representing the industrialization of IT and the end of the era of artisanal boutiques. Many of the lessons learned in the evolution of manufacturing are being applied—consciously or not— via the cloud.

In the same way that some product companies such as Apple focus on design but leverage upstream supply chain partners such as Foxconn for actual manufacturing operations, companies can leverage cloud providers to do the "operations" of IT.[15] Most companies also partner downstream for logistics and distribution: even global consumer packaged goods giants such as Procter & Gamble (P&G) don't operate their own cargo lines or retail stores; they use commercial shipping and distribute via a shelf or two at retailers such as Walmart. Using a cloud content delivery provider or getting a shelf or two in a server rack in a colocation, hosting, or cloud provider is similar.

In a reflection of the way that firms use a mix of employees, part-time workers, temporary or seasonal help, and outside contractors with specialized expertise, they can use a mix of owned equipment, virtualized resources, on-demand pay-per-use resources, and software as a service providers, with such software often encapsulating specialized expertise. Whether for human resources or IT resources, such a hybrid balances cost, flexibility, and risk.

Best practices from manufacturing correspond to cloud-based IT. Just-in-time manufacturing is akin to on-demand resources. Setup time reduction corresponds to virtual server provisioning time reduction. The convergence of design engineering and manufacturing engineering via "design for manufacturability" is similar to the "DevOps" movement, which dissolves the boundaries between software designers and developers and IT operations.[16]

In manufacturing, production lines that were uniquely optimized for a given product succumbed to flexible manufacturing cells, which were not only more fungible but also supported elastic production in the face of shifting product demand. In IT, general-purpose cloud architectures may not necessarily be optimized for a given application, but their flexibility reduces the time to get into production and the application's elasticity. Such flexibility required a focus on technologies such as computer numerical control and shop-floor control systems, corresponding to the automation of management and administration of today's information factories.

Manufacturers focused on reducing and standardizing parts through group technology and parts catalogs; IT organizations can do the same through the use of components available through PaaS and service catalogs.

The use of product platforms, such as Chrysler's K-car, mirrors the use of software platforms.

The Japanese philosophy of *kaizen* and spirit of *monozukuri*, which provide the motivation to "produce excellent products and the ability to constantly improve a production system and process," are embodied in the attention to detail that cloud providers must have.[17] Mark Thiele is executive vice president at Switch, Inc., and president and cofounder of Data Center Pulse, an organization of data center professionals. It would be hard to find someone who knows more than he does about data center design and operations. Switch operates data centers in the hot Nevada climate and has developed fundamental innovations to operate in such an environment, including adaptive systems that change the proportion of outside air used based on characteristics such as temperature, humidity, and purity. As Thiele has said, "[E]ven the coat of paint on a data center can make a difference."[18]

Such a focus on tactics and operations can ultimately be strategic, as Toyota demonstrated in its rise to become number one in global automobile manufacturing due in no small part to the Toyota Production System.[19] But the cloud can be strategic in many ways beyond production operations excellence.

Strategy

What is strategy, anyway? Edward Luttwak, a senior fellow at the Center for Strategic and International Studies, has stated that the word is used to mean everything from doctrine, to practice, to theory.[20] Generally, however, Luttwak observed that there are two key dimensions: a "horizontal" dimension related to the interactions between adversaries actively opposed to each other's objectives and a "vertical" dimension relating the macroscopic to the minute: grand strategy to theaters, operations, tactics, and technologies. Although focused on military strategy, Luttwak's insights are directly applicable to competitive strategy as well.

The leading figure in competitive strategy is arguably Michael Porter, a professor at Harvard Business School and the author of numerous books on strategy. Porter has distinguished between *corporate strategy*, the approach used in defining the portfolio of businesses that a company will have, and *competitive strategy*: how each business unit with a relatively holistic product portfolio will compete against others in a specific market.[21]

To understand the difference, consider General Electric (GE). At the firm level, GE makes decisions regarding the collection of business units that it comprises: aircraft engines, locomotives, healthcare, financial, and others. Under former CEO Jack Welch, GE developed a corporate strategy—and a basis for action—oriented around each unit being either number 1 or 2 in its industry. This formed the basis for acquisition or divestiture of units and other corporate-level investments. This is *corporate* strategy.

Disciplined frameworks have been developed to aid such decisions, such as the Boston Consulting Group Growth-Share Matrix, which assesses a company's units in two dimensions: market growth and market share.[22] It builds on the PIMS database—Profit Impact of Market Strategies—which has found a correlation between high market share and high profitability.[23] A unit in a high-growth industry that commands high market share and thus high profitability, for example, is a "star." Conversely, high-share business in a low-growth industry is a "cash cow." A low-share, low-growth "dog" wastes management time and attention and reduces overall profitability; thus, it is a candidate for divestiture. The fourth case, a "question mark" or "problem child," with low share in a high-growth industry, requires careful assessment as to whether it will become a dog when industry growth slows or can be nurtured into becoming a star. From a business portfolio and corporate strategy perspective, one might use the cash generated by the cash cows to fund investments in either stars or question marks.

Below the level of the firm, there are business units and their *competitive* strategies. GE, Porter might argue, does not compete with Rolls-Royce plc or Philips. But its aircraft engine division *does* compete with the corresponding one at Rolls-Royce, and its light bulb division competes with the one at Philips.

The head of the aircraft engine unit must decide how to sell more engines and make a higher profit on each one, while his or her counterpart at the Rolls-Royce aircraft engine unit is plotting to do the same. A new titanium alloy? Greater investment in marketing? Cutthroat pricing to build market share and become incorporated into the next generation of aircraft? Creating collaborative innovation councils with aircraft manufacturers to better determine features for the next generation?

To oversimplify Porter's work, it posits that any business can compete using one of three generic strategies: by offering products at a lower cost, with differentiated features, or based on focusing on a market niche.

Other frameworks exist, such as one from consultancy Kepner-Tregoe, who advised that companies need to focus on a specific "Driving Force": "products (or services) offered; markets served; low-cost production; operations capability; method of sale (and/or distribution), technology; natural resources; and return/profit."[24] A products-offered approach would entail finding new markets for existing products (e.g., Arm & Hammer selling baking soda not just as a baking product but as a refrigerator deodorizer), whereas a markets-served strategy might involve Neiman-Marcus looking for additional luxury items to sell to its existing set of affluent customers.

Authors and strategy consultants Michael Treacy and Fred Wiersema didn't use the term "strategy" but "value disciplines" and suggested that there are three: customer intimacy, operational excellence, and product leadership.[25]

Yet others advise that the formulation of strategy requires innovation outside of the current constraints and assumptions of the industry—recommending the pursuit of Blue Oceans—new market spaces where differentiation and low cost may be simultaneously achieved—and the pursuit of bold ideas through Big Think strategies.[26] It is important to note, however, that the process of strategy formulation, by intuition or structured framework, incremental or bold, in existing markets or new ones, does not alter the conclusion that a firm must have some source of difference to achieve an advantaged outcome.

Generally, these strategy gurus often—although not always—argue that a firm is best served by selecting one strategy to focus on rather than being "stuck in the middle." There have been dozens, if not hundreds, of variations on these ideas, and numerous critiques as well. Our purpose is not to argue the fine points but to leverage the high-level insights.

The Cloud: More than IT

Earlier we suggested that cloud computing was both cloud and computing. We argued that IT mattered: It can be just plumbing, but it can also play a key strategic role. The cloud variation of IT can also be just technical or tactical—a way of provisioning a few servers—but it may be argued that it can be strategic as well. To understand how, we'll use Treacy and Wiersema's value disciplines framework.

When Treacy and Wiersema referred to *customer intimacy*, they meant precise market segmentation and offers that are personalized and contextualized to the customer. Cloud computing can clearly fit here: Consider Amazon's book recommendations or Netflix's movie recommendations. The cloud model is of the essence: Each individual having a personal movie history locked away in their desk drawer would accomplish nothing. Hundreds of millions—if not billions—of ratings all actively—"rate what you just watched"—or passively—based on patterns of purchases or viewing—collected via the cloud and processed using sophisticated "big data" algorithms are what do the trick. Using the cloud to enhance customer intimacy can be strategic: It increases value, by providing information products that customers are more likely to enjoy; increases revenue, by recommending products that customers end up buying; and reduces cost, due, for example, to customer churn. Moreover, it creates "customer intimacy" in the true sense of the phrase: Amazon, Netflix, and Pandora "know" you the way that your hairstylist or bartender knows things about you that no one else does. Such activities shift the pattern of interaction from point transactions to a deep and long-lasting relationship.

Today, thanks to the cloud and the Internet, we can achieve what could be termed *frictionless intimacy.* Netflix can examine my movie-watching behavior, Amazon my book-buying behavior, and iTunes or Pandora my music-listening behavior, the same way that my barber, Jerry, examines my haircut preferences and thereby guide recommendations to me. What Netflix, Amazon, and Pandora do to foster their relationship with me requires no additional effort on my part (e.g., I don't need to spend hours with a survey). Rating movies requires some action, but Netflix knows which movies I stopped streaming after two minutes and which ones I've seen dozens of times (*The Matrix* and *Man on Fire*, if you must know), and Pandora knows the songs that I've skipped over. My bank can ping me with account balance updates and recommend financial products.

Customization, personalization, and contextualization are all means of achieving a higher degree of customer engagement and intimacy and can all be enabled by cloud services, above and beyond mere "IT." To put it another way, such a strategy may be based not only on a single individual's behavior, but on insights gained from its similarities to and differences from thousands or millions of other individuals, necessitating aggregation and analytics, often requiring the cloud as an enabler.

For *product leadership*, there are many ways in which the cloud can play a key role. The Apple iPad is certainly a nice product, but it wouldn't be much without the feature and function extensibility enabled by iTunes or the App Store. Products can be designed using the cloud. Drug companies may evaluate new molecules for efficacy in short amounts of time using the cloud. Design teams can collaborate on new product development. Products can be differentiated through informationalization: Consider how General Motors' OnStar helped give it an edge in a market of look-alike sedans or Nike differentiated its sneakers through Nike+, a means of monitoring workouts, uploading them to the cloud, and sharing them. Apple's iPhone 4S is differentiated thanks to Siri, a natural language interface that leverages the processing power and storage ability of the cloud, which will always be greater than that of an individual device.[27] As cheap microprocessors and hyperconnectivity become the norm, such product differentiation will become more widely used. Even light bulbs now are being built with Wi-Fi connectivity, to report back to a residential gateway and eventually to a smart grid on how much power they are consuming and accept remote commands. Products or services can be differentiated not just by color, style, and materials but by the functionality embedded in the devices acting in concert with that delivered by the cloud and its extended ecosystem.

It is helpful to distinguish between *differentiation* and *innovation*. A Coach bag may use the same leather, clasp, and design as it has for decades, and thus not be very innovative. It still is differentiated thanks to brand, design, and perhaps the quality of its raw materials. The cloud can help differentiate products but can also help innovate them via cloud-based collaboration, open source communities, contests, and so forth.

Finally, by *operational excellence*, Treacy and Wiersema were referring to low cost, high reliability, and minimal inconvenience, and the cloud can be critical in several ways. Goldcorp went from desperation to one of the leading producers by opening up its mine data to collaborators, thanks to a cloud-based contest. It was thus able to increase yield at reduced cost, surely an example of operational excellence. Companies that use the cloud to reduce IT operations costs *or* to scale up or replicate services globally to ensure service availability and performance are good examples of competition through operational excellence. If IT costs are only 3% to 4% of revenues, even a 25% reduction in overall spend will not enable a Porter-style cost leadership strategy. However, that in combination with business intelligence, enabled by cloud-based analytics for supply chain optimization and inventory reduction could create dramatic improvements. As in the Zara case, IT can enable lower costs, higher revenues, and greater customer intimacy simultaneously.

Randy Bias, chief technology officer (CTO) and cofounder of Cloudscaling, a provider of open cloud solutions, claims that enterprises and cloud providers can create a sevenfold cost advantage over legacy approaches by leveraging open cloud architectures, including building reliability in at the software layer rather than gold-plating the hardware.[28] However, Bias, who has unparalleled experience in building large open clouds, warns that it is not technology but culture that stands in the way of exploiting these best practices to achieve operational excellence. To put it another way, if most companies cannot—or will not—leverage these advantages, there is the opportunity for those that do to gain a competitive edge.

Whichever approach to strategy one prefers, it would appear that cloud computing can play an essential role. Simon Wardley is a polymath with a background in genetics, a cloud blogger, a former strategist at Canonical, and now a researcher with high-tech systems integrator, outsourcer, and consultancy CSC's prestigious Leading Edge Forum. He argues that the old assumptions—one could compete either as a cost leader, via product differentiation, or through customer focus—are giving way to new models of competition that can achieve all three.[29] An example is through the leveraging of ecosystems in a model known as ILC (innovate-leverage-commoditize). Under this model, the provision of utility IT services enables other companies to create new activities at a lower cost of failure and hence encourages creation. Through monitoring, the ecosystem is leveraged to identify activities that are diffusing. These activities are then acquired and commoditized to create further component services that enable continued growth of the ecosystem.

Using this approach, Wardley argues that firms can simultaneously be:

- Highly innovative, by pushing differentiation and the creation of new but inherently uncertain and risky activities out into a wide ecosystem
- Customer-focused, by leveraging the ecosystem to quickly identify and support emerging activities
- Highly efficient, by focusing on commoditization to achieve cost leadership

Less obvious, perhaps, is the shift in architecture that is under way. Ironically, a move to commodity infrastructure can be highly strategic in two ways. By lowering costs of entry and operations, it unleashes and democratizes the creativity of not just IT staff but personnel in the business units without specific IT skills. By eliminating custom design in favor of a standardized platform, it compresses time and thereby enables enlightened companies to use speed as a competitive weapon.

There are also unique scenarios that the cloud inherently enables beyond basic IT. We cover dozens of these—such as communities, commons, contests, and commerce—in Chapter 7.

Via the cloud, companies can eliminate the barriers to scale. Netflix realized that it couldn't build data centers quickly enough to match the pace of its growth and its globalization.[30]

Via the cloud, companies can leverage network effects, gaining first-mover advantage and then retaining customers and users through a virtuous cycle.

Via the cloud, companies can achieve global brand recognition in weeks or months and then leverage that recognition to expand into additional markets: Angry Birds evolved from an addictive game to the mechanism for Rovio to sell or license everything from coffee cups to plush toys, with millions sold at last count.[31]

Via the cloud, start-ups can latch on to high growth market opportunities, and, in a variation of Newton's second law ($F = ma$), for a given force of investment, accelerate rapidly to high numbers of users and market value, freed from the mass of building and running data centers.[32] Thus could Instagram rocket from launch through the clouds into the stratosphere, with a billion dollar exit via a Facebook acquisition in 18 months.

The Networked Organization

The pinnacle of success 100 years ago was the vertically integrated corporation. Ford's River Rouge plant was not just a plant but an entire automotive production ecosystem in a square mile, from iron ore through finished vehicle.

Today's corporation is not a single entity but what some call a network corporation, a business web, or a virtual corporation. Mobile virtual network operators are a brand and a logo, with cellular services delivered by other operators, and the hard work of deploying cell sites and laying fiber left to the operators. The operators, meanwhile, have outsourced such things as mobile device design and tower construction and ownership to others. Meanwhile, the mobile device manufacturers rarely do manufacturing but outsource production to companies such as Hon Hai Precision Industries, better known as FoxConn. P&G does some research in house but leverages open collaboration through a network of researchers and innovation marketplaces. Even the tightly integrated Inditex uses a network of madre-and-padre shops as suppliers, and Toyota is not just a firm but the glue holding together thousands of suppliers.

In an inversion of Coase's theory of the firm as an entity that would exist to minimize search and transaction costs, the new theory of the firm is that of the minimum focus needed to succeed in its chosen market.[33]

There have been seismic shifts in the global marketplace over the past years, revolutionizing organization structure as well as the thinking regarding how best to organize to respond to the environment. Organization design theorists such as David Nadler argue that there must be *congruence*, i.e., alignment, between the two.[34] For simple businesses—such as a one-person fruit stand—with a slow rate of change, a simple structure can work. When there is a high degree of environmental complexity but a slow rate of change, the traditional hierarchical organization can handle the complexity. When there is a low degree of complexity but rapid change, an entrepreneurial organization may be best. But when there is high complexity and rapid change, a network organization is required. The network organization is characterized by distributed assets and knowledge; shifting patterns of interaction; and collaboration and therefore trust and a supremacy of knowledge over authority.[35]

The *network* organization is an essential evolutionary adaptation; but in today's world of chaotic, hyperspeed change, the *networked* organization is even more critical. Rather than companies merely rearchitecting their *internal* organization designs, today they need to focus on their relationships with other players in the complex ecosystem that is the global economy. Rethinking these relationships also redefines the boundaries of the firm and thus has repercussions on internal structure.

These concepts apply to product and service development as well as more broadly in the business, whether production and service operations, distribution, or supply chain. Berkeley Haas School of Business professor Henry Chesbrough has claimed that *open innovation* is the new paradigm of the networked organization using interactions outside the firm for design and development.[36]

Chesbrough used P&G as an example of the transformation.[37] P&G initiated a program called "Connect and Develop" and created a "Director of External Innovation" with the objective of quintupling the amount of innovation that would leverage outside resources. According to Chesbrough, P&G's rationale at the time was simple mathematics: less than 9,000 scientists *inside* the company, 1.5 million *outside*.

Satish Nambisan, of Rensselaer Polytechnic Institute, and Mohanbir Sawhney, of Northwestern's Kellogg School of Management, have called this approach "network-centric innovation" and laid out four approaches to "tapping the Global Brain." They suggested that firms can leverage networks for innovation:

- By being an *orchestra*, where a conductor orchestrates specialists, as Boeing did with the 787 Dreamliner
- As a *creative bazaar*, scouting for ideas among a global talent pool
- Via an approach they call "Jam Central," characterized by emergent goals, diffuse leadership, and an infrastructure that supports collaboration
- As a "Modification Station," exemplified by open source software[38]

Considering a larger scope than just innovation, best-selling author, professor, and consultant Don Tapscott and his colleagues called the antithesis of the vertically integrated, traditional, walled organization the open networked enterprise or business web (b-web).[39] Author, economist, and Wharton lecturer Jeremy Rifkin has similarly referred to the Hollywood organizational model, where collaborators are dynamically assembled for the duration of their involvement in a movie. We have now entered the "collaborative, fragmented, demanding network-economy world."[40]

Tapscott argued that there are five variations of such webs:

1. *Agoras*, markets like eBay or NASDAQ
2. *Aggregations*, such as Amazon.com as a retailer
3. *Value chains*, such as supply chains
4. *Alliances*, for creative collaboration
5. *"Distributive"* networks, which are multiparty by definition—consider package logistics or a telecom carrier[41]

As an example of supply chain flexibility, consider the next scenario, described by Wharton's Jerry Wind, Victor Fung, group chairman of Li & Fung Trading, and William Fung, its group managing director. For a given clothing order, the yarn might come from Korea, the buttons from China, the weaving in Taiwan, and the final production in Pakistan.[42] However, they pointed out, a month later a completely different supply chain configuration might be optimal. Li & Fung has over 10,000 global suppliers, generating over $10 billion in revenue, with exactly zero factories or factory employees.

Form Follows Function, IT Follows Form

If businesses have evolved from hierarchy to network and from network to *networked*, what does it mean for IT? The nature of IT is changing because the nature of business is changing, and these changes are aligned with the inherent characteristics of the cloud.

If the corporation is now a distributed entity, what of its IT? A single company that is the dominant center of its universe, such as Toyota is with its suppliers, could certainly mandate use of a private IT infrastructure. Even major global corporations are willing to support the IT standards of their major customers, the way Walmart suppliers use Walmart Connect.

But for everyone else, the strategic architecture of the firm as a networked entity must be recapitulated by its IT: a distributed, ownerless architecture that can be embodied only by the cloud. Whether the network is a mesh of participants, such as the way that Hollywood producers, directors, actors, and agents come together to make a film, or a linear chain existing as a supply chain network, such a dynamic multi-enterprise *organizational* architecture must be reflected in a flexible multi-enterprise *information* architecture.

If the Internet was the enabler of Tapscott's b-webs, the cloud is the next step. More than just leveraging connectivity to reduce transaction costs—search, contracting, and coordination—the cloud, and its evolution to the Intercloud[43], is the IT parallel. In a world where the enterprise was a closed system, its IT could be closed as well. *But when the enterprise becomes a fungible entity and its relationships with players across the value chain are ephemeral, its IT must reflect this new organizational architecture and ecosystem.*

Moreover, in today's environment, the boundaries among IT, the networked corporation, the product or service, and even the customer are fading. As the late C. K. Prahalad, the iconic University of Michigan professor, said, "In contrast to developing stand-alone products, innovators are drawing together networks that deliver a personalized co-created experience to the customer."[44] He used Build-A-Bear Workshop, where kids design and then construct their own teddy bears as one example and also argued that General Motors' OnStar or a wireless pacemaker that is linked to doctors and hospitals is an example of the new "product." Prahalad drew this critical distinction: "[A] pacemaker is not just a product. It is the nexus of a network."[45] Prahalad, the cofounder of the theory of core competencies with Gary Hamel, argued that the original theory, formerly applicable at the firm level, must now be extended to networks of firms.

Aligning Cloud with Strategy

Different firms will find different opportunities to leverage the cloud. Today there are many companies in traditional businesses: farming, trucking, pharmaceuticals, hotels, oil and gas. IT can help these companies in different ways: irrigation optimization, farmhand tracking, route optimization, yield management. For a cost leadership strategy in such a traditional company, reducing costs *within* the IT function via the cloud is beneficial but not strategic. After all, if IT costs are an average of 4% of revenues, and the cloud could help reduce IT costs by 25%, the net impact to the corporation is only 1%, or perhaps a few percent of its cost structure, hardly a compelling enabler for a cost-leadership strategy. However, in such a company, to the extent that cloud-based services can optimize supply chains or operations logistics, the impact could be substantial.

Another case is the company that sells an informationalized offer (i.e., a product that is enhanced by IT). General Motors' OnStar is a good example. The product itself—a Corvette, say—is enhanced not just by a sunroof or V8 engine but also by features or components enabled by networked IT. It's not just products that can be enhanced: An insurance company that adjusts claims on the spot, such as Progressive, using wireless uplinks, accomplishes the same thing, as does a Personal Video Recorder such as TiVo that leverages online connections for program updates as well as recommendations.

For a cloud-native company, however—say, a Facebook, Google, eBay, Foursquare, Twitter, or Zynga—we could argue that cost reduction via the cloud could have a significant impact on burn rate and profitability. However, while such companies surely watch costs, they tend to focus primarily on revenue and growth uninterrupted by outages and unavailability due to insufficient resources. The cloud offers a means to connect with customers and users and to ensure service availability in the face of a mix of exponential growth and unpredictable, variable, demand.

Everyware, Anywhere

When viewed from the perspective of global technology trends, the cloud is becoming even more important. Digitalized, informationalized offers are becoming more pervasive. Maribel Lopez, founder of Lopez Research and a *Forbes* blogger, observed that the intersection of mobility and the cloud change what we connect, how we connect, and how we transact business, and is changing how we develop, test, deploy, and use applications.[46] There are 6 billion mobile "phones" now in use, part of a current total of 9 billion connected devices, and that total is likely to reach 24 billion within a decade, according to at least one estimate.[47] Other estimates are even higher.

As BT (British Telecom) chief scientist J. P. Rangaswami said, "You need to start from the philosophical position that everything is the end point on a network—your television, even your doorbell."[48]

This emerging era of ubiquitous, pervasive, invisible computing has been dubbed "Everyware" by author and futurist Adam Greenfield.[49] In this new world, computing and connectivity become so ubiquitous, intelligent, and low cost that they descend below conscious awareness. Your dinner plate tells the refrigerator that you ate all of your broccoli, which in turn informs the grocery store that you will need more soon, which gives the farmers a heads up. Communications within the house may not need the cloud, but collecting data from the sensors will take advantage of the rapidly materializing era of global hyperconnectivity, or what Yankee Group president and CEO Emily Nagle Green has called "Anywhere": the explosion of broadband wireless and wireline network capacity and capability combined with intelligent devices and cloud services to create new business opportunities.[50]

And, as if tablets and smartphones and laptops were not pervasive and perhaps invasive enough, not to mention wireless and smart-chip enabled cars and washing machines and photo frames, the emerging role of the cloud will be as the integrative, big-data brain behind miniaturized wireless smart-chip—enabled sensor and actuator networks for these cars and washing machines, and other mundane, pervasive artifacts of our existence. As Larry Smarr, founding director of the California Institute for Telecommunications and Information Technology, put it, this will create a "sensor-aware planetary computer," which, in turn, makes the entire world programmable.[51] Moreover, by performing calculations faster than real time, the cloud might be able to run complex simulations able to forecast the future, and not just for weather.

Alistair Croll, founder and CEO of Bitcurrent and serial entrepreneur, has a number of interesting observations about the nature of competition in such a world of near-infinite data. In today's hypercompetitive environment, survival and success belong to those who can adapt and innovate most quickly. According to Croll, military strategist and fighter pilot, John Boyd conceptualized the Observe, Orient, Decide, Act (OODA) cycle: Collect data; put it into an existing context; decide what to do; execute the decision; repeat.[52] If you can do that faster and better than your opponent, combat success will follow.

Croll argued that something similar is happening today in the world of business. We are entering a "feedback economy," an accelerating cycle of "big data" collection, analysis, decision making, and execution, which requires massive data sets to be analyzed in increasingly smaller amounts of time. Moreover, like snippets of information coming from informants and double agents, today's data are increasingly unstructured, requiring more advanced processing than merely summing row fields to determine a total or searching for records where LAST_NAME="Jones".

Leveraging such big data—becoming a "super-cruncher"—has measurable financial impact.[53] Studies conducted by Massachusetts Institute of Technology professor Erik Brynjolfsson have found that a "one-standard-deviation increase toward data and analytics was correlated with about a 5 to 6 percent improvement in productivity and a slightly larger increase in profitability."[54] Brynjolfsson argued that achieving this requires a mix of both technology and skills.

Big data is not just a means of enhancing the productivity and profitability of existing businesses. As in the case of American Airlines, where the SABRE reservation system became worth more than the physical airline, McKinsey & Company analysts have argued that "exhaust data"—the data produced as a by-product of operations—can create entirely new business opportunities, as skills and technologies for analytics are monetized.[55]

Summary

End-to-end linkages exist beginning with business goals and objectives which—based on competencies, competitive positioning, regulatory constraints, and the like—drive business strategy, which is enabled by a business system that may incorporate information technology, which may be partly or completely delivered via the cloud. These linkages are important, because *an action or capability can be evaluated only in the context of a strategy.* As seventeenth-century philosopher Baruch Spinoza observed, "[M]usic is good to the melancholy, bad to those who mourn, and neither good nor bad to the deaf."[56] Different competitors can—and must—pursue unique strategies to carve out sustainable niches within that industry competitive ecosystem, just as, for example, Hyundai, Toyota, Ford, Lamborghini, and Tesla have implemented different strategies to participate in the same market.

The cloud may sometimes be a commodity, it may sometimes merely be a tactical means of cost reduction or scalability, but at its best, it may well be a source of strategic competitive advantage, whether due to many small things done well or larger-scale initiatives focused on customer intimacy, product differentiation, operational excellence, or the innovation cycles that drive them.

Notes

1. Hunter Muller, conversation with the author, January 23, 2012.
2. Ravi Rajagopal, conversation with the author, December 20, 2011.

3. Dan Farber, "Oracle's Ellison nails cloud computing," *CNET News*, September 26, 2008. http://news.cnet.com/8301-13953_3-10052188-80.html.

4. "Billionaires Gallery 2011," *Forbes*. www.forbes.com/wealth/billionaires.

5. Gartner, "Gartner's 2011 Hype Cycle Special Report Evaluates the Maturity of 1,900 Technologies," August 10, 2011, www.gartner.com/it/page.jsp?id=1763814.

6. Nicholas Carr, "IT Doesn't Matter," *Harvard Business Review* (May 2003), (81)5, pp. 41–49, Nicholas Carr, *The Big Switch: Rewiring the World, From Edison to Google* (Norton, 2008).

7. Francis Pereira, conversation with the author, January 28, 2012.

8. Ibid.

9. www.youtube.com/.

10. www.flickr.com/.

11. Chris Anderson, *The Long Tail: Why the Future of Business Is Selling Less of More* (Hyperion, 2006).

12. John Dillon, conversation with the author, January 29, 2012.

13. John Hagel III, John Seely Brown, and Lang Davison, *The Power of Pull: How Small Moves, Smartly Made, Can Set Big Things in Motion* (Basic Books, 2010).

14. George Gilder, "The Information Factories," *Wired* (October 2006). www.wired.com/wired/archive/14.10/cloudware.html.

15. Jason Dean, "The Forbidden City of Terry Gou," *Wall Street Journal*, August 11, 2007. online.wsj.com/article/SB118677584137994489.html.

16. James Urquhart, "Understanding Cloud and DevOps—Part 2," *CNet News*, March 27, 2010. http://news.cnet.com/8301-19413_3-10470790-240.html.

17. Japan External Trade Organization, "The Mindset of Monozukuri," April 4, 2007. www.jetro.org/content/431.

18. Mark Thiele, conversation with the author, February 20, 2012.

19. Bogdan Popa, "Toyota Crowned World's No. 1 Car Manufacturer," *Autoevolution*, January 21, 2009, www.autoevolution.com/news/toyota-crowned-world-s-no-1-car-manufacturer-3439.html. Yasuhiro Monden, *Toyota Production System: Practical Approach to Production Management* (Industrial Engineering and Management Press, 1983).

20. Edward N. Luttwak, *Strategy: The Logic of War and Peace* (Harvard University Press, 1987).

21. Michael Porter, *Competitive Strategy: Techniques for Analyzing Industries and Competitors* (Free Press, 1980).

22. Samuel C. Certo and J. Paul Peter, *Strategic Management: Concepts and Applications*, 2nd ed. (McGraw-Hill, 1991).

23. Robert D. Buzzell and Bradley T. Gale, *The PIMS (Profit Impact of Market Strategy) Principles: Linking Strategy to Performance* (Free Press, 1987).

24. Benjamin B. Tregoe, John W. Zimmerman, Ronald A. Smith, and Peter M. Tobia, *Vision in Action: Putting a Winning Strategy to Work* (Simon & Schuster, 1989).

25. Michael Treacy and Fred Wiersema, "Customer Intimacy and Other Value Disciplines," *Harvard Business Review* (January–February 1993), pp. 84–93.

26. W. Chan Kim and Renée Mauborgne, *Blue Ocean Strategy: How to Create Uncontested Market Space and Make Competition Irrelevant*, (Harvard Business Review Press, 2005); Bernd H. Schmitt, Big Think Strategy: How to Leverage

Bold Ideas and Leave Small Thinking Behind (Harvard Business School Press, 2007).

27. David Daw, "What Makes Siri Special?" *PCWorld*, October 24, 2011, www.pcworld.com/article/242479/what_makes_siri_special.html.

28. Randy Bias, conversation with the author, December 14, 2011.

29. Simon Wardley, conversation with the author, December 26, 2011.

30. Jenn Webb, "How the Cloud Helps Netflix: Netflix's Adrian Cockcroft on the Benefits of a Cloud Infrastructure," *O'Reilly Radar*, May 11, 2011. http://radar.oreilly.com/2011/05/netflix-cloud.html.

31. Matt Rosoff, "Rovio Is Selling 1 Million Angry Birds T-Shirts and Plush Toys Every Month," *Business Insider*, September 12, 2011. http://articles.businessinsider.com/2011-09-12/tech/30155702_1_angry-birds-shirts-sales-manager.

32. Derrick Harris, "Why Instagram is Likely Moving on from Amazon's Cloud," *GigaOM.com*, April 9, 2012. http://gigaom.com/cloud/why-instagram-is-likely-moving-on-from-amazons-cloud/

33. Ronald H. Coase, "The Nature of the Firm," *Economica*, new series 4, No. 16, (November 1937), pp. 386–405.

34. David A Nadler and Michael L. Tushman, "Designing Organizations That Have Good Fit: A Framework for Understanding New Architectures," in David A. Nadler, Marc S. Gerstein, Robert B. Shaw, and Associates, *Organizational Architecture: Designs for Changing Organizations* (Jossey-Bass, 1992).

35. Marc S. Gerstein, "From Machine Bureaucracies to Networked Organizations: An Architectural Journey," in David A. Nadler, Marc S. Gerstein, Robert B. Shaw and Associates, *Organizational Architecture: Designs for Changing Organizations* (Jossey-Bass, 1992).

36. Henry Chesbrough, *Open Innovation: The New Imperative for Creating and Profiting from Technology* (Harvard Business School Press, 2003).

37. Ibid.

38. Satish Nambisan and Mohanbir Sawhney, "Network-Centric Innovation: Four Strategies for Tapping the Global Brain," in Paul R. Kleindorfer and Yoram (Jerry) Wind with Robert E. Gunther, *The Network Challenge: Strategy, Profit, and Risk in an Interlinked World* (Wharton School Publishing, 2009).

39. Don Tapscott and Anthony Williams, *Wikinomics: How Mass Collaboration Changes Everything* (Portfolio, 2006). Don Tapscott, David Ticoll, and Alex Lowy, *Digital Capital* (Harvard Business School Press, 2000).

40. David Friedman, "Why Every Business Will Be Like Show Business," *Inc.*, March 1, 1995. www.inc.com/magazine/19950301/2182.html.

41. Tapscott, Digital Capital.

42. Yoram (Jerry) Wind, Victor Fung, and William Fung, "Network Orchestration: Creating and Managing Global Supply Chains Without Owning Them," in Paul R. Kleindorfer and Yoram (Jerry) Wind with Robert E. Gunther, *The Network Challenge: Strategy, Profit, and Risk in an Interlinked World* (Wharton School Publishing, 2009).

43. David Bernstein, Erik Ludvigson, Krishna Sankar, Steve Diamond, and Monique Morrow, "Blueprint for the Intercloud—Protocols and Formats for Cloud Computing Interoperability," pp. 328–336, Fourth International Conference on Internet and Web Applications and Services, 2009.

44. C. K. Prahalad, "Creating Experience: Competitive Advantage in the Age of Networks," in Paul R. Kleindorfer and Yoram (Jerry) Wind with Robert E. Gunther, *The Network Challenge: Strategy, Profit, and Risk in an Interlinked World* (Wharton School Publishing, 2009).

45. Ibid.

46. Maribel Lopez, conversation with the author, January 29, 2012.

47. Om Malik, "Internet of Things Will Have 24 Billion Devices by 2020," *GigaOM .com*, October 13, 2011. http://gigaom.com/cloud/internet-of-things-will-have-24-billion-devices-by-2020/.

48. Tim Phillips, "Tomorrow's World," *Capacity* (November 15 2010). www.capacity magazine.com/Article/2758475/Tomorrows-world.html.

49. Adam Greenfield, *Everyware: The Dawning Age of Ubiquitous Computing* (New Riders, 2006).

50. Emily Nagle Green, *Anywhere: How Global Connectivity is Revolutionizing the Way We Do Business* (McGraw-Hill, 2010).

51. Larry Smarr, "An Evolution toward a Programmable Universe," *New York Times*, December 5, 2011. www.nytimes.com/2011/12/06/science/larry-smarr-an-evolu tion-toward-a-programmable-world.html.

52. Alistair Croll, "The Feedback Economy," *O'Reilly Radar*, January 4, 2012. http://radar.oreilly.com/2012/01/the-feedback-economy.html.

53. Ian Ayres, *Super Crunchers: Why Thinking-By-Numbers Is the New Way To Be Smart* (Bantam Dell, 2007).

54. "Competing through Data: Three Experts Offer Their Game Plans," *McKinsey Quarterly*, No. 4 (2011), pp. 36–47, www.mckinseyquarterly.com/Competing_through_data_Three_experts_offer_their_game_plans_2868.

55. Brad Brown, Michael Chui, and James Manyika, "Are You Ready for the Era of 'Big Data'?" *McKinsey Quarterly*, No. 4 (2011). pp. 24–35, www.mckinseyquarterly .com/Are_you_ready_for_the_era_of_big_data_2864.

56. Benedictus de Spinoza, translated by Andrew Boyle; introduction by T. S. Gregory, *Spinoza's Ethics and "De intellectus emendatione"* (Dent, 1959).

CHAPTER 4

Challenging Convention

A narrative about cloud computing and its economics has been refined after countless retellings. If you are reading this book, you probably have already internalized a substantial portion of it. The executive summary has assertions along these lines:

1. Cloud computing is a revolutionary new technology and business model.
2. "Cloud" is interchangeable with "pay per use" or "on demand."
3. Large cloud providers enjoy massive economies of scale.
4. Economies of scale are the key to cloud benefits.
5. Large economies of scale lead to large price advantages.
6. Scale and innovation enable proprietary technologies and thus sustainable competitive advantage.
7. Further benefits derive from replacing capital expenditures with operating expenses.
8. Because the largest providers drive the largest benefits, only a handful of cloud providers will survive.
9. Rational decision makers will select the lowest-cost option.
10. Therefore, all IT will move to the cloud, in the same way that all electricity has moved to the electric utility "cloud."
11. Colocation, hosting, managed services, and outsourcing will therefore be completely replaced by the cloud.
12. The cost reduction that the cloud offers will in turn drive lower IT spend.
13. However, security and availability are big issues . . .
14. . . . and so is energy use: Computing uses an increasing, nontrivial portion of the world's energy.

Not only is this story logical and plausible, it is supported by a variety of analyst reports, best-selling books, blog posts, and so forth.

Unfortunately, although the story hangs together well, many of these assertions are either debatable or more nuanced than might initially appear. Let's review the assertions one at a time.

What Is the Cloud?

In the next chapter, we define the cloud more rigorously. For now, we quickly address the cloud and its context.

> Assertion 1: Cloud computing is a revolutionary new technology and business model.

Cloud computing combines several newer technologies, such as virtualization, with new architectural approaches to scalable infrastructure. However, the business model is thousands of years old. The model of resources available on an on-demand, pay-per-use basis dates back to the Roman Republic or earlier, and is found not only in computing, but in hotels, rental car services, storage units, electrical, water, and gas utilities, among others. This is not a bad thing: It proves the durability and value of this business model.

> Assertion 2: The term "cloud" is interchangeable with "pay per use" or "on demand."

Many people use these terms interchangeably to refer to the attributes often found in cloud. However, although these concepts often coexist, from an economic perspective, they are separable. Pay-per-use pricing generates benefits in the presence of variable demand by eliminating payments for unused resources; on-demand resources generate benefits in the presence of unpredictability by ensuring that there are neither too few nor too many resources. The two are often found together but need not be. Consider a hotel room reserved months in advance. It is still pay-per-use but hardly on demand, given the long lead time. The economic benefit of pay-per-use relates to the combination of savings when the service is not used and the marginal contribution from the value that the resources provide when they are used.

Economies of Scale

The largest cloud providers leverage a variety of techniques to excel and compete, such as building reliability in at the software layer, focusing on reducing power and cooling costs via site selection and engineering, negotiating with suppliers, optimizing taxation, acquiring top engineering talent, and more. However, there is probably no phrase associated with cloud service providers more often than "economies of scale." Although there surely are such economies, the logic regarding them may not be as simple as some would suggest.

Assertion 3: Large cloud providers enjoy massive economies of scale.

There are no doubt various elements of cloud cost structure that exhibit economies of scale, but there are also scale-invariant costs and dis-economies of scale. Some aspects of cloud architecture, such as network bandwidth and power and cooling equipment, are typically "scale-up," utilizing larger components with lower unit costs. However, some key building blocks of clouds are "scale-out:" they grow by increasing their quantity. To clarify the difference: an infant grows into an adult by scaling up; an ant colony grows by scaling out. In a scale-out architecture, there can be limits to the applicability of the economies of scale concept. Scale economies require nonlinearities in cost structure, which may not always exist in some of the elements of cloud. Today the building block for many clouds is the container or pod, packed with equipment, and also available to enterprises. Depending on the specific cloud provider, this may be a different situation than, say, in air transport, where service providers have access to jumbo jets but most enterprises and consumers are unlikely to purchase them; While cloud providers run enormous data centers—the equivalent of the Airbus 380 or Boeing 787—and thus achieve notable economies for a portion of their cost structure; other elements, such as the servers and storage inside them, may be similar to or very different from the building blocks that are available to everyone. The extremes range from custom designs that are built or contracted for assembly by the largest cloud service providers, either internally or utilizing capabilities such as Dell Data Center Services, to those service providers who utilize standard servers, racks, or containers.

Large cloud providers presumably receive the best discounts, but it isn't clear how much greater these are than large enterprise discounts. Moreover, buyer cooperatives can aggregate purchasing power, getting larger discounts than any individual firm, thus matching discounts on equipment. So, while large providers presumably have cost advantages over consumers and even small businesses, it isn't clear that they always have significant and sustainable cost advantages over large, well-run enterprises.

Assertion 4: Economies of scale are the key to cloud benefits.

This is the title of a report from a well-known analyst firm and has been also argued by leading academics.[1] The cloud offers many benefits, most of which have nothing to do with cost and therefore do not require that the cloud have any cost advantage due to economies of scale. In fact, the pay-per-use pricing scheme of the cloud means that cloud services actually can have a higher unit cost and still generate a broad spectrum of benefits, such as enhanced agility, reduced risk and time-to-market, accelerated innovation, and improved customer experience. Additional mechanisms favor the cloud, such as network effects, preferential attachment, and data gravity, whereby applications migrate to where data and related applications are located.

Moreover, the term "economies of scale" normally refers to unit costs of production, with complete disregard for the nature of demand variation that can impact total delivered cost. We address this more in Chapter 8. A different effect, which we call the statistics of scale, impacts service businesses, such as cloud computing. In the same way that a hotel makes a business out of the fact that large numbers of customers have random patterns of demand, clouds can leverage the statistics of scale—or more precisely the statistics of demand diversity typically associated with scale—to generate value.

Competitive Advantage and Customer Value

Assertion 5: Large economies of scale lead to large price advantages.

There are two issues with this assertion. First, there are areas within the total cost structure of a provider that may have economies of scale, other areas where costs are scale invariant, and still other areas where there are diseconomies of scale. Consequently, it is not sufficient for there to be economies of scale; they must outweigh the areas where there are diseconomies. Second, the biggest competitor of a cloud provider may or may not be another cloud provider: It may be the do-it-yourself approach. It is not just differences in *cost* structure that matter; differences in the delivered *price* from a service provider versus the internal *cost* of do-it-yourself approaches matter. The challenge is that a service provider may exhibit net scale economies relative to, say, a midsize enterprise, but once additional elements are added to its total cost structure, a service provider actually may end up being priced higher. For example, service providers need to attend cloud computing industry events, put together brochures, hire salespeople and evangelists, hold industry analyst briefings to explain why their approach is the best, account for uncollectible or fraudulent charges where they incur cost to provide service without collecting any corresponding revenue, and so on.

Assertion 6: Scale and innovation enable proprietary technologies and thus sustainable competitive advantage.

There is no doubt that the early cloud providers have been and continue to be technology pioneers in virtually all aspects of relevant technology. As an example of such innovation, consider new approaches to hyperscale data center operations, where it is assumed that servers will fail frequently, so such failed servers are removed from the active pool by management software rather than requiring immediate manual repair or replacement. It includes new approaches to server design, eliminating components such as graphics processors that are not needed as they are not connected to displays, and putting a battery on each server for power backup. It includes new management software and tools, enabling a single administrator to remotely manage tens of thousands of servers or multiple petabytes of storage.

However, although the accelerated pace of innovation driving the industry is certainly to be applauded, from a strategy and economics perspective, the question is how *sustainable* this competitive advantage is, and for how long. Google didn't invent paid search but "emulated" GoTo.com.[2] Apple didn't invent the portable music player; it didn't even invent the portable *digital* music player. McDonald's didn't invent the hamburger, and Starbucks didn't invent the coffee shop. The major hardware manufacturers have adopted new server designs from the cloud service providers, adapted to the new architecture of highly automated, highly scalable data centers. Meanwhile, some firms are sharing their most advanced designs through programs such as Open Compute.[3] The management software vendors, whether pure-play software companies or integrated with hardware companies, are re-creating the functionality originally developed by cloud service provider pioneers required to operate, administer, and manage clouds, including specific functions, such as virtual server migration and cloud-bursting, where enterprise data center capacity is temporarily augmented by cloud-based capacity. Moreover, a major service provider—Rackspace—has released its proprietary software (integrated with NASA Nebula software) as the open source OpenStack, and fostered a community to ensure ongoing contribution and development.[4] Other cloud providers may choose to join this effort, release their own code, or sell services enabled by OpenStack as their strategies evolve.

Henry Ford may not have invented mass production, but he was the first to apply it so notably. For a while, it represented an advantage. Today there are dozens of automobile manufacturers, and mass production has diffused widely. Similarly, although various cloud service providers and tech purveyors have pioneered extremely innovative technologies, such innovations may not suffice to ensure competitive success as these technologies diffuse.

Mass production has become widespread, so automobile manufacturers now compete on sound systems and styling, ego gratification, and perhaps performance and customer care. As cloud hardware and software technologies diffuse, service providers will increasingly compete on other dimensions: customer intimacy, performance, latency, breadth of portfolio, and complementary products and services, such as systems integration, consulting, application development, and performance optimization.

Earlier we discussed the use of the cloud to achieve strategic advantage, but it is important to distinguish the means by which businesses leverage cloud providers to enhance competitiveness from the means by which cloud providers compete with each other and how they deliver a compelling value proposition to those businesses. That said, some providers will no doubt continue to wield their speed of innovation as an ongoing competitive weapon.

> Assertion 7: Further benefits derive from replacing capital expenditures with operating expenses.

Hardly an article or brochure on cloud seems to be written without pointing out this supposed advantage: Evidently, it is argued, capex (capital expenditure) is bad and opex (operating expense) is good. To be sure, for start-ups and small and medium businesses, cash flow may well be a challenge, and the cloud offers an important benefit in this regard.

In the same way that you can trade assets such as dollars for assets such as euros or trade a hundred dollars in 10s for $100 in 20s, you can also "trade" dollars for other assets, such as servers and storage, via a capital expenditure. On the books of the business, $5,000 may be debited from the cash account, and simultaneously $5,000 may be credited to the plant and equipment account. This is a capital expenditure (not "expense"). Conversely, someone may choose to pay to "rent" the asset, for example, via an operating lease. Well before the cloud arrived on the scene, customers could convert capex to opex through the expedient of an operating lease or even a managed service. Consequently, the salient factor is not such conversion, but rather, the lack of commitment that the cloud requires and thus the flexibility it offers users to adjust expense streams.

Moreover, although some of these options may be more valuable for a consumer or small business with limited cash on hand and constrained credit, large enterprises will select one approach or another based on a variety of factors, such as the current cost of capital. Companies with strong cash flow often prefer to use their cash (capital) to purchase rather than rent, because the rent is paid either to a third party or to a finance unit, either of which is presumably out to make a profit. The lessor's profit on financing is essentially the lessee's loss versus a capital investment.

Tax treatment is also an important concern. At least one large cloud customer is capitalizing expenses incurred in purchasing reserved instances, that is, pre-paid compute capacity with a pre-payment and volume discount from a large cloud provider, turning the conventional capex/opex wisdom on its head.

The key financial benefit of the cloud associated with financing choices is not capex versus opex per se but the notion that resource costs are aligned with resource demands. Hypothetically, in a liquid market, such as can be found with large-cap stocks or bonds, even capital investments could be dynamically aligned with resource needs. One could imagine a colocation vendor that also acted as a consignment shop, enabling those with excess hardware to instantly and frictionlessly sell it to and reconfigure it for those with insufficient hardware. While such a scenario is unlikely, it helps delineate where the true value is here: on-demand resources and pay-per-use pricing without commitment.

Cloud Ecosystem Dynamics

Assertion 8: Because the largest providers drive the largest benefits, only a handful of cloud providers will survive.

Large providers are likely to have price advantages, brand awareness advantages, proprietary technology advantages, and geographic footprint advantages over midsize ones.

However, price advantages due to volume buying power or statistical multiplexing of user demand may not be so compelling as to overcome other areas in which smaller providers can differentiate themselves. There are many elements of differentiation besides cost: customer intimacy and relationships, brand, specialization, proximity/latency and thus improved response time, compliance, portfolio synergies, customization support, reciprocity, and the like. Consequently, in the same way that the panoply of retail providers comprises more than just Walmart and Target, there are likely to be a number of providers leading in various niches. Walmart is surely a juggernaut, yet 7-Eleven manages to compete based on convenience, clothing shops based on tailoring and customization, tax accountants based on expertise and customer intimacy, and designer shops based on ego buyers.

Telecommunications firms or carrier-neutral interconnection and colocation facilities that can offer smaller data centers closer to customers and on net can satisfy both server huggers and challenging latency requirements. Country regulations are likely to keep much of the market fragmented: Most countries have their own airline and their own telecom carrier, after all.

And technology-based advantages are dissipating as technologies diffuse: More and more vendors are entering the market with tools that enable providers to offer cloud services, and open source software and hardware stacks are increasingly maturing and becoming available on a managed, private, on-premises basis.

Assertion 9: Rational decision makers will select the lowest-cost option.

All other things being equal, rational decision makers, if there were any such creatures, probably *would* select the lowest-cost option. However, as the last few decades of research into behavioral economics and neuroeconomics have shown, we are a mix of rationality, emotion, and intuition, subject to universal, predictable aberrations, anomalies, and biases. These human behaviors impact cloud adoption both positively and negatively. Chapter 23 addresses these in more detail.

Assertion 10: Therefore, all IT will move to the cloud, in the same way that all electricity has moved to the electric utility "cloud."

Perhaps the original proponent of this argument is Nick Carr, in his book *The Big Switch*.[5] There may be a number of reasons why most electricity consumption has moved to the cloud. There are true economies of scale in electricity generation. Turbines and nuclear power plants either have nonlinearities in their physics that drive cost advantages or have minimum operating scale: A pocket nuclear reactor that powers your toaster has not (yet) been invented.

In addition, there are differences in cost structure. Powering your own home generator means that you need to acquire, say, natural gas, which you will pay for. A utility hydroelectric power plant may not pay for each gallon of water that it "consumes" (i.e., from which it extracts potential or kinetic energy).

Actually, centrally generated power wastes energy. Only a fraction of the power that is generated gets to the end user; the rest is wasted in transmission (electric long-haul) and distribution (electric "last-mile") losses. It could be argued that something similar happens in cloud computing: There may be economic losses due to lost productivity from latency and response-time issues with remote services.

Ultimately, the question is: If, instead of paying hundreds of dollars a month for remotely generated electricity, you could buy a toaster-size fuel cell or solar panel that generated all the electricity you needed for a nickel, why would you bother with the centralized utility?

Movies were originally available *only* "in the cloud." Our grandparents went to any one of a set of shared, pay-per-use, on-demand, geographically dispersed service nodes—called movie theaters—to view content. Resources were capital intensive—both projectors and film prints. Then movies became available on premises: first by videotape; then optical discs; then virtual, digital images, and viewed on smartphones, computers, tablets, and TVs. Today content may be physical or virtual and on premises or downloaded or streamed from the cloud. So why should electric power be the relevant analogy? Aren't streamed movies a better one: a hybrid of local premises and remote cloud that seamlessly combine to make the user experience a rich one?

Virtually any industry offers dedicated ownership and on-demand, pay-per-use options. You can own a home, rent one, or stay in a hotel. You can own a car, rent one, or take a taxi. You can dine in or eat out. You can use equity or debt, and so forth. Rather than a single approach dominating, virtually all industries have a segment that is primarily dedicated and one that is "cloudy." Numerous factors drive the proportion of each, including behavioral factors, macroeconomic factors, and ease of resource accessibility. These factors may shift over time, but generally there is a balance of ownership and on demand, pay per use. With today's computing technologies and architectures, there is also likely to be a balance, leading to what is usually referred to as a hybrid cloud.

Assertion 11: Colocation, hosting, managed services, and outsourcing will therefore be completely replaced by the cloud.

I believe that this is unlikely, for two reasons. First, nothing old *ever* goes away completely. Second, and perhaps more important, hybrid models offer a chance for optimization of different architecture and pricing elements, reflecting the custom nature of some applications, requirements for performance engineering, and so forth.

That said, the nature of hosting and managed services is likely to change. Today the environment, processes, software stacks, portals, and—well just about everything that is used to support hosting—is different from that which is used to support cloud services. These environments were built in a different era. Therefore, legacy hosters that are moving into the cloud are running dual stacks, environments, and processes. However, cloud environments are inherently more flexible. Therefore, "hosting" will be transformed to be a longer-term resource commitment for resources in the same environment. The win-win collaboration between customer and provider will be that customers will receive a lower rate for a longer-term commitment, because the provider will be able to guarantee itself higher utilization of those resources for the period. Rather than a black-and-white distinction, there will be a spectrum of pricing options based on commitment levels and, ideally, seamless integration between on-premises equipment, "hosting," and a variety of cloud options. Think of it this way: You are likely to receive a lower daily rate at a hotel if you plan to stay there for a week, a month, or a year, but it is the same physical room.

IT Spend

Assertion 12: The cost reduction that the cloud offers will in turn drive lower IT spend.

This certainly sounds plausible at first glance. The cloud offers many advantages: reduced cost, enhanced agility, improved customer experience, and the like. To the extent that the cloud enables reduced cost for a unit of compute or a unit of storage, then IT spend might be expected to drop.

But it probably won't for the foreseeable future, due to price elasticity of demand. For some products—so-called Giffen goods and Veblen goods—*raising* the price tends to *increase* demand. For Giffen goods, such as some food staples, this is due to an effective lower net income due to generally higher prices driving a need to substitute the Giffen good for still higher-priced products. For Veblen goods, such as Lamborghinis, it is due to the status value of the good.

Normally, though, a *reduction* in price tends to *increase* demand. In an observation credited to Stanley Jevons, a nineteenth-century economist, the increase in demand can be greater than the reduction in price, leading to growth in total industry revenues.[6] Although this is referred to as Jevons' Paradox, it doesn't seem very paradoxical, given a little thought.

Such increased demand would certainly appear to be true of a general-purpose technology such as computing. Two drivers are important here. The first is that a reduction in total cost of computing or storage means that *more* computing can be performed for particular applications while still generating a net economic return. For example, an equity portfolio optimization algorithm can be run a little bit longer or with a little more precision or to conduct a few more what-if analyses. In other words, rather than doing the same amount of computing at lower cost, you can get more computing done for the same cost. If that extra computing generates an economic return, then you can get a larger economic benefit for a slightly increased total cost based on substantially greater computation at a significantly lower unit cost.

The second major driver is that computing, as unit cost is reduced, will increasingly substitute for other activities. For example, why travel if you can video conference? Why hire contact center representatives if an Interactive Voice Response (IVR) system can substitute? Why drive trucks around inefficiently if real-time traffic data collection and intelligent routing algorithms can optimize labor productivity, operating expenses, capital expenditures, and environmental sustainability through reduced driver hours, less idling, lower fuel consumption, and lower vehicle use? As computing gets cheaper, it can substitute for fuel, labor, trucks, and so forth.

Lest this seem like a far-fetched argument, consider the case of cellular wireless technology: also a general-purpose technology.[7] In 1980, the total industry spend on "mobility" (i.e., cell phones, "base stations" [i.e., cell sites], mobile apps, and mobile network services) was essentially *zero*. In 1982, well before iPhones and Android devices, Motorola introduced the Dynatac 8000x, a heavy brick of a phone priced at $3,995. Today the price of a phone—depending on contract terms—is more like $39.95 for a feature phone that is comparable to a Dynatac. This 100-fold reduction in price did not result in a corresponding 100-fold reduction in spend on mobility but rather an increase in the size of the mobility market from zero to what is currently about $1 trillion.

The analogous argument exists for microprocessors: The costs of a unit of compute—say, an "add" operation—have plummeted thanks to decades of Moore's Law. Consequently, rather than a computer being something that you join a tour to visit in a glass house data center, it is something embedded in a greeting card. As the price has plummeted, the total revenues for microprocessors alone have grown from zero dollars in 1971 when Texas Instruments and Intel first prototyped them, to tens of billions of dollars today.

Issues with the Cloud

A few issues are frequently discussed regarding the cloud.

Assertion 13: However, security and availability are big issues . . .

Let's take these in turn. Security is an issue in the cloud, no question. It's also an issue with personal devices and with enterprise devices and with enterprise networks and with enterprise data centers. It's *always* an issue. The question is not whether it is an issue but whether security is enhanced or weakened by the cloud.

Data are important assets. So is money. Money and other valuables such as jewelry can be kept under your mattress—a premises solution—or in a bank—a cloud solution. Which has the better security? The bank can afford stronger security in terms of vaults with foot-thick hardened steel walls, and can have a security team made up of security professionals and one or more people on payroll who stay abreast of new burglary strategies and determine and implement counterstrategies.

Not only do cloud providers have similar advantages, but they have additional ones, such as their ability to fend off hundreds of thousands or millions of marauding "bots," typically PCs that have malware running on them coordinated by software running on one or more remote servers. Although it is likely that there will continue to be security issues with the cloud, the same way that banks still get robbed, chances are your antique watch will be better off in a safety deposit vault than on your fireplace mantel.

Availability behaves similarly. Although cloud outages are well publicized, the comparison shouldn't be against perfection but against the next best alternative. It also can be argued that the inherent architecture of the cloud offers unique availability advantages via dispersion coupled with replication.

> Assertion 14: . . . and so is energy use: Computing uses an increasing, nontrivial portion of the world's energy.

This is probably true but misleading in several ways. First, cloud technologies have actually *slowed* the growth of electricity consumption by IT: Virtualization reduces the physical footprint and thus energy consumption of computing. The growth in data center energy consumption, according to the influential and well-regarded professor Jonathan Koomey of Stanford University, grew much less than predicted, due primarily to virtualization (and also, admittedly, the global economic slowdown).[8] Second, energy use is moderating thanks to greater data center energy efficiency. Each new processing architecture brings greater efficiency in terms of calculations per watt, and newer technologies that enhance power usage effectiveness are reducing wasted power. However, it is still likely that as computing—games, smart grids, surveillance, video conferencing, and other uses—becomes more pervasive in our society, and as the digital divide dissipates and all of the 7-plus billion citizens in the world have access to the digital provide, computing will consume an increasing amount of energy, up from where it stood in 2011, as this text was being written: roughly 1.1% to 1.5% of the world's consumption and 1.7% to 2.2% of that of the United States.

So? Besides the benefits of such technologies—say, telemedicine helping save lives in rural villages or social networks helping to increase civil liberties—we need to, again, compare something not against perfection but against the best alternative. If someone uses video conferencing rather than hopping on a fuel-guzzling jumbo jet, isn't that to be preferred? If someone streams a movie rather than making one or two round trips to the video store or the movie theater, isn't that better? If computing power in a smart grid control center reduces home air-conditioning use, isn't that a net gain? If the cloud can be a marketplace to enable collaborative consumption of physical goods, reducing manufacturing and its associated energy use and waste by-products, isn't that good? In short, as a *substitute* for more energy-intensive activities or by enabling *intelligence* for optimization, increased energy use in the cloud can *decrease* our total energy consumption and carbon footprint.

As a final thought, is it better to run an app on a so-called thick client, such as a laptop or desktop, or run a lot of it in the cloud and merely present an interface on a smartphone or tablet? The power consumption of a desktop plus monitor might be several hundred watts, that of a tablet 10 or 20 watts, and that of a smartphone only a few watts. Even after adding in the power needed to run the network, the cloud is still substantially more efficient.

In other words, IT as a replacement for physical activities or a means of optimizing such real world activities can lower net energy utilization, and use of the cloud to implement IT can further decrease energy use.

Summary

Whether you agree with the assertions or their counterarguments, the discussion in this chapter should make you question conventional wisdom. The traditional narrative is appealing but not necessarily completely correct. Many characteristics and behaviors of the cloud are more nuanced than simplistic arguments would suggest. And future developments will no doubt impact validity of the conventional wisdom and its counterarguments. In the rest of the book, we delve further into many of these topics, and you will be able to draw your own conclusions.

Notes

1. Daniel Sholler and Donna Scott, "Economies of Scale Are the Key to Cloud Computing Benefits," June 30, 2008, www.gartner.com/id=710610. Michael Armbrust, Armando Fox, Rean Griffith, Anthony D. Joseph, Randy H. Katz, Andrew Konwinski, Gunho Lee, David A. Patterson, Ariel Rabkin, Ion Stoica, Matei Zaharia, "Above the Clouds: A Berkeley View of Cloud Computing," Technical Report No. UCB/EECS-2009-28, February 10, 2009, www.eecs.berkeley.edu/Pubs/TechRpts/2009/EECS-2009-28.html.
2. David A. Vise and Mark Malseed, *The Google Story: Inside the Hottest Business, Media and Technology Success of Our Time* (Bantam Dell, 2005).
3. www.opencompute.org/.
4. www.openstack.org/.
5. Nicholas Carr, *The Big Switch: Rewiring the World, From Edison to Google* (Norton, 2008).

6. Andrew McAfee, "19th Century Economist Reveals Surefire Investment Strategy!" *Andrew McAfee's Blog*, January 19, 2011. http://andrewmcafee.org/2011/01/jevons-computation-efficicency-hardware-investmen/.
7. Joe Weinman, "Cloud Computing Could Boost IT Demand," *InformationWeek*, May 6, 2010. www.informationweek.com/blog/outsourcing/229202608.
8. Jonathan Koomey, *Growth in Data Center Electricity Use 2005 to 2010* (Analytics Press, 2011). www.analyticspress.com/datacenters.html.

CHAPTER 5

What Is a Cloud?

We've been talking about the cloud without explicitly describing what we mean. Before we try to define it, let's consider a few examples that illustrate the breadth of the cloud:

- Texting via your phone
- Sharing photos and updates via Facebook or Twitter
- Sending or receiving Microsoft Hotmail, Google Gmail, or Yahoo! Mail on your laptop
- Using a collaboration service, such as WebEx, NetMeeting, or GoToMeeting
- Watching a YouTube movie on your TV or smartphone
- Talking on your fixed-line or mobile phone
- Talking or video-chatting with someone using Microsoft Skype
- Sharing files via Dropbox or Box.net
- Streaming a Netflix movie to your Roku box, Blu-Ray player, smartphone, or tablet
- Participating in an audio or video conference via a conferencing service that uses multipoint conference bridges located "in the cloud"
- Using Salesforce.com or Oracle/RightNow Technologies customer relationship management capabilities to manage your accounts
- Surfing the Web, with some content being delivered by "hosted" or cloud sites and some by content delivery services, such as Akamai
- Shopping for music, videos, or apps at the iTunes Store or Android market
- Storing that music in the iCloud
- Acquiring books for your Kindle or Nook
- Having someone send a photo to your connected digital photo frame

Some will look at this list and mostly approve but raise an eyebrow over fixed-line phones, assuming that it must be an error, because those are so, well, last millennium. But it is hard to draw clear boundaries between a Voice over Internet Protocol (VoIP, or Voice over IP) connection over Wi-Fi, and one over a wired cable, and one that uses traditional circuit-switched copper wires to access a Voice over IP core, and a pure legacy plain old telephone service (POTS) connection. Ten years from now, some other technology might be in use. But none of this should matter. The point is that there is some service being offered "out there somewhere" that does something useful, in this case, connecting and switching or routing calls.

But, in addition to these human-centric scenarios, we can also include device-centric ones where a variety of endpoints connect to the cloud:

- Video surveillance cameras feeding live video to a cloud-based video archiving service for enhanced security
- Patient monitoring devices that continuously monitor blood pressure and pulse and feed it to a tele-health service
- Electric utility smart grids, where use of power-hungry devices such as air conditioners, washing machines, dryers, and dishwashers is monitored remotely and controlled in connection with grid load in accordance with policies
- Farms that monitor environmental status, such as temperature and rainfall, to ensure that crops receive exactly as much irrigation as they require

And let us not forget other devices, appliances, and equipment that may connect to the cloud:

- Servers running applications that link to cloud servers running the same or interoperable applications
- Storage, such as a local hard drive that links to cloud storage for either data protection or data distribution reasons

Defining the Cloud

As *Bloomberg Businessweek*'s Ashlee Vance quipped, "The 'cloud' refers to the amorphous, out-of-sight, out-of-mind mess of computer tasks that happen on someone else's equipment. For the past five years or so the cloud has been hyped by companies to mean anything that happens on the Web, which is how 'cloud computing' came to rival 'social networking' in overuse."[1]

Although there are literally dozens or perhaps hundreds of definitions of cloud services that attempt to capture the essence of the examples just listed and Vance's quip, one that seems to have gained traction is the definition from the National Institute of Standards and Technology (NIST), locked down after 15 iterations:

> Cloud computing is a model for enabling ubiquitous, convenient, on-demand network access to a shared pool of configurable computing resources (e.g., networks, servers, storage, applications, and services) that can be rapidly provisioned and released with minimal management effort or service provider interaction.[2]

Further, NIST defines five major attributes: on-demand self-service, broad network access, resource pooling, rapid elasticity, and measured service.

The NIST definition is quite an achievement of both semantics and compromise among a variety of constituencies. For example, it refers to "broad network access" rather than specifying a particular network technology, such as the Internet.

However, I would argue that it is semantically equivalent to a simpler definition I devised a few years ago, which is a mnemonic not restricted to computing, based on cross-domain, relevant, quantifiable, economic characteristics.

> As mentioned earlier a Cloud, may be defined as a *service* that has
> the following attributes:
> **C**ommon infrastructure
> **L**ocation independence
> **O**nline accessibility
> **U**tility pricing
> on-**D**emand resources[3]

Conveniently, this spells out an easily memorized acronym: C.L.O.U.D. These may at first glance seem like five unrelated attributes, but they all tie together in an integrated business model. Unlike inherent limitations associated with fixed resources via ownership, on-demand resources provide for nearly unlimited scalability. Your house has only a few rooms. All the hotels in your city have quite a few. Of course, if the resources have zero marginal cost—if they are free or flat rate—then customers would be wasteful. Consequently, utility pricing (i.e., usage-sensitive charging) is essential to ensure economically rational use. Such on-demand resources with utility pricing can be economically viable only if they are allocated out of a shared pool. Sharing can occur only if the resources are available regardless of location. And, if such sharing is to occur, there must be a network allowing access to resources from whichever location the customer happens to be. It all fits together.

Elsewhere I've shown that this definition can be rigorously specified, axiomatically, from the foundations of mathematics, and that there are interesting problems in computational complexity arising from the cloud, but such discussion is well beyond the scope of this book.[4]

On-Demand Resources

The term "on demand" implies that the customer can be allocated the right quantity of resources at the right time for the right amount of time at any given time. This perfect allocation of resources in an environment of shifting requirements in turn implies elasticity to increase or decrease resources as well as sufficiently fine-grained increments of resource quantity and sufficiently fine-grained increments of time. For example, if a customer has 10 servers and suddenly needs 20, or if the customer has 20 but suddenly only needs 10, resources that are on demand are able to scale up or down appropriately.

Sufficient granularity of quantity implies that if customers need 20 they can receive 20, but if customers need 1 they can receive 1 and if customers only need a quantity of .07 they can be allocated just that quantity.

Sufficient granularity of time implies that if customers need a resource for a week, they can have it for a week; if they need it for a day, they can have it for a day; and if they need it for an hour or a minute, they can have it for that long. (Note that cloud computing providers currently don't appear to offer less than one-hour increments.)

Ensuring the right quantity, in a context of demand for fractional quantities of resources, is the task of a virtualization layer or a multitenant architecture. Ensuring the right duration is the task of the resource allocation layer.

Electricity comes very close to the ideal: Flicking a switch to power a device that draws exactly a given amount of power, say, 37.3 watts, provides access to exactly that much electricity instantaneously. Cloud computing comes close but doesn't match the ideal yet. Major cloud providers might offer the equivalent of an entire core, a half core, or a quarter core but not, say, .0437 of a core. And, if you need the capacity only for 7 minutes and 14.2 seconds, you will generally still be allocated and charged as if you had it for an entire hour.

Generally, larger increments work to the advantage of the service provider; smaller ones, to the advantage of the customer. If a customer must buy an entire bottle of wine when she only wants a glass, she will be overpaying. However, service providers can gain market share by offering smaller increments of capacity. A good example is telephony, in which some carriers began to introduce six-second (a tenth of a minute) billing increments, when one-minute granularity had been the standard. Some hotels enable finer-grained increments than "days," permitting late checkout for a partial-day fee or even stays by the hour.

Having the right amount of resources at the right time is often critical to business success. Having more resources than needed signifies unproductive capital, which hurts margins and therefore impacts return on invested capital, profit, retained earnings, and market capitalization. Having too few resources impacts agility and can mean slow or no performance or delays for customers that impact the customer experience and lead to churn and bad word-of-mouth, increasing customer acquisition and retention costs.

As we explore in depth in Chapter 14, the value of on-demand resources is ultimately driven by the variability and unpredictability of demand. In the pathological case where demand is completely flat, on-demand resources are not necessary. However, when demand is more variable than static provisioning would allow, or unpredictable, there is a clear but application-dependent value.

Utility Pricing

In our definition of cloud, resources are *utility priced*. Other terms for the same approach include *pay-per-use, linear tariffs*, or *usage-sensitive* pricing or charging. Such usage may be metered over time (e.g., server hours) or based on quantity (e.g., bytes transferred) or some other "usage" metric or combination of metrics (e.g., per user or per seat per month). Subscription pricing—whether for newspapers or software as a service—is an interesting variant. It is typically flat rate per user but sensitive to the number of users. Since this is distinct from flat rate at the firm level, we consider it to be a usage-sensitive pricing model. It does illustrate, however, that granularity and context are important concerns. Is an online newspaper usage priced if there is a given rate per user? Or per user up to a number of devices? Or by article read? Or by paragraph? Sentence?

Utility pricing is in contradistinction to other pricing models, such as freemium, lifetime, nonlinear, or flat rate. An example of flat-rate pricing is the traditional enterprise license agreement for software, which is the same price regardless of the actual number of users, or so-called unlimited plans, for example, for texting or voice minutes, which have been priced so that the charge is the same whether you use the service a lot, a little, or not at all. A flat-rate plan costs the same amount each time period, typically per month, although there are flat-rate plans per day in many other industries: "unlimited" daily mileage plans in car rental services or "all-inclusive" daily rates at resorts such as Club Med, regardless of how much tennis you play or how many mai-tais you drink. A lifetime membership or subscription exists in some industries as well (e.g., Tivo Personal Video Recording services are currently available for $14.99 per month or a Product Lifetime Subscription fee of $499).

Utility pricing often goes hand in hand with on-demand services and resources. However, they are separable concepts. An omelet station at an all-you-can-eat buffet provides on-demand service but at a flat rate, and a hotel room that requires a reservation months in advance is not on demand but is still pay-per-use, based on the number of room-nights.

In cloud computing, such usage-sensitive pricing depends on the specific resource. Servers, or virtual servers, are often priced by the hour, whereas storage may be priced by the month. Time is not always part of the metric. Data transport is often measured by the number of gigabytes transferred in or out.

As we explain in Chapter 11, utility-priced—or usage-sensitive—resources can be the sole constituent of an optimal cost solution, or at least be a component of such a solution. We delineate the exact conditions under which utility pricing drives value creation.

A good way to think about on-demand, pay-per-use resources is that the demand for resources, the quantity of resources, and the charges for resources are all *exactly* aligned.

Common Infrastructure

If you were to invest in a suitably large number of dedicated, private resources, there would always be sufficient capacity, so *sufficient* resources would always be available at the right time but not the *right* number of resources in an environment with variable demand. Therefore, the only way to provide on-demand resources in an economically effective way is through common infrastructure.

"Common" in this sense implies both allocation from a *shared* pool and also *similar* (i.e., not custom). In the same way that hotels allocate rooms to guests from a shared pool of rooms, or allow them to congregate in the ballroom from a shared pool of floorspace, servers, virtual servers, or software resources are allocated dynamically and storage is dynamically partitioned. The fact that this sharing is dynamic is particularly important: Static splitting of costs is insufficient to drive the full spectrum of benefits.

A subtle point here is that such commonality suggests either common allocation in space or common allocation over time, or both. A condo might be rented by a given tenant at a given time and a different tenant at a later time. This is referred to as "time-division" multiplexing. Or two or more tenants might choose to become room- or apartment-mates (obviously at the same time), in which case it is referred to as "space-division" multiplexing.

Commonality also connotes similarity: It would be hard to allocate resources to users dynamically if each were custom-built for that user. You can put your suitcase anywhere you want in your hotel room, but you aren't allowed to renovate the bathroom or build an addition.

Common infrastructure, since it is an enabler of on-demand resourcing and utility, is an enabler of their benefits: business agility and thus revenue and market share growth as well as reduced cost.

Location Independence

Simply put, "location independence" means that a user or customer should be able to access the cloud service *ubiquitously* and *responsively* regardless of his or her location. If you are in your home, office, vacation home, boat, or car, the service should be available, and perform sufficiently similar to the service that is local.

A service that is available only, say, in Topeka, or in my living room would not satisfy this requirement.

Generally, we tend to think of clouds as being geographically dispersed rather than localized. However, upon further thought, it is clear that this is an implementation detail: We don't really care or need to know whether Amazon.com has thousands of distribution facilities including a distribution facility just down the street from us or only one, say, in Antarctica, as long as an ordered book gets to us within a desired time frame, say, one day. Similarly, we don't need to know anything about the physical locations for distributing ebooks as long as they arrive within an acceptable time frame, say one minute.

In the same way, we don't really care or need to know whether Amazon Web Services has a data center just down the street from us or only one, say, in Antarctica, as long as the compute or storage task is performed successfully within an envelope of acceptable response time. We don't need to know anything about Microsoft's Hotmail servers or Salesforce.com's data centers or Google's search query servers or Google Apps' servers.

For physical book delivery, 24 hours is acceptable, but to get hot coffee, only 1/6th of an hour (10 minutes) is. Similarly, for ebook delivery, 24 seconds is acceptable, but for keystroke mirroring, only 1/6th of a second may be. Therefore, a handful of distribution centers may work fine for books and a handful of data centers for ebooks. But for coffee and keystrokes, hundreds or thousands may be necessary. Location independence doesn't mean that location doesn't matter, it means that the behind-the-scenes engineering ensures that location doesn't matter to the customer or user.

We as *users* don't need to know; that is not to say that Amazon or Netflix or Microsoft or Google or Salesforce don't need to know. Each company needs to determine locations in accordance with meeting response-time service-level agreements or internal objectives. Each needs to site facilities to assure availability. Each needs to ensure that it is in compliance with various laws, such as the USA PATRIOT ACT and European privacy regulations.

However, that should be the service provider's problem, not the users'.

Location independence provides ubiquitous access to services and enhances the user experience and convenience; dispersion also enhances availability.

Online Accessibility

Networks are the key enabler for the other characteristics we've specified, such as common resources and location independence. Without networks, there could be no sharing (i.e., common resources) and thus no statistical multiplexing, no location independence, no on-demand resources, and therefore limited or no value creation via the cloud. Networks must be available and secure and have the capacity to enable interactions between endpoints and cloud services that create business value. Backups wouldn't work without networks; file sharing wouldn't work without networks; social networks wouldn't work without physical networks; access to remote on-demand capacity wouldn't work, and local on-demand capacity doesn't have a compelling business model.

Without networks, there is no cloud.

Difference from Traditional Purchase and Ownership

Exhibit 5.1 contrasts the on-demand, pay-per-use model of the cloud with a traditional model. As may be seen in Exhibit 5.1(a), as demand varies over time, fixed resources are overprovisioned to serve varying capacity. When a demand spike occurs, there are insufficient resources, leading to lost revenue and poor customer satisfaction and/or lost productivity and poor user satisfaction. By the time a tiger team assembles, does a postmortem, and orders additional capacity, it is too late to serve the spike, and there are now more excess resources than before. Moreover, cash outlays required to purchase and install this equipment lead to an up-front, nonrefundable one-time charge. Depending on the payment structure, the balance of up-front charges and recurring charges may not be exactly as shown, but the point is that, in this model, resources are not aligned with demand, and payment is not aligned with resources.

As shown in Exhibit 5.1(b), the cloud model has two specific characteristics that align demand, resources, and payment. On-demand resources ensure that exactly the right quantity of resources are available at exactly the right time, which I call perfect capacity, and pay-per-use—that is,

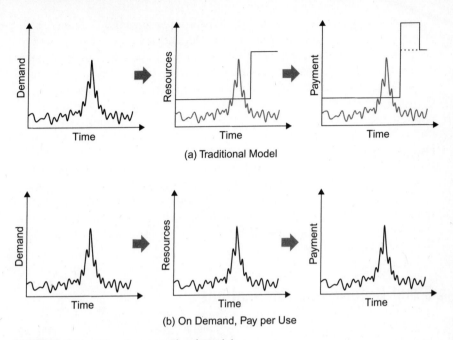

(a) Traditional Model

(b) On Demand, Pay per Use

EXHIBIT 5.1 Traditional versus Cloud Model

usage-based charging—ensures that the financial obligation incurred exactly matches the level of resources utilized. To restate things, on demand ensures that the resources curve exactly follows the demand curve, and pay-per-use ensures that the payment curve exactly follows the resources curve. All three are perfectly synchronized.

To be even more precise, we could further differentiate between resource allocation and resource use: A hotel room that is reserved for you but never used still incurs a payment if not canceled; similarly, the clock begins to tick on a virtual server the instant it is allocated, not necessarily when it begins performing useful work. We could also further differentiate between usage that incurs a payment obligation versus the actual act of payment (i.e., the transfer of money). However, the model described is sufficient to illustrate the salient characteristics.

We also note that the on-demand, pay-per-use model is not necessarily better in all respects for all users than other models. A logically inverted model can have benefits as well. For example, the variability in payment may cause budgeting challenges. Medical insurance premiums convert what could otherwise be spiky medical costs into a flat, predictable monthly charge (the premium), and some utilities offer plans to convert annual heating or air conditioning variation into a more predictable payment.

Generally, however, because in a business context demand is aligned with revenue, the on-demand, pay-per-use model ensures that costs and revenues are aligned with consistent service levels: Revenue is aligned with demand is aligned with resources is aligned with costs, stabilizing earnings.

It is also worth noting that on-demand pay-per-use can to some extent be implemented without shared resources. Some hardware vendors have implemented owned, dedicated capacity models with on-demand, pre-provisioned resources that are not charged for until turned up and used. However, while this approach is better than long delays to provision additional capacity, it may be argued that this approach is suboptimal compared to a common pool, because unused resources create economic loss, which must be recovered through higher prices to the customer for those resources that *are* used, or result in lower profitability to the vendor that is incurring manufacturing costs and costs of goods sold but not realizing revenue on that equipment.

Cloud Criteria and Implications

The five criteria—common, location independent, online, utility, and on demand—require a number of supporting capabilities.

Location independence—the ability for a person or device to use the service regardless of location—implies both ubiquity and responsiveness. As a result, it is essential to have either a robust network enabling access to one or a few locations or enough locations in enough places to overcome response time issues.

A utility—something useful and with usage sensitive pricing—implies a compelling customer value proposition ensuring utility (usefulness) and usage-sensitive pricing, which implies usage metering, rating, billing, and auditing. Note that the user doesn't always pay: Third parties such as advertisers may pay but will want to capture metrics such as click-throughs. Even offline, some combination of metering and auditing is essential; consider printed magazine circulation auditing.

On demand—the right quantity of resources at the right time—implies dynamic resource provisioning and deprovisioning, sufficient resources to handle aggregate demand, and either automated order processing (e.g., via self-service and the Web) or autonomic feedback loops that sense demand shifts and respond accordingly. Having the "right quantity" deployed can benefit from virtualization; otherwise excess will be provisioned due to the lack of fractional quantities.

While all of this could be done with multiple private siloed resources, such a method is uneconomical. Consequently, sharing resources—making them common, whether through corporate shared services or via a public model—requires securely partitioned space and/or secure reallocation of resources over time. In turn, sharing economically implies commonality of configurations rather than every customer receiving a fully custom set of resources. Customization must be performed via soft configuration rather than by physical reconstruction.

Finally, such sharing requires a network for various customers in various locations to gain access to the common pool.

Is the Cloud New or a New Buzzword?

There are some who say that cloud computing is just old technology—mainframe time-sharing, outsourcing, virtualization—wrapped up in a new buzzword dreamed up by marketers.

I think it might be more appropriate to say that it is a classic *business model*, leveraging increasingly mature technologies, applied only recently in its entirety in a convenient to use and mature way to the domain of computing.

We've discussed what cloud computing *is*; let's compare it to prior approaches with which it exhibits some similarities.

- *Cloud is not classic time-sharing*—but it certainly has similar characteristics. The cloud is based on a different scale-out architecture, whereas the time-sharing model was intended for access to a single mainframe computer. The cloud also introduces the additional dimension of geographic dispersion to support location-independent processing of highly interactive workloads.
- *Cloud is not managed services.* Managed services come in a variety of flavors, such as basic managed, performance managed, and remote management. Basic managed services are typically resources such as managed servers or managed storage. In this model, one or more physical servers, say, are provided to a customer with either basic monitoring and management (e.g., ensuring that the server is alive and responding to pings, i.e., requests to verify its health) or enhanced monitoring and management (e.g., ensuring that the server is processing at least 5,000 transactions per minute or meeting a response time objective). Cloud environments are managed for availability as well, but a key difference is that managed services traditionally offer a fixed quantity of resources under multiyear contracts as opposed to on-demand, scalable resources for extremely short durations.
- *Cloud is not outsourcing.* It's true that outsourcing has similarities to cloud, in the sense that a customer, rather than owning assets, maintaining competencies, and running an organization, shifts an entire

capability to a third party. However, in the outsourcing model, assets are transferred in their entirety as a fixed quantity. For example, 5,000 servers, two data centers, and 400 IT professionals may be moved over the outsourcer. However, outsourcing has not typically made use of shared, scalable capacity to drive benefits but rather focuses on leveraging centers of excellence to achieve economies of skill, cost management, and managing scope creep to drive costs out of the business. In short, although outsourcing appears to gain and lose favor over time but generally can drive benefits, these benefits are not the same as what the cloud offers.

- *Cloud is not virtualization.* It's true that virtualization can be important in building clouds, enhancing security, and migrating workloads between physical servers. However, the concept of virtualization is orthogonal to "cloud." A cloud service could be offered without virtualization, and virtualization can be used in many ways that have nothing to do with the cloud. From an economic perspective, virtualization generates enormous value for small workloads but has limited value for large ones. It is cheaper to send a postcard via a "virtual" or multi-tenant berth on a postal truck rather than renting out the entire truck to carry it, but when moving an entire household, there is not much difference.

- *Cloud is not grid.* The term "grid" has been used to describe desktop grids, such as SETI@home; "departmental grids," which arguably are just clusters; and global grids, such as PlanetLab and the National Terascale Facility. The primary usage of the term is to describe a heterogeneous set of entities and resources that operate in a loosely coupled fashion. Moreover, traditionally the model is a peer-to-peer resource-sharing system between entities, without cross-charging. It is true that economic concepts related to large-scale distributed systems were being explored over two decades ago[5] and that the grid computing community is increasingly moving its center of gravity toward concepts more frequently associated with cloud computing. Cloud computing is also assimilating concepts typically associated with grid: The Intercloud is an emerging heterogeneous federation of cloud providers, in the same way that the Internet is a heterogeneous agglomeration of data networks. However, a salient difference is the usage-based pricing of the cloud, as opposed to merely distributed resource allocation of grids, as is the notion that a cloud itself is a service offered by a single entity rather than a loose collection of entities.

- *Cloud is not utility computing.* Although usage-sensitive pricing grew out of utility computing, the utility computing concept did not incorporate the notion of location independence: A single server in a single location could be utility-priced.

- *Cloud is not distributed computing.* Although most clouds are distributed, the two concepts are not equivalent. Distributed computing can support location independence but doesn't necessarily incorporate common resources across multiple customers, utility pricing, or on-demand resources.
- *Cloud is not ASP.* Application service providers are perhaps one of the closest models to one type of cloud: software as a service. However, as *application* service providers, they don't expose infrastructure resources via an infrastructure as a service model.
- *Cloud is not the Internet.* The Internet is a useful network for enabling ubiquitous access to cloud services. However, a variety of other network technologies are better for certain cloud architectures, such as hybrid clouds, and for certain types of traffic, such as high-definition video.[6]
- *Cloud is not the Web.* Web 1.0 is usually viewed as the one-way display to Web surfers of static Web pages created by Web site designers, whereas Web 2.0, and its business-internal counterpart, Enterprise 2.0, is usually considered to encompass two-way interaction, for example, between blog authors and commenters. Web 3.0 is the mobile Web. Although the Web is one example of a cloud service, the cloud concept is much broader.
- *Cloud doesn't require self-service.* Some believe that self-service is somehow important to the cloud. Although the ability to immediately provision resources is surely preferable to a multi-month delay, there doesn't appear to be that much of a difference between using the Web to provision resources versus, say, calling up a customer service representative to do so. The fundamental economic value inherent in accelerated provisioning of resources is not necessarily related to the mechanism by which it occurs. Moreover, self-service is inferior to an application programming interface, where an application programmatically requests resources, or to autonomic control, where service provider logic realizes that additional resources are needed and supplies them either reactively or proactively in accordance with predefined policy or service level agreements.

In short, the cloud concept is related to and draws from other models of computing. However, it can be distinguished from them using the five C.L.O.U.D. criteria.

Summary

According to Lewis Carroll, the fictional Humpty Dumpty said "When I use a word . . . it means just what I choose it to mean—neither more nor less."[7]

We could define "cloud" to mean anything, but defining it as a common, location-independent, online, utility, on-demand service enables us to explore the economic properties of clouds in the coming chapters.

The cloud concept draws from many precursors in distributed computing, utility services, hosting and colocation, and even the mainframe era yet differs from them each in certain respects. The definition that we are using, moreover, is domain independent and applies to taxi services, hotel chains, electric utilities, and others. Therefore, much of the analysis in the rest of the book applies not only to cloud *computing* but to these other domains as well.

Notes

1. Ashlee Vance, "The Cloud: Battle of the Tech Titans," *Bloomberg Businessweek*, March 3, 2011. www.businessweek.com/magazine/content/11_11/b42190525 99182.htm?chan=magazine+channel_top+stories.
2. NIST Tech Beat, "Final Version of NIST Cloud Computing Definition Published," Information Technology Laboratory, October 25, 2011. www.nist.gov/itl/csd/cloud-102511.cfm.
3. Tony Chan, "Full Interview: AT&T's Joe Weinman," *GreenTelecomLive*, March 16, 2009. www.greentelecomlive.com/2009/03/16/full-interview-att%E2%80%99s-joe-weinman/.
4. For the mathematical foundation, see Joe Weinman, "Axiomatic Cloud Theory," Working Paper, July 29, 2011, www.joeweinman.com/Resources/Joe_Weinman_Axiomatic_Cloud_Theory.pdf; for computational complexity proof, see Joe Weinman, "Cloud Computing is NP-complete," February 21, 2011. www.joeweinman.com/Resources/Joe_Weinman_Cloud_Computing_Is_NP-Complete.pdf.
5. Mark S. Miller and K. Eric Drexler, "Markets and Computation: Agoric Open Systems," in B. A. Huberman, ed., *The Ecology of Computation* (North-Holland, 1988).
6. Joe Weinman, "Network Implications of Cloud Computing," ITU Telecom World Technical Symposium, October 26, 2011. www.joeweinman.com/Resources/Joe_Weinman_ITU_Network%20Implications%20of%20Cloud%20Computing.pdf.
7. Lewis Carroll, *Alice in Wonderland, and Through the Looking Glass* (Lothrop, 1898).

CHAPTER 6

Strategy and Value

Cloud services are worthy of consideration only if they create value for their customers. Many believe that the value of the cloud can be simply characterized by either reduced costs or increased agility. The term "agility" is often bandied about in cloud discussions, but what it actually is and how to actually quantify it never seem to get defined. Another value driver— customer or user experience—is the forgotten stepchild of cloud: Entire books have been written about business in the cloud that do not mention the customer experience even once.

"Value" is complex.

Values of the cloud, such as cost reduction and agility enhancement, may be more or less relevant depending on strategy. Strategy is not decided in a vacuum but is a function of capabilities and competencies relative to the competition, and the global environment: macroeconomic factors, regional growth, regulatory and legal constraints, and others.

Access to Competencies

When selecting a neurosurgeon or cardiologist, most patients don't make a choice based on comparing the costs of do-it-yourself versus the costs of the specialist but on the simple fact that the physician has competencies and expertise that the patient doesn't. Although you might attempt brain surgery on yourself for the cost of a knife, thus saving several hundred thousand dollars, it is not recommended.

Cloud computing can provide such access to competencies as well. Running a data center well is a complex undertaking requiring physical security, cybersecurity, certifications, configuration management, automated provisioning tools, power and cooling engineering, and the like.

At the application layer, when taxpayers access HRBlock.com or another tax preparation site, they are accessing a specific competency encoded in software, namely knowledge of and the ability to apply the complex tax code to be in compliance. This value is of course not restricted to the cloud: Individuals and companies access outside counsel who have specific legal competencies, such as expertise in bankruptcy law; investment bankers who have specific financial competencies, such as expertise in mergers and acquisitions; and also plumbers and electricians and nail artists and landscape architects and graphic artists.

As the world continues to develop increasingly specialized expertise, and as a substantial amount of this expertise becomes automated, the cloud will increasingly embody specific competencies: know-how, best practices, trade secrets, algorithms, heuristics, intellectual property, and processes.

A service provider often has the capability and competency to allocate resources, execute a process, achieve a result, or create value, and the customer simply does not. Consequently, it isn't a question of whether the provider can do the task more cheaply than the customer: The customer can't do it at all or needs to augment his own capabilities.

Implicit in this type of cloud-based value generation is the notion that there is value to leveraging the competency: Preparing your taxes correctly ensures that you get the highest possible refund without getting thrown in jail for tax evasion; evaluating restructuring options correctly ensures that maximum value can be extracted from a business unit. Consequently, leveraging external competencies costs money, but this cost is an investment in lower, say, operating costs or compliance penalties, higher revenues, or lower risk.

At one extreme are domain-specific competencies: A software as a service (SaaS) package may embody an optimal strategy for tax deductions for offshore investments or the best sales funnel management approach. At the other extreme are horizontal competencies (i.e., those not tied to a specific vertical industry): how to run a data center, how to cool it, how to secure it, how to do automated provisioning.

Relative competence can be black or white: Surely a neurosurgeon knows infinitely more about neurosurgery than you or I do. It can also be represented by shades of gray—so-called economies of skill—where greater competence can lead to shorter lead times, lower costs of production, less variability in output quality, lower schedule or cost risk. As expertise is gained and best practices and exceptions are embodied in software or operations, these economies can increase—engendering "learning curve" or "experience curve" effects.

Availability

Availability is inextricably tied to revenue. Customers can't buy and users can't work unless the services and applications that they need, and the infrastructure that supports them, are available. Often availability is also tied to cost, because downtime can result in suboptimized processes, manual workarounds, and service-level agreement penalties.

The cloud enhances availability of resources and thus business processes. Today most cloud-based services are hosted at multiple sites. If one site goes down, users and customers can be routed to and served by another site. There are two main dimensions to availability: data and services.

The cloud can create value by enhancing the availability of data in two ways:

1. Local on-premise data can be backed up in the cloud, thus ensuring that one or more copies exist even if there is a loss of the primary copy due to a "smoking hole" disaster (i.e., loss of a facility due to terrorism, a tornado, hurricane, flood, etc.).
2. Data in the cloud can be replicated to multiple locations, ensuring that the cloud has backup as well, namely the cloud.

Service availability—the availability of the business processes that deliver services, including the resources that enable those business processes—can be enhanced by the cloud too. In the same way that a hotel can be the residence for someone whose house has burned down, cloud resources can be called into service in the event of a data center disaster or significant outage. Moreover, like a hotel, a person doesn't need to pay for the resources unless and until they are used.

Capacity

Availability due to downtime is an issue, but availability may also be impacted by lack of capacity. If a Web site is not responding, does it have a software problem? Is the data center offline? Has a network connection been lost? Has the site been hit by a distributed denial of service attack? Or is it just that the capacity is insufficient?

To customers, the reason doesn't really matter—they will take their business elsewhere or rethink their purchase decision. The cloud creates value in this case through the capture of marginal revenue and the reduction of negative impacts associated with insufficient capacity.

Comparative Advantage and Core versus Context

Even if a company has the same competencies that a service provider does, the economic theory of comparative advantage—to which we owe a debt to a two-century-old treatise written by economist David Ricardo—suggests, in simple terms, that it is better to focus on what you can do best and trade for the rest.[1] Both parties to the trade benefit.

Geoffrey Moore, in what might be considered a more recent formulation of this argument, has suggested that companies focus on core activities—those that strategically differentiate them from the competition—and leave context activities—even ones that they are perfectly capable of doing—to others.[2] In other words, in today's attention economy, a frenetic world of hypercompetition where leadership time is the scarce resource, it is best to focus on those areas that mean life or death for the company rather than things that would be nice to do if only you had the time.[3]

In this case, the cloud creates value by enabling a greater focus on those activities that IT and non-IT functions within the firm can and must do uniquely well to succeed—or even survive.

Unit Cost

If both the customer and the service provider have similar competencies, unit cost can be an important differentiator. Unit cost advantages can be due to a variety of causes such as scale economies or preferential access to resources. As an example of the difference, consider running your own natural gas generator versus getting electricity generated from the Hoover Dam. The Hoover Dam's generators are larger than you might have in your backyard; they're probably larger than the backyard itself. This size surely drives economies of scale. If these larger generators were *not* more efficient, they would have been replaced long ago with many smaller ones.

Moreover, while you have to pay for the natural gas that powers your generator, they get their Colorado River water—and the kinetic and potential energy contained in it—for free.

In any case, if the cloud can do something more cheaply, it clearly can create value.

Delivered Cost

Unit cost and economies of scale are concepts that date back to the early days of manufacturing. They are generally useful but somewhat misleading when applied to service businesses, for reasons that are worth considering for a moment.

In production operations, the concept of unit cost is based on the notion of a factory that is producing at capacity and is completely decoupled from customer demand. Generally, as production facilities expand in size, various costs may proportionally increase (diseconomies), remain the same, or decrease, that is, exhibit economies of scale.

An important issue, however, is that the nature of demand does not enter the picture: Unit cost is based on total cost divided by production volume at capacity. If not sold, goods that are produced are carried as inventory, leading to inventory holding costs, which can include floor space, automatic storage and retrieval systems, labor costs to move inventory around, costs of obsolescence, and insurance or risk-adjusted costs of damage or destruction. In a manufacturing business, the price paid by the customer for a unit of production is a function of the unit cost of production, *plus* inventory carrying costs, *plus* additional components of the cost structure such as sales, general, and administrative, margin, financing operations, and so forth.

In manufacturing, output can be constant, and demand variation can be buffered with inventory throughout the process: raw materials inventory, work-in-process inventory, finished goods inventory, inventory in the distribution channel. Costs for maintaining these inventories may be borne by the manufacturer or the distributor but ultimately are paid for by the customer.

In other words, the delivered cost is based partly on production costs, which are affected by scale economies, and based partly on inventory costs, which are affected by the profile of demand relative to production. In a services business, the delivered cost is based partly on operations costs, which are affected by scale economies, and partly on perishable, unused capacity costs, which are affected by the profile of demand relative to operational capacity.

Services business—such as the cloud—don't care just about the unit cost. They must account somehow for the impact of demand variation—the fact that demand may not perfectly match output. Unfortunately, perishable capacity can't be buffered. If Boeing doesn't sell an airplane, it can keep it in a hangar at an airfield somewhere until a customer rings its bell with a check in hand.

But if an airline doesn't sell a ticket for a seat on a flight, that "seat" can't be kept in a warehouse until someone decides to fly on it, at least not until time travel is perfected.

If Boeing sells 50% fewer airplanes than it produces from January through June and 50% more airplanes than it produces from July through December, on New Year's eve, there will be no planes left: Everything balances out (except for the inventory holding costs).

If an airline sells 50% fewer seats than it has available from January through June, well, they are gone forever. Selling 50% more seats than it has in the second half of the year won't make things up; in fact, it will lead to additional costs to resolve overbooking issues.

An enterprise has the same issue with its own data center capacity and a cloud service provider with its capacity. When determining a price for a unit of capacity, it isn't only the unit cost that matters. It is obvious that for a viable enterprise, price must be greater than or equal to cost. What may be less obvious is the fact that the *price* for a unit of sold capacity must cover not only the *cost* of a unit of sold capacity but also the costs of any *unsold* capacity.

Total Solution Cost

The delivered cost of a particular set of resources under a particular pricing scheme is insufficient for a customer to clearly select between alternatives by determining their relative value. There are also training costs, information costs, transaction costs, migration costs, auditing costs, and the like. Also, there are capital expenditures and recurring operating expenses that may be relevant. For example, although the unit cost of a particular industry-standard server or performance-equivalent virtual server might be identical between do-it-yourself or a cloud service provider, as we argue earlier, the delivered price from a service provider might differ from the cost of do-it-yourself based on utilization differences or on additional structural cost elements.

But even if there were no difference, we would need to factor in those information and transaction costs and *also* consider deltas to other expenditures/expenses. In some cases, these can favor the cloud, in some cases not. For example, network infrastructure or data transport costs can add to the cost of the cloud solution. However, if the data are already in the cloud or in a so-called hybrid hosting architecture involving colocation, hosting, and cloud services, it might be substantially less than the enterprise-owned/dedicated solution.

This discussion implicitly assumes that these costs are known and thus value can be determined. There are two problems. The first is that the chief information officer (CIO) of an enterprise typically doesn't have a comprehensive analysis of every single cost element of operations at his or her fingertips to help make a rational economic cloud decision. Trying to determine how to allocate overhead costs appropriately can be a challenge, to say the least.

The second problem is that determining the cost of cloud services over a planning horizon for a financial analysis—say, three to five years—assumes that the quantity of services purchased, *and* their price, can be accurately predicted. As for quantity, this depends on the application usage profile, which is a function of everything from macroeconomic factors to the aggregate behavior of crowds of fickle users.

As for price, it is difficult—no, impossible—to predict what the price of a service provider's cloud offer will be tomorrow, much less three or five years from now. The track record of frequent price cuts among the major providers underscores this variability. And, to make things even worse, dynamic pricing has come to cloud services—several years after I predicted it would.[4] This means that some resources are priced like airline seats, changing several times per day.

The net result is that determining value requires a stochastic approach: a probability-weighted or risk-adjusted valuation.

Opportunity Cost and Cost Avoidance

Creating still further complexity, the benefits associated with one course of action must be considered not only in and of themselves but in relation to the benefits (and costs) associated with other alternatives. The opportunity cost is the cost of the loss of a benefit that might have been realized from a different course of action.

Today we live in a world of infinite choice but finite budgets. Money spent to implement application A means that application B will have to be put on the back burner, delaying or eliminating any benefits it would drive. Money saved by limiting infrastructure build-out may be exceeded by the opportunity cost due to unserved, revenue-generating demand, or reduced labor productivity.

Agility

The world is becoming more turbulent, and, consequently, yesterday's core competencies may become tomorrow's "core rigidities."[5] The sense that the world is more turbulent is not just a feeling; it can be measured in a market sector by examining shifts in relative market ranking from year to year. MIT Sloan School of Management professors Andrew McAfee and Erik Brynjolfsson, leading researchers at the intersection of IT and business, have found that not only has turbulence been increasing over the past decades but that it is dramatically greater in "high-IT" industries.[6]

These days, more and more industries are becoming high IT. The percentage of CIOs who recognize that IT is an essential part of their company's product or service is growing. Over a third of CIOs surveyed by InformationWeek Analytics said that "introducing new IT-led products and services" is among their top priorities.[7] Conversely, only 17% said that IT has no role in innovation. Beyond classic cloud examples such as Netflix or Zynga, even century-old companies are investing in cloud-based services enhancements to physical products: BMW is investing in mobile applications that provide information on parking availability and real-time traffic, thus detouring from the autobahn to the infobahn.[8]

As a result of increased incorporation of information technologies in products and services, we have entered an accelerating global race: Increased software components in the product increases the speed of change—a new car design might take a year or two, a SaaS provider can deploy a change in minutes, and firmware in a product such as a digital photo frame or set-top box can be downloaded in the same amount of time. Responding to such developments requires competitive agility, with IT capabilities—both in process and product/service—aligned to the business.

As a consequence of this turbulent, high-velocity, flat world, Kara Sprague, an associate principal at McKinsey & Company, citing recent *McKinsey Quarterly* surveys, highlighted that what business executives want from the cloud even more than economic savings are the benefits of increased business flexibility or "agility," with 70% of business respondents believing that this will be the true source of value to enterprises in deploying cloud solutions.[9]

In Chapter 14, we will precisely quantify agility in resource provisioning, but business agility more broadly entails the ability to quickly adjust to shifting customer preferences, respond to competitor actions, seize new or ephemeral market opportunities, or generally exploit or defend against any discontinuity. To the extent that products, services, processes, supply chains and innovation are all enabled or inextricably linked to information technology, the cloud at all its layers—infrastructure, platform, and applications software—can drive value through enhanced agility, in turn increasing revenue, reducing cost, and reducing risk.

Time Compression

McKinsey & Co. has conducted research suggesting that for high-tech products, being 50% over budget has little impact on overall product profitability, whereas being six months late reduces profitability by one third.[10] The reason for this is simple: the product life cycle.

When a new product enters a market, it begins a period of exponential growth before eventually the growth slows as the market matures, then growth flattens, and eventually the product becomes obsolescent, "growth" turns negative, and volume falls, perhaps to zero. This is the classic S-curve.

Early in the life cycle, margins can be relatively high. These margins attract new entrants, which often compete on price, driving margins lower and, in turn, driving industry consolidation or exits from the business. Although a fast-follower strategy can be effective, first-mover advantage typically is associated with higher margins. Moreover, network effects and virtuous cycles can result in ecosystem partners tying their fortunes to the early market participants, creating stable relationships that can make it difficult for late entrants to gain any meaningful share.

Finally, there is a time value of money: Even if there were no difference in nominal revenue, having that same revenue a year or two earlier is worth more.

The net result is that the raw speed of time to market makes a key difference in financial results through these different drivers.

Rob Shelton leads Growth & Innovation within PricewaterhouseCoopers' (PwC) Advisory practice and, before that, led the Global Innovation practice at global management consulting firm PRTM, which was acquired by PwC in 2011. Based on extensive industry studies, Shelton pointed out that unnecessary delays in new product development time push out the launch date. Getting the fully developed new product into the market as quickly as possible speeds revenue generation and turns the cash flows positive more rapidly. For that reason, many leading companies aggressively manage the time to value for new products. And the oft-heard operating rule in new product and service development is "Better to be slightly over budget than be late."[11]

Although it varies by industry, a good rule of thumb is that IT costs are 4% of revenue. This means that if *all* IT projects were 50% over budget, there would be a net difference of 2% to the bottom line. However, given the preceding logic, the revenue impact, margin impact, and time-value-of-money impact are likely to grossly outweigh this 2% difference. Moreover, in an ecosystem with winner-take-all dynamics, time can make the difference between bankruptcy and long-run market success.

Margin Expansion

Cloud services can informationalize products and services, leading to margin expansion. Some argue that the costs of processing, storage, and networking are headed to zero. Although this is an overstatement, there is no question but that costs are falling due to Moore's Law types of effects. Take any product based on physical commodities—platinum, steel, rare earths—or service based on real resources—trucks, barber shop chairs, classrooms—together with labor costs not subject to Moore's Law. If value can be enhanced or the cost structure of such components can be complemented by the value-adding zero-marginal-cost economics of information goods and services, margins can be expanded.

Customer and User Experience and Loyalty

Customer experience improvements can result in lower churn, higher prices due to perceived value-add, greater engagement and higher customer loyalty, greater willingness to repurchase, greater awareness of offline products and services, and thus increased purchase volumes.

The cloud can enhance customer experience by providing a richer, more interactive experience, whether it is at the front end—shopping, awareness, solution design—or the back end—installation, maintenance, support, returns.

Rena Granofsky, president and founder of RIT Experts, leverages a model developed by J.C. Williams Group claiming that buyers often are driven by one or two of four factors, the four E's: *economical* (cheaper), *easy* (convenience), *ego* (need for status), and *experience* (enjoyment of a multidimensional shopping process).[12] In the offline world, this explains why Walmart (economical), 7-Eleven (easy), Coach (ego), and Nordstrom (experience) can all be successful.

Online, it means that a simple, clutter-free, interaction such as Google's home page can be successful as well as a rich, multimedia, Flash, Silverlight, or HTML 5 interaction. In Chapters 16 through 20, we explore several dimensions of customer experience. For now, we note that reduced response time has been frequently correlated with increased revenue. Also, as we discussed in Chapter 3, Treacy and Wiersema's value discipline of customer intimacy can be an effective strategic focus; providing meaningful, personalized information and entertainment can enhance loyalty and thus willingness to repurchase.

For "internal" applications, we can consider the employee or user experience rather than the "customer" experience. In today's economy, the productivity of information workers is surely critical and is based partly on "quality of experience." Yet companies often underinvest in networks and servers, leading to slow computer interactions. This may often be penny wise, pound foolish. Multiply an application that takes an extra second for each Web page to load times tens of thousands of workers using that application for hundreds of transactions each day times over 200 workdays each year, and the magnitude of the user experience cost becomes clear.

Add poor user interfaces into the equation, causing incorrectly entered information requiring rework, processes that were not followed, missed opportunities, customers irritated by the customer service representative's lack of background information regarding the relationship, and the total cost of poor user experience becomes evident.

Employee Satisfaction

Employee satisfaction is partly a result of quality user experience, but it is certainly more than that. Cloud services can enhance autonomy and the perception of control by freeing employees to be creative and solve problems, whether it is something as simple as searching for an answer or using a cloud-based platform to build or extend a solution.

Although the traditional maxim suggests that "The customer comes first," there is also a school of thought that "The employee comes first."[13] Rather than a platitude, the point is that unhappy employees who lack autonomy are unlikely to drive quality customer interactions.

Revenue Growth

Revenue growth can be enhanced via the cloud, through:

- Greater value incorporated into the product or service
- Greater market penetration through the global reach of the cloud
- Greater availability through replication of data and application resources
- Greater conversion of sales through scalable online channel resources
- Greater customer engagement through richer experiences delivered via the cloud
- Greater revenue, allowing for the time value of money, by accelerating future revenue streams into the present

Community and Sustainability

Support of the community and environmental sustainability are noble goals. More than mere nobility, they also have a sound business rationale. The cloud can help in this arena, since rather than wasting owned resources, leveraging shared resources can be "greener."

Moreover, the cloud can facilitate postpurchase redistribution markets and collaborative consumption for physical goods, also enhancing sustainability. And services provided by the cloud can provide various benefits ranging from reducing physical tasks, such as transportation of goods and people; reducing energy use and water use; and optimizing transportation and distribution logistics through route optimization, real-time traffic management, and better truck packing.

Risk Reduction

The term "risk" has a variety of definitions and connotations that seem to fall into two general categories. In one, it is a measure of the variability or dispersion of outcomes: There is a low risk that the sun will not rise tomorrow; the risk associated with an investment in the tech sector is higher than that in a utility. In another, it is a measure of the likelihood of undesirable outcomes: Playing Russian roulette is risky.

In either case, the cloud can reduce risk in a number of ways. At the infrastructure level, the risk of financial loss due to excess capacity is reduced, since you need to pay only for capacity that is used. An even bigger risk is the risk of financial loss due to insufficient capacity.

Today's businesses are either IT-native businesses—think Google—or have a strong IT component. An example of the latter might be FedEx or UPS: Their core business is package delivery, but tracking and optimizing logistics, whether it is determining optimal routes or how best to pack trucks, is essential to their competitiveness, their customer value proposition, and their margins.

At the platform and software services layers, a different type of risk reduction comes into play: It is the difference between being the test pilot on an experimental rocket that you designed and built yourself versus being a passenger on a commercial jet. Enterprise customers are often faced with the choice of building a new software product versus leveraging existing components via platform as a service or using off-the-shelf software delivered as a service.

Generally, projects of any sort run into problems: Software seems to be among the domains that experience this the most. Software development projects are late, over budget, fail to meet their original objectives, or meet their original objectives, but the market has changed and those original objectives are no longer valid.

By using certified, pretested components that have been proven through use, risk can be greatly reduced. Complete, prebuilt software applications can reduce this risk even further.

Competitive Vitality and Survival

Putting a number of these benefits together ultimately can lead to an enterprise that is engineered to survive and thrive in today's environment of global competition. Winner-take-all dynamics, radical industry transformation, and the rapidity of technological change all mean that yesterday's successes mean nothing. The cloud—helping enterprises manage risk, enhancing agility, compressing time, reducing costs, growing revenues, and increasing customer loyalty—can help improve the chances of survival.

Summary

Every firm is unique at any given time in terms of goals, strategy, competencies, and relationship to competition. The cloud—as we have defined it—generates value in many ways. It is typical to list the benefits of the cloud as cost reduction and business agility. But pigeonholing benefits to these two categories is overly constricting.

Cloud computing can support a broad range of financial, strategic, employee, and customer goals, ranging from cost reduction to revenue growth, and from internal productivity and employee satisfaction to customer experience improvements.

Notes

1. David Ricardo, *On the Principles of Political Economy and Taxation* (John Murray, 1817).
2. Geoffrey A. Moore, *Dealing with Darwin: How Great Companies Innovate at Every Phase of Their Evolution* (Portfolio, 2005).
3. Thomas H. Davenport and John C. Beck, *The Attention Economy: Understanding the New Currency of Business* (Harvard Business Press, 2001).
4. Joe Weinman, "The Evolution of Networked Computing Utilities," *Business Communications Review* (November, 2007). http://joeweinman.com/Resources/WeinmanUtility.pdf.
5. Omar A. El Sawy, Arvind Malhotra, Sanjay Gosain, and Kerry M. Young, "IT-Intensive Value Innovation in the Electronic Economy: Insights from Marshall Industries," *MIS Quarterly* 23, No. 3 (1999): 305–335.
6. Andrew McAfee and Erik Brynjolfsson, "Investing in the IT That Makes a Competitive Difference," *Harvard Business Review* (July 2008). *86*(7/8), pp. 98–106.
7. Chris Murphy, "IT Must Create Products, Not Just Cut Costs," *Information Week*, March 12, 2011. www.informationweek.com/news/global-cio/interviews/229300065.
8. Ibid.
9. Kara Sprague, conversation with the author, November 3, 2011.
10. Cyril Charney, *Time to Market: Reducing Product Lead Time, Society of Manufacturing Engineers*, 1991.
11. Rob Shelton, conversation with the author, November 18, 2011.
12. Rena Granofsky, conversation with the author, January 24, 2012.
13. Vineet Nayar, *Employees First, Customers Second: Turning Conventional Management Upside Down* (Harvard Business Review Press, 2010).

CHAPTER 7

When—and When Not—to Use the Cloud

The cloud is appropriate for many things but not for everything. Here we look at the types of problems or use cases where a cloud approach applies and then consider those cases where the cloud is inappropriate. As with many things regarding the cloud, "it depends" is often the correct answer: Different companies with different strategies at different times may have different perspectives on where and why to use the cloud.

Use Cases for the Cloud

There are a number of use cases, or scenarios, for leveraging the cloud.[1] If we consider the leading cloud services—Salesforce.com/Force.com, Microsoft Azure, Amazon Web Services, the Rackspace Cloud, GoGrid, Facebook, Twitter, and Google Search, Google Apps and App Engine, Apple iTunes and the App Store, and Wikipedia, for example—they fall into one or more of these categories. Moreover, in keeping with the tone of this book— that cloud is a cross-domain concept not restricted to computing—we will allude to offline analogies as appropriate. For example, a big data repository in the cloud is analogous to the New York Public Library or the Library of Congress; collaboration via the cloud is not much different than gathering in a conference room; markets where buyers and sellers can meet online are not much different than flea markets or the New York Stock Exchange.

Complementary Capabilities and Competencies

The cloud may offer a competency that you or your firm doesn't have. This may be at the infrastructure layer—for example, data center operations; at

91

the software layer—for example, specific algorithms encoded and optimized but available only via the cloud; or at multiple layers—for example, security operations skills. Examples of specific competencies present in the cloud are tax preparation algorithms embedded in an online tax service, search algorithms and an indexed Web, information regarding flight schedules and prices but also expected delays, stock market ticker data, algorithms for finding matches, between people and movies and between people and people.

Communications

There are many types of communications in the cloud: voice, video chat, texting, direct messaging, and email, for example. Any type of communication is enabled or optimized via a cloud-based architecture, for the simple reason that a hub, or a meshed network of hubs, generates efficiencies over point-to-point communications. Although a central controller may have a strong role, such as storing files, a limited role, such as maintaining a directory of users, or no role, even peer-to-peer applications, such as Bit-Torrent and Skype, appear to be point-to-point but of course ride over the top of meshed networks. Otherwise you would need to build a direct physical network between yourself and anyone with whom you might wish to communicate. You may know that the number of point-to-point connections in a network with n users grows essentially as the square of n, whereas the number of connections in a network with a central hub or switch grows linearly with n. However, as we explain in Chapter 24, there are some trade-offs: Using a hub-and-spoke network can increase the average connection length, and thus latency, by almost half relative to a point-to-point network.

Such a strategy is not restricted to cloud computing: Airlines use hub-and-spoke networks, highways do, and even rivers and their tributaries naturally consolidate flows rather than each drop of rain finding its own path to the sea.

The value of communication cannot be underestimated: Communication enables the transmission of information, and information is required for the efficient functioning of markets. Market mechanisms drive productivity and human welfare. This is as true for the efficient allocation of capital via the financial markets as it is for the fishermen of Kerala, who now use mobile phones from their fishing boats to head to the best market to sell their catch, both based on real-time market data and dynamic prices.[2]

There are many examples of communications via the cloud. Twitter lets you easily send 140-character tweets to one user via a direct message or to millions of users—if you are @ladygaga, @KimKardashian, or @BarackObama—via a public tweet. Dropbox lets you easily send or share files. Slideshare lets you easily share slides (i.e., presentations). Instagram lets you share photos. YouTube lets you share videos.

Conversations, Connections, and Communities

A series of communications between two participants is a conversation. Conversations create persistent connections. Conversations and connections among those with shared interests, values, and goals create communities.

Communities are not new constructs. They exist among social primates, flocks of birds, schools of fish, and ant colonies. What is different now is that communities are no longer based solely on the accident of geography: Whether you were a bacterium or a polymath, where you were born defined who you were. Now global networks help forge strong bonds as well as useful weak ties between geographically disparate individuals, ties that on one hand can help unique individuals align with others of like mind and on the other hand can accentuate issues with the confirmation bias (a cognitive bias that causes people to filter out data that conflicts with their beliefs).

Sometimes online communities reflect real-world relationships. For example, Classmates.com creates a virtual community driven by which school you went to, which often is based on the accident of where you happen to live. In other cases, the real-world reflects connections created in cyberspace: I've met many people in person *after* first "meeting" them on Twitter. The cloud helps discover communities, discover members of those communities, and maintain connections within the community through directories and ongoing conversations.

Congregations, Commons, and Collections

In the real world, parks, concert halls, convention centers, and the like provide a facility for people to congregate. They also enable common, shared access to resources. In the exception that proves the rule, George Vanderbilt, in the late 1800s, was able to afford a private, 125,000-acre park as part of his unparalleled Biltmore Estate.[3] For everyone else, there are public commons, such as Central Park in New York City, coincidentally designed by the same architect: Frederick Law Olmsted. Collections, such as the Library of Congress, the Smithsonian Museum, the Louvre, or the Musée d'Orsay, have similar characteristics, only they are places where content is aggregated for shared access.

In the cloud services world, similar applications arise. Users can congregate in chat rooms or virtual worlds, such as Second Life, or online gaming sites, such as World of Warcraft. Infrastructure as a service is a type of commons available for rent: not unlike a hotel ballroom or convention center. And collections, such as Google Books or Big Data, generate benefit as they are created once, stored once (or perhaps a few times for data loss prevention and user experience enhancement), and accessed millions of times or for business intelligence and analytics.

Collections of information can be user-generated. Such information can be used not just for entertainment, as the case of sleeping cats and laughing babies on YouTube, but for social transformation. Ushahidi is a cloud-based platform and Web site for collecting information originating from cell phones and mapping it geographically. It was created immediately after social unrest grew following disputed elections in Kenya and has been described as organizing information regarding "riots, stranded refugees, rapes, and deaths . . . [collecting] more testimony with greater speed and broader reach than the media or the local officials."[4]

Consolidation

Moving to the cloud can enable "de-duplication." Rather than tens or millions of people all maintaining an exact copy of the same content, whether a PowerPoint presentation or the most recent *Saturday Night Live* on their personal video recorder, say, only one—or perhaps a handful—of copies would need to be maintained in the cloud, subject to legal and regulatory constraints. Of course, such consolidation requires highly available networks of sufficient capacity to enable a quality access experience, and can be facilitated by technologies such as EMC's Centera content-addressed storage, which identifies content based not on metadata such as file name but by a digital fingerprint based on its unique series of bits.

Collaboration, Competition, and Crowdsourcing

Collaboration can be viewed as a higher-level function built on communication: After all, it is hard to see how people could collaborate without communicating. Collaboration, however, entails additional functions similar to commons and collections, such as shared repositories of work in progress. Today, collaboration can mean a mix of synchronous and asynchronous communications across text, graphics, voice, and video, leveraging ephemeral communications as well as creating permanent archival content.

Competition is closely related to collaboration: Participants communicate with each other and share spaces with transient and permanent artifacts. The only difference is that, in collaboration, goals are aligned; in competition, they are opposed. Today's massively multiplayer online games are a blend of both, reflecting real-world constructs such as soccer teams and chess teams: Participants collaborate with each other to best other teams in games such as World of Warcraft.

Co-opetition is not restricted to wizards and space wars. Kaggle "is an arena where you can match your data science skills against a global cadre of experts in statistics, mathematics, and machine learning."[5] Teams of PhDs use arcane expertise to solve problems by designing algorithms that crunch large data sets. EdisonNation.com offers contests to design retail products, such as beach furniture and infant travel accessories. IdeaConnection.com offers collaborative workspaces for "Idea Rallies." The problem areas can be clear (e.g., "improving crop yield") or esoteric (e.g., "enhancing photosynthesis through D1 protein overexpression and enhancing stomatal response").[6] Yet2.com has numerous companies seeking solutions, such as the one seeking "products to viscosify (500 to 100Pas) aqueous acidic media pH (1.5 to 3) which contain both peroxides (2% to 8%) and biocides (0.1% to 2%), and are satable within the temperature range of 5°C to 45°C." InnoCentive offers a variety of challenges for global problem solvers to consider, such as "synthesis to 1,2,3,4-butanetetracarboxylic acid."[7] The point of these examples is to illustrate how well a cloud approach providing not just a matching service but also competitive incentives can match unique problems with the handful of people globally who might be able to solve them.

Goldcorp was able to mine the silver lining of the cloud by finding gold in its existing mine using cloud-enabled collaboration. Netflix did something similar with the Netflix Prize, which was based on an open competition to design the best movie recommendation algorithm.[8] If you liked *The Matrix* but also *The Notebook*, would you enjoy *The Shining* or *The Big Chill* more? Improving the quality of movie recommendations is important, since watching a stream of enjoyable movies helps ensure customers remain with the service. In other contexts, better recommendations increase upsell revenues.

Prediction markets, where individuals wager real or imaginary money on outcomes, and other forms of crowdsourcing,[9] such as averaging guesses or even conducting surveys, are interesting forms of unwitting collaboration. Even if participants are unaware that they are collaborating, they can still arrive at correct answers.

Commerce and Clearing

Markets that bring buyers and sellers together avoid the explosion of pairwise connections that would otherwise be required. In the 1700s, banks would settle accounts by having "walk clerks" from each bank travel to each other's bank in turn. As University of Warwick professor Martin Campbell-Kelly put it, "walking through the City of London with a large bag of money, was, to say the least, unwise," which is why the clerks eventually agreed to meet at a single location at a regular time.[10]

The London Banker's Clearing House became a hub for bank settlements early in 1800. By 1853, this approach was used in New York, with some improvements. In a sort of exchange network or human shift register, standing clerks would "speed date" by stepping once clockwise every eight seconds or so to meet their seated counterparty, finishing an entire rotation for 50 banks in six minutes. Thus, in n steps, n^2 combinations could be set up, and each pairwise settlement could occur.

The concept of money itself—whether rice as in ancient Japan, salt or coins as in the Roman Empire, gold, or rum as in colonial Australia—is relevant here: As a medium of exchange, it facilitates transactions between those holding goods that they would like to exchange and would otherwise have to barter; thus, it, in concept at least, acts as a hub. Such money enabled the first markets and market economies, which date back at least thousands of years.[11]

Marketplaces existed even before that: In ancient Greece hundreds of years earlier, the *agora* served as a general gathering place, one of whose uses was as a market.

Today, the physical market has to some extent been supplanted by online auctions; the retailer by the retailer; the physical clearinghouse by global financial payments and settlements networks; and the physical agora by the "ideagora," a term coined by Don Tapscott and Anthony D. Williams in *Wikinomics* to refer to online marketplaces of ideas that help foster innovation.[12]

"Markets" and matching are very general concepts: OpenTable.com matches prospective diners with open tables in restaurants. Kickstarter and Kiva match entrepreneurs needing funding with those having spare cash. ZocDoc matches patients with open doctors' appointments. TaskRabbit matches people with skills, time, and a desire to earn some money with errands—say, picking up dry cleaning—or tasks—say, painting the front door.

Collaborative Consumption

Rachel Botsman and Roo Rogers, authors of *What's Mine is Yours*, have suggested that there is a new economy emerging: collaborative consumption.[13] Rather than an economy based on solitary ownership of products, they argued that "communal economies" and "redistribution markets" will be a substantial portion of the economy in the coming years. The cloud plays a role as a market entity, connecting people who have goods with the people who want them, as well as an advertising entity.

Coordination, Currency, Consistency, and Control

If your watch and mine indicate different times, whose is right? Ultimately, the only way to answer questions like these is with reference to a single authoritative source. In the case of time, that source is "Coordinated Universal Time," which is delivered, via a variety of media including the Internet, to "clocks," which may include software widgets, to determine the correct time.

Besides this type of broadcast coordination, cloud services as efficient enablers of communication can coordinate events or ensure consistency of status. For example, the Arab Spring revolts that occurred in a variety of countries used Facebook and Twitter to coordinate protests. The August 2011 London riots were also coordinated via cloud services, in this case, BlackBerry messenger.[14] As a result, one way to disrupt coordination is to hinder or block the services.[15]

Other types of authorization also belong in the cloud, and enable coordination and control. Continued access to content, whether it's today's edition of *The New York Times* or *The Wall Street Journal*, or Netflix movies, requires that the software validate that your account is in good standing.

Yet another example is when multiple individuals are working on a shared document. Shipping documents, presentations, and spreadsheets around is not effective: Fred sends it to Bob and Carol and Ted and Alice. Alice makes a change that she sends to Bob and Carol, while Ted deletes a section and asks Carol to update it and only forwards it to Bob, then changes it and sends the revised version back to Fred. Chaos. With a single reference copy in the cloud, there is no doubt as to what the current version is, and changes can be rolled back, as with Wikipedia entries.

One of the key advantages of software as a service (SaaS) is that any software updates need to be applied only once, in the cloud. They are then instantaneously available to all users. This is different from what occurs with licensed software, which requires thousands, or millions, of updates, which in turn require suitable network connections, a successful download process, successful administrator permissions, and system reboots.

Cross-Device Access and Synchronization

In addition to synchronizing changes across multiple users, the cloud can help to synchronize content or applications across a single user with multiple devices, in what Forrester Research analyst Frank Gillet calls the "personal cloud," and projects to soon be a $12 billion dollar market.[16] A photo taken on your smartphone is nearly instantly available on your laptop and TV. Your Netflix queue is available via your laptop, your iPad, your smartphone, your Blu-Ray Disc players, your TiVos, and your Roku. You have access to different devices depending on what room you are in and which devices you are carrying while traveling. However, the cloud ensures that your queue is always up to date across devices and that you largely have continuous access to the current version. You can resume watching a show on a new device from the exact point you left off on a different device. Moreover, this is accomplished because Netflix—or its partners—can build interfaces or adaptors for each box or platform rather than each platform needing to ensure interoperability with the several dozen other platforms. Again, the cloud turns a difficult n^2 problem into a relatively straightforward order (n) problem.

Cash Flow

For healthy, large enterprises with billions or tens of billions in cash on their balance sheets, the fact that the cloud turns capital expenditures into operating expenses can be irrelevant or even counterproductive. However, for cash-strapped start-ups, SMBs (small and medium businesses), and even larger enterprises that are trying to conserve cash, the cash flow benefits of the cloud can be substantial.

Newline Products' chief financial officer Bill Bowers, formerly of Motorola, said that in evaluating do-it-yourself versus cloud services, "maybe from a payback analysis it's a toss-up . . . [but] in the cash-flow world, cloud is the way to go."[17]

Capacity

Capacity is a fundamental use case for infrastructure as a service. Raw capacity—Compute, network, memory, and storage—is available for rent, on a pay-per-use, on-demand basis. We explore the economics of pay-per-use in Chapter 11 and the economics of on demand in Chapter 14. If there *are* economies of scale in the cloud, such that the cloud offers more or better service—across all relevant decision parameters—at a lower cost than do-it-yourself, cloud-based capacity is the only way to go.

Instead of a pure cloud approach, cloud capacity can complement existing, owned capacity within an enterprise data center or colocation facility. In the same way that access to a hotel can prove useful when guests suddenly arrive from out of town, cloud capacity that complements owned capacity can provide a perfect mix of flexibility at minimum cost.

Continuity

The cloud can be a cornerstone of a business continuity/disaster recovery (BC/DR) or continuity of operations strategy. Not everyone lives in a house, but for those who do, very few have *another* house lying idle as a spare, *just in case* something happens to their primary house. However, a number of companies *do* have a sister site BC/DR strategy, which is equivalent: Pay for two, only use one. The cloud is enabling a new type of BC/DR, where data are replicated but the compute capacity is not. Instead, the computer resources are strictly cloud-based, on demand, pay per use. This matches what we do in the real world: Rather than owning an unused spare house, you stay in a hotel if your only house is hit by a tornado.

And if you sell your current house but your new house is not yet available, you also stay in a hotel. Companies undergoing data center migrations can potentially use cloud capacity as a temporary measure.

Checkpoints

Another use case for the cloud is the checkpoint. In the same way that Customs and Border Patrol, the Coast Guard, or NORAD protects our shores and borders, the cloud can effectively filter out everything from viruses and spam to distributed denial of service attacks. The cloud has four advantages:

1. Immense scale to protect against large-scale attacks
2. A position on the perimeter, where attacks can be stopped on ingress to core networks
3. Better resource utilization. It is better to drop unwanted traffic at the edge of the network than carry it to a destination and then drop it
4. Like the immune system, an ability to detect an unwanted signature in one place and then rapidly protect against it ubiquitously

Chokepoints

Many California highways have traffic lights to slow entry. Although these are painful when you are on the onramp, they serve to reduce congestion. Reduced congestion drives greater throughput. In other words, putting fewer cars on the road means that more cars get to their destination more quickly. The Federal Aviation Administration does the same thing with ground stops that reduce departures to reduce airspace congestion. The cloud can accomplish the same thing, throttling, policing, shaping, limiting, and/or managing data traffic in accordance with policy to ensure better service for all.

Context

Author, consultant, and venture partner Geoffey Moore is credited with distinguishing between core and context in a corporation. The idea is that core activities create meaningful differentiation—say, Apple's design efforts for its next device or Gucci's for its next dress—whereas everything else is context—say, scheduling janitors or operating the meeting room reservation system.

There is a popular line of thought that core activities should remain within the enterprise while context activities can easily move to the cloud. The latter is certainly true: Expense reporting, funnel management, and billing are just a few examples of context activities fully supported by cloud services. However, it can be argued that the cloud has grown up, and core activities can be delivered via the cloud just as well as context ones can.

Netflix has moved its members' queues, recommendations, transcoding, and video streaming to Amazon Web Services.[18] Honestly, what's left? There can't be much more that is core to Netflix than that.

Zynga leverages Amazon Web Services to deliver new games and migrates them back into its own data centers—the zCloud—after demand has stabilized.[19] Although the balance of private and public has shifted over time, Zynga does not appear to differentiate based on core versus context, but on an optimum balance of cost and elasticity. Some would say that game design is core and IT is context. Others might observe that it would be hard to find anything much more important to Zynga than ensuring successful game operations in today's world of fickle consumers. In short, while the core versus context dichotomy is plausible, its direct application to what to run in the cloud and what not to is less clear.

Celerity

"Celerity" is synonymous with "speed." Whether it is unique competencies or elastic "near-infinite" resources, various layers of the cloud can compress time. SaaS reduces the time needed to either develop similar functionality in house or deploy it in a traditional licensed software install process. Platform as a service (PaaS) reduces the time needed to write code by leveraging an assembly model on preexisting components coupled with customizability rather than writing a code a line at a time from scratch. And infrastructure as a service dynamically allocates predeployed resources rather than uncrating equipment, turning it up, and testing it.

Customer Experience

Clouds generally are geographically dispersed, enabling content and applications to be deployed closer to end users. In the same way that having a Starbucks on every corner reduces the time needed to grab a cup of coffee, having a content delivery or application delivery node on (practically) every corner reduces the amount of time required to interact with an application or retrieve a bit of content. Reduced time equals improved customer experience.

Combinations of the Above

Any or many of the above use cases can be deployed in combination. Take Twitter as an example. Certainly it is a vehicle for communications. But in addition, the billions of tweets that exist are all in a repository and can be retrieved via individuals' timelines, via search.twitter.com, or through the Twitter application programming interface. Lists and the networks of followers form communities, as do hashtags.

In short, there are many reasons to use the cloud.

Inappropriate Cloud Use Cases

Many people love chocolate, but that doesn't mean that it's appropriate as a sole source of nutrition. There is much promise and value in the cloud, but that doesn't mean it's appropriate for all applications. Knowing what belongs in the "public" cloud and what doesn't can help you develop a plan to transform your own architecture.

Constant

The cloud is renowned for scalability and for its ability to handle variable and unpredictable workloads; both on-demand resource allocation and pay-per-use pricing generate real economic value. However, in the unlikely situation that demand is flat and predictable, a perfectly viable strategy can be to bring the application in house. As we stated earlier, traditionally Zynga migrated games from the public cloud to its own data centers (the internal zCloud) once demand for a new game was stable and predictable. As the company's aggregate volume has ramped up across many highly popular games, Zynga has benefited from the law of large numbers, experiencing an increasing proportion of workloads that offer constancy, and thus brought much of the processing for that constant baseline back in house.

Generally, most demand is not inherently flat, although it can have a greater or lesser component that is flat and it can often be shaped through incentives and disincentives, or be smoothed through aggregation with other unrelated demand, or have gaps filled in with deferrable work, such as backups.

Just because an app has constant demand, though, doesn't mean that it shouldn't be run in the cloud. Other reasons, such as the cloud's ability to enhance end-user experience via a geographically dispersed footprint, should also be considered. Additional considerations include the relative unit cost of a do-it-yourself approach versus the cloud, competencies in data center operations, and cash flow.

Custom

The public cloud has many services that can be flexibly combined. The environment in which those services run, however, is shared and of necessity has limited variation, not specially engineered for unique, custom applications or modules. The widely used memcached, which enhances application performance by keeping frequently accessed data in memory, ideally requires massive memory and no disk, an unusual configuration for a general-purpose cloud.[20] Gaming company Zynga discovered that it needed only one third the resources by using specialized database, Web, and game servers.[21] Users of a custom architecture must, however, make sure that the application really is unique and that the effort and cost to run a unique architecture that may often be underutilized makes up for a potentially slight loss in performance.

Classic

A substantial base of legacy code dates back years, even decades. The effort to migrate the code to newer scale-out architectures and modern programming paradigms just may not be worth it. For example, global financial services firm Credit Suisse has thousands of software applications developed over decades. As Steve Hilton, its head of technology infrastructure services, commented, those apps are unlikely to move to the cloud "because the cost of migration is so high."[22]

It's important, however, to consider all the costs involved, including loss of business agility and poor customer experience by being tied to legacy platforms.

Close Coupling

Any applications that are tightly coupled to the aforementioned constant, custom, and classic applications, either due to high bandwidth or extreme latency constraints for interprocess communication or data transport to and from storage systems or other devices, will also need to reside in the same location. Interestingly, as more and more data migrate to the cloud, more and more applications that need to process that data will as well. Close coupling works both ways.

Content Capture, Creation, and Consumption

Content is originally captured at the edge via user devices—video cameras, PCs and tablets, mobile devices, sensor networks—and delivered, displayed, and consumed at the same edge. The cloud can't do the capture or display, only the edge devices can. Of course, the cloud can help with lots of complementary tasks (e.g., collective intelligence to gain information from captured data or support for creation such as image analysis, graphics processing, compositing, and encoding/transcoding).

Content is not only videos or digital photos but any sort of sensor data, such as temperature, pressure, humidity, and vibrations. And although graphical information may be rendered remotely, it is useful only when displayed locally.

Cryptography

Encryption of data for storage or transport begins at the point of creation. Sending unencrypted data to the cloud for encryption would be like sending a five-year-old through the woods with a paper bag full of cash to the bank for safekeeping. The same is true for decryption of received data. Today most data are stored in the cloud with protected access and/or in encrypted form. Fully homomorphic encryption schemes point the way to a possible future where data may be correctly processed in the cloud even while remaining encrypted.

As an aside, the cloud is currently being used—not without malicious intent—for decryption. Immense power at low cost means that brute-force techniques—similar to trying every possible combination to open a safe—are overturning established assumptions regarding the difficulty of breaking formerly secure codes.

Compression

Data compression for more efficient transmission should be done at the point of origin, in the same way that orange juice is concentrated near the citrus grove, not at the point of sale.

Caching

Caching can be and is done at the edge of the network very effectively. The ultimate location for cached content, however, is the device itself, or at least on premises, for example, via wide area network acceleration gear. Pay-per-use network pricing plans coupled with plummeting storage prices may tip the balance further in favor of on-premises caching. In other words, if the cost to access remote data increases, you may just want to keep the data nearby.

Covert

The legal status of your data held at a cloud provider is still uncertain. Is the data entitled to protection from warrantless search, or must they be turned over to the authorities? Someone worried about a secret fried chicken recipe falling into the wrong hands may want to keep it on premises.

Continuity

Continuity is an application for the cloud, since data loss can be avoided by maintaining a backup of the data on your device or in your data center. However, the reverse is also true: A local copy under your control can help avoid loss of data in the cloud, and local processing capability can ensure continuity of processing (i.e., continuous use) for untethered use or in the event of loss of connectivity, cloud service outages, or provider financial instability.

Summary

Most company and application can benefit from the cloud in different ways. Although there are many different compelling cases for clouds, there also are a variety of use cases where clouds may not be the best solution.

The economics of some of these solution types is not as simple as basic cost reduction or revenue growth. For example, a particular cloud service may embed a particular competency. This competency may be binary—the cloud provider has it and the customer doesn't—or graduated—a cloud provider can do something somewhat better or faster than the customer can with its own resources.

Trade-offs exist in some circumstances. For example, hub-and-spoke networks for transport or communications are more cost effective than point-to-point networks but tend to increase latency, as anyone who's waited in an airport for a connecting flight knows.

The list provided in this chapter is no doubt incomplete, as new applications and scenarios are being developed all the time. However, it serves to illustrate the power of the cloud to generate benefits in accordance with multiple canonical scenarios.

Notes

1. Joe Weinman, "Compelling Cases for Clouds," *GigaOM.com*, November 15, 2009. http://gigaom.com/2009/11/15/compelling-cases-for-clouds/.
2. Robert Jensen, "The Digital Provide: Information (Technology), Market Performance, and Welfare in the South Indian Fisheries Sector," *Quarterly Journal of Economics* 122, No. 3 (August 2007): 879–924.
3. www.biltmore.com/our_story/our_history/default.asp.
4. Don Tapscott and Anthony D. Williams, *Macrowikinomics: Rebooting Business and the World* (Portfolio/Penguin, 2010), pp. 4–5.
5. www.kaggle.com/.
6. www.ideaconnection.com/idea-rally/crop-yield/.
7. www.innocentive.com/why-solve2.
8. www.netflixprize.com/.
9. James Surowiecki, *The Wisdom of Crowds* (Anchor Books, 2005).
10. Martin Campbell-Kelly, "Victorian Data Processing," *Communications of the ACM* 53, No. 10 (October 2010): 19–21.
11. Peter Temin, "A Market Economy in the Early Roman Empire," *Journal of Roman Studies* 91 (2001): 169–181.
12. Don Tapscott and Anthony D. Williams, *Wikinomics: How Mass Collaboration Changes Everything* (Penguin, 2008).

13. Rachel Botsman and Roo Rogers, *What's Mine Is Yours: The Rise of Collaborative Consumption* (HarperBusiness, 2010).

14. Josh Halliday, "London Riots: How BlackBerry Messenger Played a Key Role," August 8, 2011. www.guardian.co.uk/media/2011/aug/08/london-riots-facebook-twitter-blackberry.

15. Kyle Vanhemert, "How Egypt Turned Off the Internet," January 28, 2011. http://gizmodo.com/5746121/how-egypt-turned-off-the-internet.

16. Frank E. Gillett, with Christopher Mines, Ted Schadler, Michael Yamnitsky, Heidi Shey, Amelia Martland, and Reedwan Iqbal, "The Personal Cloud: Transforming Personal Computing, Mobile, and Web Markets," *Forrester Research*, June 6, 2011. www.forrester.com/The+Personal+Cloud+Transforming+Personal+Computing+Mobile+And+Web+Markets/fulltext/-/E-RES57403?docid=57403.

17. Bill Bulkeley, "What CFOs Need to Hear about Cloud Computing and Consumer IT," *CIO.com*, June 14, 2011. www.cio.com/article/684314/What_CFOs_Need_to_Hear_about_Cloud_Computing_and_Consumer_IT?page=2.

18. Ryan Lawler, "Netflix Moves Into the Cloud with Amazon Web Services," *GigaOM.com*, May 7, 2010. http://gigaom.com/video/netflix-moves-into-the-cloud-with-amazon-web-services/.

19. Charles Babcock, "Lessons from FarmVille: How Zynga Uses the Cloud," *InformationWeek*, May 14, 2011. www.informationweek.com/news/global-cio/interviews/229402805.

20. Alan Kasindorf, "Troubling Memcached with the Cloud," Cloud Connect Cloud Performance Summit, February 13, 2012.

21. Charles Babcock, "Inside Zynga's Big Move to Private Cloud," *InformationWeek*, February 17, 2012. www.informationweek.com/news/hardware/virtual/232601065.

22. Ashlee Vance, "The Cloud: Battle of the Tech Titans," *Bloomberg Businessweek*, March 3, 2011. www.businessweek.com/magazine/content/11_11/b4219052599182.htm?chan=magazine+channel_top+stories.

CHAPTER 8

Demand Dilemma

Many businesses have come to accept an endemic problem: the fundamental disparity between the *capacity* to produce products and deliver services—which is fixed in the short term—and the *demand* for those products and services—which is almost always variable at *any* time scale.

By "demand," we mean users' and customers' needs and desires to acquire or consume Chinese take-out meals, Lamborghinis, plane tickets, electricity, Web content, and the millions of other products and services for sale every day, whether online or offline. By "capacity," we mean the resources that enable businesses to meet those needs: woks, tables, tablecloths, servers (as in waiters), servers (as in computers), and the millions of other resources that are required, singly or in combination. Often demand and capacity use different measures: One may measure demand for food in platefuls, but capacity is measured in woks and cooks. Sometimes they are the same: A toaster needs electricity, and a power company delivers it. Here we will keep things simple and assume that demand and capacity are in the same units.

Like a broken watch that indicates the correct time twice a day, capacity may coincidentally correspond to demand for a short while, but generally it is too high or too low, causing economic loss. Customer demand—at its heart—is volatile. Although tactical measures such as queuing and demand shaping can ameliorate the issue, only the cloud can truly solve it.

Variability and *unpredictability* are two important yet distinct characteristics of demand: The position of a thrown rock following a ballistic trajectory is variable yet predictable; that of a driven car may vary unpredictably or remain constant unpredictably. The demand dilemma—varying, apparently random demand—leads to a capacity conundrum: the challenge of determining how much production, operations, and delivery capacity should be deployed. It's a conundrum because excess capacity implies nonproductive overinvestment (i.e., costs or expenditures that are unnecessarily high). Insufficient capacity implies unserved demand (i.e., revenues that are unnecessarily low). We explore the diversity and causes of such demand to make the case in the next chapters that cloud service providers offer the only compelling solution to the demand dilemma, helping businesses address their demand unpredictability through the use of on-demand capacity and their demand variability via pay-per-use pricing.

A Diversity of Demands

Different types of demand require different management and operations strategies. Constant demand lies at one extreme but wildly varying demand lies at the other, with unpredictable timing, direction, and amplitude of gyrations and epochs of relative calm randomly punctuated by massive upheavals.

Constant demand—if there is such a thing—and equivalent fixed capacity would be a perfect fit for each other.

Periodic predictable variation is the next best scenario. A publicly traded firm knows that it needs to report earnings every quarter and can institutionalize financial data collection, aggregation, reporting, and communications processes that correspond to this cadence.

Aperiodic predictable variation is the next easiest scenario. Even if not on a regular cycle, repeatable processes, such as software upgrades or patches, can follow a standardized process. However, regardless of whether periodic or aperiodic variation is predictable, the mere existence of such demand variation can be a challenge to manage with fixed capacity.

The most challenging—and increasingly prevalent—characteristic of today's world, however, is the existence of unpredictable variation: shocks, discontinuities, disruptions, black swans.[1] Such variation may have unpredictable timing, unpredictable amplitude, or both. The date of the Barack Obama presidential inauguration or the 2008 Beijing Olympics was never in doubt, but the number of viewers certainly was. Retailers know that the month before Christmas will be their busiest time of the year, but actual store sales are a function of weather, merchandising, fads, fashions, fickle customer choices, promotions, store hours, macroeconomic factors, consumer confidence, and competitor actions. In such cases, the *timing* of peak demand is not in question, but the *size* is difficult to pin down in advance. Other events, such as the devastating Great East Japan Earthquake of 2011 or Michael Jackson's death, were unpredictable in terms of timing and impact.

Our world generally is dynamic (variable), stochastic (random and unpredictable), and/or chaotic (sensitively dependent on initial conditions) at all scales: quantum mechanical; the Brownian motion of floating particles such as dust darting about due to kinetic interactions with other particles; human behavior, where individuals randomly engage in short bursts[2] of activity; stock markets; macroeconomics; or any other complex systems from the microcosm to the macrocosm.

Full appreciation of the degree of variability in the world at large and for specific applications is hindered by blind spots in human perception and cognition. Our ability to recognize patterns is the result of highly developed visual and neural circuitry that parallel-processes the cascade of raw photons striking our eyes. However, this same capability causes us to see rabbits in clouds, faces on the moon, and heads and shoulders in stock charts. When it comes to thinking about unpredictability and variability, the list of cognitive biases (i.e., fundamental errors in thinking) is lengthy: the clustering illusion, the expectation bias, the illusion of control, illusory correlation, the hindsight bias, and others. These biases are driven by otherwise useful human capabilities as well as deep-seated psychological needs.

Dr. David Rock, cofounder of the NeuroLeadership Institute, has said that a "perception of reduced autonomy . . . can easily generate a threat response."[3] Beyond a threat response, the need for control can literally mean the difference between life and death. An oft-cited study of nursing home environments conducted by researchers from Harvard and Yale conclusively demonstrated that residents who were simply given control over whether *they* watered a flower in their room—rather than a staff member maintaining it—lived longer and healthier lives.[4]

The human need for control is at odds with the randomness and complexity of the real world. Why? California Institute of Technology (Caltech) professor Leonard Mlodinow has explained that "if events are random, we are *not* in control, and if we are in control of events, they are *not* random . . . this is one of the principal reasons we misinterpret random events."[5] In other words, there is a substantial amount of random and thus unpredictable variability in the world. The idea that somehow we can predict it and manage it successfully is largely an illusion. The demand dilemma is probably worse than we think.

Examples of Variability

Examples of the demand dilemma abound, as can be seen by looking at Web site traffic. Every online company—Facebook, Google, and eBay, but also, say, AgathasFruitJams.com—has its own distinctive pattern of variable demand, as recognizable as a heart murmur is to a cardiologist based on a glance at an electrocardiogram (EKG). This variable demand is a composite of multiple individual decisions, such as "I think I'll post my photo with Betty and Wilma now." Analyzing such traffic tells us roughly what the demand is on customer-facing Web server resources and the computing equipment supporting them, which in turn acts as a proxy for business demand volume. A currently free, easy-to-use source of such data is Alexa.com, the "Web Information Company," an Amazon subsidiary. You can receive your company's EKG in a matter of seconds by typing in its domain name (if it is large enough to track).

Alexa provides a variety of metrics for thousands of Web sites, such as global users and average page load times, but the one that is the best proxy for overall demand volume is the "estimated percentage of global page views," which Alexa can report on at various time scales. Every time a Web surfer visits a page on a Web site counts as a page view. Although a page view on YouTube may require more compute, storage, and network resources than one on Twitter, and a page view on Amazon.com may generate more or less revenue than one on AstonMartin.com, it is not the variation between sites which interests us here, but the pattern of variation on a given site, which tells us a lot about the nature of demand variability. In other domains we could use barrels of oil shipped, violins delivered, or Aston Martins purchased to determine required capacity. In the Web domain, though, demand variability information is readily available.

Alexa doesn't actually have access to the exact sites that every single person on the planet is visiting with their Web browser; rather, it extrapolates and normalizes data from a large group of Web users who have voluntarily installed the Alexa Toolbar plug-in.[6] Although this process is potentially somewhat biased due to self-selection of volunteers—users who are tech-savvy enough to install a browser plug-in may have more of a propensity to visit technology sites, for example—it is good enough to illustrate the variability of real-world use of the virtual world. Google.com is the current number-one site in the world according to Alexa. (In descending order, the rest of the top ten are Facebook, YouTube, Yahoo!, Baidu.com, Wikipedia, Windows Live, Blogspot, Amazon.com, and Twitter.[7]) Google's global page view percentage is currently about 6%. To put it another way, an estimated 1 out of every 16 pages loaded in the world is a Google Web page. In the exhibits that follow, the x-axis is date and the y-axis shows the estimated percentage of global page views.

Using Alexa charts to review the variation in page views over time shows that Google.com's demand can be eerily constant and predictable, with a weekly cycle but little change over the long term (see Exhibit 8.1).

To be sure, at this scale, data can be deceiving. For example, if all of the page views were concentrated into a single hour, with none occurring the other 23 hours, the average utilization of Google.com's resources would only be about 4%. Of course, that's an extreme and unlikely scenario, but there surely are time-of-day differences based on circadian cycles in relevant time zones. If we ignore these more dramatic variations at finer scales, it is

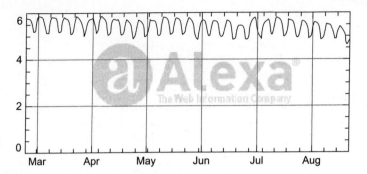

EXHIBIT 8.1 Daily Page Views (percent): Google.com
Source: © 2011, Alexa Internet (www.alexa.com). Used by permission.

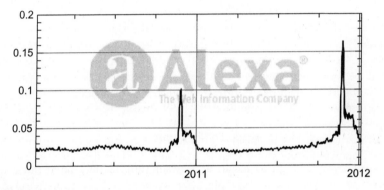

EXHIBIT 8.2 Daily Page Views (percent): Walmart.com
Source: © 2011, Alexa Internet (www.alexa.com). Used by permission.

pretty clear that Google has relatively smooth demand and can thus achieve relatively high utilization, even before considering background task such as web crawling.

However, consider full year 2010 and 2011 for Walmart.com (see Exhibit 8.2).

Walmart.com has relatively constant demand for most of the year but then runs at two to three times the baseline demand for the month leading up to winter holiday gift giving. The baseline demand for most of 2012 was not much different from that for 2011. However, the Black Friday/Cyber Monday spike was four times the baseline in 2011 but over six times the baseline in 2012.

This variability is partly a *self-inflicted wound*. Virtually all retailers with any online presence and pure-play e-tailers participate in "Cyber Monday," where online promotions serve to whip demand into a frenzy of shopping

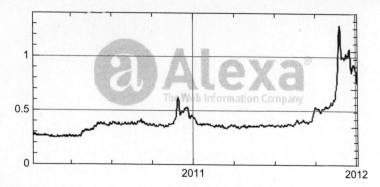

EXHIBIT 8.3 Daily Page Views (percent): Amazon.com
Source: © 2011, Alexa Internet (www.alexa.com). Used by permission.

euphoria. The bigger and nastier the spike, the worse the capacity management headache is for the chief information officer and his or her organization. However, the business units with profit and loss responsibility would like nothing better than to eclipse all previous records, as a symbol of the success of the campaign, not to mention the hard-dollar revenue gains and subsequent annual bonuses that will enable them to do their own shopping.

Amazon.com has similarities to Walmart.com but its own unique Web usage fingerprint. As can be seen in Exhibit 8.3, there was a Cyber Monday spike, but it was small compared to the dramatic increases in the fourth quarter of 2011. Be aware that although the 2011 spike is only three times the baseline, that baseline is roughly twice the size of Walmart.com's peak. These relative differences say nothing per se about relative revenues, only page views.

In the United States, the tax filing deadline for individuals as well as for companies with fiscal years aligned to the calendar year is April 15. However, the information to file is not available until January 1. Moreover, those expecting refunds tend to try to file early, and those who owe taxes—and procrastinators—tend to delay until close to the deadline.

Therefore, H&R Block's online services demand is bimodal. It appears that the early filers begin plotting how they will spend their refunds and preparing returns as tax data become available, peaking at the end of January and early February, and then drop off. Meanwhile, as awareness of impending deadlines grows exponentially, demand grows until midnight on April 15, at which point demand drops to near zero. Relative to the baseline demand of about .00025, the peak demand of about .005 represents a 20-to-1 degree of variation. This high degree of variability is *not* self-inflicted but a function of an externally imposed window (see Exhibit 8.4).

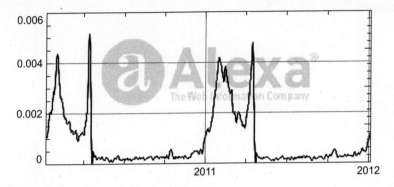

EXHIBIT 8.4 Daily Page Views (percent): HRBlock.com
Source: © 2011, Alexa Internet (www.alexa.com). Used by permission.

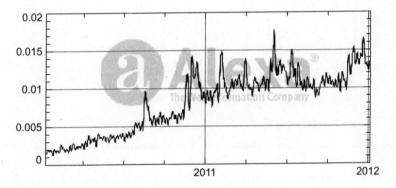

EXHIBIT 8.5 Daily Page Views (percent): Groupon.com
Source: © 2011, Alexa Internet (www.alexa.com). Used by permission.

Separate from the preceding patterns, variability may include a strong exponential baseline growth component, as with red-hot local daily special deals site Groupon.com ("Group" + "Coupon"). Note Groupon's peaks above the baseline growth, which would appear to relate to back-to-school or end-of-vacation shopping, winter holiday gift giving, Valentine's Day, and Mother's Day (see Exhibit 8.5).

Sadly, the reverse can also happen, as did with Myspace.com (see Exhibit 8.6). What goes up may eventually come down, which represents a challenging situation: A company that owns equipment faces a downturn like this with fixed costs, with dramatically reduced revenue to cover those costs, and an additional drain on funds as it defines and executes a turnaround plan.

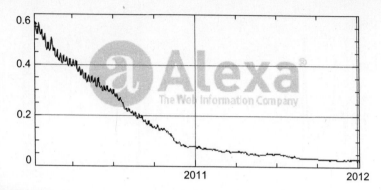

EXHIBIT 8.6 Daily Page Views (percent): Myspace.com
Source: © 2011, Alexa Internet (www.alexa.com). Used by permission.

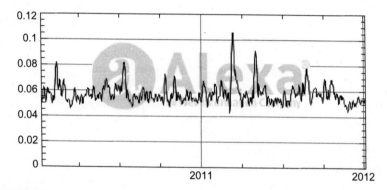

EXHIBIT 8.7 Daily Page Views (percent): CNN.com
Source: © 2011, Alexa Internet (www.alexa.com). Used by permission.

For still a different type of demand curve, consider a news site, such as CNN.com (see Exhibit 8.7). CNN has a decent amount of traffic virtually all the time. However, there can be notable spikes.

The Japan earthquake of March 11, 2011, appears to have increased demand to CNN to almost double the baseline. Although the occurrence of a large earthquake *somewhere* on the Pacific Rim at *some time* in the next, say, 10,000 years may have been predictable, the actual fact of a 9.0 earthquake and subsequent catastrophic tsunami beginning at 2:46 P.M. Japan Standard Time on March 11 was not, at least with today's technology. Widespread interest in the ongoing Fukushima reactor situation and human tragedy gave the reporting, and thus web demand, a relatively long tail measured in weeks. The other clear peak is the Seal Team Six Osama Bin Laden operation on May 1.

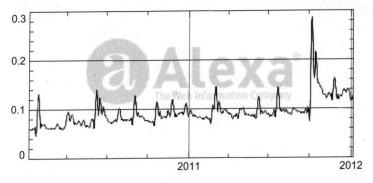

EXHIBIT 8.8 Daily Page Views (percent): Apple.com
Source: © 2011, Alexa Internet (www.alexa.com). Used by permission.

Of course, you can make your own news, as Apple did with the March 2, 2011, iPad 2 launch, the June 6 iCloud announcement, and the July 19–20 earnings and product announcements. The large spike in the final quarter of 2011 comprised the iPhone 4S and iCloud announcement on October 4 and the sad news regarding Steve Jobs on October 5 (see Exhibit 8.8).

One thing notable about many (but not all) of these cases is the steep rise of an unpredictable spike. In other words, it would be virtually impossible to respond to these spiky demands by attempting to order equipment or construct facilities as the initial rise was detected.

Even when spikes are predictable, their magnitude may not be.

On January 20, 2009, there was a spike in traffic: the historic inauguration of President Barack Obama. At CNN.com, the traffic spike was characterized by 160 million page views and 25 million video streams within a 12-hour period. Trying to predict this demand might have been difficult. The prior CNN.com record, set on Election Day a few months earlier, was only *one fifth* as large. And the total count over 12 hours doesn't reflect the instantaneous peak reached during the actual inauguration, not to mention that the demand peak was higher than the served peak: Some users were unable to view the stream. Other sites, such as Twitter, were also inundated, processing five times as many tweets per second than usual. As Shawn White, director of external operations for Keynote Systems, a Web and mobile performance measurement firm, wryly commented: "It's difficult to prepare for something that's unprecedented."[8] Even if you had perfect knowledge of the exact number of users every second for the day, Matt Poepsel, vice president of performance strategies at Gomez, a division of Compuware focues on web performance benchmarking, pointed out that "it would be financially imprudent for companies to always maintain . . . enough capacity to handle such events."[9]

Bill Tancer, the general manager of Global Research at Web traffic online competitive intelligence and research firm Hitwise, provided examples of other events that have caused traffic spikes[10]:

- The April 2005 airing of an *Apprentice* television show episode featuring a competition requiring development of a brochure for the soon-to-be-released Pontiac Solstice automobile. This resulted in a fourfold increase in searches on the car versus the prior week and a sixfold increase in searches compared to the prior month.
- The 2003 Super Bowl Janet Jackson "wardrobe malfunction," resulting in a dramatic increase in visits to her site.
- Dana Reeve's death from lung cancer in March 2006, causing a tripling of searches on "lung cancer" the week of her death.
- The death of Anna Nicole Smith in February 2007, when she became the fifth most popular search term for U.S. Internet searches.

The *New York Times* Web site (nytimes.com) has been crippled several times due to unexpected demand: during the 9/11 disaster; an American Airlines crash in Queens, New York, two months later; and in March 2008, when news of then New York Governor Eliot Spitzer's prostitution scandal broke.[11]

Spikes in demand may also be based on Internet floods, sometimes referred to as the Slashdot effect, where a mention on a popular site such as Slashdot.org or a tweet by a widely followed Twitter user can cause a site to suddenly receive a flood of thousands or millions of visitors. Often the flood itself becomes newsworthy, driving yet more traffic.

Of course, such spikes in demand are not restricted to the Web; they also occur in other domains. The Monday after Thanksgiving is the busiest day of the year for phone calls, Mother's Day is the busiest holiday for phone calls and for Kentucky Fried Chicken, and Father's Day is the busiest day for collect phone calls. Super Sunday is the busiest for ordering pizza, the day after Christmas is the busiest for emergency rooms, Black Friday is the busiest for . . . plumbers, New Year's Eve is the busiest for Disney, Valentine's Day is the busiest for florists and . . . Applebee's, Christmas is the busiest day for . . . Chinese restaurants, January 7 is the busiest for divorce lawyers and travel agents, July 4 is the busiest for boaters and firefighters, and the busiest day for in-person shopping is not Black Friday but the last Saturday before Christmas.[12]

AT&T reported its largest text-messaging spike in history to that point on Election Night, 2008, with total text messaging jumping 44% as the results were called.[13]

This broke the prior record that occurred earlier that year, when AT&T reported record text messaging—78 million text messages—due to demand based on *American Idol*, then the most popular show on television. In an interesting twist, not only did the show generate a substantial burst of traffic, but one fifth of respondents to a survey indicated that *American Idol* was the reason they *learned* to text message.[14] This volume was a combination of votes to a central site as well as messages to friends and family.

Data from Sonus Networks shows the spike in calling volume for one telecommunications operator when a large earthquake hit the East Coast, on August 23, 2011 (see Exhibit 8.9), and on New Year's Eve 2010 (see Exhibit 8.10).[15]

September 11, 2001, was an extreme example of unusual and unpredictable demand loads. Calling volume began to depart from the normal Tuesday morning pattern the minute that news reports began to air regarding the first plane hitting the North Tower of the World Trade Center. For Verizon, with a strong local service presence in New York City and the surrounding region, this resulted in *twice* the normal calling volume for

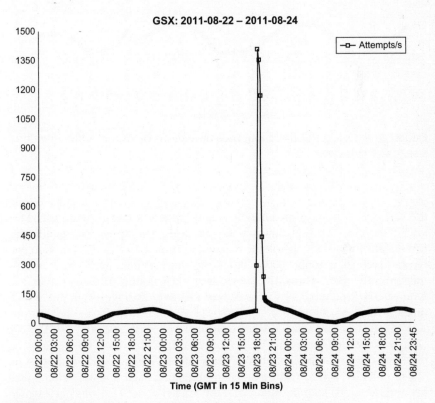

EXHIBIT 8.9 Calling Volume during the August 23, 2011, Earthquake

Source: Sonus Networks.

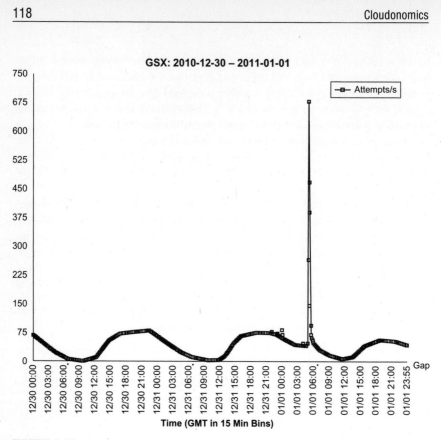

EXHIBIT 8.10 Calling Volume during December 31, 2010
Source: Sonus Networks.

the day, even though, presumably, many people were glued to their TV set.[16] For AT&T, at that time having primarily a long-distance telephony focus, nationwide calling volume reached 431 million calls, even though the typical average is "only" 300 million, and the previous peak day was 330 million.[17] In other words, the previous peak was only 10% over average, whereas on September 11 the peak was 44% over average—four and a half times as large a difference.

As my former colleague Dave Johnson, a spokesperson for AT&T's Global Network Operations Center observed, "'When you have a sizable disaster—and it can be what happened to us in New York, a bomb blast in Oklahoma City, a major earthquake in Seattle, or a hurricane in Florida—you get a tremendous leap in calling *into* the impact area.' This was particularly true in the case of the World Trade Center attacks, 'because [New York City] has a community of interest that stretches out across the whole country.'"[18]

In a pattern we often see, where a post on Slashdot leads to an Internet flood at a unsuspecting site, or where a broadcast in one medium—say, *American Idol*—drives a flood in a different medium—say, text messaging— it turns out that it was broadcast coverage, not the actual attack, that caused the spike. If anything, the attack itself would have actually *reduced* calling volume, as a substantial number of networks were routed through the basements of the World Trade Center destroyed by the building collapses, neighboring carrier switching centers, or were impacted by subsequent power outages and cuts. Thanks to television broadcast media, said Johnson, "people knew instantly. If you saw my call chart for the day, it literally takes off like a spaceship—at about 9 A.M. it just takes off and climbs right on up."[19]

The Internet was also impacted. Online news sites suddenly got hit with three to ten times normal traffic, with one news site reporting a doubling of traffic every few minutes. By just 15 minutes after the first plane—American Airlines Flight 11—hit, all the major news sites had begun to slow noticeably, due not to network issues but to insufficient IT capacity.[20]

There is more to the world than the World Wide Web and tele-communications, so let's consider automobile production capacity—plants, equipment, personnel, materials—during the financial crisis that began in 2008. A strong global economy and increased demand from emerging countries, such as China, spiked the price of oil in less than 18 months, with a barrel of West Texas Intermediate crude costing $54.51 in January 2007 and $133.88 by June 2008, according to the Energy Information Administration of the U.S. Department of Energy.[21] This cost increase alone reduced demand for gas-guzzling but previously popular and profitable SUVs.

Then, beginning in early September 2008, the collapse of Lehman Brothers and related domino effects triggered a bear market, subprime mortgage crisis, credit default swap issues, global liquidity problems, and a global financial crisis, which eliminated the price increase in oil and then some (with oil plummeting to $41.12 in six short months), and virtually halving the Dow Jones Industrial Average in six months as well: from a high of 11,715 at the end of August 2008, to a low of 6,547 on March 9, 2009. With an estimated $25 trillion lost in just three months—$10 trillion in home values globally, $7 trillion in equities losses in the United States, and another $5 trillion internationally, plus $1 trillion dollars here and there—spending declined drastically.[22]

Unfortunately, as former Ford Motor Company chief economist Martin Zimmerman put it, "I cannot think of an industry more cyclical or more dependent on the business cycle than the automotive industry."[23] Zimmerman further explained that cars are "postponable" purchases, and therefore, when household income falls, as during a recession, or during oil price shocks or interest rate shocks, the number of units sold falls precipitously.

His comments were made years ago, but unsurprisingly, 2008 was no different: U.S. automotive and personal light truck sales declined from a run rate of roughly 17 million vehicles per year prior to the recession, to barely over 10 million. The percentage decline in volume was exceeded by the 60% decline in new housing unit construction over the same period, where the pre-recession run rate of about 1.5 million new units each year dropped to 600,000 in 2010.[24]

The impact of these shifts in demand volume, driven by a variety of business cycle discontinuities, is well known: unemployment in the automotive sector, the shuttering of legacy brands, government bailouts, dealership closures, and the like. From an IT perspective, systems are designed to handle the volume of IT that is aligned with the volume of business. When customer demand nosedives, so do many IT workloads, and thus utilization. Again, fixed capacity is a poor match for variable demand.

To make things even worse, supply chains exhibit what is known as *volatility amplification*, or the *bullwhip effect*, since a small flick in the handle of a bullwhip causes dramatic changes at the end of the whip. If automotive sales are down, you can bet that the companies that supply machine tools such as presses and painting robots to automobile factories will experience a dramatic fall-off in revenue, since automotive companies will postpone capital expenditures to refurbish and upgrade manufacturing facilities, much less undergo new plant construction. Consequently, a small shift in consumer income can cause a medium shift in business-to-consumer sales and a large shift in business-to-business sales.

In other words, in a kind of supply chain variation of chaos theory, a butterfly flapping its wings at the tail end of a supply chain can cause a hurricane at the beginning.[25]

Chase Demand or Shape It?

Given that variable demand is a given in virtually any business, the question is what to do about it. One strategy is called "chase demand" (i.e., assume that the demand is what it is, and attempt to use a mix of fixed and variable capacity to meet that demand). The other approach is to shape the demand to meet the capacity of the system by smoothing the peaks and filling the troughs.

Users often exhibit emergent aggregate demand smoothing, for example, leaving the house early to avoid rush hour. Businesses and governments shape demand to maximize revenues and profit or to disincent use during peak periods through dynamic pricing. Hotel rooms in Las Vegas on fight night and airline fares during spring break and Christmas are higher than average; some cities charge congestion fees to reduce rush hour traffic.

During periods of light use, demand can be incented. Promotions, such as sales and special offers, can increase discretionary demand. You may not have had any plans this weekend, but if an all-inclusive airfare plus hotel deal to Palm Springs is offered at the right price, that could rapidly change.

Also, certain *deferrable* workloads can be executed when exogenous demand is low. For example, network connections can be used off-peak to update digital signs or preload caches with content that is expected to be accessed, voluminous data can be backed up.

It is important to realize that various workloads have differing priorities and different degrees of deferability. Someone hit by a truck has an urgent need for health care; someone else pondering cosmetic surgery may be able to wait longer. Long-term activities, such as network capacity planning and design, can be delayed by a month or two; news sites responding to peak loads during breaking events have different considerations. Many workloads are increasingly interactive—online gaming, collaboration, stock transactions—but it also may be argued that there is an emerging category of discretionary applications. Like a trip to Palm Springs that is not *necessary* but at the right price can generate value, running an algorithm to the next decimal point of precision may not be *necessary* but at the right price point can generate value. If the price of cloud services is highly variable, due to the application of yield management algorithms by service providers, such *discretionary computing* may become more prevalent.

If we can shape demand by avoiding it, promoting it, disincenting it, or deferring it, we simplify the demand dilemma. However, often such demand shaping is not an option.

Summary

Demand variation can be caused by a number of factors: seasonal or macroeconomic variation, chaotic and stochastic individual choice, natural events, feedback loops and bullwhip effects, windows of opportunity, business growth or decline, scheduled events, unscheduled events, or just about anything. Variations may be gentle or have a sharp rise and a gentle fall, as with news stories, or a slow rise and a sharp fall, as with tax filing.

Although some demand can be shaped, in today's world of instant gratification, there would appear to be less and less opportunity to defer workloads, so variable and unpredictable demand creates a real dilemma.

🖳 ONLINE

Alexa Internet, at www.alexa.com/, collects data from millions of users to offer a broad variety of information on site traffic, global rankings, page views, page views per user, and more.

Notes

1. Black swans are a concept first associated in the context of highly unexpected event probability distributions by Nassim Nicholas Taleb, *Fooled by Randomness: The Hidden Role of Chance in Life and in the Markets* (Random House, 2005) and its sequel, *The Black Swan: The Impact of the Highly Improbable* (Random House, 2007).
2. Albert-László Barabási, *Bursts: The Hidden Pattern Behind Everything We Do* (Dutton, 2010).
3. David Rock, "Managing with the Brain in Mind," *strategy+business*, August 27, 2009. www.strategy-business.com/article/09306?pg=3.
4. Ellen Langer and Judith Rodin, "Long-Term Effects of a Control-Relevant Intervention with the Institutionalized Aged," *Journal of Personality and Social Psychology* 35, No. 12 (1977): 897–902.
5. Leonard Mlodinow, *The Drunkard's Walk: How Randomness Rules Our Lives* (Vintage Books, 2008), p. 186.
6. www.alexa.com/company/technology.
7. www.alexa.com/topsites.
8. Matt Hamblen and Juan Carlos Perez, "Inauguration Buckles, but Doesn't Break, the Internet," *ComputerWorld*, January 26, 2009, p. 12. www.computerworld.com/s/article/332829/Inauguration_buckles_but_doesn_t_break_the_Internet.
9. Ibid.
10. Bill Tancer, *Click: What Millions of People are Doing Online and Why It Matters* (Hyperion, 2008).
11. Rachel Sklar, "Spitzer Traffic Crashes *NYT* Website," *Huffington Post*, March 28, 2008. www.huffingtonpost.com/2008/03/10/spitzer-traffic-crashes-n_n_90819.htm.
12. "The Busiest Day of the Year for . . . ," www.dailyfinance.com/photos/busiest-day-of-the-year/3661335/.
13. "AT&T Reports Largest Text Messaging Spike in Company History on Election Night," November 6, 2008. www.att.com/gen/press-room?pid=4800&cdvn=news&newsarticleid=26287.
14. "AT&T Announces FOX's "American Idol" Seventh Season Breaks All-Time Record for Text Messaging: AT&T Records More Than 78 Million "American Idol"-Related Text Messages," May 22, 2008. www.att.com/gen/press-room?pid=4800&cdvn=news&newsarticleid=25731.

15. Dave Connolly, "Of Earthquakes, Clouds and Auld Lang Syne," *Sonus in Session*, November 21, 2011. http://info.sonusnet.com/bid/68277/Of-Earthquakes-Clouds-and-Auld-Lang-Syne.

16. Chuck Yaunches, "Zurich Risk Engineering Global Workshop 2004: When It All Falls Down and You Have to Stay Up." www.risk-engineering.com/rep/d/gho/attachments/attachments_news/re_workshop04/presentations/nw_gho_20040924_en_zregws04_pres18_chuck_yaunches.pdf.

17. P. J. Aduskevicz, "AT&T Response Terrorist Attack September 11, 2001: Presentation to NRIC V," Network Reliability and Interoperability Council, October 30, 2001. www.nric.org/pubs/nric5/appendixd.ppt.

18. Richard Grigonis, *Disaster Survival Guide for Business Communications Networks: Strategies for Planning, Response and Recovery in Data and Telecom Systems* (Focal Press, 2002).

19. Ibid.

20. Committee on The Internet Under Crisis Conditions: Learning from September 11 and National Research Council of the National Academies, "The Internet Under Crisis Conditions: Learning from September 11," (National Academies Press, 2003), www.nap.edu/openbook.php?record_id=10569&page=R1.

21. www.eia.gov/dnav/pet/hist/LeafHandler.ashx?n=PET&s=RWTC&f=M.

22. Heather Landy, "The Stock Slump of 2008: Wrecking Ball to Wealth," *The Washington Post*, January 11, 2009. www.washingtonpost.com/wp-dyn/content/story/2009/01/10/ST2009011001747.html.

23. Martin Zimmerman, "A View of Recessions from the Automotive Industry," in Jeffrey C. Fuhrer and Scott Schuh, eds., "Beyond Shocks: What Causes Business Cycles," Federal Reserve Bank of Boston, Conference Series 42, June 1998.

24. Steve Shefler, "What Auto Sales Tell Us About Future Economic Growth," *Mutual Fund Research Newsletter* (September 2010). http://funds-newsletter.com/sept10-newsletter/sept10-steve.htm.

25. James Gleick, *Chaos: Making a New Science* (Penguin, 2008).

CHAPTER 9

Capacity Conundrum

The demand dilemma of variability and unpredictability described in the last chapter leads to the capacity conundrum: unsatisfying options for the amount of fixed capacity to deploy to meet such demand. As shown in Exhibit 9.1, if a company builds capacity to match its peak demand, or higher, it will have substantial excess capacity during off-peak periods. Moreover, peak demand often can be determined only in hindsight; there is no guarantee that the next peak won't be much larger than any prior peak. This excess capacity represents either nonproductive capital—somewhat akin to stuffing cash under your mattress rather than investing it, only worse, because it is invested in depreciating resources—or unnecessary expense—like paying for a gym membership that you don't use.

Conversely, if capacity is sized to the baseline or any other level below peak, there will be insufficient resources to handle spikes. Customers or other users either won't conclude their transactions, like music fans who won't be spending money on a sold-out concert, or will be forced to *queue*, that is, wait in line, negatively impacting the customer experience.

Transactions not served represent demand for the products or services that the business would have monetized: either directly, as in e-commerce, or via third parties or two-sided monetization models, such as serving ads as part of a free service. If the system is internal, rather than a loss of revenue, such insufficient capacity can result in a loss of productivity, as workers stare at blank screens waiting for them to load. Often it can result in both: A customer hangs up rather than making a purchase because the contact center agent has just admitted that "our systems are slow today," and both labor productivity and revenue suffer.

In addition to direct loss of revenue, there are other context-dependent issues caused by insufficient capacity, as, for example, when customers who would like to be served cause trouble for the ones who are already there. In

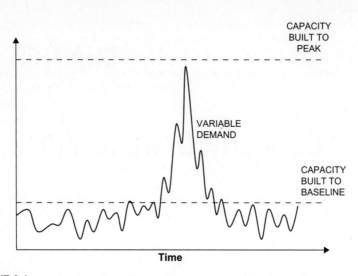

EXHIBIT 9.1 Fixed Capacity Is a Poor Solution to Variable Demand

a restaurant filled to capacity, clientele waiting for tables clog the aisles, impeding the servers, that is, wait staff, worsening the user experience for all. In a computer system filled to capacity, additional clients attempting to begin a session clog the networks and servers, that is, computers, worsening the experience for all as well. Then there is bad word of mouth, as customers complain about the bad service and don't recommend it to prospects. And there is bad publicity, which damages the brand and reduces still other prospects' propensity to buy, not to mention the additional load from rubberneckers who want to see for themselves if the site is down.

If demand is deferred due to limited capacity—as when customers queue to get into a restaurant—there can be a nonlinear impact on service quality due to waiting. Very short waits aren't noticed; short waits are accurately perceived, but after a couple of minutes, the perception of wait time begins to expand well beyond the actual passage of time, negatively impacting the customer experience.

Online, tolerance is much lower; a few seconds is about all that anyone will wait these days. Customers will *renege*—abandon a line after some waiting—or *balk* entirely—go to another site and avoid the problem all together.

In an environment of variable demand, fixed capacity causes problems one way or another.

Service Quality Impacts

The leading thinkers in understanding service quality are longtime collaborators Leonard Berry and A. Parasuraman, of Texas A&M, and Valarie

Zeithaml, of Duke University. As Berry and Parasuraman have emphatically stated: "Service quality is the foundation for services marketing because the core product being marketed is a performance. The performance *is* the product; the performance is what customers buy."[1]

To understand the importance of service quality and reliability, consider this math regarding the "iceberg of ignorance," from Chuck Chakrapani, president of the largest independent research company in Canada, Leger Marketing. Receiving only 50 complaints might indicate a loss of 2.5 million impacted customers. This math is based on the number of dissatisfied customers and the percentage of those who actively complain.

A satisfied customer may tell 5 to 8 potential customers about how great a company is. Unfortunately, a dissatisfied customer will tell twice as many people—10 to 16—how awful the company is. Consequently, one dissatisfied customer can cost a firm up to two dozen: the 16 people they complain to and the 8 to whom they don't recommend the firm.[2]

That was the traditional math, anyway. Today there is a new dynamic. A single unsatisfied customer—such as Dave Carroll—with a single incident—such as having his guitar damaged by an airline—can tell over 11 million people—not accounting for duplicate views—about his experience.[3]

The relationship between dissatisfaction and complaint is somewhat complex. There appear to be two main types of responses: private actions and public actions. A public action is one where, for example, a customer complains to management or a customer service representative. A private action is one where the customer either stops patronizing the establishment or complains to others (e.g., friends, family, or even random acquaintances). The decision of which action to take appears to be based on a number of factors: the degree of dissatisfaction with the service received, the consumer's attitude toward complaining, the importance of the situation, and the customer's perception of the likelihood of success ("You can't fight city hall!").[4] Interestingly, the level of dissatisfaction itself is not strongly correlated to public complaint actions. In other words, just because someone is extremely unhappy with terrible service, they may not stop to fill out a form or complete an online survey. They may be happy to vilify the firm and its miserable service to anyone who will listen, though, like Dave Carroll.

Fixed Capacity versus Variable Demand

In the world of manufacturing, inventory is used to buffer the difference between production and demand. A plant can produce plush toys all year round, warehouse them, and meet the holiday rush. There are carrying costs associated with inventory, but these can be rolled up into the final price, with an optimal trade-off determined between perfect factory utilization and zero inventory.

A "service" is usually defined as something intangible that is consumed and produced at the same time. This is a convenient oversimplification. Various services occur along a *tangibility spectrum*[5]; for example, an uncomfortable seat on a long flight (a transportation service) is very tangible, as is a tasty meal at a restaurant (a food service). The criterion of *inseparability*—that is, that production and consumption occur simultaneously and capacity is thus perishable—is also not strictly true. After all, a tax preparation service or audio transcription service may do its work "offline."

Generally speaking, however, inseparability and thus perishability are a core characteristic of services. You can't store cab rides or rental car days or compute cycles in a warehouse for when they are needed.

If there is only so much capacity to deliver a given quantity of services, and demand exceeds that capacity, then customers may queue. However, customers may not want to wait and thus revenue associated with that demand is lost; or customers may be dissatisfied during the wait and thus have a poorer experience leading to a lower propensity to repurchase.

The service quality literature has tended to focus on physical experiences in retail environments, such as grocery stores and fast-food restaurants. However, similar issues apply to online environments, where milliseconds may mean millions of dollars. We explore this topic in Chapter 16. For now, it's worth noting that major e-commerce providers have conducted experiments and determined that a few hundred milliseconds' delay in serving Web pages (i.e., a few tenths of a second) can cause revenues to decline by 20%.[6]

Given that variable demand rarely matches fixed capacity, and that there are issues with overcapacity and undercapacity, we need to either shape demand to meet available capacity or shape capacity to chase demand.

Shaping demand is like using a bulldozer to level a field: The idea is to shave the peaks and use the excess to fill the valleys. If demand can be deferred, this strategy is effective. For example, many doctors and dentists schedule patients to fill their fixed capacity. However, if the patient has a gunshot wound, it may not be effective to mention that there is an open slot on the doctor's schedule in a couple of months. Similarly, in the online world, you do not expect to run a query at a major search engine only to be told to come back the following Tuesday.

Demand can also be shaped via pricing and promotions. Advanced yield management algorithms used by hotels and airlines maximize revenue and utilization by using dynamic pricing and charging more when demand is high and offering discounts when demand is low. Cloud computing is beginning to follow this direction, as I predicted, introducing spot pricing to incent off-peak use.[7] However, doing so requires price elasticity of demand—the level of demand must increase when the price is lower and decrease when the price is higher. This is not always the case: I won't be able to use an airline ticket to Cleveland this afternoon even if it *is* only $10, and the total quantity of caskets I plan to purchase for my own use is no more than one.

For many services, capacity is somewhat inherently elastic, with customer experience sometimes degrading near its maximum. After all, the absolute maximum number of passengers that can fit into a subway car is partly a function of how forcefully they are being stuffed in.[8] Capacity can also be made somewhat fungible. Taxicabs in London don't have trunks: The luggage space is inside the passenger area. Although somewhat disconcerting at first, it is effective, since fold-down seats enable the same space to be used for large suitcases or for passengers. Employees can be cross-trained, making them a type of flexible capacity as well.

Virtualization is a technology used to enable sharing of computer servers or data storage, where each application "thinks" it has sole use of a resource, but this resource is actually a "virtual" one, and two or more of these virtual resources may reside on a single physical resource. This may sound confusing, but the same approach is used in the offline world as well: When you share a cab with someone, their virtual cab ride and your virtual cab ride are both mapped to the same physical vehicle for a time. Sharing is more efficient than using one taxi for each ride. Or think about less-than-truckload (LTL) shipments. Prior to this, a "shipment" meant a "truckload." But, with LTL, multiple "shipments" can be mapped to a single "truckload."

Some in the industry appear to believe that since virtualization can reduce resource requirements and enhance utilization, it alone can solve the capacity conundrum. A moment's thought, however, shows that while virtualization is a very effective technology with sound benefits and that it can reduce the magnitude of the capacity conundrum, it can't comprise the entire solution.

Virtualization is effective in reducing the total resource requirements but doesn't do much about the variability. Suppose at peak, 60 resources are required but there normally is an average of 20. Virtualization that achieves a 2-to-1 compression ratio is helpful in reducing the peak requirement to 30 resources and the average to 10, but there still will be a 3-to-1 peak-to-average ratio.

In other words, virtualization can shrink the total *size* of the problem but won't do much about the *nature* of the problem: unused capacity when demand is low and/or insufficient capacity when demand is high.

Splitting the Difference

If someone says you *must* pick a capacity level to meet a given demand profile, what level should you pick? We'll look at the problem a simple way and then in a more realistic way.

We've already mentioned that if capacity is greater than demand, we incur a penalty due to excess capacity. It would be like buying three plane tickets, when we only need one, or buying three cars, when we can only drive one at a given time: We are unnecessarily incurring costs such as leases, financing, or depreciation.

Conversely, if we need a car, but we have none, we end up paying some kind of penalty by not having it. For example, if we need the car to get to work, we lose the wages associated with the job.

To keep things simple, we will assume a few things for now. First, we will assume that the cost of excess capacity is exactly the same as the cost of insufficient capacity. In effect, if we have one car too many, we are paying a penalty that is identical as having one car too few.

Second, we will assume that the penalty cost is linear. In other words, having three cars too many costs three times as much as much as having one car too many.

Last, we will assume that the demand is uniformly distributed. In other words, every level of demand between two select numbers is equally likely. For the sake of simplicity, let's assume that a demand of zero units—say, cars—is as likely as one unit is as likely as two units is as likely as three units is as likely as . . . is as likely as nine units is as likely as ten units. Since there are 11 possible outcomes—0, 1, 2, 3, 4, 5, 6, 7, 8, 9, 10—that are each equally likely, the probability of any of them is 1/11, or about .091. Suppose that we set the capacity to be zero. Then 1/11 of the time we would be exactly right. Another 1/11 of the time we would be off by 1. Another 1/11 of the time we would be off by 2.

We can see where this is going: The expected value of the total penalty depends on the probability of each outcome and the penalty given that outcome. This weighted, or probability-adjusted, penalty is

$$\frac{1}{11} \times 0 + \frac{1}{11} \times 1 + \frac{1}{11} \times 2 + \frac{1}{11} \times 3 + \frac{1}{11} \times 4 + \cdots + \frac{1}{11} \times 9 + \frac{1}{11} \times 10$$

This can be rewritten by moving the 1/11 to the side and summing, giving just $\frac{1}{11} \times 55 = 5$.

Not bad. It should also be obvious in this case that if we set the capacity to be 10 instead of 0, with the same demand distribution we would end up with a penalty of 10 when the demand was 0, 9 when the demand was 1, and so forth. This is the same equation as the one just given, resulting in the same expected value, 5.

Can we do better than this? In this case, it turns out that we can. If we pick a point right in the middle—a capacity of 5—the penalty function is reduced. When the demand is 0, the penalty is only 5, and when the demand is 10, the penalty is only 5. Consequently, the new penalty function is:

$$\frac{1}{11} \times 5 + \frac{1}{11} \times 4 + \frac{1}{11} \times 3 + \frac{1}{11} \times 2 + \frac{1}{11} \times 1 + \cdots + \frac{1}{11} \times 4 + \frac{1}{11} \times 5$$

This is, $\frac{1}{11} \times 30 = 2.73$. This approach tells us that under the circumstances we've described—symmetric penalties for over- and undercapacity, a linear penalty function proportional to the size of the difference, and uniform distribution of demand—a better strategy to solve the capacity conundrum with fixed capacity, which turns out to be the best that we can do, is to pick a capacity value right in the middle of the distribution.

The "expected value" tells us the weighted penalty given the probability distribution. When the distribution is uniform across *discrete* values, such as 1, 2, 3, 4, as when rolling a die, we can use an approach like this to determine the answer. Mathematically, the expected value is the sum of probability adjusted outcomes, as in the calculations just given.

There are also *continuous* probability distributions. For example, the temperature outside might be 81, 82, 83, 84, but it also might be 81.1, 81.2, 81.3, or even 81.274566228790. In this case, we make use of the fact that the expected value can be determined using calculus. For our purposes here, we can just eyeball the areas to get a sense of the size of the penalty, which is the magnitude of the shaded area seen in Exhibit 9.2.

As can be seen in Exhibit 9.2(a), when the capacity is set at 0, the penalty grows as the demand increases. In Exhibit 9.2(b), when the capacity is set at 10, the penalty grows as the demand decreases. In Exhibit 9.2(c), the capacity is set at 3, and there are costs in either direction. When the capacity is set in the middle, as in 9.2(d), there are still penalties in either direction, but the total penalty—the size of the shaded area—is minimized.

Better Safe than Sorry

In the analysis just described, we assumed a *symmetric* penalty function. In other words, being one resource too high cost us exactly as much as being one resource too low; being 100 resources too high cost us just as much as being 100 resources too low. Typically this is not the case, though. We invest in resources to receive a net return.

We don't spend an extra dollar on computers to receive an extra dollar in income from the Web site that they power. By "spend," here, let's assume that we have converted investments and the income generated from them into similar units; otherwise, we will have to worry about the weighted average cost of capital and depreciation schedules and the time value of the net operating profit after taxes and things like that. But let's keep it simple.

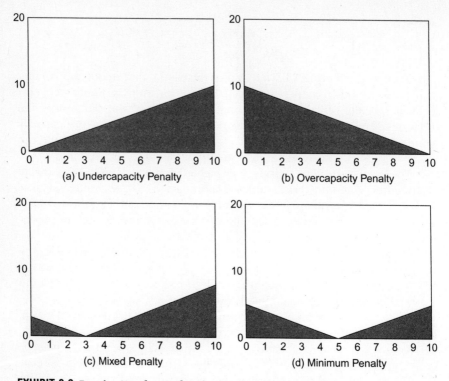

EXHIBIT 9.2 Penalty Size for Uniformly Distributed Demand Served by Fixed Capacity with *Symmetric* Penalty Costs

If spending $1 only returned us $1, we wouldn't be any better off than not spending that dollar. Instead, we would expect that spending a dollar would gain us $2, $3, or $10, for example.

Therefore, an *asymmetric* penalty function makes more sense. Let's take a look at the same set of capacity strategies as before, but this time, assuming that the net cost of resources is only 50 cents, but the net revenue that they generate is $2. Then, having two unneeded resources costs us $1, but being two resources short loses us $4. What happens under those assumptions?

Exhibit 9.3 graphically illustrates the effect: Triangles that slope to the left (indicating overcapacity) are shallower than those that slope to the right (indicating undercapacity). As can be seen in Exhibit 9.3(a), if we set capacity at zero, we pay an increasing penalty up through $20 when we are 10 resources short.

However, if, as in Exhibit 9.3(b), we set capacity at 10, we pay an increasing penalty as the actual demand decreases, but the worst case is only $5.

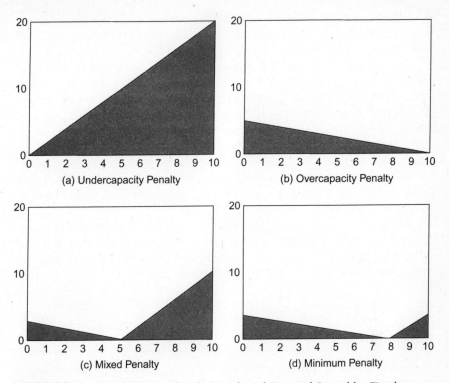

EXHIBIT 9.3 Penalty Size for Uniformly Distributed Demand Served by Fixed Capacity with *Asymmetric* Penalty Costs

If we try the same strategy as in the case of the symmetric penalty function, namely a capacity at the midpoint of 5, as shown in Exhibit 9.3(c), we are better off than at zero capacity, but we can do better yet.

The optimal capacity in this case, as shown in Exhibit 9.3(d), is at 8, where in the worst case we are overcapacity by eight resources for a penalty of $4 or undercapacity by two resources also for a penalty of $4.

We'll derive these results more completely in Chapter 14,[9] but briefly, when demand is characterized by a uniform distribution, you should select a capacity that errs on the side of excess capacity by a ratio that is the cost of insufficient capacity divided by the sum of the cost of excess capacity and the cost of insufficient capacity.

This logic means that the higher the ratio of the penalty cost of insufficient capacity to the penalty cost of excess capacity, the better it is to be safe rather than sorry (i.e., to err on the side of caution, by deploying capacity nearer to the peak demand).

This quantitative rationale supports most companies' intuitive strategy of building infrastructure to handle peak demands or, actually, peak expected demand plus some headroom (i.e., margin of safety).

This simple analysis doesn't take into account all the complexities of the real world, such as the fact that we don't really know what the future distribution of demand is; at best, we can attempt to extrapolate from history, modulated by exogenous risk and trend analysis. The penalty function may not be linear; you can manage through a little bit of insufficient capacity in many cases (e.g., having people stand in the subway car a little bit more closely together).

However, the most important lesson is this: Given assumptions on underlying demand distributions and penalty functions and related factors, we can find an optimal solution.

But, no matter how good this solution is, it will not solve the capacity conundrum. In other words, there are bad solutions and there are less bad solutions, but there is no excellent solution to the issues inherent in using fixed capacity in an attempt to satisfy dynamic demand.

Capacity Inertia

Even if demand is variable and unpredictable, it would not represent a problem if it were possible to rapidly purchase or sell the owned capacity needed to fulfill demand. Unfortunately, there typically is friction or inertia in increasing capacity. It may take time to realize that there is a gap and determine how much additional capacity is needed. Companies must forecast to try to predict how much capacity will be needed by the time the demand arrives. Ordering the capacity and deploying it requires additional time. However, after a peak subsides, there is friction in decreasing it. Some equipment may be on a three-year lease, which is a problem if the peak lasts only a few days or months. If the equipment is owned, it has almost certainly depreciated. There are transaction costs associated with disposal (e.g., sale or auction, contracts, transportation).

Capacity may not just be equipment, such as servers. If it is people, the same principles apply: It takes time to post job ads, interview, select, onboard, and train. In some countries, workers may not be downsized without a lengthy process, severance, and works council approvals. So, human resources are not that different from other resources when it comes to increasing or decreasing "capacity." Some businesses do not have these constraints: In employment at will, in many cases for day laborers such as, say, some construction work or farmwork, a truck picks up as many workers are needed that day, with no commitment and no complex skills evaluation or worker selection. This, of course, is not fixed capacity, but on-demand capacity acquired from the "labor" cloud.

Some capacity, such as manufacturing and power plants, may take years to deploy, between planning and design, site selection, permitting, construction, equipment deployment, and the like, and of course it also may take years to decommission and dispose of. In short, fixed capacity is problematic, driving an imperative to use the cloud.

Summary

There are numerous drivers of variable and unpredictable demand, which cause the capacity conundrum: how to deploy capacity to respond to the demand. If capacity is too high, money is wasted. Either capital expenditures tie up funds that could be used elsewhere, or an expense stream is not generating any useful returns. If capacity is too low, however, revenue can be lost, labor productivity impaired, and customer experience degraded. There also may be secondary effects, such as impact to reputation and loss of existing customers or future prospects.

Depending on assumptions regarding the relative cost of overcapacity and undercapacity and the probability distribution of demand, some fixed capacity solutions may be *better* than others, but there will not be a perfect solution that minimizes the total cost, without relying on the on-demand, pay-per-use nature of the cloud, which we examine in the coming chapters, beginning in Chapter 10 with an exploration of the relative cost of such capacity relative to fixed capacity.

Notes

1. Leonard L. Berry and A. Parasuraman, *Marketing Services: Competing Through Quality* (Free Press, 1991), p. 5.
2. Chuck Chakrapani, *How to Measure Service Quality and Customer Satisfaction: The Informal Field Guide for Tools and Techniques* (American Marketing Association, 1998).
3. www.bigbreaksolutions.com/events/?utm_source=UnitedBreaksGuitarscom.
4. Beatriz Moliner Velazquez, Gloria Berenguer Contri, Irene Gil Saura, and Marie Fuentes Blasco, "Antecedents to Complaint Behaviour in the Context of Restaurant Goers," *International Review of Retail, Distribution and Consumer Research* 16, No. 5 (December 2006): 493–517.
5. Irena Ograjensek, "Service Quality," in Shirley Coleman, Tony Greenfield, Dave Stewardson, and Douglas C. Montgomery, eds., *Statistical Practice in Business and Industry* (John Wiley & Sons, 2008).

6. James Hamilton, "The Cost of Latency," *Perspectives: James Hamilton's Blog*. www.perspectives.mvdirona.com/2009/10/31/TheCostOfLatency.aspx.

7. Stacey Higginbotham, "Dynamic Pricing Comes to Amazon's Cloud," *GigaOM.com*, December 14, 2009. www.gigaom.com/2009/12/14/dynamic-pricing-comes-to-amazons-cloud/.

8. User d0b33, "Japanese Train Station During Rush Hour", uploaded December 3, 2007, www.youtube.com/watch?v=b0A9-oUoMug.

9. Joe Weinman, "Time is Money: The Value of On-Demand," January 7, 2011. www.joeweinman.com/Resources/Joe_Weinman_Time_Is_Money.pdf.

CHAPTER 10

Significance of Scale

One significant aspect of today's leading providers is their scale and scope. They may support millions or even hundreds of millions of users each month, often have global reach, and can exploit the economics of large facilities. This scale can shift relative costs, and can also offer unique advantages beyond cost.

If we are considering using the cloud, one factor impacting our choice is surely the cost relative to the do-it-yourself option. The major cloud computing providers have outdone themselves in building large multi-football-field-size data centers. Author and futurist George Gilder called these "the Information Factories," and as he put it, "[W]e're all petaphiles now, plugged into a world of petabytes, petaops, petaflops."[1] The art and science of designing and siting these data centers involves many different insights and best practices in a variety of areas: property acquisition; tax incentives; power and cooling engineering; regional electric power cost differentials; immunity from earthquakes, floods, and other disasters; and high-bandwidth network connectivity, to name a few. A major reason to build such enormous facilities is to exploit economies of scale.

According to economics textbooks, "economies of scale" are "increases in productivity, or decreases in average cost of production, that arise from increasing all the factors of production in the same proportion."[2] The conventional wisdom regarding economies of scale in the cloud is that larger cloud providers realize this lower average cost of production, translating into an enormous advantage over enterprise do-it-yourself approaches. Some have argued that such a cost advantage, in fact, is the main benefit of the cloud.[3] The implications of this would be staggering, if true: Enterprise IT would cease to exist in a world of rational economic decision makers; the cloud market would consolidate to fewer and fewer players, subject only to antitrust constraints; and the market would stabilize—perhaps even become sclerotic—as the barriers to entry would be insurmountable.

Such economies-of-scale arguments, however, are more nuanced than might appear at first glance, and drawing any such conclusions may be premature. Understanding scale arguments is somewhat tortuous and torturous, unfortunately, but absolutely essential to correctly defining the role of the cloud. Making the analysis more difficult is that cloud prices have been dropping, costs of technology used by enterprises and cloud providers have been dropping, and cloud service providers are using a variety of architectural approaches. Some are using commercially available racks and servers or blades, some are using containerized architectures, and some are building to their own designs, building data centers that look less like a collection of equipment than a single enormous computing monolith.

The key points are these:

- "Economies of scale" is not a sufficiently holistic concept, because it ignores the crucial interplay of production with demand in determining delivered cost.
- Cloud service providers certainly have economies of scale in parts of their operations; however, these may exhibit diminishing returns. Moreover, they have diseconomies in other areas.
- Diffusion of existing technologies and the emergence of new ones may reduce the differences in the relative cost structures of enterprises, medium-size providers, and large providers.
- As profit-seeking commercial concerns, service providers have additional cost structure elements that an enterprise IT shop, as a cost center, doesn't have.
- Therefore, how much it costs a cloud provider to "produce" a unit of IT may actually be *higher* than it costs a "well-run" enterprise.
- But this higher unit cost ultimately doesn't matter, because for certain application profiles, it is not only the unit cost but the pay-per-use difference in cloud pricing and the statistics of demand aggregation that generate *total cost* benefits.
- Beyond *total cost*, scale generates additional benefits such as cyber-attack resilience, and thus the cloud is an important component of any enterprise strategy.

In summary, the traditional argument might be phrased like this: "You should use the cloud because it exhibits scale economies." The more nuanced argument is: "The cloud may have a lower unit cost or a higher unit cost but can still save you money *and* deliver other benefits." We address some elements of this argument now and some in the next few chapters.

Is the Cloud Like Electricity?

Electricity is a pay-per-use, on-demand, ubiquitous utility; so is cloud computing. Of course, there are salient differences—data are not undifferentiated the way that electrons are—but can we learn anything by examining their similarities?

Bestselling author Nick Carr argued that an important similarity between the two is the historic migration from private, owned facilities to the public utility.[4] He pointed out that, as the industrial era dawned, factories used on-premises power plants: typically a large water wheel to capture the kinetic energy in flowing water and a system of belts and pulleys to transport that power from the water's edge to the various tools in the factory, such as drills.

To paraphrase Carr's argument, this strategy of "enterprise power centers," if we can call them that, requiring local, owned, capital resources, evolved to a pay-per-use, on-demand service model: what we might call "the electric cloud," where the huge economies of scale and other benefits associated with enormous "cloud electric centers" dwarfed what could be achieved locally. The argument posits the inevitability of this transformation. In effect, nobody but some sort of Luddite or survivalist living in the wilds generates their own electricity or does without.

The thesis of this line of argument is clear: An industry's evolution to a pure service model delivered from highly consolidated and vertically integrated facilities exhibiting immense economies of scale is inevitable.

Or is it?

Erik Brynjolfsson of the Massachusetts Institute of Technology and his colleagues argued that there are salient differences between computing clouds and electric utilities, for both technology and business model reasons.[5] Brynjolfsson claimed that not much has happened in electric power generation technology evolution, whereas the rapidity of innovation in computing is unparalleled, and thus requires talented people, in contradistinction to stable technologies. He also observed that the cloud is very good at some types of applications, such as highly parallel ones. But there are other applications—such as online transaction processing, requiring consistency of data and performance—that may not be well suited to the cloud. He also argued that "latency is not dead," and location can be critical for some applications, such as high-frequency trading of equities. In his view, this last model argues *against* the cloud; I will argue in Chapter 18 that it is often *aligned* with the cloud and the cloud's inherently dispersed architecture. After all, because of the requirement for low latency, that is, convenience, there is a coffee shop on every corner (i.e., a dispersed architecture).

Moreover, Brynjolfsson and his colleagues argue that there are even more substantive business model differences than the preceding technical differences:

1. IT is an enabler of new business models and new organization designs and thus is much more strategic than mere electricity.
2. The elements of the cloud—interfaces, data formats, and the like—inhibit interoperability and markets.
3. Security issues in the cloud are very different: As Brynjolfsson quipped, "No regulatory or law enforcement body will audit a company's electrons."

I think that most of Brynjolfsson's points are valid but that there is an even more blatant issue with drawing analogies between electricity and cloud computing. This issue has to do with the economies-of-scale argument and the implication that the cloud will inevitably take over all IT.

There certainly are differences between the two domains, but perhaps the first question to ask is the simplest: Is there a fundamental cost advantage deriving from the cloud model, is the cloud equally as expensive as do-it-yourself, or could it even be more expensive?

Distributed Power Generation

For the past century, we've gotten electricity from service providers for a variety of reasons: It's easy and convenient to do so; it requires no up-front capital investments; and running our own generator would require allocation of space, personnel, and skills. But perhaps the biggest reason is that it's *relatively inexpensive*. But let's do a thought experiment. Suppose that someone invented a safe, shoebox-size power generator that you could buy for a dollar and self-install in your basement in minutes. Let's also assume that it ran for a decade or two. Not only would it save money, but it would be inherently more efficient since power transmission and distribution waste resources: Much of the electric energy goes to heating up the power line rather than rather recharging your tablet.

Such a scenario is not that far-fetched, after all. Nuclear submarines have been in service for half a century, sales of solar cells are going through the roof, and we can't rule out a disruption such as fuel cells or cold fusion or something that would make the scenario work. In other words, rather than computing increasingly replicating the electric utility model by moving into the cloud, electricity might increasingly parallel pre—cloud computing environments, deployed on consumer and enterprise premises.

Right now, though, the power utility has the upper hand, for several reasons. First, there truly *are* economies of scale in power generation. Power utilities use enormous turbines for the simple reason that their physical performance exhibits nonlinearities: Larger generators are more efficient than smaller ones. There is also a minimum size required for some technologies, such as nuclear power plants. The third reason is that some power companies get some of their raw materials for free: No one is counting the amount of kinetic and potential energy in each gallon of water that the Hoover Dam uses. These benefits have traditionally overcome the disadvantages of transmission losses.

But suppose that electric power companies, instead of using enormous turbines, used the same generators that you or I could buy at Home Depot and paid the same rates for raw materials—say, coal or natural gas. Would kilowatt-hours be cheaper or more expensive? The electric company might have some cost advantages, such as economies of scale in administering the generators or getting a bigger discount from Home Depot, but it also would have disadvantages: The chief executive officer of the utility needs to fly around to give dinner keynotes on the state of the electric power industry and meet with important customers.

Is electricity the right analogy, or is rental car services?

Is the Cloud Like Rental Cars?

Whether to buy equipment to deploy in your own data center or rent the resources from the cloud is similar to the buy versus rent decision for homes or cars. Let's consider the latter.

A typical midsize car can be financed for a few hundred dollars per month. Let's call it $300. This works out to a cost of $10 per day to own. Equivalently, you could pay cash and depreciate the vehicle at about the same rate. This doesn't include fuel or insurance.

Instead of the $10-a-day rate, you could also go to a leading car rental service and pay $30 or $40 per day, also excluding fuel and insurance.

To put it more bluntly, the unit cost of a "world-class service provider" costs three to four times as much as that of a do-it-yourself solution. This is true even though such a service provider presumably has enormous economies of scale, highly repeatable service operations, optimized processes, and immense volume purchasing power leverage over automobile manufacturers. Moreover, unlike you, who has your eye on that hot little red sports car at any price, a rental company can populate a portion of its fleet with cars that are attractively priced because auto manufacturers can't sell them, and often utilizes manufacturer buyback programs where it can sell the car back to the manufacturer.

What's going on? How are electric cloud services currently cheaper from a service provider than owning the means of production yourself whereas rental car cloud services are more expensive than owning? And how can this be when both are arguably commodities and the benchmarks are versus mature, well-run firms.

It would appear that a key difference is that rental car companies largely utilize a scale-out architecture with limits to scale economies, whereas electric utilities and other service providers such as airlines have a scale-up architecture that benefits from cost nonlinearities.

In other words, when Hertz or Avis wants to beef up its business, it doesn't buy *larger* cars, it buys *more* cars. Sure, the companies get a volume discount, but this discount exhibits diminishing returns. You or I might be able to negotiate a good price on a car, someone buying 10 could do better and someone buying 100 probably still better. But how much better can Avis do? Large enterprises run their own "private car cloud": the corporate fleet. Enterprise buyers, in short, can get pretty good deals themselves.

Conversely, in the airline business, when United Airlines wants to expand on a route, it goes from a regional jet to a Boeing 737 to a 757 to a 777 and soon a 787. Flying 300 passengers via a 777 is less expensive per mile than ferrying them in two-seater planes, one at a time. And, while a typical individual or enterprise might be able to afford a Cessna, few could or would own and operate a jumbo jet.

Depending on the industry, there are certainly additional factors and tradeoffs: resource provisioning and deprovisioning costs and fixed and variable costs required to use either your own or service-based resources. To acquire a rental car, you have to get to the rental car facility somehow. If you own a car, you have to allocate space to garage it or pay for street parking. To hail a cab takes an indeterminate amount of time. The bottom line is that in a variety of domains, *even leading service providers in competitive markets may not necessarily offer equivalent goods and services at a lower unit price than the unit cost of a do-it-yourself strategy.*

Does this mean that once word gets out that rental car services are priced higher than do-it-yourself they will all have to close up shop? No, because the other key insight to be garnered from this analogy is that *a major component of the rental car value proposition versus do-it-yourself is not necessarily a lower equivalent day rate, but the pay-per-use pricing model, coupled with the absence of commitment and minimal or no additional charges.*

To understand whether the power utility has an advantage over home generation, we'd need to compare the *cost* of do-it-yourself—all-in, including time spent evaluating which generator to buy and scouting deals (search and information costs), time spent to drive to Home Depot to buy it (transaction costs), purchasing fuel (cost of goods sold), traipsing down to the basement

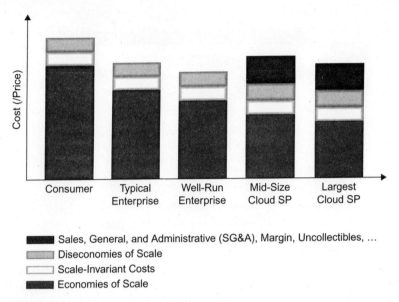

EXHIBIT 10.1 Illustrative Example of Delivered Costs

every Sunday to make sure it hasn't blown up (operations, administration, and management)—relative to the *price* that the utility was selling it at. We'd need to do the same for owning versus renting cars.

Exhibit 10.1 illustrates how these factors can impact the relative delivered unit costs of various sizes of customers and various sizes of service providers (SPs). There may be economies of scale, diseconomies of scale, scale-invariant costs, and additional costs associated with commercial operations. These costs may be explicitly represented in a service provider's price or implicit in a customer's additional costs to enter into commercial external relationships: search and contracting costs, for example. Moreover, the components of price for a commercial firm include additional elements such as sales, general and administrative (SG&A) expenses, margin, etc. The exhibit is illustrative but shows that, even in the presence of scale economies, the relative *unit* cost of doing it yourself should not be blithely assumed to be higher than that associated with using a cloud provider.

Capital Expenditures versus Operating Expenses

Some have argued that one of the benefits of the cloud model is that companies can avoid large capital expenditures (capex) and translate them into operating expenses (opex) using the cloud. As shown in Exhibit 10.2,

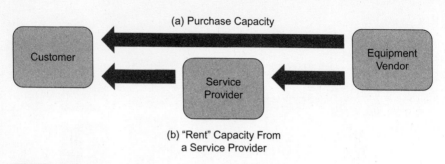

EXHIBIT 10.2 Apparent Capex versus Opex Decision

the choice appears to be that between Exhibit 10.2(a), a large up-front capital investment, and Exhibit 10.2(b), a more manageable payment stream.

Healthy companies, some of which are today sitting on enormous piles of cash, don't necessarily consider capital expenditures bad and operating expenses good; rather, such expenses are among a variety of viable ways of financing operations. Choosing one versus the other involves trading off considerations such as the weighted average cost of capital, tax implications, covenants, EBITDA (Earnings Before Interest, Taxes, Depreciation, and Amortization), and assorted budgetary targets. There are additional subtleties: IT strategist Chris Potts advised that "if an IT plan is part of a major corporate project like building a big factory, trying to expense IT could affect depreciation schedules for the whole plan."[6] In such cases, migrating from capex to opex might have larger—and negative—repercussions.

Moreover, as seen in Exhibit 10.3, a company doesn't need to have a cloud computing service provider handle the conversion of capex to opex for it; rather, it can use a "loan service provider"—such as a bank—to do it. Exhibit 10.3(c) shows an expense stream—loan interest servicing—going to a bank that provides the capital to buy the equipment. Exhibit 10.3(d) shows the use of leasing company, and Exhibit 10.3(e) is the nearly equivalent vendor financing of the equipment, where the vendor is not only the manufacturer but a lessor. There are assorted options, such as capital leases and operating leases with a variety of tax implications. We could expand this even further to include other sources of funds, such as commercial paper, public equity market financing, private equity, venture capital, angel investors, and the like.

The point of this discussion is that the salient difference is not capex versus opex—that conversion was enabled millennia ago via the lease—but the ability to acquire and release resources frictionlessly, the lack of commitment, and the pay-per-use model in the context of variable demand. Cloud approaches are increasingly complementing other opex approaches, such as leasing and managed services, so it is not the use of opex that is the

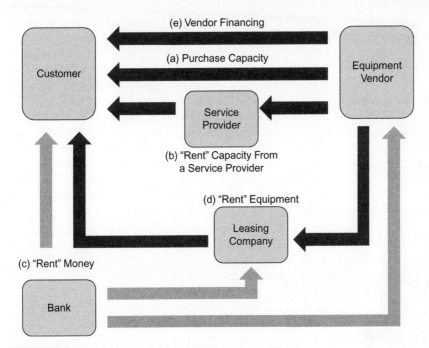

EXHIBIT 10.3 Illustrative Options Available to a Customer

salient difference. In highly liquid markets with minimal costs associated with market transactions and title transfer costs, and zero or minimal transportation costs, ownership (and disposal) can be on demand. The stock market is a good example: A person can own stock, expending capital to do so, and then trade it.

What about depreciation? When an asset is owned, it may depreciate; in fact, given Moore's Law, depreciation is guaranteed. That's true, but it doesn't impact anything. The same asset is depreciating at the same rate on the service provider's books, and those costs are built in to the cost per hour of the "rental."

To really understand the wisdom of either strategy over time, we'd need to understand each of the cost drivers and their trends.

Benchmark Data

Ideally, these arguments help us think better about whether there are economies of scale that drive price advantages, but are somewhat theoretical. What do the actual data show?

McKinsey & Company is perhaps the most prestigious management consulting group in the world, found in the boardrooms of the Fortune 500 on a daily basis. At McKinsey, Will Forrest is a principal and is responsible for the bombshell report "Clearing the Air on Cloud Computing."[7] Forrest and his colleagues continue to do in-depth analyses, relying not only on their strategy insights but also in-depth multiclient studies.

What Forrest showed was that the total cost of assets for a "typical data center" in a larger enterprise was almost always less than on-demand resources from a major cloud provider, regardless of the instance size—small, medium, large, or extra-large—and regardless of the operating system—Microsoft Windows or Linux. The assumption regarding total cost of assets included a very realistic 10% utilization, 10 cents per kilowatt-hour, and $14,000 per server for a two-way, four-core server.

Forrest also showed that for very small compute jobs, with prepaid instances running Linux, this leading service provider could cost one quarter to one half the typical data center price.

Forrest included a 15% reduction in labor costs by moving to the cloud, after looking at a variety of roles: application support and development, architecture, business analysis, client services, database administrators, desktop support, facilities, help desk, IT administrators, management, quality assurance, real estate, and telecommunications.

Since then, a variety of analyses with mixed conclusions have been conducted by industry insiders and vendors as well as objective third parties.[8] Making such analyses even more challenging, the numbers change frequently, as service providers regularly cut prices and introduce options offering additional discounts for volume and commitments.[9] Some service providers claim that customers can save money "regardless of the size of their operations."[10] But industry consultant David Linthicum, CTO of Blue Mountain Labs, argues that "The myth is that cloud computing is always cost-effective, [but in] many instances, it's not."[11] Moreover, as we will see in Chapters 11 and 12, cost advantages are highly dependent on the application and its demand: As Gartner analysts Lydia Leong and Ted Chamberlin have directly stated, "Customers do not usually save money by using cloud IaaS . . . For larger businesses with existing internal data centers and IT operations teams, public cloud IaaS for steady-state workloads is often no less expensive, and may be more expensive, than an internal private cloud."[12]

Finally, an apples-to-apples comparison can be a challenge: It is easy to find list prices for service provider offers; difficult to accurately account for all internal costs and correctly evaluate other attributes such as performance, security, and availability. Such an evaluation would require not only the determination of, say, relative availability, but a precise projection of the *economic value* of this difference.

Results from Vijay Gill, a blogger and executive with Google at the time, showed that buying cloud services from a leading provider could be 68% more expensive than doing it yourself in a colocation facility.[13] Some argued that Gill should have used different assumptions, but focusing solely on the price of a delivered unit of capacity on a per-hour, on-demand, pay-per-use basis, his analysis showed a price premium rather than a reduction due to the oft-assumed economies of scale.

Gill is very well aware of the implications, assumptions, and limits of his analysis, and has observed that the duty cycle is what makes the difference. As Carl Brooks, an experienced technology writer with TechTarget at the time, put it: "Renting an apartment can seem like a waste of money if you own a home, not so much if you need a place to live."[14] The point stands, though, that the cloud *may* be more expensive on a unit cost basis.

Cost Factors

Developing a robust model of provider pricing versus do-it-yourself pricing to understand where or whether there truly are economies of scale and how they will evolve over time requires an understanding of factors that may increase or decrease a service provider's unit costs relative to your own. Here is a list of cost drivers. They can be categorized differently, you may have different or additional costs, but it's a start.

- *Computing equipment.* This equipment includes servers, storage, and networking gear such as switches, routers, and load balancers. Some of this functionality may be virtually implemented as software running on other hardware, but any function requires a physical embodiment and thus equipment.
- *Power and cooling equipment.* This equipment includes power distribution, generators and uninterruptible power supply systems, heating, ventilation, and air conditioning.
- *Supporting equipment.* This includes miscellany, such as cable troughs and fire suppression equipment.
- *Physical plant and access control.* The building itself and/or containers, fences, physical access control and security mechanisms, administrative offices.
- *Power costs.* This includes electricity, the fuel to generate electricity, and costs to contract for guaranteed delivery across one or more grids or fuel suppliers. These costs are of the utmost concern: Google's engineers have disclosed that "one of the most important factors [is] energy efficiency . . . [which] is key at our scale of operation."[15]

- *Virtualization software and support.* License and support fees for virtualization software must be assessed. Even "free" open source software can incur costs for testing, integration, support, modification, and community contributions.
- *Network transport.* This may be a cost for physical gear, indefeasible rights of use (IRUs), which are essentially leases for subsea cable fibers, leased lines, network services, or bandwidth charges.
- *Security.* Security costs include costs for security hardware, such as firewalls, and security operations costs, such as personnel and security management, incident monitoring, and intrusion detection and prevention.
- *Management and administration tooling.* This area spans management for servers, storage, load balancers, firewalls, configuration management databases, provisioning tools, trouble ticketing software, and intelligent correlation engines.
- *Management and administration labor.* The tools don't run themselves; administrators must be hired, trained, and paid.
- *Purchasing power and discounts.* How much leverage is there on suppliers? What are the volume discounts, market development funds, or reciprocal agreements?
- *Skills, knowledge, expertise.* What skill level can you afford to hire and maintain? Will employees be motivated? Will turnover be high?
- *Learning curve effects.* How do these skills improve over time? How much investment can you make in process improvement and standardized documentation?
- *Training costs.* What are the costs to train staff, develop training materials, allocate personnel to act as instructors, or hire outside "train the trainers," i.e., trainers to train your training personnel?
- *Proprietary processes, patents, trade secrets.* Cloud service providers have developed tricks of the trade. Some, such as Facebook, are willing to share some of them[16]; others are not.
- *Capacity quantization effects.* How big is the increment of capacity required, and how much does it cost? Traditionally, this was the data center; now it may well be the container. There are other discontinuities, such as the cost of a rack versus the equipment that goes in it.
- *Statistics of scale and effective utilization.* What is the pattern of demand, and how does that impact utilization? Chapter 15 explores these effects in more detail. Can there be overbooking or "thin provisioning," and how does that impact costs?
- *Sales, general, and administrative.* How much, if any, is allocated to the internal IT shop? What are the selling, general, and administrative costs for commercial operations?

- *Provider operations overhead.* How much effort is required to design, develop, operate, and maintain commercial portals?
- *Service-level agreements, payments, and credits.* What are the levels that a provider is willing to commit to versus what you may achieve yourself? Who is responsible for detection? What is the cost of an outage? What is the likelihood of an outage?
- *Engineering.* These costs include a variety of research, technology assessment, design, engineering, development, planning, integration, migration, of physical data centers, their interconnection, and the solution stacks within them.
- *Vendor selection, trials, certification, interoperability testing.* What is the cost to write requests for proposals, quotations, or information, hold meetings with vendors, test new equipment, run a test lab, certify current applications on new systems, validate performance?
- *Margin.* What margin is the provider incorporating? Is it sustainable, or will it increase or decrease over time? How intense is the competitive rivalry within the specific cloud industry subsegment of interest?
- *Technical support.* What are the costs to provide help desks, frequently asked questions, and maintain a knowledge management system?
- *Accounts Receivable and Uncollectibles.* Customers who delay payment or never pay.
- *Search and information costs.* These costs include determining equipment and software vendors and evaluating financing options for a do-it-yourself strategy or assessing cloud service providers for a cloud strategy. They also include modeling and projecting costs in either scenario based on application profiles.
- *Transaction costs.* These are the costs of procurement operations, contracting, legal fees, and transaction fees.
- *Migration costs.* These are the costs of renegotiating contracts, early termination fees, bandwidth for data migration, and application rewrites.
- *Generally accepted accounting principles and financial practices.* Some companies are depreciating payments for reserved instances. This may tip the buy-versus-rent balance one way or another.
- *Taxes and tax credits.* Investment tax credits alter breakpoints.

As if this weren't a complicated enough list, it is constantly in flux. Provider pricing changes, sometimes for the better, but not always, depending on your applications portfolio. Application demand shifts. Labor costs shift. Tax law changes.

Technology also changes: Data centers usually have been buildings. Some alternative designs are asphalt parking lots or cleared fields in emerging countries with the IT in rugged, containerized pods. In the middle are data centers, such as Microsoft's latest in Chicago, a $500-million, 700,000-square-foot shell with prebuilt double-decker containerized servers and storage.[17] One benefit of this approach is that it reduces up-front fixed investments, aligns costs better with growth in demand, and enables more efficient cooling—the need to cool containers, not buildings, speeds provisioning—2,000 servers can be turned up in eight hours—but also changes the size of the minimum capacity increment; thus, if you only need 2,001 servers you will still need to buy 4,000. There may well be no "best" architecture, but a best one at a point in time for a given set of requirements, highlighting that there are many different variables that can be adjusted based on business needs.

The other point is that enterprises and cloud providers can also determine the degree of vertical integration that they desire. Some service providers are buying their own subsea cable capacity; others are happy with buying services. Some are purchasing off-the-shelf industry standard servers; others are engaging traditional vendors to build to custom requirements; still others are designing their own servers, in some cases in utmost secrecy, but in the case of Facebook's Open Compute Project, releasing detailed specifications as open source hardware.[18] Some are building their own proprietary tooling and software stacks; others are buying them from management software providers; still others are participating as both users and contributors of open source initiatives.

There are two points here:

1. There is still tremendous room for innovation, from the ground up through the management software.
2. Cost comparisons are a moving target.

In a way, though, all this complexity is a strong argument for moving to the cloud. Certainly a small business—say, a pizza shop or realtor—doesn't want to be configuring routers and making tweaks to server motherboard designs. However, some large enterprises may have the expertise and motivation to so invest their time and money. As the list above shows, there are many factors to consider in determining cost tradeoffs alone.

Benchmarking the Leaders

Beyond looking at long lists of factors, one way to determine the right approach might be to benchmark the industry leaders. The easiest way to do this might be to consider the top four "Cloud Computing Leaders of 2011," named by TechTarget's SearchCloudComputing.com.[19]

At the number one position is Adrian Cockcroft, the cloud architect at Netflix. Under his direction, Netflix migrated *out* of its data centers and into the public cloud for most if not all of its IT.[20]

David Nelson, at number two, chief cloud strategist at Boeing, directed efforts that leveraged the cloud for special projects, such as a secure supply chain and logistics portal built in a matter of weeks, and a near-virtual-reality interactive experience to let customers visualize the 737, by stitching together tens of thousands of images.[21]

Number three, Allan Leinwand, is chief technology officer of infrastructure engineering at Zynga, the social gaming powerhouse. He set Zynga on a course that leverages the cloud initially when game uptake is uncertain, then moves processing in house once demand stabilizes.[22] Now that Zynga has a strong base of demand, Leinwand has moved even more processing off of the public cloud and into the company's private zCloud, reserving the public cloud for additional elasticity.[23]

Number four, Christian Reilly, formerly manager of global systems engineering at Bechtel, pursued a fully private cloud strategy—using cloud technologies on dedicated, owned infrastructure.

In other words, Cockcroft went fully public and Reilly went fully private. Nelson's strategy was mostly private with the use of the public cloud for special projects, and Leinwand's was to start in the public cloud but eventually return to Zynga's own data centers.

Four different companies. Four different leaders. Four different approaches. What gives? Who's got the *right* answer, who is misguided, the victim of the wrong paradigm?

As we'll see, it turns out that they may well have all adopted the right strategy *given their objectives and constraints*. In addition to soft factors, such as enterprise culture, specific individuals with specific personalities in the organization, and so forth, a major consideration is the nature of the application.

After all, if you need to transport a 30-foot pine tree, you wouldn't use a Smart Car; if you were traveling by yourself, you wouldn't select a tractor-trailer. If you needed a car for just one weekend, you wouldn't buy one, and if you needed one every day to commute to work, you wouldn't rent one.

The need—the strategy and the application—defines the solution—how and where to use the cloud.

Size Matters

Regardless of whether there are economies of scale in the cloud that translate into a unit cost advantage, size does matter. Think of it this way: If you are leading an army that is fighting hand to hand, it doesn't matter whether you received a volume discount on the cost of the soldiers' uniforms. And if you are trying to park a jumbo jet in a hangar, it doesn't really matter whether the cost per brick is higher or lower in smaller buildings; you need a minimum size to accomplish the task.

There are two scenarios that we will briefly touch on where size is key: the case of defense and the case of minimum requirements. The cloud can uniquely help with both.

In military operations, there are two general approaches to battle: *attrition* and *relational maneuver*. Attrition is a brute-force numerical contest, which may exist in several forms. Generally, the larger army beats the smaller one, although depending on the nature of the battle, various stochastic system dynamics may unfold.

In maneuver, subterfuge, indirection, and deception may be at play. Rather than victory merely being based on the logic of probability and proportionality, insights into the weak points of the enemy are relevant. As military strategist, historian, and author Edward Luttwak, a senior associate with the Center for Strategic and International Studies wrote, the point of maneuver is "to incapacitate by systemic disruption—whether the 'system' is the command structure of the enemy's forces, their mode of warfare and combat array . . . or even an actual technical system."[24]

Luttwak observed that there are a number of examples of attritional warfare in history, such as trench warfare in World War I, where "battles were dominated by highly symmetrical brute-force engagements,"[25] and air battles between the Royal Air Force and the Luftwaffe in World War II. Attrition need not have symmetry in offensive-defensive configurations: In World War II, German U-boats were trying to destroy the Allied surface-ship-based resupply capability. Still, it was a battle of numbers: More U-boats meant the result could have gone one way; more surface ships meant that the actual result went the other way.

Military strategist Carl von Clausewitz argued 200 years ago that "In tactics, as in strategy, superiority of numbers is the most common element in victory."[26] Although strategy defines the time, place, and character of conflict, and strategy in turn is defined by the goals of the military engagement, Clausewitz observed that "if we . . . strip the engagement of all the variables arising from its purpose and circumstances, . . . we are left with the bare concept of the engagement, a shapeless battle in which the only distinguishing factor is the number of troops on either side."[27]

Even then, the course of a military battle of attrition is not just a matter of mere superiority in numbers: An army with 10,001 troops is not guaranteed a victory over an army with 10,000 troops. Frederick Lanchester, a British engineer who co-invented the field of Operations Research, used today in areas ranging from factory floor layout to flight scheduling, observed that there were two types of warfare. In a simple linear battle—say a tug-of-war or hand-to-hand combat between contestants of equal strength—perhaps such a result would hold. This was the domain of Lanchester's Linear Law. However, in many other types of battles, where forces of a given strength were shooting at forces of lesser strength, the change over time could be described as a simple system of differential equations leading to a square rather than linear factor: Lanchester's Square Law. To put it simply, a force that was twice as large had four times the effective strength.

Even 2,000 years ago, these insights were understood. The legendary Sun Tzu, in *The Art of War*, wrote: "If you outnumber the opponent ten to one, then surround them; five to one, attack; two to one, divide . . . If you are equal, then fight if you are able. If you are fewer, then keep away if you are able. If you are not as good, then flee if you are able."[28]

In the case of cybersecurity, both types of attack are present. Maneuver—the use of surprise or deception—occurs in social engineering, phishing, or clicking on an apparently harmless link that leads to a virus or other malware.

Attrition, though, is as simple as the U-boat/supply ship war of numbers or Lanchester's Linear Law: An attacking force larger than a defending (or counterattacking) force wins; one smaller, loses.

Security is typically a priority for any CIO, and cloud security is often listed as the number one concern that CIOs have about using the cloud. Yet the cloud can often enhance security across its multiple dimensions, sometimes referred to as CIA: confidentiality, integrity, and availability; and sometimes further expanded to CI5A, adding authentication, authorization, accounting, and anonymity.[29] With all of these dimensions, cloud security requires a book of its own. We'll touch on a few aspects here: cyberattacks and security event analysis.

The number of cyberattack incidents seems to be growing: Sony's PlayStation and Entertainment networks have had data on 100 million accounts hacked; an attack in South Korea left 30 million banking customers unable to access their accounts; the U.S. Government experiences 15,000 attempted intrusions every day, and Citigroup experiences twice that number.[30]

Today, large botnets—thousands or millions of PCs that have been infected and are under a single malevolent command-and-control structure—are harnessed to form an attacking force causing a denial-of-service (DoS) attack. Such an attack is intended to be disruptive to a computing resource or service. As Ed Amoroso, AT&T senior vice president and chief security officer, said, a distributed DoS attack, termed DDoS, is "akin to asking a group of people to begin shouting at some victim all at once. The noise coming from the distributed sources becomes overwhelming."[31]

Some of the largest botnets (e.g., Conficker and Mariposa) have over 10 million bots. Here's where von Clausewitz, Sun Tzu, and Lanchester come in. There are two ways to defend or counterattack. One is maneuver: figuring out how the malicious code operates and taking control of it. The other is attrition—or simple superiority in numbers (i.e., managing to deploy an equal or greater force). In this case, the force need not be symmetric: The objective is not a DoS attack against the bots, after all. Instead, the objective is to differentiate between malicious bot traffic and legitimate traffic, letting the legitimate traffic through while "killing" the malicious traffic by dropping those packets. As Bill Woodcock, research director at Packet Clearing House, states, "DDoS is very much a numbers game . . . If the target has more than the sum of the attackers' capability and normal day-to-day traffic, then it is fine."[32]

Achieving this superiority in numbers is key: A large botnet can generate so much data traffic—in effect, a hail of bullets—as to overwhelm a smaller defender, even a large enterprise. A botnet of 1 million PCs, each generating an average of 1 megabit per second of attack bandwidth, say, could generate a terabit per second, thousands of times more bandwidth than a typical enterprise is likely to have. Large cloud providers, however, have the network bandwidth to continue functioning even in the face of such an attack. Large network providers that have the network capacity and packet filtering capability—network-based firewalls and network-based anti−DDoS attack capability—can repel the onslaught or, more specifically, "scrub" or "surgically mitigate" the attack, letting valid traffic through.[33] One terabit per second is a lot of traffic, but by comparison, data network vendor Juniper's new packet transport switch series can handle nearly 4,000 terabits per second.[34] There is clearly an arms race: More network capacity enables both larger DDoS attacks and stronger defenses.

Size is also important in early detection of anomalies that can portend an attack. The larger the amount of traffic sampled, correlated, and analyzed, the more likely early detection is possible. The same principle applies to spam filtering. In the same way that you wouldn't want to have junk mail delivered to your house, only to throw it away, it doesn't make sense to pay for a high-bandwidth connection and have most of the traffic on it delivered to a premises-based firewall or spam filter that then discards it.

The scale at which cloud providers operate can also be used to simulate large numbers of users, for load testing of Web sites and related applications. As Tom Lounibos, chief executive of SOASTA, a cloud-based testing firm, pointed out, the cloud transforms the economics of load-testing for applications.[35] Thousands of servers can be used on a short-term basis to simulate loads, and the capacity of the cloud can also be used to analyze the incredible volume of data produced.

Another case where the cloud is helpful is in processing very large workloads. In some cases, the duration may be limited, such as a finite element analysis of a new physical structure. In other cases, the cloud may be called on for a continuous large task, such as streaming Netflix movies. The larger the task, the more useful a large cloud is. In fact, the cloud ideally should be many times the size of its largest workload, because otherwise variability of that single workload could wreak havoc on either the performance or economics of the other workloads in the shared environment: If an elephant is running amok, you don't want to be inside a closet with it.

Summary

It is safe to say that larger cloud providers are likely to experience economies of scale, as well as other advantages such as denial-of-service attack resilience and exceeding the minimum scale required for certain functions. Whether these economies of scale translate into a cost advantage relative to do-it-yourself approaches is difficult to determine due to all of the cost drivers involved, and is also dependent on application workload profiles and other factors.

As we'll see in more depth in the next chapter, however, regardless of whether the unit cost of doing IT yourself is higher or lower than the price offered by service providers that can leverage economies of scale, the cloud should almost always be a part of your overall IT architecture and strategy, even ignoring other benefits of cloud usage such as user quality of experience.

> **☐ ONLINE**
>
> Amazon Web Services provides a number of spreadsheets and white papers at http://aws.amazon.com/economics.

Notes

1. George Gilder, "The Information Factories," *Wired* (October 2006). www.wired .com/wired/archive/14.10/cloudware.html?pg=1.
2. Paul A. Samuelson and William D. Nordhaus, *Economics*, 14th ed. (McGraw-Hill, 1992).
3. Daniel Sholler and Donna Scott, "Economies of Scale Are the Key to Cloud Computing Benefits," June 30, 2008. www.gartner.com/id=710610.
4. Nicholas Carr, *The Big Switch: Rewiring the World, From Edison to Google* (Norton, 2008).
5. Erik Brynjolfsson, Paul Hofmann, and John Jordan, "Cloud Computing and Electricity: Beyond the Utility Model," *Communications of the ACM* 53, No. 5 (May 2010): 32–34.

6. Bill Bulkeley, "What CFOs Need to Hear about Cloud Computing and Consumer IT," *CIO.com*, June 14, 2011. www.cio.com/article/684314/What_CFOs_Need_to_Hear_about_Cloud_Computing_and_Consumer_IT?page=2.

7. Will Forrest, "Clearing the Air on Cloud Computing," McKinsey & Company March 2009.

8. For a variety of analyses, see Rolf Harms and Michael Yamartino, *The Economics of the Cloud* (Microsoft Corporation, 2010). http://www.microsoft.com/press pass/presskits/cloud/docs/The-Economics-of-the-Cloud.pdf; Vijay Gill, "Cloud Economics," https://vijaygill.wordpress.com/2010/08/09/cloud-economics/; or Charlie Oppenheimer, "Which is Less Expensive: Amazon or Self-Hosted," February 11, 2012. http://gigaom.com/2012/02/11/which-is-less-expensive-amazon-or-self-hosted/.

9. Gill, "Cloud Economics."

10. Jeff Barr, "Dropping Prices Again—EC2, RDS, EMR and ElastiCache," *Amazon Web Services Blog*, March 5, 2012. aws.typepad.com/aws/2012/03/dropping-prices-again-ec2-rds-emr-and-elasticache.html.

11. Nancy Gohring, "Cloud economics improving for users in wake of price cuts," *Computerworld.com*, March 9, 2012. www.computerworld.com/s/article/922 5069/Cloud_economics_improving_for_users_in_wake_of_price_cuts.

12. Lydia Leong and Ted Chamberlin, "Magic Quadrant for Public Cloud Infrastructure as a Service," *Gartner*, December 8, 2011. www.gartner.com/technology/reprints.do?id=1-18CIS0X&ct=111215&st=sb.

13. Chris Kanaracus, "Amazon Web Services enacts 'significant' price cut," *Infoworld.com*, March 6, 2012. http://www.infoworld.com/d/cloud-computing/amazon-web-services-enacts-significant-price-cut-188054.

14. Carl Brooks, "Did Googler Jump the Gun with Cloud Calculator?" *Troposphere*, September 7, 2010. http://itknowledgeexchange.techtarget.com/cloud-computing/did-googler-jump-the-gun-with-cloud-calculator/.

15. Luiz André Barroso, Jeffrey Dean, Urs Hölzle, "Web Search for a Planet: The Google Cluster Architecture," IEEE Micro, March-April 2003, pp. 22–28. static.googleusercontent.com/external_content/untrusted_dlcp/research.google.com/en/us/archive/googlecluster-ieee.pdf.

16. http://opencompute.org/.

17. Rich Miller, "Microsoft Unveils Its Container-Powered Cloud," *Data Center Knowledge*, September 30, 2009. www.datacenterknowledge.com/archives/2009/09/30/microsoft-unveils-its-container-powered-cloud/.

18. Amir Michael, "Inside the Open Compute Project Server," *Facebook*, April 8, 2011. www.facebook.com/note.php?note_id=10150144796738920.

19. Staff, "Top 10 Cloud Computing Leaders of 2011," SearchCloudComputing.com. http://searchcloudcomputing.techtarget.com/feature/Top-10-cloud-computing-leaders-of-2011.

20. http://cloudscaling.com/blog/cloud-computing/cloud-innovators-netflix-strategy-reflects-google-philosophy.

21. Paul Desmond, "Boeing Makes Effective Use of Cloud Services to Augment Internal Resources," NTTCOM TV. http://nttcom.tv/on-the-wire/articles/year/boeing-makes-effective-use-of-cloud-services-to-augment-internal-resources/.

22. Charles Babcock, "Lessons from FarmVille: How Zynga Uses the Cloud," *InformationWeek*, May 14, 2011. www.informationweek.com/news/global-cio/interviews/229402805.

23. Charles Babcock, "Inside Zynga's Big Move to Private Cloud," *InformationWeek*, February 17, 2012. www.informationweek.com/news/hardware/virtual/232601065.

24. Edward N. Luttwak, *Strategy: The Logic of War and Peace* (Harvard University Press, 1987), pp. 93–94.

25. Ibid, p. 93.

26. Carl von Clausewitz, *On War*, edited and translated by Michael Howard and Peter Paret (Princeton University Press, 1976), p. 194.

27. Ibid, p. 194.

28. Sun-Tzu, *Art of War*, translated by Thomas Cleary (Shambhala Publications, 1988), pp. 74–75.

29. Asoke K. Talukder, Lawrence Zimmerman, and H. A. Prahalad, "Cloud Economics: Principles, Costs, and Benefits," in Nick Antonopoulos and Lee Gillam, ed., *Cloud Computing: Principles, Systems and Applications* (Springer, 2010).

30. Robert N. Charette, "More Cyberattacks or Just More Media Attention?" *IEEE Spectrum* (July 2011). spectrum.ieee.org/computing/networks/more-cyberattacks-or-just-more-media-attention.

31. Ed Amoroso, *Cyber Security* (Silicon Press, 2007), p. 40.

32. Somini Sengupta, "With Advance Warning, Preparing for Hackers' Attack on the Internet," *New York Times*, March 31, 2012, p. B4, www.nytimes.com/2012/03/31/technology/with-advance-warning-bracing-for-attack-on-internet-by-anonymous.html.

33. Arbor Networks, "Distributed Denial of Service Attacks: Global Insights and Mitigation Techniques," n.d. www.arbornetworks.com.

34. Caroline Chappell, "Juniper: Disruptive Innovation," *Capacity* (May 2011). www.capacitymagazine.com/Article/2824793/Search/Juniper-Disruptive-innovation.html

35. Tom Lounibos, conversation with the author, February 13, 2012.

CHAPTER 11

More Is Less

It is certainly possible that the cloud is capable of delivering resources and services at a *lower* unit cost than an enterprise. By "unit cost," we mean costs for server-hours or gigabyte-months. It is also possible that the cloud costs *more* on a unit-cost basis, the way that a midsize car that one can own for $10 per day will go for $30, $40, or even $50 per day from a rental car company. Whether the unit cost is higher or lower between cloud service providers and enterprises depends on a multitude of factors.

All other things being equal, if the cloud is less expensive than an enterprise, then an optimal financial decision would be to use the cloud. *Counterintuitively, even if the cloud is more expensive on a unit-cost basis, the cloud still can cost less*, in terms of total cost. In considering relative costs of do-it-yourself versus the cloud, it turns out that the most important number is not necessarily the cost when you use the cloud but may well be the cost when you don't: zero.

In the case of the renting versus owning, the two cost drivers are the cost when you use something and the cost when you don't. Suppose that you are evaluating owning a car for $10 a day versus renting a car for $50 a day. Suppose further that you need the car for three days per month. Over 30 days, the "cheaper" car will cost $300, whereas the "expensive" rental will cost only $150.

In other words, one way to save money is by paying more—some of the time—and paying zero—most of the time.[1] For many complex workloads, a few criteria determine whether a dedicated resource strategy, a pure cloud strategy, or a hybrid strategy is best.

Is the Cloud Less Expensive?

As Lori Mac Vittie, cloud evangelist with F5, a computing and networking company, said, it's called "cloud computing, not cheap computing."[2] She advised that whether the cost-benefit-risk equation favors the public cloud is ultimately unique to each customer. Further confusing things is the challenge of separating arbitrary costs from inherent ones.

Therefore, an apples-to-apples, "all-in" cost comparison can be challenge. James Staten, research vice president and principal analyst at Forrester Research, observed that apparently low costs per employee per month can add up as more employees use software as a service, and low costs for infrastructure per hour also accumulate as more infrastructure is used on a regular basis, including charges for additional services, such as data transport, load balancing, and security. Moreover, in what Staten called "the uneven handshake," all enterprise costs don't drop to zero just because the cloud is used; as in any partner-based initiative, there are ongoing costs for architecture, integration, testing, monitoring, governance, and the like when using the cloud.[3]

This handshake may be uneven in the other direction as well. Lew Moorman, president of Rackspace's Cloud business, has argued that there are many hidden costs that enterprises incur when they build and manage their own infrastructure: evaluation of new technologies such as solid state drives and liquid cooling, design, architecture, testing, and integration.[4]

Randy Bias, chief technology officer and cofounder of Cloudscaling, an open cloud infrastructure solutions provider, has suggested that high costs for enterprise IT infrastructure are partly an outcome of organizational culture and behavior. He said that gold-plating is the result of risk-averse organizational silos that overbuild, without giving sufficient thought to the overall cost structure. Ironically, he argued, this approach to system availability, performance, and security increases complexity and therefore can reduce uptime, hinder performance, and increase risk. Moreover, he said, highly custom architectures, vendor lock-in, and a performance optimization culture often lead to delays in software and systems delivery. In other words, enterprise costs may be higher than open cloud approaches due not to any salient, inherent disadvantage in, say, volume discounts, but due to adding the cost of suspenders to that of a belt.[5]

Will Forrest from McKinsey & Company noted that after extensive work and client effort they have detailed economic models that show moving to any type of cloud creates large-scale cost advantages (upward of 20% of total IT spend) and that hybrid deployments will be the most economical of all (25% cost savings) when they achieve widespread deployment.[6]

Forrest also anticipated that the relative cost advantages of the biggest players directly from infrastructure actually will shrink over the next five years but that operational efficiencies and service quality will become the key differentiator for a significant set of buyers. He argued that competitors will continue to lower their physical costs as they grow and adopt more scalable solutions and have a material opportunity to imitate operational improvements in the market, the largest players have only limited ability to further exploit existing (physical) scale benefits and will increasingly rely on operational and other sources of innovation, which are more fungible.

The bottom line: Making an exact comparison between internal costs and external prices is complex, given hidden costs on both sides. Moreover, such costs may be as much a matter of culture and practices as they are data on price sheets or accounting ledgers.

To summarize the complexity of comparing enterprise do-it-yourself costs to cloud costs: We need to make sure that we are comparing the same things, put the comparison that in context of overall value, and consider trends. However, in this chapter, we explore a key insight: The unit cost of the cloud relative to enterprise IT unit costs may impact the *degree* of cloud utilization but not *whether* to use the cloud.

Characterizing Relative Costs and Workload Variability

To decide which approach to use, we need to characterize a few main parameters. The first is the unit cost of an on-demand, pay-per-use cloud resource relative to the unit cost of a dedicated resource, which may be owned and incur a cost for depreciation, may be leased and incur a monthly fee, or may be financed, and represent an ongoing principal plus interest fee to the bank. We will define a "utility premium," U, as the ratio of the cloud unit cost to the do-it-yourself unit cost. In an example where an owned car costs \$10/day and a rental costs \$50/day, the premium for the rental car is $U = 5$, since the rental car costs five times as much.

If $U = 1$, the cloud costs the same as ownership. It is like getting the rental car for \$10 per day. And if $U < 1$, the cloud is cheaper, which certainly can happen as well. The utility premium, U, may vary over time, due both to improvements or one-time charges in your own operations and to price reductions or increases that the cloud provider may implement. However, here we adopt the convenient fiction that U is constant. We assume that the cost of the "ownership" model for a resource for a unit time is c_r and therefore that the cost of the utility pricing in the cloud is $U \times c_r$. For a given amount of time, T, the total price incurred for an owned resource is $c_r \times T$, and the total price for that in the cloud is $U \times c_r \times T$. These formulas are just a way of formalizing what we've already discussed. In the rental car case where the fee for three days was \$150, we had $U = 5$, that is, the rental cost five times as much as owned car; $c_r = \$10$ per day; and $T = 3$ days.

The other characteristic that we want to consider is the degree of variability of demand. Normally, statisticians use measures such as variance and standard deviation. For now, we use a much simpler characterization: peak, P, and average, A, which we can combine into a peak-to-average ratio: P/A.

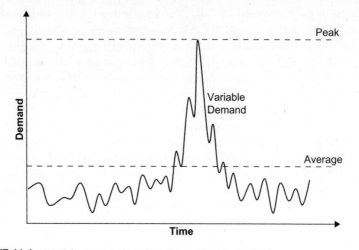

EXHIBIT 11.1 Variable Demand and Peak and Average Metrics

Exhibit 11.1 illustrates a typical variable demand for a Web site, an internal application—or it could be electricity utilization or automobile purchases or anything. As can be seen, over this time horizon, there is a peak and an average.

You may remember from Chapter 8 that Google's demand over a several-month period was almost as flat as a midwestern plain. Its peak was basically its average (i.e., $P \cong A$). However, the retailers tended to have a mountain beginning around Thanksgiving, which rises from the mesa that is their everyday demand. The baseline demand is not the average but in most cases will be relatively close, because if we were to "bulldoze" the mountain and spread the rubble around, it wouldn't raise the surface of the mesa by very much. A good example of a ratio of a medium-size peak to average is Walmart.com from Chapter 8, with an approximate average of .025% of daily page views, and a peak of .16% of daily page views, for a P/A of 6.4.

Then there are the really high peak-to-average workloads, such as the spike in telephony traffic that the Sonus Networks data in Chapter 8 showed on New Year's Eve. The Olympics Web sites are another example, with large numbers of visitors for two weeks every couple of years but much less the rest of the time. One thing to note is that the peak must always be greater than or equal to the average. When the peak equals the average, demand is perfectly flat.

Armed with only this information, we can make a number of intelligent decisions. In Chapter 9 we discussed the optimal resourcing strategy for a simple case of uniformly distributed demand, which is partly dependent on the nature of the workload and partly dependent on the relative penalties associated with excess resources versus unmet demand. Of course, there are other demand distributions as well, such as normally distributed (bell curve) demand. We assume that a better-safe-than-sorry strategy is deployed, such that an enterprise has enough dedicated resources to meet its peak demand.

Given all this, if an enterprise has resources that are built to peak, P, for a given amount of time, T, the enterprise cost is simply $P \times c_r \times T$. With the pay-per-use strategy of the cloud, the price each day, or hour, or minute may vary, and this may seem like a challenge to model. However, the average encodes the impact of this variation. Having one rental car for one day and then three rental cars the next day costs no more or less than having two cars—the average quantity—for the two days. Either way costs four rental days (we are ignoring volume discounts, getting the fifth day free, or other promotions and deals).

Consequently, the cloud cost is just the average quantity of resources used times the cloud price, which is the base resource cost times the utility premium, times the duration for which those costs were incurred: $A \times U \times c_r \times T$.

Armed with nothing more than these two equations for enterprise cost and cloud cost, we can draw some important conclusions.

When Clouds Cost Less or the Same

If $U < 1$—that is, clouds are less expensive per unit of resource per unit oftime—the cloud is always a good idea, regardless of the application profile. This is easy to see. The cloud cost is $A \times U \times c_r \times T$, and the dedicated cost is $P \times c_r \times T$. Since $A \leq P$, by definition, and $U < 1$, we know that $A \times U < P \times 1$. Multiplying both sides by $c_r \times T$ gives us $A \times U \times c_r \times T < P \times c_r \times T$; in other words, the cost of the cloud is less than the cost in the enterprise.

If clouds cost the same, $U = 1$. The relative total cost then depends on whether $A = P$ (i.e., the demand is flat) or $A < P$ (i.e., there is some variation). There *always* is some variation, but let's assume there is not. Then $A = P$, and since $U = 1$, we know that $A \times U = P \times 1$. Therefore, again by multiplying both sides by $c_r \times T$, we see that $A \times U \times c_r \times T = P \times c_r \times T$. In other words, the cost of the cloud and enterprise approaches are identical. This makes sense. If the cloud costs the same on a unit-cost basis as dedicated resources, and the flatness of the demand means that we aren't really using the special pay-per-use benefit, both approaches cost the same.

However, if there is *any* variation, even if the cloud costs the same, the pay-per-use benefit kicks in. Specifically, when $U = 1$ and $A < P$, we know that $A \times U < P \times 1$ and therefore $A \times U \times c_r \times T < P \times c_r \times T$. In other words, the cloud is the better option.

Under all of these circumstances, where either the cloud costs less or the same, the cloud is often a better option. Only under an atypical assumption that the demand is perfectly flat is the cost of the dedicated option the same as the cost of the cloud. Small and medium businesses are likely to have higher unit costs than cloud service providers, not to mention the fact that they lack requisite competencies. Analyst and commentator Ben Kepes related the example of Gregory/Richochet, a New Zealand fashion retailer. Not including hardware, a private strategy cost NZ\$30,000 per year; after migrating to a portfolio of cloud software services, the cost dropped to about NZ\$4,000.[7]

If Clouds Are More Expensive

Suppose that the cloud *is* more expensive on a unit-cost basis. The key then becomes the magnitude of the peak-to-average ratio compared to the utility premium. If the demand is *spikier* than the cloud is *relatively expensive*, the cloud still can be cheaper overall. Specifically, suppose that $U < P/A$. By multiplying both sides by A, we see that $A \times U < P$. Multiplying both sides as usual by $c_r \times T$, it turns out that $A \times U \times c_r \times T < P \times c_r \times T$, and again the cloud solution is less expensive. Suppose that it costs \$200 a day to rent a car. If you need the car only for one day a month, it still makes sense. The peak requirement is one car, but the average demand is only 1/30. Therefore, the peak-to-average ratio is 30, whereas the utility premium, even at that exorbitant rate, is only 20. Since the peak-to-average ratio is larger than the utility premium, the utility pricing model of the cloud is preferable. Conversely, if the demand is flat, at least compared to the utility premium (i.e., where $U > P/A$), a dedicated solution would be less expensive than the cloud. Then $A \times U \times c_r \times T > P \times c_r \times T$. However, under such circumstances, it turns out that a hybrid solution of both dedicated and on-demand resources is optimal, as we'll explore next.

Beauty of Hybrids

If the demand is variable, a hybrid is almost always best. The key is to think of the demand as having separable components. A typical family, for example, might need between zero and four cars at any given time. The schedule might be as shown in Exhibit 11.2.

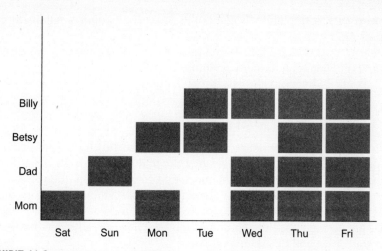

EXHIBIT 11.2 Illustrative Varying Resource Needs by Individual Driver

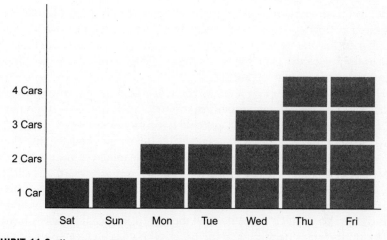

EXHIBIT 11.3 Illustrative Varying Aggregate Resource Needs

Given that Billy can drive Betsy's car, and Betsy can drive Dad's car, we can think of this demand curve as multiple tranches of demand: the demand for a first car, the demand for a second car, and so forth, as shown in Exhibit 11.3.

Now consider the decision regarding the first car. The family has flat demand for the first car, so a dedicated car—for example, via a lease or ownership—would make sense. However, the need for four cars is infrequent, so that fourth car might be best served via a rental. And for the second and third cars, it depends on where the breakeven point is, based on the value of U.

Simply put, demand can be partitioned into three mutually exclusive tranches of demand across any given time period, T.

1. The duration of need, let's call it t, satisfies $t > T/U$.
2. $t = T/U$.
3. t is relatively short-lived (i.e., $t < T/U$).

Consider a tranche where $t < T/U$. For that tranche, the level of demand is 1 for t of the time and is 0 for $T - t$ of the time. The peak, $P = 1$, and the average is t/T. Since $t < T/U$, we know that $t/T < 1/U$. But then $A < 1/U$. Since $P = 1$, we can divide by it, getting $A/P < 1/U$. Multiplying both sides by $U \times P/A$, we see that $U < P/A$. For this tranche, then, the peak-to-average ratio is greater than the utility premium, and we have already seen that that's when the cloud will be less expensive.

Inverse logic holds for the other extreme. The middle case, where $t = T/U$, turns out to be a "don't care." Whether we use a dedicated resource or a rental doesn't matter.

What this analysis means is that for the tranches of demand that get a long enough duty cycle, it makes sense to use dedicated resources, if they are cheaper. For the tranches of demand that are of short duration, it makes sense to use the cloud, even if it is more expensive, as long as the duration is shorter than the cloud is expensive.

How does this argument relate to the real world? In the empirical data, depending on assorted configurations, instance sizes, and so forth, a cloud might be less expensive. When it appears to be more expensive, it might be 20% or 40% more costly. Let's exaggerate to make a point and give the cloud a two-to-one disadvantage. Even with that disadvantage, it means that the cloud is still useful for those resources that are needed less than half the year. Remember the tax preparer example from Chapter 9? The resources above the baseline are needed only between January 1 and April 15: 3.5/12ths of the year, which is well below the 6/12 threshold. Retailers have a tranche of resources needed only for 1/12 of the year. In fact, some of their resources are needed only for 1/365 of the year, even if cloud providers decided to charge, say, 300 times as much as do-it-yourself costs, it *still* would be wise to use them for that spike.

This logic means that cloud computing must be at least a part of your IT strategy, essentially regardless of how much it costs. More is less.

It also means that, all other things being equal, some sort of hybrid architecture is likely to be best—a mixture of dedicated, cheaper resources, and short-term, pay-per-use resources that may be charged at a higher rate. As Jens Lapinski, CEO of aiHIT, a business information services company, first put it, it's smart to "own the base and rent the spikes."[8]

Also note that this mixture does not pertain only to dedicated, owned capital resources sitting in your own data center versus cloud-based, pay-per-use resources. The same logic holds in minimizing costs by leveraging a mix of rates with different commitment levels from a single cloud or "hybrid hosting" provider that can offer some mix of colocation, managed services, and/or various rate plans for various degrees of commitment.

Cost of the Network

A hybrid architecture is more than just a simple combination of enterprise resources and cloud resources, and thus its total cost is more than the sum of those two resource types. For example, there may be additional load balancing needed, a cloud operating system or hybrid cloud management software, performance and usage monitoring, each of which adds to the cost of the hybrid and shifts the breakeven point. Perhaps the most important additional cost in implementing a hybrid is that of the network.

Returning to the car example, a hybrid mix of owned cars and rental cars sounds good, but to implement it, we have to have some way of accessing the rental cars. If we happen to live next door to a rental car location, that would be particularly handy, but such a fortuitous situation is unlikely. The optimal cost of implementing a hybrid solution depends on the network costs, which may vary. Moreover, as author and cloud expert Barrie Sosinksy has said, "If any cloud-computing system resource is difficult to plan for, it is network capacity."[9]

The total or marginal costs associated with a network are highly dependent on existing network services and infrastructure, the application architecture, and the pattern of demand.

In the *best* case, the application doesn't need any additional networking between the dedicated, flat-rate resources and the on-demand, pay-per-use resources. This scenario can arise in three ways:

1. The application doesn't require much data to flow between the two locations.
2. The two locations are one and the same, as in a hybrid hosting environment.
3. The network costs something, but that network is needed anyway for something else, such as business continuity, and therefore the marginal cost of the network is zero.

In the *worst* case, network costs associated with implementing a hybrid solution are relatively large. This means that saving a little by using pay-per-use resources can't overcome a large expense. It would be akin to being able to save a nickel at a different store, but needing to pay a $10 cab fare to take advantage of the savings. In such a case, a comparison of a pure, dedicated, flat-rate build-to-peak solution versus a pure cloud solution must incorporate network costs.

These costs, or affordable performance, can be a real concern. Bernard Golden, chief executive of Hyperstratus, pointed out that the network bandwidth limitations—the "skinny straw"—can be a constraining factor in the emerging reality of hybrid clouds. He observed that proper placement of workloads will be the key to a hybrid strategy.[10]

Conversely, the network can act as an enabler instead of a constraint. According to Deb Osswald, vice president of next-generation network operations with technology research firm IDC, the proliferation of increasingly robust fixed and mobile broadband networks will permit the true potential of the cloud to be unleashed. Osswald envisioned a vastly wider audience now able to affordably access advanced applications and services that have the power to enable economic growth and enhance productivity. Service providers, Osswald said, have a key role to play in such a transformation.[11] She observes that with penetration rates hovering at or around 100%, service margins rapidly compressing, and already-fierce competition intensifying, many service providers are rushing to embrace the rich value-creation capabilities that the network-centric cloud offers.

Somewhere in between the extremes of hybrid architectures requiring large network investments and those available at zero marginal network cost, we have a variety of network costs and a variety of charging schemes. For most applications, network usage is proportional to demand and thus is also proportional to the quantity of servers or storage. Such proportionality has the effect of shifting where the pure cloud solution makes sense and where the partition in the hybrid should be. In effect, rather than a utility cost of $U \times c_r$, we now have a new $U' > U$. This means that the duration, t', must not only be smaller than $t=T/U$ but smaller than T/U'.

There are a variety of options to consider, which can shift the logic regarding optimization.[12] Moreover, we can't look at such pricing logic in a vacuum but relative to the best alternative. Such analyses can get very complex: For example what is the marginal cost of expanding the current network into the data center based on a risk-adjusted view of data transport volumes over a planning horizon of three years assuming a given cost of capital but unknown uptake for the new application?

Although we've focused on on-demand, pay-per-use processing, let's turn briefly to storage. On a straight apples-to-apples comparison, a local hard drive would outperform the *exact* same cloud-based drive—if there were such a thing—in important dimensions—access latency, cost, reliability, availability, and security—for the same reason that Oreo cookies in your pantry are easier to get to than ones across the country. Rather than fetching data over a network and incurring a response-time penalty, the data can be accessed locally. The availability of the drive is much better than the availability of a drive combined with a network, and so forth. This is not a current technology snapshot but inarguable, eternal logic.

The cloud becomes advantageous when other dimensions are included. For example, a local drive can't de-duplicate the same content that may be owned by thousands or millions of other users (if it did, the data would no longer be local for most users), and can't offer higher availability through geodiversity. The storage capacity of a local drive is limited but that of the cloud is essentially boundless. And if the local endpoint is a (relatively) underpowered mobile device, there is no comparison between it and the cloud. Consequently, we can't look simply at straight comparisons but need to consider the architectural and application context.

To make the analysis even more challenging, we can include a variety of additional factors: volume discounts; price discrimination, where different users may be charged different amounts; dynamic pricing, where the price for a given amount of resources may change from one moment to the next; and industry pricing dynamics, such as price wars or collusion.[13]

Summary

We have come full circle. The conventional wisdom is that cloud computing is less expensive on a unit-cost basis, and that's why you should use it. If it *is* less expensive, and all other considerations—security, availability, etc.—are equal, then you should use it. Perhaps surprisingly, the argument we've explored here is that even if cloud computing *is* more expensive (on a unit-cost basis), you can still use it and save money.

If you take nothing else away from this book, it's that cloud computing should be at least part of your overall enterprise IT strategy. And the logic becomes even more compelling when we add in the fact that we may not know what our resource requirements will be and when we consider additional benefits that the cloud can offer, such as enhanced user experience.

The other lesson of this chapter is that under many scenarios, a hybrid architecture is likely to be best. We explore a variety of hybrids next.

🖥 ONLINE

"The Value of Utility Resources in the Cloud," at http://complex-models.com/Utility.aspx, illustrates the cost implications of various capacity strategies relative to differing demand profiles.

Notes

1. Joe Weinman, "Mathematical Proof of the Inevitability of Cloud Computing," January 8, 2011. http://joeweinman.com/Resources/Joe_Weinman_Inevitability_Of_Cloud.pdf.
2. Lori MacVittie, "It's Called Cloud Computing not Cheap Computing," *F5 DevCentral*, December 6, 2010. http://devcentral.f5.com/weblogs/macvittie/archive/2010/12/06/itrsquos-called-cloud-computing-not-cheap-computing.aspx.
3. James Staten, with Khalid Kark and Eric Chi, "The Three Stages of Cloud Economics: How to Maximize Savings and Increase Profits For Your Organization," Forrester Research, April 28, 2011. http://h20195.www2.hp.com/v2/GetPDF.aspx/4AA3-8122ENW.pdf.
4. Lew Moorman, conversation with the author, January 2, 2012.
5. Randy Bias, conversation with the author, December 14, 2011.
6. Will Forrest, conversation with the author, November 3, 2011.
7. Ben Kepes, "Cloudonomics: The Economics of Cloud Computing," *Diversity Limited*, 2011. broadcast.rackspace.com/hosting_knowledge/whitepapers/Cloudonomics-The_Economics_of_Cloud_Computing.pdf.
8. Jens Lapinski, commenting on Joe Weinman, "Why McKinsey's Cloud Report Missed the Mark," *GigaOM.com*, April 21, 2009. http://gigaom.com/2009/04/21/why-mckinseys-cloud-report-missed-the-mark/.
9. Barrie Sosinsky, *The Cloud Computing Bible* (John Wiley & Sons, 2011), p. 128.
10. Bernard Golden, "Cloud Computing: 2011 Predictions," *CIO.com*, December 9, 2010. www.cio.com/article/645763/Cloud_Computing_2011_Predictions.
11. Deb Osswald, conversation with the author, January 29.
12. Oleksiy Mazhelis and Pasi Tyrväinen, "Role of Data Communications in Hybrid Cloud Costs," in S. Biffl, M. Koivuluoma, P. Abrahamsson, and M. Oivo, eds., SEAA2011, *Proceedings of the 37th EUROMICRO Conference on Software Engineering and Advanced Applications* (IEEE Computer Society, 2011), pp. 138–145, preprint.
13. Oleksiy Mazhelis and Pasi Tyrväinen, "Economic Aspects of Hybrid Cloud Infrastructure: User Organization Perspective," *Information Systems Frontiers* 13 (2011), preprint.

CHAPTER 12

Hybrids

A hybrid is "anything derived from heterogeneous sources, or composed of elements of different or incongruous kinds."[1] In cloud computing, a variety of architectures meet that definition. As we've seen, in the presence of variable demand and a utility premium for cloud resources, hybrids can be cost optimal. However, rather than just one hybrid, there are several different permutations of users, dedicated flat-rate resources, and on-demand pay-per-use resources, and several different means of linking them together.

For example, one such permutation is a mix of owned resources in a data center with flexible resources in the cloud. Another is owned resources in colocation space with physically adjacent flexible resources sold on a pay-per-use basis. Yet another type of hybrid is the Web app or cloud-enabled app. For example, the Dragon Naturally Speaking dictation app on a tablet converts spoken words to text. The client-resident functionality is limited primarily to an interface; the spoken words are captured as an audio stream, compressed and encoded, and then transmitted to the cloud for speech-to-text processing, and then the text stream is sent back to the device. Google or Bing search running in the cloud is accessed via a client interface—a dynamic HTML page or a smartphone widget, say—but the heavy-duty processing is done in the cloud, and search results are returned to the device. Or those functions can be combined and semantic analysis included, which is what Apple's Siri (Speech Interpretation and Recognition Interface) smartphone interface does: Voice is captured, coded, compressed, then transmitted to, processed in, and responded to by the cloud.[2] Whether we are considering massively multiplayer gaming; complex processing and data-intensive applications such as search, speech interaction, and semantic analysis; or mundane activities like watching TV, there is a often a role for both dedicated, local equipment and remote, shared resources.

In Chapter 11, we concluded that flat-rate, fixed capacity mixed with pay-per-use capacity often can be cost optimal. However, a number of factors can impact that conclusion. One is the relative cost of flat-rate resources versus pay-per-use resources. Another is the variability of the demand. The inherent architectural characteristics of the application turn out to be another, because they will impact the network requirements and therefore the breakeven points or decision financials.

Complicating things even further is that the cost drivers for owned network resources may not match the cost drivers for data transport in the cloud: An owned network might involve an up-front nonrecurring cost coupled with monthly recurring costs for fixed capacity, whereas data transport in the cloud may be priced based on the quantity of data transferred in plus data transferred out of the cloud.

In this chapter, we examine a few hybrid architectures and their relative costs and explore the impact of those costs on breakeven points.

Users, Enterprise, and Cloud

There are many variations on network architecture, each with differing cost implications, depending on the pattern of use of the applications residing on that architecture and their data transport requirements. We can generally partition the multitude of architectures into six generic combinations of users, enterprise data center(s), and cloud data center(s).

We use the term "users" very broadly to mean any endpoints outside of the cloud or enterprise data center. Users may be individual consumers, business partners, or corporate employees, using laptops, tablets, smartphones, personal music players, set-top boxes, streaming video devices, immersive videoconferencing setups, electronic whiteboards, etc. Increasingly, "users" may be sensors or actuators, tied to individual people, such as patient monitoring devices; tied to vehicles, such as GPS tracking systems or video surveillance devices; on pets; embedded in air conditioners, dryers, and thermostats; or even laid out in open fields, such as farm temperature and irrigation sensors.

A small to medium business, enterprise, or government may have one or more data centers or equipment closets. And the "cloud" typically will comprise several data centers, which may have one or more data links that are used to communicate with users and enterprises, between cloud providers (the Intercloud), or between data centers within a given cloud provider (the intracloud). We can simplify this complexity and consider the variations shown in Exhibit 12.1.

- *User(s) to enterprise resource(s)*. Exhibit 12.1(a) illustrates the traditional (non-hybrid) baseline, originating with mainframe connectivity and continuing today, in cases where users connect only to the enterprise.

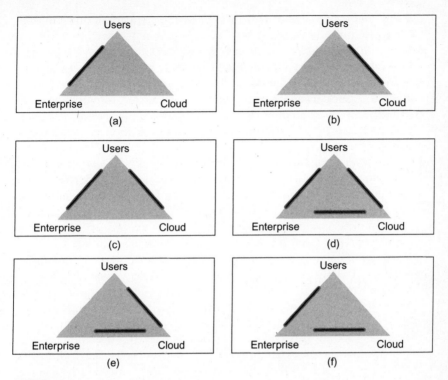

EXHIBIT 12.1 Generic Architecture Options

- *User(s) to cloud resource(s).* Exhibit 12.1(b) is the new cloud paradigm in its purest (non-hybrid) form: watching YouTube on your iPad, Netflix on your Roku, gaming "live," or accessing Salesforce.com from your Android smartphone.
- *User(s) or transactions to enterprise resource(s) or cloud resource(s).* Exhibit 12.1(c) is an architecture where users may access either the enterprise or the cloud, but there is minimal or no data traffic between the cloud and the enterprise data center. One workload runs in the data center; one in the cloud. Charles Babcock, an editor-at-large for InformationWeek, described Sony's strategy: Always send buyers to the Sony data-center-based online store but, during peaks, send information seekers to the cloud rather than Sony's data center.[3]
- *User(s) to enterprise resource(s) and cloud resource(s).* In Exhibit 12.1(d) users are load-balanced between owned, dedicated, enterprise resources and pay-per-use, on-demand cloud resources. As demand varies, resource utilization in the cloud is adjusted upward or downward, as in cloudbursting, where limited enterprise data center capacity is dynamically complemented by on-demand cloud capacity.

A key element of this approach is often the network connecting the enterprise and the cloud.

- *User(s) directly to cloud resource(s) and then to enterprise resource(s).* In Exhibit 12.1(e), the cloud has the front end: Web servers, app servers, content delivery servers, and so forth. The cloud typically offers proximity to users through geographically dispersed resources, which enhances users' experience for highly interactive applications. The back end comprises legacy systems or single-instance applications or databases of record.
- *User(s) directly to enterprise resource(s) and then to cloud resource(s).* The mirror image of the prior case is shown in Exhibit 12.1(f), where the enterprise is the front end and the cloud sits behind the enterprise. Storage mirroring and replication for business continuity would be an example.

These options are the main logical permutations of users, enterprise resources, and cloud resources or services. However, there are different ways of implementing them physically, resulting in different cost trade-offs.

We naturally think that on-demand, pay-per-use implies a cloud data center and that a dedicated, flat rate implies an enterprise data center. Generally this is true. However, capabilities such as HP's LocalBurst enable pay-per-use to a certain extent in an enterprise data center, and colocation, managed service, or hybrid hosting capabilities from service providers can provide flat rates and dedicated equipment in a provider location. The math that proves that hybrids typically are best economically says nothing about the exact location where the hybrid is resident. In other words, a hybrid may involve both an enterprise data center and a cloud location, just an enterprise data center or centers, or just a cloud center or centers.

Hybrid Architecture Implementations

As we've seen, even if the unit cost of cloud resources is higher than that of "owned" ones, a pure cloud-based solution still can deliver a lower total cost. Generally, a hybrid of dedicated, flat-rate resources and on-demand, pay-per-use cloud resources will be cost optimal. However, additional architectural elements required to implement the hybrid can alter the cost structure and therefore the points of cost optimality. We can distinguish a few major variations of the hybrid architectures illustrated in Exhibit 12.1(c) through (f).

Colocated Hybrid

When we visualize the hybrid clouds shown in Exhibits 12.1(c) through (f), we tend to think of an enterprise data center networked to a cloud service provider. However, some service providers offer hybrid hosting, a mix of colocation, managed services, *and* cloud services. An enterprise customer can maintain owned, dedicated, and thus flat-rate resources in a single facility. These resources can have a flat-rate cost based on a variety of financing mechanisms: a capital expenditure with straight-line depreciation from purchase price through to residual value, or as a constant operating expense stream via leasing or financing options. These resources can interoperate with managed services elements, such as managed servers or managed storage, where a slightly higher flat rate is paid, but value delivered can include everything from basic server monitoring and management up through performance-managed servers, where the provider may guarantee throughput or response-time service levels.

From an economic analysis perspective, the costs of the network to link the pay-per-use resources with the dedicated resources are essentially zero, since both types of resources are in the same location, perhaps connected by a short length of cable or virtual interconnect.

It is possible to imagine an even closer relationship between the enterprise and the cloud, where the interface is contained in a single chip. I have proposed a variation on homomorphic encryption, where there is a high frequency of interaction between logic "belonging" to the enterprise and that "belonging" to a cloud provider as a trusted third party, running an algorithm belonging to a software provider. Through encryption implemented via shared registers on the chip, the party with the algorithm need not have visibility into the data, the customer owning the data need not have visibility into the algorithm, yet both can collaborate to achieve a computational result.[4]

Partitioned-Data Hybrid

In the partitioned-data hybrid model shown in Exhibit 12.1(c), there are enterprise resources and there are cloud resources, but they have minimal or no data communication needs between them. In this model, different locations may have the same type of data for different users in a type of load balancing, or different types of data and applications for the same user, as with the Sony example. As a result, the marginal cost associated with data transport due to the separation of the resources is inconsequential.

One example might be an application where each user uploads photos to a service, and the service returns a video of those photos set to music. The data traffic is between the users and the servers running the application, *not* between the enterprise servers running the application and the cloud servers running the application. Consequently, there is no need for an expensive network tying the enterprise data center to the cloud data center(s). Of course, if there are costs per megabyte transferred to and from the cloud, and these are greater than the costs of transfer to and from the enterprise data center, there can be a cost differential. As always, however, even if the unit cost to transfer a megabyte is greater in the cloud, variable data transport requirements may drive a lower total cost.

If it is feasible to partition the data but run a portion in the enterprise and a portion in the cloud, there may not be any net new charges. Rather than 100% of the data being transported to and from the enterprise data center for customers whose last names begin with A through Z, for example, A through M might be served out of the enterprise and N through Z via the cloud, leading to two locations but each requiring only half as much data.

The problem is that such a simple solution is unlikely to work for a number of reasons. There is likely to be *some* data traffic between the enterprise data center and the cloud, to coordinate and synchronize virtual machine instances as well as, say, maintain customer account metadata or transaction logs.

The nature of the charging is likely to vary as well. For enterprise data networks, there typically is a fixed cost; for the cloud, there typically is a charge based on data transferred. The same logic regarding cost structure applies as always: The service provider needs to earn a fair return for shareholders, so these charges can add up. However, network prices seem to be one of the areas where there really are nonlinearities in cost structure and thus economies of scale, so whether the cloud network charges are more expensive than the enterprise network charges will depend on a number of factors that might end up favoring one approach or the other, depending on the application.

But there can be additional concerns with this approach. If the rationale for the hybrid is based on a cost-optimal solution driven by variable demand, the point of the hybrid would be that, say, 100% of the transactions are handled in the enterprise data center during low periods of use and then, as the climb up a demand spike occurs, an increasing number of transactions are handled by the cloud. During low demand, all customers need to be handled by the enterprise data center; during high demand, there is a mix. Consequently, relevant customer records would need to migrate from the enterprise to the cloud as demand increases and return to the enterprise as it ebbs: In other words, there will be data transport charges. Consequently, it may be preferred to either just do it all in the cloud, or use a Sony-style solution, where cloud elasticity is used in conjunction with relatively static data.

Monolithic Hybrid with Remote Data Access

The approach shown in Exhibit 12.1(d) appears straightforward, but doesn't capture the economic and performance complexity of data management. An enterprise may have an enormous data warehouse or collection of datasets sitting in its own data center. The reverse may also hold: the "Big Data" may be cloud resident. If the servers running in the cloud need access to enterprise-resident data or vice versa, either a fixed-cost network or pay-per-use data transfer charges will impact the breakeven points between pure enterprise or pure cloud at either extreme and hybrids in the middle. Beyond cost, another challenge is the potential performance or response-time impact due to the additional network round-trip time required to access and/or update the data remotely rather than locally.

Monolithic Hybrid with Dynamic Data Migration

Another means of implementing the approach illustrated in Exhibit 12.1(d) is to use a monolithic hybrid model with dynamic data migration, where data migrate to and from the cloud as cloud resources are increasingly exploited and released based on increasing and ebbing demand. This migration may be asymmetric: If a customer is to be handled by the cloud, all of her information may need to migrate to the cloud; after a customer uses the cloud, perhaps only updates or a transaction log needs to migrate back to the enterprise data center.

Current solutions to this need to migrate data fall short when the quantity of data is nontrivial. Major cloud providers can spin up virtual servers in minutes or even seconds, but once the quantity of data hits gigabytes, they suggest express mailing the data on a portable hard drive. In other words, although the server is available in, say, 24 *seconds*, the data that the server needs to be useful aren't available for 24 *hours*.

In an ideal world, a firm would like to increase the bandwidth between its location and the cloud to an enormous level for a matter of a few seconds but not pay any extra. Existing and emerging networking technologies may begin to enable this nontraditional capability, at least through the network core; they include the link capacity adjustment system, virtual concatenation, the generic framing procedure, reconfigurable optical add-drop multiplexers, and the optical transport network. One challenge is for telecommunications carriers to link the network capabilities to a billing layer. A bigger challenge is what to do with the "last mile." Carriers won't deploy dedicated expensive high-capacity facilities and equipment, including paying for rights of way and rights of entry, through the last mile to customer premises on the off chance that they will be able to bill for services used for a few seconds or minutes per year.

Monolithic Hybrid with Data Synchronization

A potential approach to implementing the strategy illustrated in Exhibit 12.1(d) that could solve the data transport problem in dynamic hybrids is based on the observation that if the data are needed to support applications and services, then they are valuable, and if they are valuable, they are worth protecting against loss. A standard approach to such data protection in transactional environments is synchronous mirroring, whereby each local data write is copied to a remote location, which must acknowledge receipt before the local write can be acknowledged and the input/output transaction can complete. There are also asynchronous approaches that make remote copies without delaying the local write, potentially at the risk of losing a very small amount of data were a disaster to strike just as the data was being copied.

If "the cloud"—which might be a mixed colocation/hosting/cloud center—is being used for this data mirroring, a copy of the data would *already* be in the cloud. And this copy would be *exactly* current. The network required to achieve this data mirroring would not need to burst to near-infinite capacity end to end to nearly instantaneously copy from scratch an entire enormous database. Instead, the copy of the data would be built up over weeks, months, or years, as each transaction used information essentially simultaneously at both the local and the remote location.

If the application instances in the cloud are merely reading data, the cloud environment only has to support simultaneous local reads as well as remote writes from a primary array. However, if the cloud-resident application were also writing, challenges would exist in either distributed locking or bidirectional updates, where for some data the enterprise is primary and the cloud is secondary and for other data the cloud is primary and the enterprise is the mirror. Newer products such as EMC's VPLEX virtual storage platform are beginning to enable this scenario; where updates applied at any of several locations are nearly simultaneously applied elsewhere.

Another consideration is that for highly transactional environments with a business constraint for zero data loss, a distance limit of 30 to 40 miles is typical for synchronous mirroring; otherwise, the application begins to slow down noticeably. For such applications, balancing application performance with elasticity implies that "cloud" data centers, rather than being enormous, consolidated facilities, need to be much more distributed geographically. There is nothing wrong with this: We argue in Chapter 19 that such an approach is likely to occur for some cloud facilities due to user experience reasons as well. However, there are trade-offs between centralization and dispersion, which we address at length in Chapter 20.

Eventual Consistency

Given all these trade-offs and issues, another approach to the model in Exhibit 12.1(d) is to give up on making lots of data instantaneously available in multiple places and instead utilize more of a best-efforts approach. "Eventual consistency" means that the data will get there when they get there. After all, it's not the end of the world if a few tweets are temporarily unavailable.

Front-End/Back-End Hybrids

We've looked at a variety of ways of implementing hybrids where users may connect to either the cloud or the enterprise data center. Another approach that can be considered is a hybrid of a front end in the cloud, handling customer-facing interactions, with a back end in the enterprise data center, as shown in Exhibit 12.1(e). Relatively static data, such as product catalogs and room rates per night, can be maintained on a distributed basis in the cloud, and transactions of record can then be passed through to back-end databases. From a network cost perspective, this means that front-end customer-facing transactions potentially move from a flat-rate basis to a consumption basis and that what was local data networking between app servers and database servers within the enterprise data center becomes a remote interaction, which may occur on a pay-per-use basis or over a fixed network connection.

This general approach is not new to the cloud: "Web hosting" has provided such an architecture for years, just not via a dynamic, pay-per-use, on-demand provisioning model. It is also a model with a strong rationale: Distribute the highly interactive portion of the application to be closer to customers and thus improve the customer experience; consolidate the back end where response time is not as critical. This same model is used in delivery of more mundane services: Starbucks has thousands of globally dispersed service delivery nodes—"coffee shops"—but back-end operations, such as roasting coffee beans, are centralized and consolidated.

On-Demand BC/DR

One last hybrid worth mentioning is where the front end is the enterprise and the back end is the cloud, as shown in Exhibit 12.1(f). In this case, the cloud may be used for data mirroring, as in the monolithic hybrid with data synchronization scenario, but also for on-demand compute capacity in the event of a smoking-hole disaster. This model is something like staying in a hotel if your house burns down. The cost is incurred only in the event of a disaster, which makes it substantially less expensive than owning a second "spare" house in the event that yours experiences a catastrophe. Although such a scenario sounds ridiculous, it is exactly what companies often do: They maintain a costly "sister site" for disaster recovery. The hotel stay—and using the cloud for on-demand recovery—makes much more sense financially, if the application architecture permits.

Other hybrids are certainly possible. For example, a hybrid over time may make sense: Zynga uses the cloud for new games and then migrates them back in house as demand becomes more level and predictable. The reverse approach can also work, where apps are developed and tested in house and then deployed in the cloud. Then there are variations of the above. In one, sometimes referred to as "tethering," data may be transported first from an enterprise location to a cloud location, and then to one or more locations within that cloud or other clouds. Copies at other locations can support geographic diversity for business continuity, or proximity to a distributed user base for enhancing the user experience.

Summary

We've seen that hybrids can be cost optimal, but there are many varieties of hybrids, and technology is evolving rapidly, shifting the boundaries between the architectures that are visionary and the ones that have been proven. Architecture must be driven by performance, user experience, elasticity, and availability goals, the relative costs of various cloud services and dedicated and thus flat-rate resource strategies, an assessment of the unique demand variability and architectural requirements of the application, and ancillary costs, such as network costs and pricing plans.

Finally, dedicated, flat-rate resources can be combined with on-demand, pay-per-use resources in many ways, ranging from dedicated resources in data centers interacting with pay-per-use resources from a service provider, to pay-per-use resources in an enterprise data center interacting with flat-rate resources in the cloud, to a combination of multiple rate plans in either the enterprise data center or the cloud.

Notes

1. http://dictionary.reference.com/browse/hybrid.
2. www.smartplanet.com/blog/smart-takes/say-command-how-speech-recognition-will-change-the-world/19895?tag=content;siu-container.
3. Charles Babcock, *Management Strategies for the Cloud Revolution* (McGraw-Hill, 2010).
4. Joe Weinman, "Methods, Systems, and Computer Program Products for Performing Homomorphic Encryption and Decryption on Individual Operations," Published U.S. Patent Application 20120066510, Filed March 15, 2012. appft1 .uspto.gov/netacgi/nph-Parser?Sect1=PTO1&Sect2=HITOFF&d=PG01&p=1&u=% 2Fnetahtml%2FPTO%2Fsrchnum.html&r=1&f=G&l=50&s1=%2220120066510%22 .PGNR.&OS=DN/20120066510&RS=DN/20120066510

CHAPTER 13

Fallibility of Forecasting

The world descended into financial chaos in the fall of 2008, driven ostensibly by the subprime mortgage crisis and marked by the implosion of Lehman Brothers in mid-September. Dominique Strauss-Kahn, now perhaps better known for his May 2011 Sofitel New York hotel stay but then head of the International Monetary Fund, predicted a recovery beginning in 12 to 18 months, but this forecast, he admitted, was "plagued with uncertainty."[1] To his credit, at least he acknowledged it was basically a guess.

John Kay of the London Business School has argued that economists rarely disagree significantly in their predictions. The salient differences are not *among* economists but *between economists and reality*: "[W]hat [economists] say is almost always wrong . . . the consensus forecast failed to predict any of the most important developments in the economy."[2] No wonder author and economist John Kenneth Galbraith quipped that economic forecasting makes "astrology look respectable."[3]

There surely are increasingly sophisticated technologies being used for forecasting—exponential smoothing, chaos theory, state-space models, crowdsourcing, and prediction markets, Box-Jenkins autoregressive moving average models—and many of these can be aided by the immense computational ability of the cloud. However, while these models may often apply, fundamental folly of forecasting is the fantasy that the future can be foretold, often leading to catastrophic flame-outs, such as Lehman Brothers, Long-Term Capital Management (LTCM), or MF Global. These firms discovered the hard way that the market could stay irrational longer than they could stay solvent, as legendary economist John Maynard Keynes allegedly observed.[4]

Exacerbating matters is the fact that people generally have a belief in their exceptionalism: an *assumption of uniqueness*. They irrationally, optimistically, and incorrectly believe in their ability to predict—if not outright control—the future. They believe that they have an edge at dice games if they toss the dice themselves and a greater chance of winning the lottery if they get to pick the numbers. Even Ivy League students believe that predicting the outcome of a random coin toss is a skill that can be honed with practice.[5] In the classroom, this is a humorous delusion; it is not so useful in the boardroom.

The fallibility of forecasting accentuates the importance of *on-demand* capacity, which is like a variation of roulette where you place your bet *after* the ball lands: You can't help but win. Since forecasting is fallible, it's best to respond in real time.

Even Stranger than Strange

Yogi Berra's quip that it is difficult to make predictions, especially about the future, is highlighted by rogue traders, such as Nick Leeson at Barings Bank, Jérôme Kerviel at Société Générale, Yasuo Hamanaka at Sumitomo, and Toshihide Iguchi at Daiwa Bank, who each lost at least a billion dollars for their respective employers betting on stock market index futures, commodities, or bonds.[6] We might discount these cases as exceptions to a normally functioning system. But consider LTCM, led by John Meriwether, the former head of bond trading at Salomon Brothers, advised by Nobel Prize winners Myron Scholes and Robert Merton, and employing a stable of quantitative analysts building sophisticated financial and risk models. LTCM lost nearly $5 billion in a few months and then permanently closed its doors.

It's not just LTCM. Over a 15-year period, virtually all mutual fund and bond fund managers *underperformed* the broader market.[7] Nobel economics Laureate Daniel Kahneman conducted a simple analysis of finance professionals in a leading firm: The interyear correlation of results was essentially zero.[8] Such data can be interpreted as suggesting that winning a lottery is not proof of skill in winning lotteries.

California Institute of Technology (Caltech) professor Leonard Mlodinow has similar data showing a regression to the mean for money managers, underscoring that past performance is no guarantee of future results.[9] One problem with forecasting financials, as author, professor, and trader Nassim Nicholas Taleb has famously noted, is that black swans—unusual, extreme events—can and do occur, and concepts such as "average" and "normal" may not be sufficient to fully characterize such systems.

Even so, companies such as the Prediction Company, now a division of banking and investment giant UBS, have tried to use—and improve on—chaos theory, complex adaptive systems theory, general equilibrium theory, neural network algorithms, and who knows what else, to predict the direction of the markets in the intermediate term as well as to support real-time trading.[10]

As Norman Packard, cofounder of the Prediction Company, observed:

One of the fundamental truths about markets is that the dynamics are non-stationary. We see no evidence for the existence of an attractor with stable statistical properties. This is what characterizes chaos—having an attractor with stable statistical properties—so what we are seeing is not chaos. It is something else. Call it an "even-stranger-than-strange attractor," which may not really be an attractor at all. The market might enter an epoch where some structure coalesces and sits there in a statistically stationary pattern, but then invariably it disappears. You have clouds of structure that coalesce and evaporate, coalesce and evaporate.[11]

Stock prices behave like a flock of birds that arrive out of nowhere and chirp about your backyard for a while and then without warning fly off to a randomly selected new destination, say, Toledo. Such systems behave in complex ways that may be chaotic (i.e., deterministic, but with sensitive dependence on initial conditions) or stochastic—truly random—or, as Packard says, even stranger than strange.

Turbulence is inherent to such systems. Researchers have found that markets can fluctuate erratically even in the *absence* of any external influences. They mathematically modeled three types of traders: *fundamentalists*, who focus on the current price relative to the fundamental value; *optimists*, who believe the trend is up; and *pessimists*, who believe the reverse. Traders were free to switch strategies. With *just these three types* of traders buying and selling *just one* stock in a simulated market, periods of relative quiet were suddenly punctuated by *wild swings*: either bull market rallies or crashes.[12]

Now add exogenous drivers to this inherent instability. Thus, do we have Lehman Brothers disappearing in a weekend, presidential elections being won or lost on a chad, consumer confidence and jobless claims and home sales rising or falling or staying the same, gold booms and busts, terrorist attacks and peace talks, typhoons and frosts impacting food prices and thus political stability, offhand comments from Federal Reserve chairmen, planned comments from Federal Reserve chairmen, or any of a trillion other things that might impact the economy, and therefore demand, and therefore IT workloads.

Demand for Products and Services

Volatility in financial markets drives volatility in the broader economy, and the broader economy returns the favor. Such stranger-than-strangeness is what makes forecasting so difficult. In their 876-page textbook, *Retailing*

Management, Stanford and Harvard professors and Price Waterhouse consultants had this to say about sales forecasting:

> [The] following are *advised cautions* since sales forecasting involves *substantial judgment* as well as established technique . . . [in] an *attempt* to predict the future. The *best that can be hoped* for are *educated guesses*. . . . Generally, past sales [tell] the retailer only what *has* happened, *not what will* happen [given] a *wide variety of factors*, many *beyond the retailer's control*.
>
> If this process seems filled with *estimates* and *quite imprecise*, be reminded of the professionalism inherent in large-scale retail management. . . . *Executive judgment* is the final ingredient in any sales forecast. A sales forecast is, therefore, a *human estimate* [that] may prove ultimately very accurate or *quite wrong*, but it is the best *starting point* available.[13] (emphasis added)

To make things worse, reliance on "executive judgment" may not be sufficient. Studies have shown that with executives, as with mutual funds, past performance is no guarantee of future results. Caltech's Mlodinow observed that everyone understands that "genius doesn't guarantee success, but it's seductive to assume that success must come from genius."[14] But at least in some industries, he argued, executives can't do much better "than an ape throwing darts at a dartboard."[15]

As a measure of forecast accuracy, consider that, typically, 7% of products are out of stock. And during promotions (when *extra special effort is being made to sell these products*), that number rises to over 15%.[16] Retailers that are winning in the market today are those such as Inditex—owner of the popular Zara fashion chain—that have shortened inventory refresh cycles dramatically. In other words, rather than futilely forecasting, they are rapidly responding.

Conversely, consider Missoni, one of the most exclusive Italian designer labels, selling haute couture clothing and accessories selling for hundreds, thousands, or in some cases over $10,000. It was quite a coup when Target introduced Missoni for Target. Unfortunately, on September 13, 2011, "in an unusual fumble for the large retailer, Target was unprepared [and the] Target.com site was wiped out for most of the day."[17]

Only a couple of months later, on November 25, "fire sales turned into a firestorm for Walmart . . . as the company's web servers buckled under Black Friday traffic. Shoppers . . . waited until the middle of the night for sales only to experience broken checkout pages, emptied shopping carts, and login errors."[18]

Walmart.com's capacity hitting a wall and Target's being off target are cautionary tales. As the largest retailers in the world, they benefit from the law of large numbers and a strong executive bench. If they can't accurately forecast, how are the rest of us supposed to?

System Dynamics

The root cause of issues with forecasting lies in the turbulent, unpredictable nature of complex systems. The gravitationally driven trajectories of two bodies, whether rocks or planets—the earth and the sun, say—can be determined easily using Newtonian physics. Add in a third body—Jupiter, say—and the general problem becomes unsolvable due to a basic issue: *sensitive dependence on initial conditions*. Such "chaotic behavior" occurs in many realms, including weather, which has been described as subject to the *butterfly effect*, where a butterfly flapping its wings in Asia might eventually cause a hurricane in the United States. Lest this seem abstract, consider that the 35 million casualties of World War I were arguably precipitated by the death of Archduke Franz Ferdinand of Austria and his wife, Sophie, Duchess of Hohenberg, when their car turned down the wrong street in Sarajevo and encountered an opportunistic assassin.

If the best scientists in the world can't figure out what happens to three rocks, what are the chances that the rest of us will be able to figure out what 7 billion people will cause to happen when they are shopping and buying and selling at various prices in the complex, chaotic, dynamical system we call the global economy? Each of them is subject to mood swings, cognitive biases, bounded rationality, emotions, fear, uncertainty, irrational behavior. As John von Neumann, the inventor of game theory and the modern computer, wryly commented, "It is unlikely that a mere repetition of the tricks which served us so well in physics will do for the social phenomena, too."[19]

There are just too many ways things can get crazy. According to Charles Fine of the Massachusetts Institute of Technology (MIT), there are a number of disruptive forces impacting virtually all companies: shocks to the business environment, such as business regulation, economic shocks, technological shocks, and innovative competitor models.[20] In the world of ecommerce, Google's fine-tuning of the PageRank algorithm—the so-called Google Dance—can cause a company that counts on search engine referrals to shift from success to bankruptcy. A mention of one Web site in a blog post can catapult the referenced site from obscurity to millions of page views.

Sizing and resizing infrastructure and other resources effectively depends on accurately characterizing demand. But demand for most if not all products and services is inherently unpredictable, due to exogenous factors, such as consumer sentiment and global economic conditions, but also due to internally generated patterns of individual behavior that create emergent erratic system behaviors. Better forecasting with more comprehensive models calculated on the most powerful high-performance computing environments on the planet can perhaps help a little bit with the short term, but these models are *ultimately doomed to failure because the problem lies not with inadequate models or computing power but with the unpre-dictable nature of reality itself.*

The issue is not that future demand is not *known*; it's that it is *unknowable*.

Whips and Chains

Peter Senge, director of the Systems Thinking and Organizational Learning program at MIT's Sloan School of Management, has run a business school simulation called "the beer game" thousands of times.[21] His students play retailers, wholesalers, and brewers and are told to maximize revenues and profits, which means ensuring that there is sufficient product without car-rying excess inventory. To keep things manageable, there is only one brand of beer offered by one brewer.

Things run well for a while, until a slight uptick in demand causes the craziness to begin. The retailer orders more beer from the wholesaler, who orders more from the brewer. When it doesn't arrive quickly enough, the retailer orders even more. The wholesaler, seeing increased demand, orders even more. As stock-outs ensue, players keep ordering, and the brewery keeps ramping up production.

Finally, all the beer arrives downstream, and the retailers, now inun-dated with too much, cut their orders back to zero. The brewery, mean-while, has been ramping up production, until the messages that orders have been cut to zero work their way through the distributors back to the brewer. Money is lost throughout the entire system, due to the opportunity costs of lost sales due to unfulfilled customer demand, excess inventory and its carrying costs, and capital expenditures as the brewer expanded.

Moreover, not only is there variability, but MIT's Fine pointed out that firms that are farther upstream in the supply chain experience *vol-atility amplification*, or a bullwhip effect. He illustrated this with the auto-motive industry. During a three-decade period, the U.S. gross domestic product varied by a few percentage points, automobile manufacturer's revenues varied by 20%, and those of machine tool manufacturers by 60% to 80%. If a consumer sees the economy hitting a speed bump, he or she will slow down car purchases, and when automotive manufacturers see reven-ues going downhill, they will slam the brakes on major capital investments.

Exogenous Uncertainty

Taleb, who catapulted the phrase "black swan" into the contemporary lex-icon of risk managers, has related a story about the four biggest losses at a casino based on risk consulting work that he conducted.[22] They weren't defined by the statistics of win-loss percentages for craps or blackjack, or even predictable causes, such as card counters or brazen daylight robberies.

Instead, they were costs and lost revenue due to: the premature end of the Siegfried and Roy show from a tiger's alleged attack[23]; a contractor upset over a proposed workplace injury settlement who then tried to dynamite the hotel; the inexplicable failure of an accounting clerk to file reports with the Internal Revenue Service, which led to a huge fine; and a ransom payment for a kidnapped casino owner's daughter.

In the world of IT, uncertainty can come not just from sudden customer demand spikes but data center outages due to floods, fires, hurricanes, and tornados; distributed denial of service attacks; disgruntled former or current employees with root passwords, network outages due to backhoe attenuation, and other causes. In other words, both the level of demand and the level of capacity can experience unexpected discontinuities.

Behavioral Cloudonomics of Forecasting

Forecasting in the broadest sense—our ability to imagine the future, evaluate potential scenarios, assess the impact of our actions without executing them—is perhaps one of the capabilities that makes us most human. As part of a so-called executive function of the brain, it has roots in the prefrontal cortex and the anterior cingulate cortex. These areas are involved in "cross-temporal perception-action cycles," that is, mingling past experience with future planning.

A slew of cognitive biases impact forecasting. We devote Chapter 23 to a survey of those impacting cloud computing, but ones relevant to forecasting include a bias for certainty; the clustering illusion, where randomness—such as stars—appears to have a pattern—such as a constellation; selective recall and the confirmation bias (i.e., a preference for proving that we were right); and illusory control, the belief that we can control inherently random outcomes.

Pattern Detection

The brain encodes information for efficiency, predicts trends, *becomes stimulated when those predictions are not met*, and then attempts to work the new exceptions into its predictive model of reality. Learning is intimately associated with the neurotransmitter *dopamine* and the structure and dynamics of those neurons that leverage this chemical communications system. As bestselling author Jonah Lehrer explained, "If everything goes according to plan . . . dopamine neurons secrete a little burst of enjoyment. [If not, they] instantly send out a signal announcing their mistake and stop releasing dopamine. The brain is designed to amplify the shock of these mistaken predictions."[24] The brain is designed for the comfort of predictable patterns and sounds alarms otherwise.

In the Iowa Gambling Task, an experiment conducted by two neuroscientists, Antonio Damasio and Antoine Bechara, each subject could draw cards either from a deck that, unbeknownst to them, contained many high-payoff but also high-loss cards or from a deck with low-payoff and low-punishment cards.[25] After about 50 cards they started drawing from the safe deck and after 80 they could explain why.

But galvanic skin response equipment showed that the subjects began to have increased skin conductivity—a measure of fear and anxiety—after drawing only a few cards from the "bad" deck. They subconsciously detected the pattern.

Humans are exquisite pattern detectors. Unfortunately, they are so good that they detect patterns *even when they aren't there*. According to Dutch psychologist and expert witness Willem Wagenaar, "People have a very poor conception of randomness: they do not recognize it when they see it and they cannot produce it when they try."[26] For example, they tend to overly accentuate the degree of alternation—heads, tails, heads, tails, heads, tails, heads, tails—than would appear in a truly random sequence.[27]

Lehrer called the stock market "a classic example of a random system. This means that the past movement of a particular stock cannot be used to predict its future movement . . . all of the esoteric tools used by investors to make sense of the market were pure nonsense."[28] However, the same way that people find big and little dippers in random star fields, Lehrer argued that "dopamine neurons are determined to solve the flux, but most of the time there is nothing to solve. And so brain cells flail against the stochasticity, searching for lucrative patterns."[29]

According to Read Montague, director of the Human Neuroimaging Laboratory at the Virginia Tech Carilion Research Institute, "People enjoy investing in the market and gambling in a casino for the same reason that they see Snoopy in the clouds. When the brain is exposed to anything random, like a slot machine or the shape of a cloud, it automatically imposes a pattern onto the noise. But that isn't Snoopy, and you haven't found the secret pattern in the stock market."[30]

A classic study examined whether basketball players were streaky—that is, *made* lots of shots when they were "hot" but missed them when they were "cold."[31] Using statistical analysis, the authors showed that the players' performance didn't deviate from what you'd expect from tossing a coin weighted with their likelihood of making shots. For example, if a player had an 80% probability of sinking a shot, you'd expect many successful sequences, but a number of sequences where they missed attempt after attempt wouldn't be unlikely.

When neuroscientists perform imaging during experiments similar to the Iowa Gambling Task when there is no pattern, they discover that the same dopamine-rich pattern-finding areas in the brain are firing like crazy.

In other words, specific subsystems in the brain will leave no stone unturned trying to find patterns, and therefore *the brain will find those patterns whether they are there or not.* Forecasters, looking at random data, will find patterns and thus believe that future demand is predictable, even if it is not.

Illusory Superiority

Dartmouth Tuck business professor Sydney Finkelstein, author of *Why Smart Executives Fail*, observed that there are two major recurring themes in major business disasters: "the remarkable tendency for CEOs and executives of new ventures to believe that they are absolutely right, and the tendency to overestimate the quality of managerial talent by relying on track record, especially in situations that differ markedly from the present new venture."[32]

Illusory superiority—the notion that we are better at something than we actually are—is a pervasive human characteristic. The average person believes themselves to be anything but. For example:

> a large survey of American high school seniors revealed that a full seventy percent thought they had higher than average leadership ability, while a mere two percent judged themselves to be below average. All of the one million students surveyed thought they had an above average ability to get along with others . . . while twenty-five percent considered themselves to be in the highest one percent. These figures cannot simply be attributed to youthful inexperience: a survey of college professors revealed that all but seven percent believed that they were better than average at their work.[33]

Harvard University professor and author Daniel Gilbert wryly observed: "Ironically, the bias toward seeing ourselves as better than average causes us to see ourselves as less biased than average too. As one research team concluded, 'Most of us appear to believe that we are more athletic, intelligent, organized, ethical, logical, interesting, fair-minded, and healthy—not to mention more attractive—than the average person.'"[34] Not only are we unable to see into the future, we are unable to see that we are unable to see into the future.

Bias for Certainty

People have an irrational fear of the unknown, partly driven by their need for control. Author and lecturer David Rock said that the brain conserves energy by acting on auto-pilot normally, relying on "long-established neural connections in the basal ganglia and motor cortex that have, in effect, hardwired this situation and the individual's response to it." This is how we can walk while chewing gum while texting. "But the minute the brain registers ambiguity or confusion . . . the brain flashes an error signal. Uncertainty registers (in a part of the brain called the anterior cingulate cortex) as an error, gap, or tension: something that must be corrected before one can feel comfortable again." He observed that this discomfort in turn "diminishes memory, undermines performance, and disengages people from the present."[35]

Studies have shown that cognitive control—that is, awareness and detailed information—regarding medical procedures to be performed reduces stress and accelerates recovery. And behavioral control—that is, simply enabling intensive care patients to determine when they received visitors and when they ate—also turned out to be key to enhancing recovery.[36]

More broadly, Wharton Business school professor J. Scott Armstrong, in evaluating the accuracy of experts in forecasting, wrote: "Overall, the evidence suggests there is little benefit to expertise, [so] claims of accuracy by a single expert would seem to be of no practical value."[37] Armstrong has formulated what he calls the "seer-sucker theory," namely that regardless of the evidence showing that there is no such thing as a seer, there are suckers who believe that they exist.

James Shanteau, a professor at Kansas State University, is an expert, on, well, experts and is one of the founders of the Cochran-Weiss-Shanteau metric for expert performance. His analysis showed that experts in a variety of fields, ranging from financial advice, to clinical psychology, are about as likely to agree as not. Experts disagree not only with others but with themselves: They are just as likely to give the same opinion as a different opinion from what they had given earlier. Finally, not only were these experts often wrong, they had such a high degree of overconfidence that they routinely believed that they were right.[38] As James Surowiecki, author of *The Wisdom of Crowds*, summed it up, there is "little correlation between an expert's confidence in his judgment and the accuracy of it. In other words, experts don't know when they don't know something."[39]

Summary

The world is stranger than strange, subject to chaotic sensitive dependence on initial conditions, stochastic phenomena, recursive system dynamics, network feedback effects, and volatility amplification. Our ability to forecast can appear to work for some time, only to fail at the worst possible time.

Moreover, a variety of cognitive biases make us see patterns in this chaotic randomness where none exist and make us be confident in our ability to either predict or control that which we cannot. And because we believe ourselves to be better than we are, and experts believe themselves to be better than they are, and prefer the illusion of certainty regarding the future rather than accepting its innate unpredictability, we cannot fully appreciate the degree to which we are unable to forecast.

The way to manage unpredictability is not with faulty models worsened by cognitive biases but by on-demand resources, the subject of Chapter 14.

Notes

1. "IMF Sees U.S. Recovery in late 2009," *Reuters*, December 18, 2008. http://ca.reuters.com/article/idUSTRE4BH0ZL20081218.
2. John Kay, "Cracks in the Crystal Ball," *Financial Times*, September 29, 1995, quoted in Mark Buchanan, *Ubiquity: Why Catastrophes Happen* (Three Rivers Press, Random House, 2001), p. 139
3. Toby Poston, "The Legacy of J.K. Galbraith: Analysis," BBC News, April 30, 2006. http://news.bbc.co.uk/2/hi/business/4960280.stm.
4. "The Market Can Remain Irrational Longer Than You Can Remain Solvent," Quote Investigator, August 9, 2011. quoteinvestigator.com/2011/08/09/remain-solvent/.
5. Leonard Mlodinow, "The Limits of Control," *New York Times Opinionator*, June 15, 2009. http://opinionator.blogs.nytimes.com/2009/06/15/the-limits-of-control/?ref=opinion&apage=1.
6. Marketwatch, "Rogues gallery: From Leeson to Kerviel: Five of the most notorious rogue traders in market history," *Marketwatch*, October 5, 2010. http://www.marketwatch.com/story/from-leeson-to-kerviel-rogues-gallery-slide-show-2010-10-05.
7. James Surowiecki, *The Wisdom of Crowds* (Anchor Books, 2005).
8. Daniel Kahneman, "Don't Blink: The Hazards of Confidence," *New York Times Magazine*, October 19, 2011. www.nytimes.com/2011/10/23/magazine/dont-blink-the-hazards-of-confidence.html?pagewanted=4&_r=2.
9. Leonard Mlodinow, *The Drunkard's Walk: How Randomness Rules Our Lives* (Pantheon, 2008).
10. Thomas Bass, *The Predictors: How a Band of Maverick Physicists Used Chaos Theory to Trade Their Way to a Fortune on Wall Street* (Owl, Henry Holt, 1999).
11. Ibid., p. 207.
12. Buchanan, *Ubiquity*, pp. 152–154.
13. William R. Davidson, Daniel J. Sweeney, and Ronald W. Stampfl, *Retailing Management*, 6th ed. (John Wiley & Sons, 1988), pp. 369, 372. Emphasis added.
14. Mlodinow, *The Drunkard's Walk*, p. 11.
15. Leonard Mlodinow, "Chaotic," *LA Times Magazine West*, July 2, 2006. http://articles.latimes.com/2006/jul/02/magazine/tm-random27

16. Doug Henschen, "A Matter of Survival," *InformationWeek*, March 2, 2009, p. 29.

17. Stephanie Clifford, "Demand at Target for Fashion Line Crashes Web Site," *New York Times*, September 13, 2011. www.nytimes.com/2011/09/14/business/demand-at-target-for-fashion-line-crashes-web-site.html.

18. Josh Constine, "Walmart's Black Friday Disaster: Website Crippled, Violence in Stores," *TechCrunch*, November 25, 2011. http://techcrunch.com/2011/11/25/walmart-black-friday/.

19. John von Neumann, Oskar Morgenstern, Harold William Kuhn, and Ariel Rubinstein, *Theory of Games and Economic Behavior (Commemorative Edition)* (Princeton University Press, 2007), p. 638.

20. Charles Fine, *Clockspeed: Winning Industry Control in the Age of Temporary Advantage* (Basic Books, 1998).

21. Peter M. Senge *The Fifth Discipline: The Art and Practice of the Learning Organization* (Doubleday Currency, 1990).

22. Nassim Nicholas Taleb, *The Black Swan: The Impact of the Highly Improbable* (Random House, 2007).

23. "Siegfried: Tiger Wanted to Help Roy," www.cnn.com/2003/SHOWBIZ/10/08/siegfried.roy/index.html.

24. Jonah Lehrer, *How We Decide* (Houghton Mifflin, 2009), p. 37.

25. Ibid.

26. Leonard Mlodinow, *The Drunkard's Walk: How Randomness Rules Our Lives* (Pantheon, 2008), p. 174.

27. Maya Bar-Hillel and Willem Wagenaar, "The Perception of Randomness," *Advances in Applied Mathematics* 12, No. 4 (December 1991): 428–454.

28. Lehrer, *How We Decide*, p. 67.

29. Ibid.

30. Ibid.

31. Thomas Gilovich, Robert Vallone, and Amos Tversky, "The Hot Hand in Basketball: On the Misperception of Random Sequences," *Cognitive Psychology* 17 (1985), pp. 295–314. http://teacherweb.com/MD/RiverHill/Hugus/AP-Stat-Gilo.Vallone.Tversky-Hot-Hand-Basketball.pdf

32. Surowiecki, *Wisdom of Crowds*, p. 220.

33. David Livingstone Smith, *Why We Lie: The Evolutionary Roots of Deception and the Unconscious Mind* (St. Martin's Press, 2004), p. 25.

34. Daniel Gilbert, *Stumbling on Happiness* (Vintage Books, 2007), p. 252.

35. David Rock, "Managing with the Brain in Mind," *Strategy+Business* (Autumn 2009). www.strategy-business.com/article/09306?pg=3

36. John E. G. Bateson, "Perceived Control and the Service Encounter," in John A. Czepiel, Michael R. Solomon, and Carol F. Surprenant, eds., *The Service Encounter: Managing Employee/Customer Interaction in Service Businesses* (Lexington, 1985). pp. 67–82.

37. J. Scott Armstrong, "The Seer-Sucker Theory: The Value of Experts in Forecasting," *Technology Review* 82, No. 7 (June/July 1980): pp. 16–24.

38. Surowiecki, *The Wisdom of Crowds*, p. 33.

39. Ibid., p. 278.

CHAPTER 14

Money Value of Time

If forecasting the future is fallible, what is the alternative? Although it's often advised that it's better to be predictive and proactive than reactive, perhaps this wisdom needs to be turned on its head. If we can react instantaneously to any condition with as many—or as few—on-demand resources as we need, forecast error is irrelevant.

To the extent that exactly the right resources are available at exactly the right time, unpredictable variability becomes a nonissue. It is clear that this is the best possible solution and one that, increasingly, the cloud is ready to handle.

However, suppose that instead of instantaneous dynamic response, there is a delay. How much does such a delay cost? The answer is: It depends.[1] It depends on a variety of factors, such as the penalty associated with insufficient resources and that associated with excess resources, as well as the degree to which the demand is unpredictably volatile. It also depends on the interaction between customers (or users) and the service process: If there are insufficient resources, is the revenue (or productivity) lost forever, or are transactions queued until resources are available. If they queue up, what is the order in which customers are served? At a high level, if the demand doesn't vary very much, being slow to respond isn't that critical: Even a sloth can catch a snail. If application demand is highly volatile, the resource-provisioning function needs to be equally agile: It takes a tiger to catch an antelope.

Most businesspeople know that there is a time value of money; there is also a *money value of time*. Time *is* money, and in this chapter we explore exactly how much.

Demand and Resource Functions

Often demand and resources are measured in separate units—for example, the demand is for sweaters, and the resources needed are knitting machines, operators, and wool. Sometimes resources are in integer units, say, planes, but demand is in fractional quantities, say, plane seats; or the reverse may occur. Here we ignore all these complicating factors and simply assume that demand and resources are in the same units, for example, kilowatts of demand for electricity and kilowatts of electrical generating capacity. This assumption does not impact the generality of the insights that we derive in the next few pages.

We assume that the demand for resources over time is a function, $D(t)$, and the resources available to meet that demand is also a function, $R(t)$. At any given time, say, t_1, one of these must hold:

- $D(t_1) < R(t_1)$—We have excess resources deployed
- $D(t_1) > R(t_1)$—We have too few resources (i.e., excess demand)
- $D(t_1) = R(t_1)$—The amount of resources we have is just right

In the best of all worlds, at all times we would have _exactly_ the correct amount of resources to satisfy demand or $D(t) = R(t)$. We can call this _perfect capacity_. However, depending on the demand function and the resource function, it certainly is possible—or even likely—that the resources will be either insufficient or excess, and this situation will incur a penalty, or cost.

In attempting to match resources to capacity, there are six major areas to consider.

1. _Frequency of demand assessment._ Are we checking the level of demand only once a week, or continuously?
2. _Accuracy of this assessment._ How good is our process for evaluating demand?
3. _Underlying variability and unpredictability of the demand curve._ Is it flat, linearly growing, random but distributed normally, or something else?
4. _Accuracy of the forecasting process._ Being able to exactly forecast demand a month from now gives us provisioning advantages over not knowing what will happen in the next nanosecond. As discussed in Chapter 13, it is unlikely in the general case that our forecasting will be perfect.
5. _Response time of the capacity adjustment._ If we know instantaneously that the demand has changed, but it takes us a month or two to respond to the change, we may be in trouble. Such response time may be a predictable duration (e.g., nine months), stochastic (e.g., between two and five months), nearly instantaneous, or something in between.
6. _Granularity of the adjustment._ If demand varies in tens or hundreds of watts, but capacity is available only in kilowatt or megawatt increments,

there will be a difference between demand and capacity. Thanks to virtualization, we assume that both demand and capacity are available at the same level of granularity: If a customer needs 4.23 servers, we can provide exactly that.[2]

There may be additional subtleties in some capacity models, such as ownership. For example, excluding supply chain disasters or creditworthiness issues, it generally is easy to increase capacity by ordering new equipment. It is harder to dispose of used equipment. We ignore those asymmetries in this analysis.

Cost of Excess Capacity

As we initially explored in Chapter 9, there are costs to excess capacity as well as insufficient capacity. There are major economic costs to excess capacity, such as the leasing, loan servicing or the opportunity cost of the capital that is employed, the administration of the assets, and any additional costs required due to the excess capacity, such as power and floor space.

Suppose that we lease or buy $2 million worth of servers when we only need $1 million worth. The opportunity cost of that decision is the income that could have been earned using that $1 million to do something else. We could put it in a checking account and earn interest. We could buy back our stock, driving the share price higher. We could invest in a new business or a new product. At the end of several years, we might have turned that million into $2 million or $5 million or $50 million.

Even if we did none of that and just kept the $1 million under the corporate mattress, at the end of three to five years we still would have the $1 million (less any losses in purchasing power due to inflation). If we had bought wine—Bordeaux first growths, say—and kept it cellared properly in its original wood cases, the wine might have *appreciated* in value. However, the servers, storage, and switches—even if cellared properly and still in their original boxes—would have depreciated in value. Given the rate of technology evolution, the residual value of high-tech equipment after three years might be only 10% or 20% of the original cost. In addition, although cash is liquid, getting rid of used equipment can incur additional costs, such as administration, packaging, and shipping. We have essentially thrown away the money.

And, depending on the scenario, there are additional costs in owning such technology assets: installation, turn up, testing, power, floor space, heating, ventilation, and air conditioning for the equipment.

In short, having more capacity than we need is costly.

Cost of Insufficient Capacity

However, running out of capacity can be even *more* costly because the capacity is needed to do something. It may be used to reduce cost or grow revenue.

In IT, examples of use for cost reduction might be the technology used to optimize a supply chain or reduce fraud.

Most businesses use IT to maximize revenues: E-commerce is an important channel; applications for yield management and dynamic pricing can maximize revenue; usable and helpful customer support can maintain customer loyalty and therefore reduce churn or erosion of revenue. IT even can be used to optimize receipts from collectible accounts: The timing and text of letters or e-mails to customers can increase the percentage of responses and amount of money collected.

Insufficient capacity negatively impacts revenues in many ways: Consider the direct revenue loss, where a hotel reservation site is unable to accept bookings so the guest goes to a competitor, or an e-commerce site where, deprived of the instant gratification of ordering, the purchaser thinks better and cancels his plan to purchase. There are also indirect costs, such as loss of the customer and her lifetime value for good; the negative reviews the customer may spread, thus causing the firm to lose additional customers; bad press; and legal actions.

The exact cost of $1 of excess capacity will vary, but generally we might argue that the cost of a misallocated dollar might be 30 or 40 cents each year, based on an opportunity cost of a nominal risk-adjusted rate of return of, say, 10% and a straight-line depreciation cost of, say, 30% per year over three years with a 10% residual.

In the case of insufficient capacity, however, rather than a cost of 30 or 40 cents annually by misallocating a dollar, there may be a greater cost in such a misallocation. The penalty will vary depending on the exact situation.

A recent study by Sunil Mithas, an associate professor at the Robert H. Smith School of Business at the University of Maryland, and his colleagues, used rigorous statistical analysis of data from over 400 large global firms to show that "an increase in IT expenditure per employee by $1 is associated with $12.22 increase in sales per employee."[3] They showed that this amount was larger than the return from other discretionary expenditures such as on advertising and research and development. Moreover, according to Mithas, a dollar in expenditures was associated with between $1.20 and $1.90 in profits.[4] This matches what one might expect for not just IT projects, but any useful project: There is no reason to spend a dollar to get back ninety cents. Firms invest to achieve nontrivial risk-adjusted returns: A revenue-oriented IT investment must generate enough marginal revenue that the marginal after-tax earnings produced achieve an internal rate of return that is greater than the corporate hurdle rate for such projects.

Asymmetric Penalty Functions, Perfect Capacity, and On Demand

Given these arguments, we can formalize a penalty cost for incorrect capacity. We denote the unit cost of an excess resource by c_r and denote the unit cost of an insufficient resource by c_d. In some cases, we keep things simple and assume that $c_d = c_r$. Generally, though, we assume that $c_d \gg c_r$.

In other words, there is a cost associated with having too little or too much capacity. Having the exactly correct amount of capacity at all times—which we call perfect capacity—ensures that this penalty function is zero. We can formalize this cost over the period $[t_1, t_2]$ as:

$$\int_{t_1}^{t_2} [D(t) - R(t)] \times c_d \, dt | D(t) > R(t) + \int_{t_1}^{t_2} [R(t) - D(t)] \times c_r dt | R(t) > D(t)$$

In other words, the penalty function is the cost of undercapacity times the amount of undercapacity over time, plus the cost of overcapacity times the amount of overcapacity over time.

On-demand capacity is one way of achieving perfect capacity. If we can respond to any shift in demand by instantaneously adjusting the resources, we will always have the correct capacity. However, on-demand capacity is *not* equivalent to perfect capacity: For some types of demand curves and resource provisioning strategies (e.g., flat demand and fixed capacity or step-increasing demand with enough forecast visibility to meet it and provision capacity), it is possible to achieve perfect capacity without on-demand resources. Generally, however, the ability to dynamically ensure the correct capacity on demand is useful when demand is unpredictable.

Other formulations are possible, for example, where insufficient capacity leads to user or transaction queueing.

Flat Demand

If demand is flat, say, $D(t) = k$, where k is a constant, setting resources correctly is easy: Simply set $R(t) = k$ as well. This is the simplest case that can be imagined. Unfortunately, it is unlikely to correspond to many real-world scenarios.

Uniformly Distributed Demand

As we previewed in Chapter 9, suppose that $D(t)$ is uniformly distributed between 0 and P. For a discrete uniform distribution, sample values will look something like Exhibit 14.1.

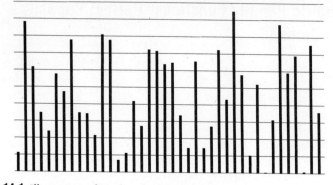

EXHIBIT 14.1 Illustration of Uniformly Distributed Demand

We are going to explain the solutions using the example of singles tennis, where the demand is represented by where our opponent hits the ball and our capacity is represented by where we stand. We don't know where the opponent is going to return the ball. If we stand on the left sideline, there's a chance that our opponent will hit it directly to us, but it could be anywhere on the court, including the right sideline. The minimum distance we'd have to run is zero, the maximum is one court width, but, assuming that return volleys are evenly distributed, we would expect to have to run *half* the width of the court. Conversely, if we are on the right sideline, the same logic holds in reverse, and our expected distance to run to hit a return shot is still half the width of the court.

But, if we stand in the middle of the court, the minimum is still zero, but the maximum distance is only half a court width. The expected distance to run for a ball on the left half court is only one half the half-court width, or one quarter the width of the court, and the same for the balls on the other side. By standing in the center of the court rather than on a sideline, we can reduce the expected distance we need to run by half.

Let's return to the world of capacity. We could set $R(t) = 0$, but then we would be almost always short of resources. Since $D(t)$ is uniform on [0,1], we would have an expected value $E(D(t))$ of $\frac{1}{2}$. Under our assumptions, this means that we would be paying a penalty over a duration of time T of $\frac{1}{2} c_d \times T$. Conversely, we could set resources to be exactly 1—that is, $R(t) = 1$—but then we would have *excess* capacity. Again, since the expected value of $E(D(t))$ is $\frac{1}{2}$, this amount over a duration of time T would be $\frac{1}{2} c_r \times T$. It turns out that we can do better than this: Rather than the extremes of permanent undercapacity— $R(t) = 0$—or permanent overcapacity— $R(t) = 1$—we can identify a point in between with a minimal penalty (translation: the least bad).

Using tennis court logic, let's pick a point F—our capacity choice and our decision as to where to stand—somewhere in the range from 0—the left baseline—to *P*—the right baseline. The chance that the "ball"—user demand—lands to our right—that is, in the interval *F* through *P*, is just $(P - F)/P$, the proportion of the court to our right. Conversely, the chance it is on the left is F/P. If it lands on the right, the expected value of the distance is $(P - F)/2$, and the penalty that will be paid is c_d. If it lands on the left, the expected value of the distance is $F/2$, and the penalty that will be paid is c_r. Multiplying probabilities, expected distances, and penalties, the expected value of the penalty is:

$$\frac{F}{P} \times \frac{F}{2} \times c_r + \frac{(P - F)}{P} \times \frac{(P - F)}{2} \times c_d$$

We can multiply things out and rearrange terms somewhat, to arrive at:

$$\frac{1}{2P} \times \left[\left(F^2 \times c_r \right) + \left(\left(P^2 - 2PF + F^2 \right) \times c_d \right) \right]$$

Taking the derivative of this equation with respect to *F*, since *P*, c_d, and c_r are constants, and using the rules of calculus, such as that the derivative of x^2 is $2x$, and then setting the derivative to zero, which is where the minimum will be, we find that:

$$0 = Fc_r - Pc_d + Fc_d$$

More simply:

$$F = P \frac{c_d}{c_r + c_d}$$

If the cost of unserved demand is equal to the cost of excess resources, the optimal point is one half the peak—that is, the middle of the court. However, as the cost of unserved demand gets higher and higher relative to the cost of resources, the least cost fixed point gets closer and closer to the peak (in other words, it becomes increasingly better to be safe than sorry). To return to our tennis analogy, if missing a shot on your left costs you the point, but we change the rules so that missing a shot on your right immediately costs you the match, it makes sense to stand closer to the right sideline.

Better Never than Late

A well-known maxim advises "Better late than never," but in the world of capacity management, the reverse can often be true. Boston Consulting Group vice presidents George Stalk and Thomas Hout addressed the problems of overcorrection based on a model originally discussed in a 1958

Harvard Business Review article by Jay Forrester, the inventor of system dynamics.[5] When demand is cyclical, responding slowly can be worse than not responding. As demand grows, capacity is added, but by the time it is added, demand has fallen off, so there is even more excess capacity. As Stalk and Hout observe in analyzing a production response to a demand increase, if you attempt to "smooth the demand by advertising and promoting in the troughs and raising prices in the peaks, the oscillations would actually increase."[6]

If we consider the "better safe than sorry" analysis, we realize why "better never than late" can in fact be a good strategy. If we try to chase random fluctuations, we will end up picking points *other* than *F*. But we already have seen that *F* is the best choice when we don't know what's coming. Since we don't know what's coming, any other choice is worse. In the tennis game, if we were to use a shot on the right sideline as an indicator that *all* coming shots will be on the right, we have just worsened our position in returning the uniformly distributed shots that may be as far off as the left baseline.

Although we are addressing capacity here, these insights apply to the stock market as well, where attempting to respond to a trend is like buying high and selling low. Professors Brad Barber and Terrance Odean, then at the Graduate School of Finance at the University of California, Davis, quipped that "trading is hazardous to your wealth" and determined, in a study now cited over 1,000 times, that active investors during a five-year period earned 11.4% *per annum*. A terrific return, if it weren't for the fact that the broader market in this same period increased by 17.9% annually.[7]

MAD about Being Normal

There are a couple of other scenarios worth touching on. One is a normal distribution. Let's assume that we are playing tennis from the center of the court and the person on the other side of the court is actually a friend, just out to hit balls with us. She is a decent player but not an expert, so she tries to hit balls back to us but doesn't always succeed. If the distribution of volleys is normal with a mean at the center of the court but with standard deviation σ, the expected distance that we will have to travel from the center is the mean absolute deviation (MAD)—which, for a normal distribution, is $\sqrt{\frac{2}{\pi}}\sigma$ or roughly $.798\sigma$. If the distribution of demand is normal we can determine the likely penalty function: $.798\sigma(\frac{1}{2}c_d + \frac{1}{2}c_r)$. We expect to have to sidestep about four fifths of the standard deviation, and half the time it will be to the left, half the time to the right (i.e., if we pick capacity at the expected value of demand, half the time we will be under and half the time we will be over).

Triangular Distributions

It is unlikely that demand actually will be normally distributed, because the tail of the normal distribution goes out to both positive and negative infinity. We can approximate such demand, though, by a triangular distribution, also known as a triangle distribution. In the simplest case, the distribution is symmetric. For each half-triangle, the expected value is one third of the way from the peak to the base. For an isosceles triangle, the mean absolute deviation is therefore one third of the base of each half-triangle or one sixth of the base. To contrast this with a sideline strategy, even if our colleague across the net is trying to hit toward us, the expected distance we'll need to shuffle is one third of the length of the baseline. By moving to the center, the expected distance we'll need to shuffle (i.e., the penalty cost) will only be half as large, namely one sixth.

Linear Growth

We've looked at uniform, normal, and triangular demand distributions, but suppose we are fortunate in that our customer demand growth is steady, that is, demand is linear, of the form $ax + b$. If the growth is definitely steady and we can ratchet up capacity, we are in good shape. If we are running a rental car service and the first day of operation we have one customer, the second day of operation we have two, and so on, we just need to buy cars at a rate of one per day, and we will have perfect capacity. Even if it takes a month to order and receive a car, it's no problem if we can forecast accurately; we just order cars one month ahead of time, and we still have perfect capacity.

If, however, we are more conservative, there is a problem. Suppose we don't really trust our forecast, and we wait until there is proof of demand before increasing capacity. Then, there is a direct relationship between the time it takes to acquire a car—that is, to provision capacity—and the penalty we will pay for insufficient capacity. If we are always one day behind, we will always be one car short. If we are always two days behind, we will always be two cars short. If we are always n days behind, we will always be n cars short.

As shown in Exhibit 14.2, since we are always short, we always pay a penalty proportional to c_d. Consequently, the total penalty is proportional to the length of the delay, the size of the penalty, and the duration for which we pay the penalty:

$$Penalty = n \times c_d \times T$$

Note that this delay can be based on two drivers: recognition and response. If we recognize that demand has increased immediately, but it

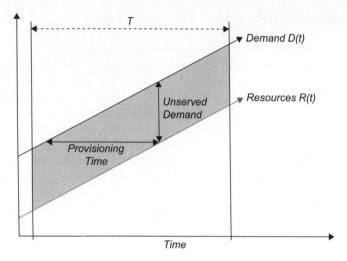

EXHIBIT 14.2 Linear Demand Growth with Constant Resourcing Delay

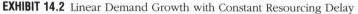

takes three days to respond, this is not any different from a situation where it takes us three days to recognize the change and we can respond immediately or if it takes one day and two days for each function, respectively.

In the case of linear growth, where we either don't attempt to anticipate and forecast this growth or maintain a conservative capacity provisioning or allocation strategy, the bottom line is that the size of the penalty is exactly proportional to the size of the delay.

In the reverse case—where demand is declining linearly—the same conclusion holds: The size of the penalty is linearly proportional to the size of the delay. Here, though, of course, the constant of proportionality reflects c_r rather than c_d, and instead of the processes reflecting activities such as ordering, installation, and turn-up or, in an allocation environment, virtual provisioning, they reflect asset disposal or deprovisioning.

Exponential Growth

Suppose instead of a linear growth environment there is exponential growth, as many hot start-ups and even some companies that are no longer quite start-ups seem to have. At first glance, the situation—as illustrated in Exhibit 14.3—seems identical to the linear growth case; after all, the curves are following each other.

However, there is something very different going on. The horizontal distance stays the same—at any "altitude," the demand curve and the resource curve are separated by the same horizontal distance. But, over

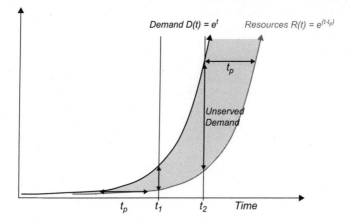

EXHIBIT 14.3 Exponential Demand Growth with Constant Resourcing Delay

time, as we move farther to the right, the vertical drop increases. In other words, rather than always being one server or one car short or two cars short, we start off one car short then we are a few cars short then we are dozens and then thousands and then millions. The difference over time, rather than being constant, is *exponential*.

When the demand function is exponential—that is, $D(t) = e^t$—any fixed provisioning interval for deploying resources in accordance with the current demand level (i.e., there is no forecasting) will fall exponentially farther behind. This is easy to show. Let the fixed provisioning interval be p. Then, in chasing the demand function $D(t)$, we set resources $R(t) = e^{t-p}$. Thus, the difference between the two is:

$$D(t) - R(t) = e^t - e^{t-p} = e^t(1 - e^{-p}) = ke^t,$$

where $k = 1 - e^{-p}$ and thus the penalty cost is $c_d \times ke^t$. In other words, unlike the earlier case where the penalty function grows linearly, the penalty function grows exponentially over time. Referring to Exhibit 14.3, it is clear that the vertical gap at time t_2 is much greater than that at t_1.

This type of growth is a particularly strong argument for using the cloud. Even if you have virtual server, storage, or network provisioning under control, soon the gap grows large enough that you need to speed up physical provisioning. Once you have physical provisioning under control, soon you have to accelerate data center siting and construction, a challenging task. This is not a theoretical issue but a real one.

According to Adrian Cockcroft, cloud architect at Netflix and one of the driving forces behind the company's move to the public cloud, "We've stopped building our own data centers. We couldn't predict where

we were going to be" in terms of demand volume when they were completed.[8]
As *InformationWeek* editor-at-large Charles Babcock commented, Netflix
decided to move to a public cloud "because it saw its growth accelerating so
rapidly that it faced a staggering task in building data centers to keep up."[9]

The reverse scenario has different characteristics. When the decline—
instead of the growth—is exponential (i.e., $D(t) = e^{-t}$), the biggest losses are
at the beginning. Literally, in the thermodynamics of the physical world and
figuratively in business, this is what happens as a hot thing cools off:
The level of decrease is proportional to the difference from the baseline.
As demand drops precipitously, you just can't shed capacity fast enough.
The good news is that the absolute level of decline slows as the exponential
decay flattens. The bad news is that when such a business catastrophe
occurs—due to shifting customer preferences, macroeconomic discontinuities, or competitor moves—there is a triple whammy: You have lost a
large portion of your revenue as customer demand has fallen off of a cliff;
and you can't shed cost structure fast enough; *and* you now need to invest in
a response: new products, new features, new marketing. In such cases, you
may go out of business before you can enjoy the leveling off of the decline.

Here's a case where human behavior gets in the way of sound risk
management. Youngsters don't ponder their own mortality, and start-ups
in their growth phase don't ponder the eventual slowing of growth or the
inevitable new entrants. Interestingly, many start-ups today are doing
the right thing without necessarily consciously realizing it: By avoiding
physical infrastructure from day 1 so as to maximize cash flow and con-
centrate management attention on areas core to their business, they are also
saving themselves potential headaches down the road.

Random Walks

Rather than the simplicity of flat demand or linear growth or the monoto-
nicity of exponential growth, often demand variation is more like the stock
market. Up a little, flat, up a little more, down a little, up a lot, flat again, . . .
In the same way that stocks fluctuate as buyers and sellers enter and leave the
market, the aggregate level of demand for some applications can be modeled
as users arriving at a site, engaging in some activity—say, searching or
shopping—and then moving on to do something else.

Albert Einstein is known for the theory of relativity. But in 1905, he not
only developed the special theory of relativity, explained the photoelectric
effect, and equated matter with energy, he also managed to explain Brownian
motion, first observed by Scottish botanist Robert Brown, where particles
suspended in the air or a liquid tend to bounce about. One of the key things

that Einstein showed was that the "displacement" of a particle (i.e., how far it moved) was proportional to the square root of the elapsed time.

In Brownian motion, a particle can be jostled in any direction. In a one-dimensional random walk, picture a particle that can move either left or right. In some variations, the particle can move exactly one step either way; in others there is some distribution of potential distances, say, uniform, or perhaps normal.

In general, though, here's what happens. It is certainly possible that a particle moves to the left continuously, say, L—L—L—L—L—L . . . It is also possible that it moves to the right continuously, say, R—R—R—R—R—R. However, these sequences become increasingly unlikely. The chance that the first move is to the left is 1/2. The chance that the first two moves are *both* to the left is 1/4. The chance that the first three moves are *all* to the left is 1/8, so on. It is much more likely that there are some moves to the left and some to the right, and they cancel each other out to some extent.

Exhibit 14.4 shows some sample simulation runs. Not surprisingly, the exhibit looks like the effluent from a smokestack in a breeze. This is not a coincidence. The breeze causes the particles to "age" in time from left to right. Although Brownian motion would normally create a spherical cloud about the smokestack, in the breeze, the speed of the wind outweighs the Brownian motion, and thus the particles' vertical position more or less reflects a random walk in two dimensions that is then perceived in one (from the side).

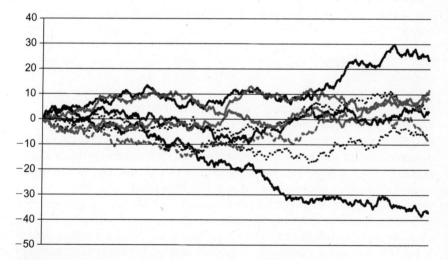

EXHIBIT 14.4 Monte Carlo Simulation of Random Walks over Time

As Albert Einstein surmised, after a sequence of n steps, a random walk can be expected to have a translation distance proportional to $\sqrt{n}$. Specifically, when the step size follows a random distribution with standard deviation σ, the translation distance asymptotically approaches $\sqrt{\frac{2}{\pi}}\sigma\sqrt{n}$.

The sublinear relationship between expected translation and number of steps implies that when there is a process where the value is a random plus or minus delta from the prior interval, as we've discussed, there is a moderate benefit from time compression. Specifically, reducing process intervals by a factor of n results in loss being reduced to a level of $1/\sqrt{n}$ of its prior value. Thus, a twofold reduction in cost requires a fourfold reduction in time. Or to put it the other way, achieving a fourfold reduction in provisioning time doesn't give us a fourfold reduction in the penalty cost, only a twofold reduction. We could view this as a slightly disappointing return on investment in process improvement or view it as strong support for the importance of on-demand resourcing.

Variable Penalty Functions

We have kept things simple by assuming that the opportunity cost of a missed customer stays constant, regardless of the number of customers whose demand is ignored, and that the cost of resources is the same, regardless of how many aren't used.

If only the real world were that simple, but of course it's not. If there's one customer who can't get through to your Web site or one employee who can't get online to your internal application, it may be their problem. If there are 10 or 100, it's a serious problem, and if there are 10,000, it's a public relations nightmare. Conversely, being a little over on capacity is inefficient, but being a lot over can cause the corporation to miss earnings targets, the stock to plummet, a takeover to ensue, and regrets to arise that we hadn't studied the equations just presented more carefully.

There are also other ways to consider what happens when there is excess demand. Rather than a penalty function based on the excess and the assumption that the unserved demand is lost, the unserved demand can be delayed until later. This delay has a cost to the customer that is application dependent. Moreover, the cost in this case is related to the delay, but the delay is related to the quantity of overage *and* the subsequent demand. If demand levels immediately following the overage are high, the delay may be pushed out for a long time: This is the three-hour wait for a dinner table at a popular restaurant. However, if the demand immediately following the excess demand is lower than the available capacity, the queued demand can be served relatively quickly.

There are many ways to model variable penalties, but the simplest one is to assume that the degree of penalty is proportional to the error. In other words, rather than c_d being a constant, we would have $C_d(x) = kx$, a linear function in the degree of the error. We could also use a monotonically nondecreasing sigmoid (S-shaped) curve: Not much penalty for being a little bit off, but an increasing penalty for being somewhat off that then flattens out.

This type of analysis can be expanded, as researchers Sadeka Islam, Kevin Lee, Alan Fekete, and Anna Liu have, by considering only provisioning delays that exceed a threshold, considering differences between quantities allocated and quantities billed, or considering nonlinear penalty costs.[10] As they point out, charging for cloud services often begins the instant they are requested, even if there is a delay in actual resource availability; conversely, when resource use is terminated, the resources may continue to incur charges until a minimum increment is reached. This finding matches everyday experience: Leaving a hotel room hours before checkout time does not typically entitle you to a refund.

Summary

Forecasting can work—in some industries better than others—at least until a black swan flies into town. However, rather than attempting to forecast, it's easier to exploit the benefits of on-demand capacity. A true cloud—which among other things entails a service provider offering on-demand capacity to customers—thus can achieve real business value by minimizing the penalty cost due to the wrong capacity to zero.

Although the analysis in this chapter has been somewhat abstract, the business benefits are real. Using on-demand capacity—that is, elasticity—to meet unpredictable, accelerated growth is one of the main benefits of the cloud, found in examples literally from A to Z: Consider Facebook application company Animoto, which scaled from 50 instances to 3,500 instances in less than three days, on an exponential trajectory.[11] Zynga grew from zero to 42 million users in 30 days with its Empires & Allies game by leveraging public cloud elasticity.[12]

🖳 **ONLINE**

"Random Walks," at http://complexmodels.com/Brownian.aspx, illustrates the evolution of systems driven by processes such as Brownian motion and random walks.

Notes

1. Joe Weinman, "Time is Money: The Value of 'On-Demand,'" January 7, 2011. http://joeweinman.com/Resources/Joe_Weinman_Time_Is_Money.pdf.
2. Note: This is a slight oversimplification due to the computational complexity of bin packing.
3. Sunil Mithas, Ali Tafti, Indranil Bardhan, and Jie Mein Goh, "Information Technology and Firm Profitability: Mechanisms and Empirical Evidence," *MIS Quarterly*, Vol. 36, No. 1, p. 214.
4. Ibid., p. 215–216; Sunil Mithas, conversation with the author, April 16, 2012.
5. Jay Forrester, "Industrial Dynamics: A Major Breakthrough for Decision Makers," *Harvard Business Review* (July–August 1958), pp. 37–66.
6. George Stalk Jr., and Thomas M. Hout, *Competing against Time: How Time-Based Competition Is Reshaping Global Markets* (Free Press, 2003), p. 64.
7. Brad Barber, Terrance Odean, "Trading Is Hazardous to Your Wealth: The Common Stock Investment Performance of Individual Investors," *Journal of Finance* 55 (2000): 773–806.
8. Charles Babcock, "Netflix Finds Home In Amazon EC2," *InformationWeek*, March 8, 2011. www.informationweek.com/news/cloud-computing/infrastructure/229300547.
9. Ibid.
10. Sadeka Islam, Kevin Lee, Alan Fekete, and Anna Liu, "How a Consumer Can Measure Elasticity for Cloud Platforms," University of Sydney, School of Information Technologies Technical Report 680 August 2011.
11. Jason Hsiao, "Amazon.com CEO Jeff Bezos on Animoto," April 21, 2008. http://animoto.com/blog/company/amazon-com-ceo-jeff-bezos-on-animoto/.
12. Charles Babcock, "Zynga's Unusual Cloud Strategy Is Key to Success," *InformationWeek*, July 1, 2011.www.informationweek.com/news/cloud-computing/infrastructure/231000908.

CHAPTER 15

Peak Performance

One reason that financial advisors recommend diversification is that while a single stock may be a dog or a single industry may have issues, it is less likely that all the stocks in your portfolio will simultaneously collapse if you have diversified across companies and across industry sectors. Of course, the same effect works in reverse: You may have been better off solely holding Apple, or Google, or Microsoft during certain periods than a basket of stocks. In other words, diversification drives higher lows but also lower highs. This smoothing effect has nothing to do with stocks per se; it is a *mathematical* characteristic of the sum of independent random variables. Cloud service providers can use this statistical effect to generate a real, compelling, economic customer value proposition.

Of course, often the movements of individual stocks are highly correlated: It is a rare stock that can swim upstream during a market crash, and, often, a rising tide lifts all boats, even if some of the boats are dogs, to use an awful mixed metaphor. Demand for computer services has similar characteristics. There is *some* degree of correlation: Increasing Internet access via increased broadband wireline and wireless penetration across a growing global population is certainly driving a healthy increase in Web usage, and the decreasing price of hardware, the increased availability of open source software, and advancing technology in areas ranging across search algorithms, voice recognition, semantic analysis, facial recognition, recommendation engines, and big data analytics implies a general increase in computing.

But once we get past these macroscopic aggregate trends, there are individual variations in the demand for specific services, such as payroll, tax preparation, and search queries, as we illustrated in Chapter 8. Whether we deal with each of these variations individually—as in owning a single stock—or in aggregate—as in owning a mutual fund or index fund—makes a big difference in financial results for cloud service providers and their customers.

Relationships between Demands

We can categorize four interesting relationships between two or more demand functions: (1) independent and uncorrelated, (2) negatively correlated, complementary, and/or countercyclical, (3) positively correlated, (4) generally uncorrelated but with simultaneous peaks. These relationships impact service provider Cloudonomics.

Independent

When demands are independent, aggregation creates a smoothing effect, in the same way that a diversified portfolio has a lower volatility than the most volatile stock in the portfolio. Aggregating the demand from increasing numbers of customers results in increased smoothing—sanding the jagged edges of volatility, as it were—that can be easily characterized, as we shall see.

Negatively Correlated

When demands are negatively correlated—either complementary or countercyclical—it only takes two or three demands to potentially create a relatively smooth aggregate demand. Winter ski resorts that turn into golf and tennis resorts in the summer maintain relatively high occupancy compared to those resorts that are just ski resorts. Such complementary demands may be achieved through luck or planning. Samuel Insull, for example, built and ran one of the first electric utilities, Chicago Edison, in the early 1900s. He strategically balanced the demands of the "traction" companies—streetcars and elevated railways—whose peak demand was during morning and evening rush hours, with offices and factories—whose peak demand was during the day—and residences—whose peak demand was evenings and early mornings.[1] In IT, demand for business applications, such as customer relationship management, is likely to be negatively correlated with demand for television entertainment. Exploiting Insull's strategy would suggest that both services be delivered out of the same pool of resources.

Positively Correlated

As demands are increasingly correlated, aggregation has less and less value. Cloud providers may still generate value through economies of skill, scope, and scale, as well as through uniquely cloud-centric use cases, as listed in Chapter 7. A good example of demands with high-positive correlation are the demands among retailers, e-tailers, and credit card payments and processing firms. In early November, people begin their holiday shopping, both in traditional bricks-and-mortar locations and at online sites. They ramp up their buying seriously around Thanksgiving, and this continues up until Christmas. The details vary, but the same general trend occurs with Amazon.com, Walmart.com, and Target.com: A disproportionately large fraction of a retailer's business occurs in the month before Christmas. It is also a safe bet that many of those purchases are conducted via credit card. Consequently, banks and credit card companies are likely to see their transaction volume rise and fall in tandem with retailers.

If independent, uncorrelated demand is akin to a diversified portfolio of stocks, the case of perfect correlation is more like buying additional shares of the same stock. There is no smoothing effect or volatility reduction.

Weakly Correlated, Simultaneous Peaks

Somewhere in the middle is the case of generally uncorrelated demand with one or more simultaneous peaks. Whether the service provider can generate real economic value ultimately depends on the approach to service-level agreement (SLA) payouts and the nature of the simultaneous peak: predictable or not. Consider the hypothetical case of a cloud service provider that targets only tax preparation firms and online florists. The two businesses would appear to have independent demand functions; after all, they have nothing to do with each other.

As it happens, however, the three main times of the year when people buy flowers are the winter holidays, Valentine's Day, and Mother's Day. As we've mentioned, the two main peaks for tax preparers are the early filers and the late filers. Companies mail out annual financial statements beginning in January, so the early filers—expecting a refund or else wanting to get the pain over as quickly as possible—end up generally filing in early to mid-February. As a result, although not on exactly the same day, the peak for Valentine's Day flowers predictably aligns with the peak for early tax filers.

However, a celebrity death that drives traffic to news sites or microblogging social networks is unpredictable and may or may not correspond to a peak in, say, a weather site, due to a blizzard or hurricane. Such a simultaneous peak is unpredictable.

If a service provider adopted the approach of building sufficient capacity to meet peaks, then its utilization would be no better than the weighted average constituent utilization of those workloads if handled by the individual enterprises themselves. To put it another way, no economic value short of potential net economies of scale would be created.

If, however, the service provider underbuilds capacity but pays out on SLA misses due to insufficient capacity, it may be able to generate value through statistical multiplexing to a sufficient extent that it overcomes the value destroyed by the SLA payout and the negative impact to the customer—and thus itself—from lack of available capacity. Of course, customers generally don't want payouts for SLA violations; they want reliable services on which to build their businesses. And although knowingly having insufficient capacity to meet predictable simultaneous peaks perhaps is legal and even sound engineering, its ethics are questionable. But not much can be done about unpredictable simultaneous peaks. Customers generally don't want to pay for "perfect" protection from simultaneous peaks, any more than they want their state and local taxes increased to enable protection from not just the 100-year flood but the 1,000-year or even 10,000-year flood. A number of cognitive biases cause this, including the neglect of probabilities—an inability for humans to correctly calculate risks intuitively—and hyperbolic discounting—which weights current costs and benefits more highly than ones in the distant future. We tend to choose an immediate, certain benefit over a potential future one.

Size, Diversity, Capacity

All of these factors become greater or lesser issues based on the relative size of individual variation. Con Edison won't really care that both you and your neighbor happen to use your toasters at the same time. However, for even the largest cloud service providers, there are some companies that use a substantial fraction of their total capacity and whose use of that capacity is the service provider's lifeblood. So the question becomes: How many customers with what types of variation in relative demand of what size relative to overall capacity does a service provider need to acquire to have a sound business?

Lessons from Rolling Dice

Before we delve into some statistics, we explore what happens when rolling dice, as in the game of craps. What happens in Vegas . . . can form the basis of a deeper understanding of statistical phenomena. Let's consider how the likelihood of a given total shifts as the number of dice increase.

If we roll *exactly one* six-sided die, the number of permutations, and thus expected relative frequency of outcomes, is equal, as shown in Exhibit 15.1. There is exactly one way to roll a total of 1, which is by rolling a "1." There is exactly one way to roll a total of 2, which is by rolling a "2," and so on. The distribution of outcomes is flat: A high result is just as likely as a low one. Each outcome has a theoretical probability of 1/6.

If we play craps and roll *two* six-sided dice, the relative frequency of outcomes follows a triangular distribution (see Exhibit 15.2). As is well known, 7 is the most likely total, with a 1 in 6 chance of happening (6 ways

ROLL

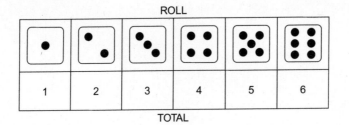

TOTAL

EXHIBIT 15.1 Outcomes from Rolling One Die

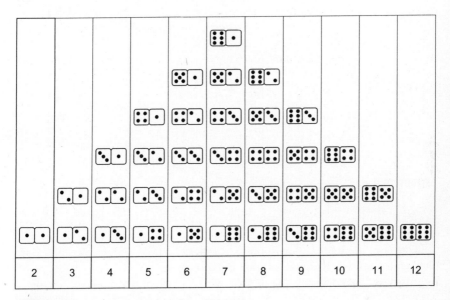

EXHIBIT 15.2 Outcomes from Rolling Two Dice

out of 36 combinations), and snake eyes—2—and boxcars—12—have only a 1 in 36 chance.

Now it gets interesting. Exhibit 15.3 shows the possible outcomes of rolling three six-sided dice. There is only one way to make a total of 3 ("1," "1," and "1") and only one way to make a total of 18 ("6," "6," and "6"). However, there are plenty of ways—27, in fact—to make a total of either 10 or 11.

As we roll an increasing number of dice, the distribution of permutations shifts from flat to triangular to bell-shaped.[2] As we roll more and more dice, the proportion of outcomes that is in the middle increases. If we scaled the results so that the minimum and maximum were aligned, we'd see the

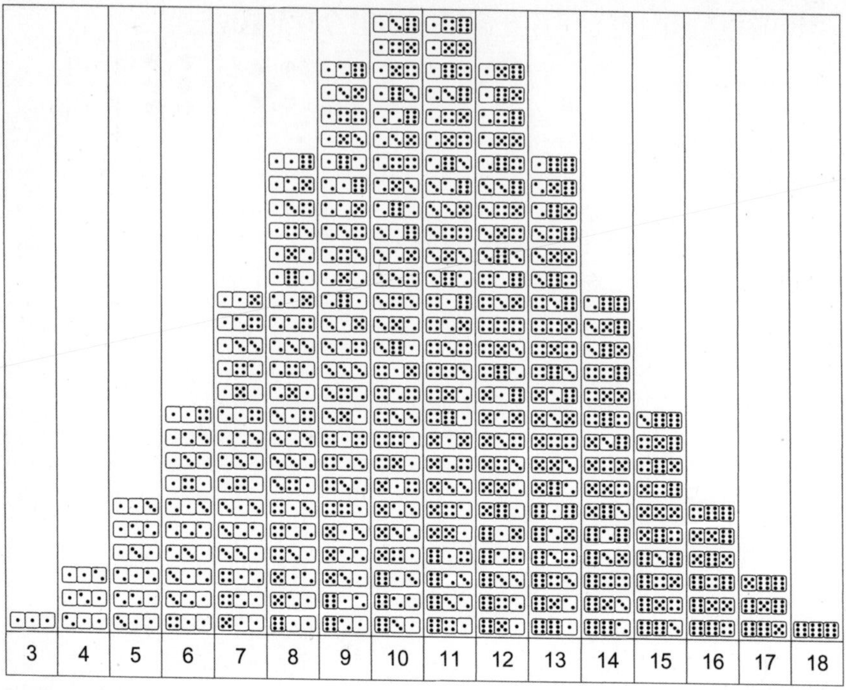

EXHIBIT 15.3 Outcomes from Rolling Three Dice

normal distribution being squished, to use a highly technical term—becoming narrower and taller. In short, as we increase the number of dice rolled, there are increasingly more ways to make the central outcomes than the outliers as a percentage of total outcomes.

Another way to state this is that with lots of dice rolled, the chances are very good that there will be some high numbers and some low numbers and they will cancel each other out, leaving a total somewhere in the middle.

Similarly, in the cloud computing context, when we "roll the dice" on levels of *independent* customer demand, at any given time the chances are that there will be some customers with heavy usage—the sixes—and some with light usage—the ones—and that they will balance each other out. As the number of customers with independent demand increases, the relative likelihood decreases that they *all* are at minimum or that they *all* are at maximum at the same time.

For a service provider, this is great news. It implies lower aggregate capacity requirements, lower payouts on SLA violations, or both. Regardless of whether there are *any* economies of scale, this effect—the statistics of scale—generates real value.

Coefficient of Variation and Other Statistics

Whenever a mathematical function varies over time, there are a number of useful measures—or statistics—of interest. They may not tell *everything* there is to know about the function, but they can tell us some useful things.

One useful statistic is the mean, or average value. For a discrete series, the mean is the sum of the values divided by the number of terms. For a continuous function, the mean is the integral of the function divided by the length of the interval.

However, this doesn't tell us how variable or flat the function is. For example, the set of values 100, 100, 100, 100, 100, 100 has the same mean as this set: 0, 200, −1000, 1200, 150, 50. Consequently, statisticians use metrics such as variance and standard deviation to describe variability.

However, standard deviation presents us with an issue. The series 0, 100, 0, 100, 0, 100 has the same standard deviation and variance as the series 1000, 1100, 1000, 1100, 1000, 1100. This may not seem like a big deal, but when we are considering real-world metrics, such as data center utilization, it represents a huge difference. Suppose that the values in the series represent the equivalent demand for servers over time. In the first case, if we build to peak and deploy 100 servers, we will only achieve 50% utilization (since the mean is 50 and the total number of servers deployed is 100). This 50% utilization means that, on average, for every server we have productively employed, there is one that we paid for that is not generating any value. In the second case, if we build to peak and deploy 1,100 servers, since the mean demand is 1,050, we will achieve a utilization rate of over 95%: world class by any measure.

This tells us two things. The first is that the utilization of owned, dedicated resources has something to do with how well the data center is run and the quality of the capacity management process. After all, if we had deployed 2,100 servers, we still would be getting only 50% utilization. However, once we are managing our data center properly, the utilization that we will achieve is a function of the nature of our demand. A retailer with high workload variance shouldn't beat itself up if it has low utilization. And, of course, the cloud offers a way out of this dilemma: a way for customers to achieve 100% utilization by only using on-demand resources and a way for service providers to come close to that through demand aggregation.

The second thing it tells us is that standard deviation or variance is insufficient to tell us much about what kind of utilization we can expect and is therefore insufficient to characterize the benefits due to aggregating demand and serving it out of common, pooled resources.

Consequently, a key metric that we will use is called the *coefficient of variation*.[3] It is the ratio of the standard deviation (which is always positive) to the absolute value of the mean. This measure has its own problems (e.g., it is unhelpful if the mean is zero), but it is very helpful to characterize customer demand variation. In the cases we will be looking at, we consider only demand that is positive. It won't be negative (a customer won't want -3 virtual servers or -5 gigabytes of storage). Since the values won't be negative, and we aren't interested in customers whose demand is always zero, we know that any customer's demand is always nonnegative and not always zero; therefore, the mean must be positive.

If the standard deviation is small relative to the mean, we have a relatively smooth or flat function. If the standard deviation is large relative to the mean, we have a relatively variable function.

These are generalities: Functions that are "flat" everywhere except for a single enormous spike of nontrivially short duration may be "generally flat," yet have a large standard deviation and thus a large coefficient of variation. If, however, that spike is instantaneous but drives a build to peak strategy, we will have a low coefficient of variation yet very low utilization. We can draw only general conclusions about utilization, but we are going to assume that the functions are not overly pathological (e.g., 1 server needed for 3 years, except for a nanosecond where 7 trillion servers are required).

Consequently, we use the coefficient of variation as a measure of how good or bad the environment is. The lower the coefficient of variation, c_v, is, the lower the relative variability and therefore the better our utilization is likely to be.

Statistical Effects in Independent Demand Aggregation

Suppose that we are a service provider with m customers, which conveniently are named 1,2,3, ... m.[4] Let's also suppose that we can characterize each of their demands over time as $D_1(t)$, $D_2(t)$, $D_3(t)$, ... $D_m(t)$. To illustrate the smoothing effect of statistical multiplexing, suppose that these demands are independent and uncorrelated; in other words, knowing that one customer has a given demand at a given time is of no help in determining what the demands of any of the other customers are at that time. Moreover, to keep things simple, let's assume that the demands have identical variances (and thus standard deviations) and identical means. Note that the underlying distributions don't need to be the same—one can be a triangular, one can be normal, one can be uniform, one can be exponential; all we are looking for is the same mean and standard deviation.

Under those circumstances, since the standard deviations and means of each customers demand function are identical, the coefficient of variation of each function is identical.

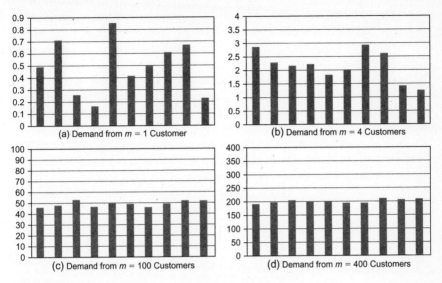

EXHIBIT 15.4 Smoothing Due to Demand Aggregation

What is the aggregate variation if we multiplex the m demands into a shared resource pool offered by a service provider?

To solve this, we note that the standard deviation of each customer's demand function is identical, say, σ, where $\sigma = \sigma(D_i(t))$. Similarly, the mean of each customer's demand function is identical, say, μ, where $\mu = \mu(D_i(t))$. Therefore, the coefficient of variation of any demand function is the standard deviation over the mean, that is, $c_v = \sigma/\mu$, which of course means that $c_v = \sigma(D_i(t))/\mu(D_i(t))$.

Let the aggregate demand be represented by $D^+(t)$, which is the sum of the demands as a function of time. Of course, $D^+(t) = D_1(t) + D_2(t) + \cdots + D_m(t)$. To visualize this, consider Exhibit 15.4. It illustrates samples from a single uniformly distributed demand (Exhibit 15.4(a)), 4 aggregated such demands (Exhibit 15.4(b)), 100 aggregated demands (Exhibit 15.4(c)), and 400 aggregated demands (Exhibit 15.4(d)).

What is c_v^+ the coefficient of variation of the aggregate demand? If it is the same as c_v we haven't realized any gain; if it is higher, demand aggregation would be a bad idea; and if it is lower, demand aggregation results in smoothing and thus utilization improvements and therefore favorable economics.

To answer this question, we need to know two things that apply to *any* independent random variables $X_1, X_2, X_3, \ldots X_m$. One is that the mean of the sum is the sum of the means—that is, $\mu(X_1 + X_2 + X_3 + \cdots X_m) = \mu(X_1) + \mu(X_2) + \mu(X_3) + \cdots \mu(X_m)$. The other is that the variance of the sum is the sum of the variances—that is, $\sigma^2(X_1 + X_2 + X_3 + \cdots X_m) = \sigma^2(X_1) + \sigma^2(X_2) + \sigma^2(X_3) + \ldots \sigma^2(X_m)$. The last thing we need to remember is that the standard deviation is the positive square root of the variance. With this in mind, we can see that the mean of the aggregate demand is just the sum of the means of the individual demands and, therefore, $\mu(D^+(t)) = m \times \mu$. Similarly, the variance of the aggregate demand is just the sum of the individual demand variances and, therefore, $\sigma^2(D^+(t)) = m \times \sigma^2$. These equations may be annoying, but all we are saying is that for the case of mean and variance, as long as the random variables (i.e., demands) are independent, the whole is just the sum of the parts.

Now, here's where something very interesting happens. Recall that the coefficient of variation is the standard deviation divided by the mean and that the standard deviation is the positive square root of the variance. To figure out the coefficient of variation c_v^+ of the aggregated demand, we know that $c_v^+ = \sigma(D^+(t))/\mu(D^+(t))$. For the numerator, $\sigma(D^+(t)) = \sqrt{\sigma^2(D^+(t))}$, which is just $\sqrt{m \times \sigma^2(D(t))} = \sqrt{m} \times \sqrt{\sigma^2(D(t))} = \sqrt{m} \times \sigma$. The denominator $\mu(D^+(t))$ is just equal to $m \times \mu$. As a result, $c_v^+ = \frac{\sqrt{m} \times \sigma}{m \times \mu}$, which is $\frac{\sqrt{m}}{m} \times \frac{\sigma}{\mu}$. This clearly equals $\frac{1}{\sqrt{m}} \times c_v$.

Such an analysis may seem somewhat abstract, but it explains an interesting phenomenon that is easy to understand: In the same way that the relative height increases and the bell curve becomes relatively narrower as we look at outcomes from rolling increasing numbers of dice, the variation in aggregate demand becomes narrower as well.

Significance of $1/\sqrt{m}$

For independent demands with the same mean and variance, the inverse square root $1/\sqrt{m}$ has implications on IT strategy and ecosystem evolution. As we've discussed, there may or may not be compelling economies of scale in the cloud. If there are no compelling economies of scale—that is, unit cost reduction in production or service operations—there still may be economies associated with the statistics of scale. If, as we've seen, the penalty costs associated with under- and overcapacity can be reduced merely through the expedient of demand aggregation and resource pooling, then bigger is better, assuming that bigger means more diverse.

However, this benefit has diminishing returns. Exhibit 15.5 shows the relative penalty cost of incorrect capacity compared to a single, unaggregated demand. As can be seen, the penalty is reduced by 30%, merely by going from one workload to two. It can be reduced to only 50% of the single-demand level by aggregating demands from four sources, since $50\% = .5 = 1/\sqrt{4}$. If we want to aggregate demands to get a 75% reduction, we need 16 sources, since a 75% reduction equals a remaining $25\% = .25 = 1/\sqrt{16}$.

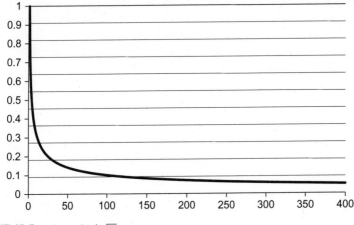

EXHIBIT 15.5 Value of $1/\sqrt{m}$

What this curve shows is that in a company with just two independent workloads, a 30% savings (in the relative penalty cost) can be realized by the use of a "private cloud." Since terminology is often ambiguous in the cloud market, what I mean by "private cloud" is the use of technologies that enable dynamic elasticity, which may include virtualization. Virtualization—such as that provided by VMware vSphere, Citrix XenServer, Microsoft Hyper-V, and the open source KVM—drives several important economic benefits: One by letting two workloads, even ones of constant size, use less space via mere *sharing*—as when two roommates share an apartment; and a second one by enabling dynamic allocation of fixed resources between the workloads, enabling these aggregation benefits. Another, more subtle one, is the ability to migrate workload.

It also means that a large, diversified company can gain substantial savings through private clouds, where the IT shop acts as an internal service provider aggregating these demands to achieve a benefit through statistical multiplexing. The key word in the last sentence is *diversified*, either statistically independent businesses or customers with diverse demands: An enormous company by any measure—revenues, locations, personnel, IT budget—still may be in a single sector, say, retail. Then, from the perspective of demand variation, the size won't help much. It also means that a small company that just isn't large enough to be diversified may have difficulty achieving these gains.

In terms of service provider advantage, this logic also argues that mid-size service providers have an excellent shot at being competitive against the behemoths. The reason is that with 100 customers, the diversification leads to a penalty cost reduction to $1/\sqrt{100}$, or 10%, and one with 400 customers gets to 5%. Put differently, a midsize provider with a few hundred customers gets to within a few percentage points of the theoretical best possible capacity penalty cost of zero, or $1/\sqrt{\infty}$, that, hypothetically, an infinitely large provider with an infinite number of customers with diverse demands could theoretically achieve.

Issues with Perfectly Correlated Demand

We have examined the beneficial effect in aggregating independent demands. But what if the demand is correlated—in fact, what if it is *perfectly* correlated? Rather than the normalized compression toward the center, the distribution would remain proportionally similar.

What happens to the coefficient of variation metric? Let a demand curve $D(t)$ have $\sigma = \sigma(D(t))$ and $\mu = \mu(D(t))$. Therefore, the coefficient of variation of this demand function is $c_v = \sigma/\mu$. However, since $D^+(t) = D_1(t) + D_2(t) + \ldots + D_m(t)$, now $D^+(t) = m \times D(t)$. The mean is $\mu(D^+(t)) = m \times \mu(D(t))$. However, the variance $\sigma^2(c \times X)$ of a constant times a random variable is the square of the constant times the variance of the random variable: $\sigma^2(c \times X) = c^2 \times \sigma^2(X)$. Therefore, $\sigma^2(D^+(t)) = \sigma^2(m \times D(t)) = m^2 \times \sigma^2(D(t))$ and the standard deviation is $\sigma(D^+(t)) = m \times \sigma(D(t))$. Rather than the $\sqrt{m}$ factor that we discovered earlier, the new coefficient of variation is $c_v^+ = \frac{m \times \sigma}{m \times \mu} = \frac{\sigma}{\mu} = c_v$. In other words, there is *no change to the coefficient of variation*. Put another way, there is no smoothing effect through aggregation.

In most cases, there is likely to be a mix of correlated demand and independent demand, so the penalty cost reduction benefit of demand aggregation will be somewhere between none and the reduction to $1/\sqrt{m}$.

Community Clouds

For the case of perfectly correlated demand, there is no *statistical* benefit to aggregating demand and serving it out of pooled resources. If there *are* any economies of scale, *and* they are significant enough to overcome the diseconomies of scale *and* cost structure disadvantages to result in a delivered price advantage versus do-it-yourself, *then* there *would* be benefits to aggregating demand to exploit these economies. If the customers are all interconnected in some way, there also might be benefits to colocating them—for example, reducing the distance and delay associated with data sharing and application interconnection. But there is little *statistical* benefit to aggregating customers with highly correlated demand, unlike the situation with independent demand.

A concept often discussed among cloud strategists is so-called community clouds. There are two ways to interpret this notion. One is that the community might involve a business Web or virtual network of collaborating organizations—for example, physicians, hospitals, health insurance firms, diagnosticians, and pharmacies. Another example might be consumer packaged goods manufacturers, transportation companies such as trucking and shipping firms, customs clearinghouses, retailers, and credit card companies. At the software layer, this can make sense; for example, the medical network could provide secure access to electronic patient records including medical diagnostic images, that are HIPAA (Health Insurance Portability and Accountability Act) compliant or compliant with the medical privacy and records retention laws of other countries. The supply chain network could provide end-to-end optimization, offer chain-of-custody tracking, etc.

However, if the community cloud focused only on, say, retailers, the demand will be highly correlated and, thus, cost savings will be limited to scale economies, and won't reflect statistical economies. The way out of this dilemma is for a community cloud to be implemented as a virtual layer built on top of an infrastructure cloud with a more diverse set of customers. This is not unlike a mall, where rather than only aggregating Halloween costume stores that would be in use for a few weeks out of the year, the individual boutiques and stores that cater to various types of needs are a "virtual" layer built on top of the actual physical infrastructure of the mall.

In such a case, any unique compliance, performance, or security requirements at the vertical services layer may be inherited by the physical infrastructure enabling those services, potentially creating challenges as well.

Simultaneous Peaks

In the preceding discussion, we've assumed highly correlated demand. However, even when the demand is not highly correlated, there is a pathological case worth reviewing that has implications on both service provider economics and on customer agreements.

Consider two customers with varying demands $D_1(t)$ and $D_2(t)$ that are independent and uncorrelated: Their correlation coefficient is 0. Suppose, however, that for a single instant they simultaneously reach a peak. The correlation coefficient is still 0, but we now have a problem. If we are comparing a strategy of *absolute assurance of sufficient resources* via a build-to-peak strategy for each customer relative to a build-to-peak strategy for the aggregate demand for the service provider, there will be no net gain in utilization, and therefore no gain from statistical multiplexing. Although there still may be some net gain from economies of scale, as we've discussed, if the customers are both large enough to achieve substantial economies, there may not be enough of a further gain from consolidation to be either meaningful in and of itself or to overcome additional transaction costs, such as contracting for external services and the ongoing costs of service management and oversight.

This is a serious implication. If both customers *must guarantee* that sufficient resources are available *and* they have a simultaneous peak, *regardless* of what happens during 99.9999% of the time, that one instant can kill all the benefits of statistical multiplexing and common resource pooling. This is a further issue with a community cloud that services only one vertical: Retailers and e-tailers will share cyber Monday and tax preparation firms will share April 15.

There are two ways out of this dilemma. One is to have a sufficiently large and diverse base that, say, even if 10 or 50 customers have simultaneous peaks either due to predictable seasonal cycles or for completely random reasons, there are another 100 or 1,000 or 10,000 thousand customers to balance things out and generate favorable economics. However, a challenge with this strategy is that regardless of weekly, monthly, or seasonal cycles, there is one cycle that tends to correlate workloads from many verticals: the macroeconomic cycle. There are some countercyclical businesses—it's great to be a repo man during a recession—but most businesses are correlated: Growth in housing sales means growth in construction means growth in dishwasher and refrigerator sales and growth in disposable income so growth in scarves and bicycles and automobile purchases and so forth.

If there is a penalty for lack of availability, a service provider can achieve gains through statistical multiplexing *most* of the time and offset those gains with the occasional penalty. If the penalty for SLA violations is small enough relative to the gains through multiplexing, this is a good deal for everyone.

Peak of the Sum Is Never Greater than the Sum of the Peaks

When we aggregate demands $D_1(t)$, $D_2(t)$, and so on, the aggregate demand will never be *greater* than the sum of its individual components: We will never have a situation where 1 plus 1 equals 3. In the worst case, where there are simultaneous peaks, the peak or maximum value of the sum will equal the sum of the peak values of each of the individual demands. However, if that doesn't happen, the peak of the aggregate demand will be less than the sum of the peaks of the individual ones. In case this logic is a little tough to follow, let's consider a simple example.

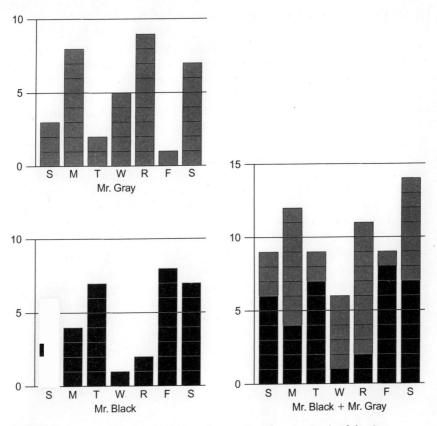

EXHIBIT 15.6 Sum of the Peaks Is Less than or Equal to the Peak of the Sum

As seen in Exhibit 15.6, Mr. Gray and Ms. Black have varying demands through the week.

For Mr. Gray, the peak occurs on Thursday, when he needs 9 resources. This leads to a peak demand for him of 9 and therefore a capacity requirement of 9. For Ms. Black, a peak occurs on Friday, when she needs 8 resources, leading to a capacity requirement of 8 resources for her. If we were to sum the demands via pooling resources and multiplexing resource requirements, we end up with the aggregate demand shown on the right of the exhibit. The peak of that aggregate demand is on Saturday, but the 14 resources required are less than the capacity of 17 resources—a max of 8 for Mr. Gray and a max of 9 for Ms. Black—that would otherwise be needed if the demand *wasn't* aggregated into pooled capacity. This is another way of looking at how much overhead is required in aggregated versus unaggregated scenarios.

Utilization Improvements

The larger a container is, the more difficult it would seem to be to fill it up. But between statistical multiplexing effects and dynamic pricing, utilization of consolidated environments can get very high. If the check-in lines in Vegas always seem crowded, perhaps that's because they are. The MGM Grand Hotel & Casino—still one of the largest hotels in the world—manages to nearly fill over 5,000 rooms on a daily basis, achieving an occupancy rate of 96.8% in a recent quarter.[5]

The impact of smoother demand is fundamental: improved utilization, which in turn leads to either higher profitability at the same price or maintained profitability at lower prices. Lower prices can mean higher share in markets with intense rivalry or the preservation of share as competitors lower their prices. If demand is smoother, there also can be few payouts or credits on SLAs at a given level of resourcing or less uncaptured revenue, which improves the bottom line directly and, by enhancing customer satisfaction, reduces churn and increases competitiveness.

Smoother demand increases utilization by reducing the quantity of unused capacity. As can be seen in Exhibit 15.7(a), when the demand is highly variable, utilization is low (the white space under the actual capacity

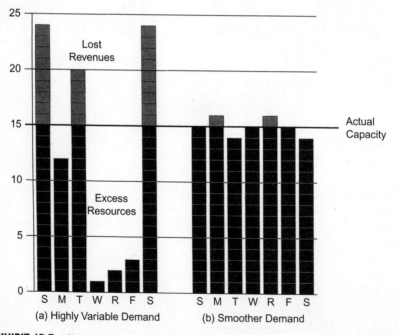

EXHIBIT 15.7 Effect of Demand Smoothing on Utilization

line) *and* lost revenues or SLA payouts are substantial. If the capacity is increased, say from 15 to 25, the SLA violations or lost revenues drop, but the utilization goes even lower. However, in Exhibit 15.7(b), it is clear that average utilization is extremely high without substantial SLA violations.

The economic impact can be substantial. Suppose a fruit seller bought five peaches for each one he sold, throwing the other four away. It means that the cost of each peach sold must account for the costs of the other four. Such a fruit seller either will not be competitive with the stand across the way, because prices will of necessity be higher, or else the other stand will be able to charge the same price but without the same unfortunate cost structure, reaping higher profits.

In the world of the cloud, unsold server hours and storage gigabyte-months are the unsold peaches. Paying customers must pay not only for their own resources but for the lost server-hours and storage-months that are tossed in the Dumpster. Consequently, demand aggregation, and the utilization benefits it creates, drives economic benefit to either the customer or the provider or both.

Summary

It can be challenging to deal with variable demand using your own capacity. By aggregating demand—as a service provider can do—benefits arise through smoothing, as long as the individual demands are uncorrelated. These smoothing benefits drive higher utilization and thus a lower cost per *delivered* resource. Consequently, even if a service provider doesn't have advantaged economics in terms of *unit* costs, benefits can be generated via lower aggregate capacity requirements.

This strategy will work as long as demands aren't correlated and don't have simultaneous peaks. If they do, the service provider will generate fewer or no benefits via demand aggregation but still may be able to generate benefits via economies of scale, less any additional provider cost structure elements.

🖳 ONLINE

"The Central Limit Theorem and Combinatorics," at http://complex-models.com/CentralLimit.aspx, "The Value of Aggregation in Variability Smoothing and Peak Reduction," at http://complexmodels.com/Aggregation.aspx, and "The Value of Resource Pooling and Load Sharing Across a Grid," at http://complexmodels.com/Grid.aspx, illustrate the benefits of demand aggregation: reduction in peak capacity needed as well as increased utilization.

Notes

1. Nicholas Carr, *The Big Switch: Rewiring the World, From Edison to Google* (W. W. Norton, 2008).
2. Thanks to Ben Black for first observing this.
3. Thanks to Chris Volinsky for suggesting this metric.
4. Joe Weinman, "Smooth Operator: The Value of Demand Aggregation," February 27, 2011. www.joeweinman.com/Resources/Joe_Weinman_Smooth_Operator_Demand_Aggregation.pdf.
5. Andrea Petersen, "How a Megahotel Tries to Seem Small; 20 Brides in a Weekend," *Wall Street Journal*, September 22, 2011. online.wsj.com/article/SB10001424053111903791504576584944173766266.html.

CHAPTER 16

Million-Dollar Microsecond

In August 2008, Michael Phelps swam into the history books, winning eight gold medals at the Beijing Olympics, an unsurpassed record. Immediately after, the endorsement value of such an accomplishment was estimated to be $100 million.[1] Each medal, of course, contributed to the total of eight, but his closest victory was the one in the 100-meter butterfly, which he won by 1/100 of a second—10 milliseconds—in a photo finish.[2]

In the world of trading—currencies, commodities, or equities—it isn't just milliseconds that matter, but microseconds and soon nanoseconds. The New York Stock Exchange (NYSE) Euronext's Nouveau Système de Cotation (New Quotation System) delivered performance of 1.5 milliseconds per round trip. But that wasn't good enough, so the exchange upgraded, developing the Universal Trading Platform, which can deliver up to ten times faster performance: 150 microseconds.[3] As NYSE Euronext chief information officer Steve Rubinow responded to a vendor pitch regarding submillisecond performance, "Do you mean 900 microseconds or 100 microseconds? Because that's a world of difference to us."[4] This is because of the "million-dollar microsecond,"[5] where increasing performance by 1 microsecond—1 one millionth of a second—is worth $1 million—every day. The concern around microseconds has "come up in pretty much every customer meeting I've had," claimed the CME Group's Craig Mohan, who is responsible for the colocation services of the Chicago Mercantile Exchange.[6]

Phelps only had to win a few races a year; traders have to win their financial races every day. By being the first to take advantage of fleeting opportunities, traders thus make millions each day, which turn into billions over time. Soon microseconds will seem meandering: nanoseconds are next.[7]

This escalating competition has been dubbed "the race to zero"[8]: an attempt to get as close as possible to the shortest possible time. Virtually all of the data transmission time budget is spent in physical propagation delays, with only 8% associated with the opto-electronics and characteristics of the optical waveform itself.[9] Consequently, the only choices are these:

- Move the user closer to the service.
- Move the service closer to the user.
- Shorten the route.
- Attempt to speed transport along a route (which ultimately is limited by the speed of light in a given medium).

Locating facilities close to optimized network routes to key services is an essential strategy in the race to zero in financial services and in other sectors. According to Eric Shepcaro, chief executive officer (CEO) of Telx, which provides cloud computing and colocation as well as network-neutral interconnections to dozens of carriers, customers are migrating to such facilities to minimize the latency that end users experience for interactive services regardless of their network service provider.[10]

Speed is significant not just in medaling and finance, but in the world of the Web and also in the workplace.

On Time

Robert Buzzell, of the Harvard Business School, and Bradley Gale, of the Strategic Planning Institute, created a comprehensive database—PIMS (Profit Impact of Market Strategies)—to conduct research into the performance of hundreds of companies and thousands of strategic business units in these firms and determined that "the most important single factor affecting a business unit's performance is the quality of its products and services, relative to those of competitors."[11] Superior quality correlated with higher prices and market share growth, in turn driving economies of scale leading to higher margins.

Quality, then, is good, but what is it? It can be aesthetics, brand, unique, distinctive materials, customer return on investment, emotional value, function, perceived quality, personal preference, practical value, price, responsiveness, service quality, technical quality, transaction value, trust, or who knows what. Frequently, however, it is tied to convenience, which in turn is related to time.

Paco Underhill, the CEO of Envirosell, a retail consultancy, argues that the "single most important factor in determining a shopper's opinion of the service he or she receives is waiting time . . . a short wait enhances the entire shopping experience and long one poisons it."[12] The impact of waiting time on service quality is not just of hypothetical academic interest: Americans alone spend tens of billions of hours waiting each year.[13] Making things worse, perceptions of waits can be overestimated, not by just by 10% or 20%, but by 600%.[14]

The human experience of time is, well, *complex*. There are two ways of spending time, *hedonic* and *utilitarian*. Hedonic time is that spent in an enjoyable activity, say, wine tasting or the movies; utilitarian time is less exciting: waiting in line at the department of motor vehicles (DMV) or the check-out lane. You might be willing to pay extra to shorten your wait at the DMV, you probably wouldn't appreciate a movie theater that offered to fast-forward you through the new two-hour-long Oscar contender in less than five minutes. Specifics vary by individual: To paraphrase a maxim, one man's hedonic time is another's utilitarian time.

For waiting customers, however, the *perception* of time is different from the actual *passage* of time. Underhill, who has consulted for Starbucks, claims that customers don't mind waiting in line for coffee for about 90 seconds; after that, the perceived wait increasingly exceeds the actual delay.[15]

Different people tend to perceive time differently, use time differently, and value time differently. For example, some people appear to be more poly-chronic, or what we now more typically call multitaskers.[16] Such people might listen to an iPod while watching television while putting on makeup while instant messaging friends while sorting through iTunes while surfing the Web while eating a snack. There is a theory that the apparent multitasking of the new generation represents a new mode of cognition, but Clifford Nass, a professor at Stanford University, claims that multitaskers are "suckers for irrelevancy" because "everything distracts them."[17] His research has found that multitasking results in poorer memory and cognition than a single-minded focus.

And the cognitive complexity of a task can interfere with or eliminate the perception of the passing of time. Mikhail Csikszentmihalyi, University of Chicago professor and former chair of its Department of Psychology, calls a unique, time-insensitive state that the mind can enter "flow." Flow is the state that we enter when doing a crossword puzzle, watching a movie, or listening intently to music. If the task is too easy, boredom sets in. If the task is too hard, frustration does. When it is somewhere in the middle, the mind happily engages and apparently allocates all available resources to the task, *including those that are responsible for tracking the passage of time*. Consequently, as Csikszentmihalyi says, "the sense of the duration of time is altered; hours pass by in minutes, and minutes can stretch out to seem like hours."[18]

Some people seem to be more aware of time and treat it as a scarce resource; others appear to be less concerned. This trait, referred to as *time consciousness*, differs among cultures as well as between people.[19] Some people are "time-buyers," who spend money to buy time; others are "time-sellers," who spend time to save money. The former are the people who pay a premium for convenience; the latter are those who spend afternoons clipping coupons. Convenience-focused time-buyers tend to be a more profitable segment for the businesses that serve them, since saving money is not their primary goal; time-sellers tend to be more problematic, since these customers vanish whenever there is a better deal. Author and Olympic contender Vince Poscente argues that we have entered the Age of Speed, observing that inflation-adjusted incomes have tripled in the last half-century, but life expectancy has only increased 10 percent; consequently, each minute of our life has become substantially more valuable.[20]

So convenience is generally good, but turns out to be a multi-faceted concept. Boston College professor Kathleen Seiders and her colleagues have proposed that there are five main areas where convenience plays a role in the overall service relationship.[21] Some of these attributes of convenience apply to the cloud.

1. *Decision* convenience—how easily someone can acquire information to make a decision. Sites that aggregate information and clearly compare alternatives help.
2. *Access* convenience—24/7, location-independent, easy availability. ATMs and 7-Elevens accomplish this in the real world; high-availability, globally dispersed services accessible from a multitude of mobile devices do so in cyberspace.
3. *Benefit* convenience—being able to drop 10 pounds while eating chocolate is a more convenient way to realize the benefit of getting in shape than doing an excruciating six-hour workout every day for a year.
4. *Transaction* convenience—a mouse click is easier than filling out reams of forms in triplicate; surfing is easier than driving to the big box retailer.
5. *Postbenefit* convenience—how easy are returns and exchanges?

Seiders and colleagues' research was originally applied to the offline world, but its extensibility to both the sale and use of cloud services is apparent.

Convenience—being easy to do business with—enables companies to charge more and earn higher margins, enhances customer "repatronage *intentions*"—their willingness to repurchase—and increases their *actual* repatronage and even the amount that they spend when they return. Convenience is valuable, but how does it apply to computing?

Rapidity Drives Revenue

On the Web, rapidity drives revenue. Consultancy and research firm Aberdeen Group surveyed 160 companies with average annual revenue of over $1 billion. The results indicate that a one-second delay in response time would cause an 11% decrease in page views, a 7% decrease in "conversions" (i.e., converting a visitor into a customer), and a 16% decrease in customer satisfaction.[22]

Google conducted experiments between two different page designs for displaying search results, one with 10 results and one with 30 results per page. In the case of the larger design, the page took a few hundred milliseconds more to load, reducing search usage by 20%. For Google, traffic is correlated with click-throughs, and click-throughs are correlated with revenue, so the 20% reduction in traffic would have led to a 20% reduction in revenue. Reducing Google Maps 100-kilobyte page weight by almost a third increased traffic by over one third. As Google vice president Marissa Mayer said, "Users really respond to speed."[23]

The relationship between response time and revenue is not restricted to Google. Greg Linden, formerly at Amazon, claimed that Amazon.com—the retailing portion of Amazon, not cloud services—discovered that 100 milliseconds of delay reduced revenues by 1%.[24] At Amazon.com's current annual revenues, that would equate to hundreds of millions of dollars annually. According to Yahoo! Inc. performance engineer Stoyan Stefanov, Yahoo! found that 400 milliseconds of delay led to a 5% to 9% drop in "full-page traffic," as visitors left the site.[25]

Authors and management consultants Michael Treacy and Fred Wiersema argued that competitive success in business requires a focus on one of the value disciplines of customer intimacy, product leadership, or operational excellence, and that it was hard—although not impossible—to succeed at two.[26] On the Web and in the cloud, though, all three seem relevant: customer intimacy via personalization, including recommendations; product leadership via better prices and more relevant information and more engaging entertainment; and operational excellence via user and Web performance engineering.

Phil Dixon, former vice president of engineering at Shopzilla, an online comparison shopping engine, asserts that a few seconds' reduction in page load time led to a 12% increase in revenue, which may be attributed to several interrelated factors.[27] First, if a site takes too long to load, the user will balk, or renege: abandon the interaction and go somewhere else. It is easy to compare the number of click-throughs to a site to the number of customers who remain at the site. This performance increase led to a reduction in abandonment from 6% for Shopzilla.com and 9% at sister site Bizrate.com to only about 4%. Second, with more customers remaining on the site, and with faster response times, more pages were viewed—*25% more pages*. And finally, with more pages viewed by more customers, customers were more likely to find what they were looking for, leading to the revenue increase. These factors mirror rules for bricks and mortar retailers: Get customers in the store, give them great customer service, and help them find what they are looking for. Ka-ching.

In the workplace, employee applications may be Web based. Beyond the revenue considerations, there are also labor productivity opportunities.

Consider an inbound or outbound call center or other work center—say, for insurance claims processing—with a few hundred employees. If the time spent interacting with an application—data-entry screen pops, data lookups, page loads—is reduced, leading to a 10% reduction in total transaction time, it is equivalent to increasing labor productivity by 11% or being able to reduce or reallocate 10% of those workers' aggregate fully loaded wages. Application speed can thus equate to millions of dollars.

Built for Speed

Given the importance of load times on revenues, we might ask what causes them to be longer than desirable. There are dozens of rules of thumb, such as "Don't dynamically scale images in the browser."

Generally speaking, the end-to-end time is based on time spent:

1. On the client *endpoint*—smartphone, tablet, laptop, or PC and its browser or app
2. In the *network*, which is a function of network latency (i.e., delay) and the number of round trips across the network
3. In the cloud or at the corporate data center

To reduce the first is usually a matter of user interface design (and increasing the computing power of the endpoint device, if possible); to reduce the second is a function of reducing the distance between the client and the cloud and reducing the number of sequential round trips; and to reduce the third is a matter of improved application design and improved architecture, including the use of parallel processing.

To better understand the issues surrounding the number of round trips, it's important to understand how Web pages load. One key factor is the total size of the page, but of perhaps greater relevance is the number of objects, which tend to be images, and thus the number of image requests.[28]

According to Web performance optimization company StrangeLoop Networks, the average page size is now over a half a megabyte and contains about 80 individual objects, such as banner ads and illustrative graphics and logos.[29] The more objects that need to be fetched, the longer it takes to fetch them. Current browsers usually request two to four objects in parallel to reduce total page load times. Unexpectedly, trying to increase this number appears to be counterproductive: Yahoo! research shows that attempting to fetch too many page objects in parallel actually *reduces* performance.[30] Partly for this reason, newer approaches are attempting to do more processing in the cloud. Amazon CEO Jeff Bezos has described the synergies between the Kindle Fire, its Silk browser, and Amazon's cloud, observing that what "makes mobile web browsing slow is the fact that the average website pulls content from 13 different places on the Internet." Using a "split browser," where normal browser functions are divided between the device and the cloud, Bezos argues that "What takes 100 milliseconds on Wi-Fi takes less than 5 milliseconds . . ."[31]

Summary

Time is of the essence. For financial firms, time is money, and even a microsecond can make a difference in the race to complete a trade. But in virtually any interaction on the Web, time is important. For hedonic activities, such as streaming movies or playing games, slow response time can impact the perceived quality of user experience. For utilitarian activities, such as those of knowledge workers, slow response time can impact labor productivity. In the experience of online retailers, response time is directly correlated with revenue.

Strategies for response time improvement in the cloud and on the Web match everyday experience. Speed up local processing, reduce distances and round trips, and parallelize where possible. In the next few chapters, we look in depth at leveraging parallel processing and reducing network latency.

Notes

1. Marcus Baram, "Michael Phelps Expected to Become Biggest Money-Making Olympian," *ABC News*, August 20, 2008. http://abcnews.go.com/Business/story?id=5612292.
2. sportsillustrated.cnn.com/multimedia/photo_gallery/0808/oly.phelps.sequence/content.1.html.
3. www.nyse.com/press/1234869395643.html.
4. Patrick Thibodeau, "Stock Exchanges Start Thinking in Microseconds," *Computerworld*, August 4, 2008. www.computerworld.com/s/article/323391/Stock_Exchanges_Start_Thinking_in_Microseconds.
5. Jacob Goldstein, "The Tuesday Podcast: The Million-Dollar Microsecond," *NPR Planet Money*, June 8, 2010. www.npr.org/blogs/money/2010/06/08/127563433/the-tuesday-podcast-the-million-dollar-microsecond.
6. Chris Murphy, "Create," *InformationWeek*, March 14, 2011. www.techweb.com/news/229300065/it-must-create-products-not-just-cut-costs.html.
7. *Information Week Reports*, "Accelerating Wall Street 2010—Next Stop: Nanoseconds." reports.informationweek.com/abstract/106/3255/Financial/accelerating-wall-street-2010-next-stop-nanoseconds.html.
8. Richard Irving, "The Race to Zero," *Capacity* (May 2011). www.capacitymagazine.com/Article/2828418/The-race-to-zero.html.

9. Ibid.

10. Eric Shepcaro, conversation with the author, January 30th, 2012.

11. Robert D. Buzzell and Bradley T. Gale, *The PIMS (Profit Impact of Market Strategy) Principles: Linking Strategy to Performance* (Free Press, 1987), p. 7.

12. Paco Underhill, *Why We Buy: The Science of Shopping* (Simon & Schuster, 1999), p. 189.

13. Christopher Lovelock, *Services Marketing*, 3rd ed. (Prentice-Hall, 1996), p. 217.

14. Lovelock, *Services Marketing*, p. 219.

15. Taylor Clark, *Starbucked: A Double Tall Tale of Caffeine, Commerce, and Culture* (Back Bay Books/Little, Brown, 2007), p. 107.

16. Carol Felker Kaufman, Paul M. Lane, and Jay D. Lindquist, "Exploring More than 24 Hours a Day: A Preliminary Investigation of Polychronic Time Use," *Journal of Consumer Research* 18 (December 1991), pp. 392-401. www.business.camden .rutgers.edu/FacultyStaff/research/Kaufman-Scarborough/JCR%20PAI.pdf.

17. Adam Gorlick, "Media Multitaskers Pay Mental Price, Stanford Study Shows," *Stanford Report*, August 24, 2009. http://news.stanford.edu/news/2009/ august24/multitask-research-study-082409.html.

18. Mihaly Csikszentmihalyi, *Flow: The Psychology of Optimal Experience* (Harper & Row, 1990), p. 49.

19. Mirella Kleijnen, Ko de Ruyter, and Martin Wetzels, "An Assessment of Value Creation in Mobile Service Delivery and the Moderating Role of Time Consciousness," *Journal of Retailing* 83, No. 1 (2007): 33−46.

20. Vince Poscente, *The Age of Speed* (Ballantine Books, 2008), p. 17−18.

21. Kathleen Seiders, Glenn Voss, Andrea Godfrey, and Dhruv Grewal, "SERVCON: Development and Validation of a Multidimensional Service Convenience Scale," *Journal of the Academy of Marketing Science* 35 (2007): 144−156.

22. Bojan Simic, "The Performance of Web Applications: Customers Are Won or Lost in One Second," Aberdeen Group, November 2008. www.aberdeen.com/ aberdeen-library/5136/RA-performance-web-application.aspx/.

23. Dan Farber, "Google's Marissa Mayer: Speed Wins," *ZDnet.com*, November 9, 2006. www.zdnet.com/blog/btl/googles-marissa-mayer-speed-wins/3925.

24. Greg Linden, "Make Data Useful," www.scribd.com/doc/4970486/Make-Data-Useful-by-Greg-Linden-Amazoncom.

25. Stoyan Stefanov, "YSlow 2.0," presented at the CSDN Software Development 2.0 Conference, December 6, 2008, Beijing. www.slideshare.net/stoyan/yslow-20-presentation.

26. Michael Treacy and Fred Wiersema, *The Discipline of Market Leaders: Choose Your Customers, Narrow Your Focus, Dominate Your Market* (Basic Books, 1997).

27. http://blip.tv/oreilly-velocity-conference/velocity-09-philip-dixon-shopzilla-s-site-redo-you-get-what-you-measure-2305633.

28. http://httparchive.org/interesting.php#onLoad.

29. www.strangeloopnetworks.com/assets/images/infographic6.jpg.

30. http://yuiblog.com/blog/2007/04/11/performance-research-part-4/.

31. Steven Levy, "CEO of the Internet," *Wired*, December, 2011, p. 214. www.wired .com/magazine/2011/11/ff_bezos/all/1.

CHAPTER 17

Parallel Universe

To specify any event in our universe—a car accident, a flight departure, or a royal coronation or presidential inauguration—requires both a location in space—9233 Elm Street—and a time—4:00 P.M. ET on November 3, 1932. Albert Einstein and his teacher Herman Minkowski proposed that space and time are components of an integrated entity: the space-time continuum. Rather than merely combining two unrelated concepts, their point was that, at relativistic speeds, time slowed down, so that space and time are inextricably linked.

What does relativistic physics have to do with cloud computing? Plenty.

Although the term "space-time" originated in physics, computer scientists have co-opted it. The complexity of a problem can be measured by the amount of time it takes to solve it as well as the amount of space— for example, storage or memory.[1] Moreover, as with real space and time, one quantity can be related or converted to the other. More processing can be used to make up for a lack of storage space, or more space can be used to save processing time.

Here we use the term "space-time" even more broadly to relate to general trade-offs between resources and time, in the spirit of the aphorism that "Many hands make light work." Specifically, with more processors— central processing units, cores, or graphics processing units—available to perform a calculation, often processing time can be decreased.

In the easiest case, time and space can be inversely proportional to each other. If a project requires 100 staff-hours, one person needs to work 100 hours, 100 people need to work 1 hour, or there is some other combination, say, 10 people for 10 hours.

In effect, we can combine relativistic physics—space-time is a continuum— with armchair economics—time is money—to generate customer value and competitive advantage. Briefly, we use additional computing power—"space"—to accelerate time and thus create customer value. Google uses this strategy every time someone runs a search. Rather than poking along on a single processor, Google uses 1,000 or more, thereby returning results in milliseconds, in turn increasing click-throughs, thereby ringing the cash registers in Mountain View to the tune of $40 billion each year.

IBM's famous Jeopardy!-winning computer, Watson, uses IBM's DeepQA, a "massively parallel probabilistic evidence-based architecture," running on thousands of IBM POWER7 cores in parallel to implement 100 simultaneous approaches to question-anwering, processing 80 trillion operations per second, thus reducing the time to answer a Jeopardy! question from two hours on a single core to mere seconds.[2] Of course, Watson competed against contestants that were also running simultaneous heuristics on a parallel processing architecture: the human brains of Jeopardy! champions Ken Jennings and Brad Rutter, but using neurons instead of transistors. Virtually any company in any industry can use a similar approach.

Limits to Speedup

Einstein also argued that the speed of light in a vacuum is the ultimate speed limit. As a result, no object with mass can be accelerated to the speed of light, although it can get arbitrarily close. Unfortunately, the amount of force required becomes greater and greater as the speed of the object gets closer to the speed of light. Enormous amounts of effort are required to achieve infinitesimal speed increases.

Gene Amdahl, a computing pioneer, suggested something similar for attempting to speed up applications.[3] Some initial gains might result, but, at some point, near-infinite effort would be required to achieve infinitesimal speed increases. Amdahl's line of thought hinges on the difference between parallel and serial processing. A classic serial task is making a baby. One woman takes nine months to do it, and no matter how many women (or men) you add to the project, the baby won't arrive any sooner. Decorating the nursery, however, is highly parallelizable: Someone can be painting while someone is assembling the crib while someone else is placing toys on the shelves.

What Amdahl realized was that most applications are a mix of parallel and serial code. Although the parallel portion could be sped up, the serial portion could not be. In effect, no matter how many relatives are fixing up the nursery, the baby won't arrive any more quickly. We might say that in the same way that Einstein observed that increasing physical force exhibited diminishing returns in accelerating an object that could never equal, much less surpass, the speed of light, Amdahl observed that increasing the computing force exhibited diminishing returns in accelerating a calculation that could never equal, much less surpass, the speed of the serial portion. In going from 1 processor to 2, the total processing time might be dramatically decreased, but after 50 or 100 processors were added, adding a million more processors might not have a very noticeable impact.

The pay-per-use model of the cloud dramatically alters the *economic* implications of some of these laws: rather than acceleration being increasingly costly, as both Einstein and Amdahl observed, speedup in the cloud can be free. And, while Amdahl's Law is still technically correct, it no longer tells the whole story in today's distributed architectures serving global user communities, an important dimension we explore in Chapters 18, 19, and 20.

Amdahl versus Google

Amdahl worked at IBM and then founded his own companies, including Amdahl and Trilogy. Interestingly, he was arguing *against* expecting too much from parallel processing, which at the time—the mid-1960s—was beginning to attract substantial interest. He argued for "the continued validity of the single processor approach and of the weaknesses of the multiple processor approach in terms of application to real problems," basing his analysis on the proportion of computation that was typically sequential at that time, such as data management housekeeping.[4]

His argument may have been true at the time, but, today, loosely coupled parallel processing is used to great benefit in a variety of important computing tasks. One that we all use several times each day—without necessarily realizing or appreciating—is online search.

Suppose that you were in a large public library, say, with 1 million books, without any Web access or online catalog. Moreover, suppose that you needed to find the exact book and exact page number with a specific unusual phrase. You might get lucky and, accidentally, immediately pull the correct book off the shelf and turn to the right page. Generally, it would take quite a while to read through each book in search of the text fragment. In fact, you might be extremely unlucky and find that whatever order you picked meant that you were extremely *unlucky* and searched through all 1 million books before you found the phrase. On average, for a given random phrase occurring in only one book, you would expect to read through half the books before finding the phrase: 500,000 books. A very time-consuming process indeed.

However, suppose that you had 999 friends that were willing to help you. Each of you would be assigned 1,000 books, and rather than the worst case being 1 million books read and the average being 500,000, each of you would need to read only through 1,000 books in the worst case and 500 books on average. Using such a divide-and-conquer approach, assuming that you all have more or less the same reading speed, both the average and worst case have been sped up by a factor of 1,000: the exact number of parallel readers.

Google and the other major search engines use something like this process to speed up queries. Actually, rather than reading through all the pages on the Web sequentially to respond to a search query, the pages are preindexed based on keywords, which are matched against search terms. However, the principle of leveraging parallel processing remains[5]: Rather than using a single processor to process a query, on the order of 1,000 are used in parallel.[6]

There is a diversity of computational tasks, ranging from highly parallel computational tasks, such as search query processing; at the other, there are sequential tasks, such as making a baby, but also certain types of recursive computation, where the next result is dependent on the current result. In the middle, there are tasks that are a mix of serial and parallelizable, and occasionally, debate over whether certain types of computation can benefit from parallelization.[7] A computation for someone wiring money might require entry of a value, conversion of that value to a foreign currency based on an exchange rate, and debiting one account while crediting another. The exchange rate conversion is serial, but the debit and credit can occur sequentially (serially) or in parallel.

Let the total processing time to do the potentially parallel transactions be P and the number of processors utilized be p. It is clear that the time to perform the processing is P/p. On two processors, the time taken is half as long as on one. This is a simple case; p might be 1,000 or 50,000 processors, and for the right type of so-called embarrassingly parallel task, the speedup will occur.

If we add in a time, S, for the serial portion, then the total time, T, to execute code on a single processor that consists of a serial portion, S, and a parallelizable portion, P, is just $T = S + P$. But on p processors, it is only $S + P/p$. In the baby plus nursery example, let's assume that the parents don't want to know the gender of the baby. They need to wait until the baby is born to determine how to decorate the nursery. S is nine months, P is the time to decorate the nursery, and p would be the number of people working on the nursery. Since the decoration must await the arrival of the baby, the total time is $S + P/p$.

For many tasks, this is a slight oversimplification, because the exact speedup may be dependent on the amount of interprocessor communication required as various parallel portions execute. Even in the nursery case, two people may not do all the work in half the time, because the person painting may get in the way of the person placing toys, or they may spend part of the available time chatting about where to move the changing table. However, we'll ignore those second-order effects.

Amdahl's Law states, in effect, that the maximum speedup is the ratio of the serial plus parallel portion to the serial portion. The first insight that may be derived is a restatement of his observation: No matter how many processors we deploy, we are never going to go faster than the serial portion of the code. If the serial portion is a large percentage of the code, parallelism won't get us very far. If all that needs to be done in the nursery is to push the crib against the wall, 1,000 extra people helping out won't mean very much relative to the baseline of nine months.

As may be seen in Exhibit 17.1, the serial portion of the computation remains constant while the parallel portion takes a time inversely proportional to the number of processors. Due to the high percentage of the work that is serial, the first few processors reduce the total time by 30% or 35%, but the next few *dozen, million,* or even *trillion* processors will reduce things only by another few percentage points.

What Amdahl didn't focus on, though, which is also a result of this equation and is frequently exploited today, is that *if the serial portion of the code is small or nonexistent, we can get whatever speedup we desire* simply by deploying more processors, but with diminishing returns.

For "embarrassingly parallel" applications such as processing search queries, forget Amdahl; think Einstein-Minkowski. The *space* (i.e., the number of processors) can be traded off for *time*—the time needed to run the computation. As may be seen in Exhibit 17.2, the time to run such a task is inversely proportional to the number of processors.

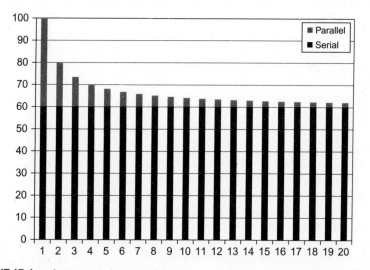

EXHIBIT 17.1 A 60% Serial, 40% Parallel Task on an Increasing Number of Processors

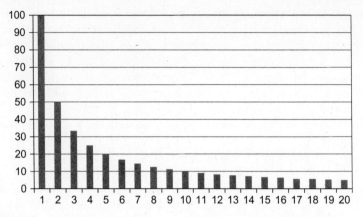

EXHIBIT 17.2 A 100% Parallel Task on an Increasing Number of Processors

To put these numbers in context, if a search query running on a single processor took 60 seconds, running it on 10 processors would take 6 seconds, on 100 processors would take .6 seconds, and on 1,000 processors would take only .06 seconds, or about 60 milliseconds.

It's not just search, but many computational tasks that can be sped up this way, such as graphics calculations used for digital animated movies or "cracking" encryption used to secure computing and mobile telephony. One widely used approach, called MapReduce by Google and implemented in open source as Hadoop, involves a few steps: dividing up the task, executing it on multiple processors in parallel, organizing and integrating the results, and determining a final answer. In the case of the library search example, this would entail assigning specific library aisles to specific friends, everyone flipping through pages in parallel, and then holding a meeting to determine who found the phrase.

Free Time

Without the cloud, speed kills. Specifically, attempting to speed things up kills your IT budget. If an application takes too long on one server, you *could* buy 1,000 more and speed it up significantly. The good news is that you have just sped things up by three orders of magnitude. The bad news is that you had to spend 1,000 times as much to achieve this acceleration. Exhibit 17.3 illustrates that, without the cloud, the diminishing returns from increasing parallelization are not accompanied by diminishing costs but rather linear costs as more and more processors are added.

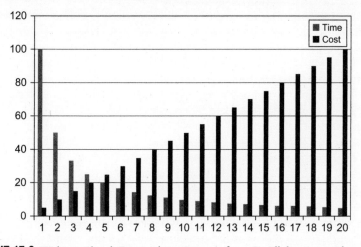

EXHIBIT 17.3 Without Cloud: Diminishing Returns from Parallelization with Linear Costs

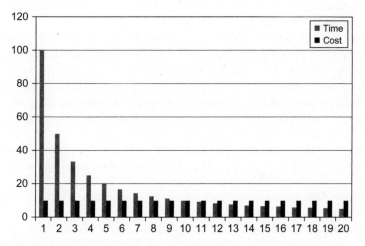

EXHIBIT 17.4 With Cloud: Constant Costs Regardless of Parallelization

With the cloud, something beautiful happens, as shown in Exhibit 17.4. Your acceleration is free: Regardless of the number of processors, the cost remains constant.

Getting something for nothing is quite surprising and important. To understand this principle, consider a wedding with 100 couples, at least traditionally one held before the baby/nursery portion of our scenario. We need to get these couples from the ceremony to the reception. We *could* have one cab drive back and forth. If the reception is only 3 minutes from the ceremony, it takes 3 minutes to drive the first couple over, 3 minutes for the cab to drive back. It takes another 3 minutes for the second couple to be transported, another 3 minutes for the cab to drive back. After 100 couples take 6 minutes each in total, 600 minutes have passed, which is 10 hours. The early-arriving couples eat all the shrimp and drink all the good wine. Tired, they leave. The last 50 couples wonder why there is no food or drink and never hand over their wedding gifts. It is a disaster.

Instead, 100 cabs could be hired, and 3 minutes after the ceremony ends, everyone could jockeying for position at the open bar or the hors d'oeuvres.

Whether there is only 1 cab hired for 100 rides or 100 cabs that each provide one ride, the total cost for cab rides is exactly the same.

In other words, by trading off space for time, we speed up the application, and pay no more for the privilege if we use the cloud.

In today's hypercompetitive world, such acceleration can be the basis for competitive success. The Web search firm that can provide meaningful query results faster than its competitor will gain more traffic. The brokerage that can exploit an arbitrage opportunity a few microseconds ahead of its competitor will enhance its profitability.

Such cost-effective parallel processing can also undermine the basic assumptions of our cybersociety. For example, encryption that protects everything from e-mail accounts to financial and government systems is based on the computational difficulty and thus infeasibility and cost of certain operations, such as prime factorization of large numbers. But the immense calculating power that the cloud provides at low cost implies that formerly secure codes no longer are. Thomas Roth, a German security researcher, was able to decipher 14 supposedly secure passwords in 49 minutes for $2.10. Roth observed that "cloud-based cracking really has a future . . . as you split the task . . . onto multiple instances, you can divide the time you actually need to crack the hash by the number of instances you rent—without having more costs."[8]

One caveat is the minimum billing increment. If the minimum "rental" for a server is one hour, space-time is no longer a continuum from an economic perspective. We can conduct two server hours of parallel computation on one server for two hours, two servers for one hour, or four servers for half an hour. However, if the minimum billing increment is one hour, the first two scenarios will cost the same but the third one will cost twice as much.

One predictable result of this discontinuity is that cloud service providers may begin to compete on offering shorter minimum billing increments, in the same way that telecommunications carriers went from one-minute billing increments to finer-grained measures.

Summary

In many markets, time is a critical competitive advantage. Generally, you get what you pay for, but in the world of the cloud and its pay-per-use resources, acceleration can be free.

For companies trying to accelerate time to value—that is, "competing in time"—the cloud can be a cost-effective weapon of choice. This fact has two implications.

1. Companies should leverage parallelism where possible to accelerate relevant business processes, reduce cycle times, and enhance customer responsiveness.
2. They can accomplish this for free using the cloud.

As more companies accelerate their processing, computing workloads placed on cloud providers will mutate from longer tasks on fewer processors to shorter, spikier tasks requiring more processors. Some service providers may see a shift in individual and aggregate demand characteristics.

Moving to shorter times will create opportunities for some service providers to offer shorter billing increments, just as some telcos bill by six-second increments and some hotels bill by the hour.

Notes

1. Michael R. Garey and David S. Johnson, *Computers and Intractability: A Guide to the Theory of NP-Completeness* (W. H. Freeman, 1979).
2. "Watson: A System Designed for Answers: The Future of Workload Optimized Systems Design," IBM Systems and Technology, February, 2011. www-03 .ibm.com/innovation/us/watson/what-is-watson/a-system-designed-for-answers .html
3. Gene M. Amdahl, "Validity of the Single Processor Approach to Achieving Large Scale Computing Capabilities," *AFIPS Conference Proceedings*, Vol. 30 (Atlantic City, N.J., Apr. 18–20), AFIPS Press, Reston, Va., 1967, pp. 483–485. turing.eas.asu .edu/cse520fa08/Alaw.pdf.
4. Ibid.
5. Luiz André Barroso, Jeffrey Dean, and Urs Hölzle, "Web Search for a Planet: The Google Cluster Architecture," *IEEE Micro* (March–April 2003): 22–28. static. googleusercontent.com/external_content/untrusted_dlcp/research.google.com/en/ us/archive/googlecluster-ieee.pdf.
6. Stephen Shankland, "We're all Guinea Pigs in Google's Search Experiment," *CNet News*, May 29, 2008. http://news.cnet.com/8301-10784_3-9954972-7.html?tag= mncol;txt.

7. Kai-Hui Chang and Chris Browy, "Parallel Logic Simulation: Myth or Reality?" *Computer*, April, 2012, pp. 67–73. www.computer.org/csdl/mags/co/2012/04/mco2012040067-abs.html.

8. Paul Roberts, "The Cloud Makes Short Work of Strong Encryption," *threatpost*, Kaspersky Lab, November 19, 2010. http://threatpost.com/en_us/blogs/cloud-makes-short-work-strong-encryption-111910.

CHAPTER 18

Shortcuts to Success

Revenue relates to response time, which, as we saw in the last chapter, can be improved through parallelization. But when an application has a global base of users—employees, customers, or partners—network latency—delays due to signal transmission time over distance—is a critical factor as well. Taking the shortest path between the user and the application helps, as does reducing round trips. After that, the only thing left to do is to reduce the distance between the user and the service: As the saying goes, either the prophet must go to the mountain, or the mountain must come to the prophet.

The first strategy involves bringing the users closer to the data center. Most people think that the New York Stock Exchange (NYSE) is on Wall Street, but, for many, it is in Mahwah, New Jersey: Almost half of the equity and options trading in North America is processed there. There we find users such as hedge funds, which make use of the NYSE's Capital Markets Community Platform, a colocation/cloud data center that *guarantees* a round-trip message time of 70 *microseconds*.[1] For the entire system to perform in times measured in microseconds, various components must be even faster. Microseconds have been shaved end to end by using ultra-high-performance network switching gear that guarantees less than 700 *nanoseconds*—billionths of a second—to aid in the routing of messages from a buyer to a seller, for example.[2]

This strategy—migrating the user to the data center—works for traders or, more specifically, for their platforms, given the money at stake and the microsecond time frames. Of course, asking the average Web searcher to travel to Google, Microsoft, Yahoo!, or Baidu's data center to conduct a search might not be as effective. As we've discussed, location independence—ubiquitous access to services—is a key characteristic of the cloud.

245

Rapid Transit

The rescue of Captain Richard Phillips of the *Maersk Alabama* could not have been more dramatic. After days of tension, three U.S. Navy SEAL snipers, using night-vision goggles, on a ship tossing about in rough waters, each took one shot, "picking off" three Somali pirates, one of whom was behind a window, in a boat 100 feet away, in a split second.[3] The rescue was notable, but the hijacking and hostage taking were typical: The European Union Naval Forces have reported that thousands of hostages have been taken over the years, with hundreds held at any given time.[4] You might ask why ships keep plying the Somali coast or, more generally, the Gulf of Aden. The answer is simple: Although money may be lost in hijacked cargo and ransom payments, more money would be lost by taking a longer route.

A trip through the Red Sea and the Gulf of Aden is inevitable when traversing the Suez Canal. And the Suez Canal is the shortcut between parts of Asia and the Indian subcontinent and the Mediterranean and the North Atlantic for ships headed to or from Europe or even the East Coast of North America. The only currently viable alternative is to round the Cape of Good Hope and all of Africa, which adds thousands of miles and several days to the voyage: Days in which extra fuel is used, days in which crews must be paid, days in which produce can rot, days in which inventory holding costs will be incurred.

Time is money; thus, delay is costly. Yet exploiting a shortest path can be associated with death and destruction. Both Somali pirates and their hostages have died in the prevention and pursuit of shortest paths, and this number pales in comparison to the thousands of workers who died in the construction of the Suez Canal. However, the search for shortest paths in the pursuit of commercial benefit can also be considered among humankind's most important achievements: Christopher Columbus discovered America and initiated the Age of Discovery in a quest to find a shorter path to acquire Asian metals, silks, and spices.

Such shortest path discovery and exploitation is so important that it offers evolutionary advantage among even lesser creatures. Honeybees famously use a waggle dance to communicate the nearest food source. Slime molds can connect food sources via the shortest path.[5] Even the common black ant, *Lasius niger*, will exploit the shortest path: In simple yet profound experiments, ants could reach a food source via a shorter or longer route. After initial random meandering, emergent behavior based on denser deposition of pheromones led to a vast majority of the ants preferentially utilizing the shortest path.[6] Researchers have observed that such behavior is likely to be evolutionarily beneficial, enabling ants to minimize travel time and energy costs and to consume a rich food source more quickly, offering competitive advantage over neighboring colonies—not much different than in the world of online rich media.[7]

Sending Letters

As the world becomes increasingly virtual, routing and distance concerns might appear to less critical. After all, who cares about ships and the Cape of Good Hope when data packets can be whisked from one corner of the earth to another in mere milliseconds?

The answer: just about everyone. Milliseconds matter in many, if not most, applications. For brokerage operations, even microseconds matter. Since milliseconds matter, miles matter also, in turn often driving a requirement for dispersed infrastructure and optimized routing.

Some simple calculations show why this is true.

Only a few years ago, when the Web was young, usage entailed a straightforward loop: Request a Web page, load the page, look at the page, click on a link and thereby request a Web page, load that page, look at the page, click on a link. A page might take seconds to load. Although users didn't particularly enjoy the "World Wide Wait," that was what the processing power of the endpoint, the bandwidth limitations of dial-up access, and other factors conspired to provide.

Today, the page-at-a-time paradigm has been replaced by a more highly interactive usage model. For example, today's search engines begin providing suggestions with each keystroke—so-called autocomplete or incremental search. If you type "C-l-o-u-d-o-n-o-m-i-c-s" into a search engine query box, each letter generates some suggested returns. As you type "C," your search engine might suggest "Craigslist," "Chase," and "CNN." After the "l," it might suggest "Club Penguin," "Club Monaco," and "Clearview Cinemas," and after the "o," "Cloisters," "Cloud Computing," and "Clockwork Orange."

The objective of such high interactivity is user convenience and employee productivity, and the objective of convenience and productivity is monetization and profit: Studies have shown a direct link between speed and revenue for Web interactions. Why force you to type such a long word if the engine can make an intelligent guess on your behalf? Of course, for this approach to work, the suggestions need to be generated in the instant of time between typing each letter, or else the search engine will still be providing suggestions such as "Craigslist" and "Chase" long after you've typed "Cloudonomics."

There are only two ways to enable this functionality: One is to preload your device with every possible word or phrase; the other is to dynamically generate the suggestions on a remote server as you type. The former approach might work in this particular example, but it won't work as a general solution because this strategy is increasingly being used to generate not just suggested search term phrases but also snippets of Web pages that change all the time. Preloading would require local caching (copying) most of the entire Web into your device. Storage is cheap, but not that cheap, and the amount of information continues to explode.

What happens is this: As you type each letter, the code in your browser (or in an app) interprets the keystroke and triggers a bit of code that then sends the letter, "C," say, over one or more networks to the cloud server(s), which then process the letter by running some other code. This code then determines the one or two handfuls of most likely words that begin with the string typed so far and sends them *back* over those same networks. Your device and the browser or app then receive the response and display it.

All of this must happen before the next letter is typed. A skilled typist can type 120 words per minute.[8] If a computer user types only half that—60 words per minute—which many of today's users can, especially for short bursts—that works out to one word every second. By the way, accuracy doesn't matter, since the search engine still needs to generate suggestions ("Did you mean . . . ?") as well as process backspaces. One word each second is six letters or spaces each second, which means that there are only 166 milliseconds in the total time budget to execute the request-response loop just detailed: Hit a key, generate a keystroke event, process the event, send the letter over a network, generate responses, send the responses over a network, display the responses.

Other applications have similarly stringent requirements. Remote virtual desktops, where single keystrokes or mouse moves cause not just search phrases to appear but replace sections of screen real estate wholesale, have only 150 to 180 milliseconds of time budget. Here, rather than just text phrases, such keystrokes can delete sections of text, jump to new document sections, or replace charts or graphics.

Interactive video conferencing permits a maximum of 200 milliseconds or so of delay for conversations to appear natural and collaboration to be maximized. Today, videoconferencing merely entails sending a video stream from one location to another. Tomorrow, all kinds of advanced processing can be imagined, where multiple individuals in different locations are composited to appear as if they were all together, and three-dimensional-perspective views are generated by compute-intensive electro-holographic processing.

We are also moving beyond talking-head videoconferencing into an immersive world of multiplayer gaming, where physical actions, such as dancing and tennis strokes, must be interpreted and generate game or "mirror"-world results. The human nervous system is specifically designed to compensate for slow transmission of nerve pulses and slow reflexes by projecting and anticipating trajectories. This fact puts the necessary speed of response down into the tens of milliseconds.

Consequently, the route and the distance to the destination matter to both boats and bits. For boats, the right routing can shave dozens of hours;

for bits, it can shave dozens of milliseconds. Either way, the time savings can generate hundreds of millions, if not billions, of dollars in value.

Short on Time

Unfortunately, targets of 150 to 200 milliseconds are roughly the time needed for the network round trip *alone* for worst-case city pairs such as, say, New York and Singapore.[9] In other words, we use up all of our available time budget just for the network portion of the work, with no time left over for any other of the tasks in the request-response cycle. This is like blowing your vacation budget on the plane ticket, having no money left for hotel, food, wine, and recreation. It just won't work.

But technology marches forward. Won't global network speeds get better over time? Not without some revolutionary breakthrough, such as data transport based on quantum entanglement, or wormholes through hyperspace, because currently, the speed of light—186,282 miles per second—is the limiting factor. This is certainly fast, but it is not fast enough on a planet as large as earth populated with humans with reaction times and granularity of perception in the range of tens of milliseconds. Making things worse, the speed that light travels is not always the speed of light: In an optical fiber, light travels only at two thirds that speed, so we are down to 124,000 miles per second, which works out to 124 miles per millisecond in a fiber. This means that a round trip from say, Newark, New Jersey, to Trenton, New Jersey, takes about 1 millisecond.

Taking only 1 millisecond to go 124 miles is pretty snappy, but at that rate, the 9,500 miles between New York and Singapore takes almost 80 milliseconds *one way* and therefore close to 160 milliseconds round trip.

And this is the best-case round-trip time for the simplest possible transaction, not unlike using the top speed of your car to determine how long it will take you to drive cross country. Traffic jams, speed limits, and detours may impact the result. If you wanted to determine exactly how long a trip really would be likely to take, you might keep a record of how long it usually takes you, and ask your friends to do the same.

Thanks to the wonderful folks at Internet performance monitoring firm Cedexis—Marty Kagan and Greg Unrein—we have empirical data on Web performance, such as Hypertext Transfer Protocol (HTTP, the mechanism that enables web pages to be loaded and online forms to be submitted). They have billions of sample measurements passively and automatically generated by users all over the world, which they can slice and dice in every which way. An example measurement they took from over 140 countries on 11/11/11 (November 11, 2011) on the distribution of average response times can be seen in Exhibit 18.1.

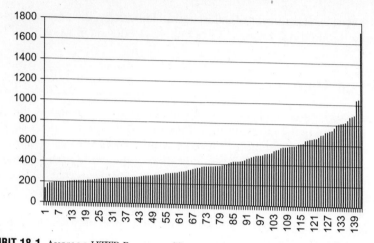

EXHIBIT 18.1 Average HTTP Response Times to East Coast United States by Country
Source: Cedexis (www.cedexis.com). Used by permission.

A few averages are below 200 milliseconds, but the distribution stretches out to an average of over 1 second in Senegal and Zambia and closes in on 2 seconds for Syria. Note that these data per se do not give a sense of the distribution of response times that a randomly selected global individual might expect, as it's not population adjusted.

Cedexis can also slice things by network, which is where it is also apparent that there is variation, due to a combination of factors: regional footprint of the network; coarse technology, such as wireline versus wireless; fine technologies, such as 3G versus 4G wireless; routing; and congestion, among others. The point is that real data network latency is not deterministic, any more than figuring out Lincoln Tunnel or Route 101 delays.

Exhibit 18.2 shows results just for the United States, showing internetwork variation. In other words, knowing that the average response time to the United States from within the United States is much lower than, say, from within Syria is interesting, but the average response time in the United States is not important to any individual, only the response time that that individual is receiving at that moment. The nearly 1.5-second response time is across a satellite network, where the response time from point A to point B is four links: uplink and downlink for the request, and uplink and downlink for the response.

The key insight for our purposes, though, is how *slow* these round trips are most of the time. As Exhibit 18.1 shows, just for a single round-trip transaction, a vast majority of the time from a vast majority of places in the world, we can't possibly meet the time budget limitations for even the simplest of transactions: sending a letter (i.e., a single character) and receiving some suggested phrases.

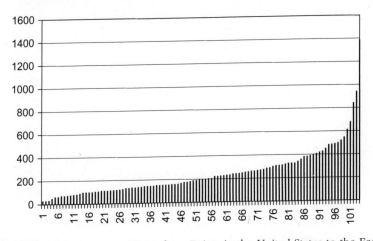

EXHIBIT 18.2 HTTP Response Times from Points in the United States to the East Coast by Network

Source: Cedexis (www.cedexis.com). Used by permission.

To make matters worse, even with today's technology, most Web pages take a long time to load, even the famously sparse Google home page. The reason is that rather than one cross-country trip, each Web page requires many. The "body" of the Web page is retrieved, but then another request and round trip is required for the corporate logo, and then another one for the nifty graphic, and another one for each banner ad, and another few for each image. Even the Google home page has over a dozen independent objects; load the *Huffington Post* (www.huffingtonpost.com) to see what a lot of objects looks like. Even though it is in the top 25 most visited sites in the Unites States, Alexa Internet Services rates it in the bottom 8% of sites in terms of average load time at this writing.[10] This is merely a reflection of the quantity of rich content and its interplay with the current Web technologies.

To recap the challenge, look at it this way. The response time of the wetware that is the human nervous system depends on a variety of factors, including blood alcohol levels. Autonomic responses, such as the knee-jerk reflex, take about 50 milliseconds, as opposed to consciously flexing the knee, which takes hundreds of milliseconds.[11] There are two insights to be drawn here. One is that evolution itself has engineered the body to use a distributed processing architecture for latency reduction. Because the round trip to the brain to pull your hand away from a hot stove—a situation in which time is of the essence—would take too long, processing the reaction is done "offsite" at "the edge" in the spinal cord. In fact, the body also has specially engineered data communication networks, using a type of cable cladding—myelin sheathing—to speed transmission. Myelin speeds up nervous system impulses from 1 meter per second to about 100 meters per second, which works out to about 224 miles per hour—about the speed of a Formula 1 race car.

The other key point about the human nervous system is that it doesn't just rely on *responses*. If a soccer player waited until the ball was right near his or her foot to command a knee-flex, the player would miss the ball every time. Instead, humans *predict* trajectories. This function is so important that even three-month-olds can do it.[12] Interactive systems that mimic physical phenomena must perform at the same or better responsiveness as humans do.

The fastest response times needed are not the 200 milliseconds of video interaction or the 150 milliseconds of keystrokes or even the 50 milliseconds of knee-jerks but in the realm of the zero milliseconds of predictive interactions. Next-generation applications are not just videoconferencing or remote virtual desktops but telesurgery and interactive video gaming, such as remotely playing tennis or air hockey with someone over a network using Nintendo Wii or Microsoft Kinect types of interfaces.

Bandwidth Isn't Enough

If a Web page takes five seconds to load at 1 megabit per second, how long does it take to load at 5 megabits per second? Obviously, the answer is one

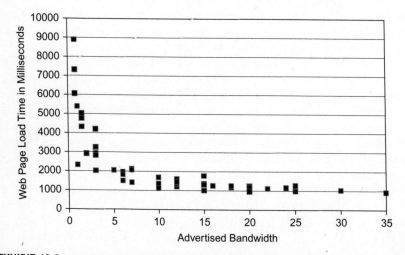

EXHIBIT 18.3 Web Page Loading Time by Advertised Bandwidth

Source: Federal Communications Commission, Office of Engineering and Technology and Consumer and Government Affairs Bureau, "Measuring Broadband America: A Report on Consumer Wireline Broadband Performance in the U.S.," 2011. www.fcc.gov/measuring-broadband-america.

second. How about at 35 megabits per second? Obviously, the answer would be 1/7 of a second.

Unfortunately, the obvious answers are not the correct ones. Exhibit 18.3 from the Federal Communications Commission shows download times for a Web page based on the advertised bandwidth of several vendors.

In other words, even at infinite bandwidth, a Web page still may not load all that much faster than at a megabit per second of bandwidth, due to the effect of latency. To put it another way, even if there were an infinite number of lanes on Route 80 (bandwidth), it still is going to take a few days to drive from the East Coast to the West Coast due to the speed limit and distance (data rate, speed of propagation, latency).

Summary

Many tasks today require fast response times and low latency; these tasks range from keystroke mirroring for remote virtual desktops to video conferencing to interactive Web pages.

Customers tend to focus on bandwidth, believing that higher bandwidth will mean faster response times. Although more bandwidth can result in faster times for some tasks, latency is often the culprit. Keys to improving response time thus include reducing latency by reducing the physical distance between the client device and the server, thus reducing propagation delay, and reducing the number of round trips for a given transaction. As we see in the next chapter, reducing the physical distance for users who may be globally distributed requires a dispersed infrastructure.

Notes

1. Patrick Thibodeau, "In Fortified Data Center, NYSE Runs 'Gated' Trading Cloud," *Computerworld*, August 31, 2011. www.computerworld.com/s/article/9219668/In_fortified_data_center_NYSE_runs_gated_trading_cloud.
2. InformationWeek, "Accelerating Wall Street 2010—Next Stop: Nanoseconds," *InformationWeek Analytics*, June 2010. reports.informationweek.com/abstract/106/3255/Financial/accelerating-wall-street-2010-next-stop-nanoseconds.html.
3. Robert D. McFadden and Scott Shane, "In Rescue of Captain, Navy Kills 3 Pirates," *New York Times*, April 12, 2009. www.nytimes.com/2009/04/13/world/africa/13pirates.html.
4. EU NAVFOR Public Affairs Office, "Merchant Ship Crews Held Hostage in Somalia," December 20, 2011. www.eunavfor.eu/2011/12/merchant-ship-crews-held-hostage-in-somalia/.
5. Toshiyuki Nakagaki, Hiroyasu Yamada, and Ágota Tóth "Intelligence: Maze-solving by an amoeboid organism," *Nature*, 407 (28 September, 2000), p. 470.

6. James Kennedy and Russell Eberhart with Yuhui Shi, *Swarm Intelligence* (Morgan Kaufmann Publishers, 2001), pp. 105–106.

7. Scott Camazine, Jean-Louis Deneubourg, Nigel Franks, James Sneyd, Guy Theraulaz, and Eric Bonabeau, *Self-Organization in Biological Systems* (Princeton University Press, 2001), p. 225.

8. Robert U. Ayres and Katalin Martinas, *On the Reappraisal of Microeconomics: Economic Growth and Change in a Material World* (Edward Elgar, 2005), p. 41.

9. http://ipnetwork.bgtmo.ip.att.net/pws/network_delay.html.

10. www.alexa.com/siteinfo/huffingtonpost.com, accessed April 19, 2012.

11. Jeffrey S. Nevid, *Psychology: Concepts and Applications* (Houghton-Mifflin, 2009).

12. Reneé Baillargeon and Julie DeVos, "Object Permanance in Young Infants: Further Evidence," *Child Development* 62 (1991): 1227–1246.

CHAPTER 19

Location, Location, Location

Every realtor knows that the three most important characteristics of any property are, in priority order: location, location, and location. This is important not only in residences, but logistics centers, malls, factories, coffee shops, and of course, data centers. Tim Harford, author of *The Undercover Economist*, pointed out:

> Starbucks' most significant advantage is its location on the desire line of thousands of commuters. There are a few sweet spots for coffee bars—by station exits or busy street corners. Starbucks and its rivals have snapped them up. If Starbucks really did have the hypnotic hold over its customers that critics complain about, it would hardly need to spend so much effort getting people to trip over its cafés. The nice margin that Starbucks makes on their cappuccinos is due neither to the quality of the coffee nor to the staff: it's location, location, location.[1]

In other words, when time is of the essence, we can either do what New York Stock Exchange Euronext did, and bring the users closer to the processing, or do what Starbucks and Web sites do, and bring the Java closer to the end user. However, since users are globally dispersed, service nodes must also be globally dispersed. But how many nodes is enough: 5? 10? 20? 20,000?

In this chapter, we explore how increasing the number of service nodes reduces latency, but with diminishing returns.

Latency and Distance

Generally, latency, or time delay, is based on speed and distance; traveling at twice the speed, or for only half the distance, can halve the latency.

However, there are a number of complicating factors in the real world, for both speed and distance.

There is—at least with current physics—a limit to speed: the speed of light in a vacuum. This theoretical speed is not actual speed: Light in a fiber travels significantly more slowly than light in a vacuum, and traffic congestion impacts real speed.

Another issue is that the distance as the crow flies is not necessarily the same distance that a routed network covers. There are all kinds of anomalies in routed networks due to cable routes that follow everything from rights-of-way on train tracks and bridges to terrain topology constraints due to mountains, valleys, rivers, lakes, and coastlines to where cities happen to have sprung up—often due to those same constraints. Undersea, there are topological anomalies to be managed, areas of seismic activity requiring wide berth, and fishing areas—where cables tend to be dug up—to be avoided.

TeleGeography, a telecom market research firm covering international networks, was kind enough to provide Exhibit 19.1, a map of undersea cable routes. Although the routes don't exactly follow the paths shown due to some liberty taken with graphics for readability, a quick glance at the map shows the uneven deployment of routed networks. In some cases—say, New York to London—there are multiple cables on direct paths. In other cases—say, Johannesburg, South Africa, to Perth, Australia (on the southwest coast)—there is no direct route, only one via India and Indonesia, that is roughly twice as long as the actual distance.

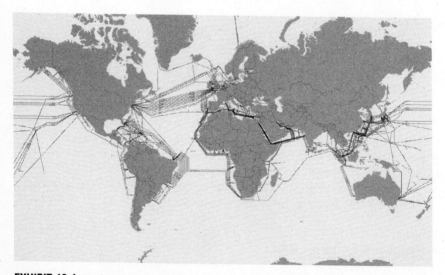

EXHIBIT 19.1 Undersea Cable Map

Source: © 2012 TeleGeography (telegeography.com). Used by permission.

Within the United States, there are network routing anomalies as well.[2] A north—south route from Boston to Orlando is more or less a straight shot: Boston to New York to Philadelphia to Washington, D.C., to Atlanta to Orlando. An east—west route from Orlando to Los Angeles via Dallas is relatively straight. However, trying to get from Orlando to Seattle can be a challenge: You can go north to New York and then west through Chicago, or west to Los Angeles and then north via San Francisco, but either way is much longer than a crow would choose.

Unless we want to determine an *exact* solution for a given network, as a first cut at the problem, however, we can assume that latency is proportional to distance. Therefore, although direction and routing are important, we will simplify the problem to assume that direction and routes *don't* matter and that if we are trying to meet a given latency constraint—say, 1-millisecond worst case—we can treat it as an equivalent distance constraint—say, 124 miles.

Circle Covering and Circle Packing

To further abstract the problem, we consider what happens as we adjust the radius, r, of a circle about a given service node or multiple service nodes. This is a way of viewing the problem of finding a nearby "node," such as a hamburger joint, coffee shop, or mobile base station: If you want to find one less than a mile away, say, you must be situated within the circular area swept by a radius of one mile about the node. It turns out that for a circle with *worst-case* distance r, the *expected* value of the distance to the center of a point selected at random within the circle is $\frac{2}{3}r$. This means that when we talk about distance on a plane, we needn't exactly specify worst-case versus expected, as they are the same except for a scaling constant.

Coverage impacts more than just latency. Placing cell sites—or related technologies such as picocells, femtocells, wireless access points, or distributed antenna systems—is more about ensuring reception than addressing latency. Moreover, sometimes we prefer less coverage rather than more. Since the capacity of cellular base stations and wireless access points is constrained, more users can be served by more sites each covering less area. The general abstract coverage problem—determining whether k sites can cover an arbitrary set of points on a plane—is computationally intractable.[3] In the real world it is somewhat easier: Service providers prioritize the most relevant countries economically, then the most important locations within those countries. In any event, whether it is latency or accessibility that we are concerned with, we need to determine the tradeoff between investing in locations and the area served.

Suppose that we want to try to lay out hockey pucks on a pool table as densely as possible. This is the circle-packing problem. We could randomly

place hockey pucks without moving them and end up with a fairly inefficient packing. However, regular tilings are more likely to be dense. A square
packing looks like Exhibit 19.2.

Square packing is how wine or beer bottles are laid out in a case, but
such a packing is not the most efficient. As you might expect, the best—or
closest—possible packing is hexagonal, and looks like Exhibit 19.3.

Conversely, suppose that instead of hockey pucks, we are laying down
paper doilies on the pool table, and we'd like to ensure that not even the
slightest portion of the pool table is uncovered while using the minimum
number of doilies. This is the circle-*covering* problem. It turns out that the
optimal circle covering is based on scooching the circles a little closer
together from the hexagonal packing, to eliminate the little curved triangles
at the interstices. (See Exhibit 19.4.)

Inverse Square Root Law

It should be clear that regardless of the approach that we use—packing or
covering—the area, A, that is covered is proportional to the number of

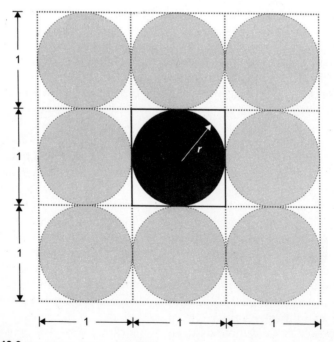

EXHIBIT 19.2 Square Packing of Circles

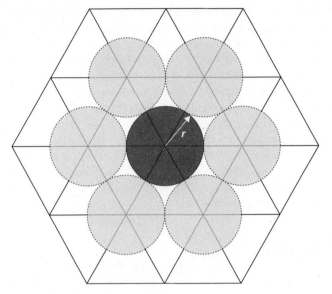

EXHIBIT 19.3 Hexagonal Close Packing of Circles

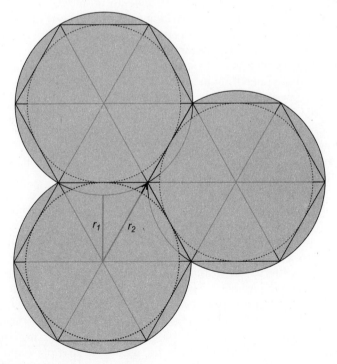

EXHIBIT 19.4 Optimal Circle Covering

circles, n, and is also based on the radius of each circle, r. Specifically, $A \propto nr^2$, where the constant of proportionality depends on the packing strategy that we use and thus what is referred to as the packing density, η (eta). And we've stipulated that latency is proportional to distance. But this means that for a given area A, $r \propto \frac{1}{\sqrt{n}}$, or, in other words, on a plane, the average latency and therefore also the worst-case latency are both proportional to the inverse square root of the number of nodes.

This is very powerful for small n but rapidly leads to diminishing returns. If global round-trip response times are, say, 160 milliseconds, by using a couple of dozen or so nodes, we can get round-trip latencies way down, say, to 10 or 20 milliseconds. However, it becomes increasingly difficult to reduce latencies through node build-outs: At some point, for example, reducing latency by a microsecond or so might require billions of service nodes. This is too many even for McDonald's or Starbucks.

Spherical Caps and the Tammes Problem

If we want to be even more precise, we must recognize that we don't live on a plane; the earth is not flat. On a sphere, there are additional complications. The general analog to doing circle packing or circle covering on a sphere is the Tammes problem, named after a problem originally formulated in 1930 by botanist Pieter Merkus Lambertus Tammes, which originally addressed the layout of pores on grains of pollen.[4] As can be seen from Exhibit 19.5, which is a grain of pollen from the Heavenly Blue morning glory flower, the layout of these pores (at least for spherical grains) is identical to packing nonoverlapping circles onto a sphere and also that of distributing points—service nodes—"evenly" on a sphere, so as to maximize the minimum distance between centers.

Tammes also concluded that there was a $\sqrt{n}$ effect at work (he termed it $\sqrt{a}$), writing:

> the variation in number of places of exit was statistically traced and a typical correlation appeared to exist between the size of the pollen and the number of places of exit, in that . . . Diam. $= (\sqrt{a \text{ to } a + 1}) \times V$, when the places of exit are distributed over the whole surface, *Diam.* representing the diameter of the grain, *a* the observed number of places of exit, and *V* a constant for pollen-grains of one species being under equal circumstances.
>
> He continued: To the arrangement of the places of exit in the pollen, however variable it may be, yet a general rule obtains: that equidistance is observed in which the distance from a place of exit to the nearest places of exit is nearly equal in value. . . . [W]e might

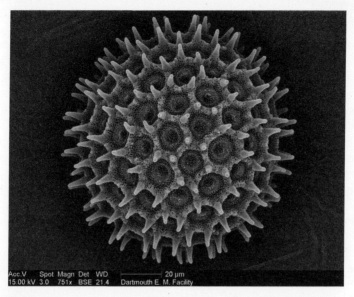

EXHIBIT 19.5 Heavenly Blue Morning Glory Pollen Grain, Magnified

Source: Dartmouth Electron Microscope Facility, Dartmouth College, http://remf.dartmouth .edu/pollen2/pollen_images_4/images/03%20Pollen%20MGlory-3.jpg.

infer that the arrangement and the number of places of exit only depends on the closest covering of the space occupied by the places of exit.

Tammes was close, but not exactly right due to anomalies in translating results from a plane into results on a sphere, which we briefly explore. A similar problem arises in a surprising variety of domains: packing dimples onto the surface of golf balls; the "Coulomb Potential" problem, where charged particles such as electrons constrained to a sphere try to push themselves away from each other (i.e., maximize the minimum distance between them) to reduce the total potential energy; and other areas of physics, such as baryon density isosurfaces.[5]

Unlike the planar problem, the problem on a sphere is as much art as science; various mathematicians have come up with a few provably correct solutions[6]—for 1 to 12 circles (or spherical caps) and 24 circles—and quite a few best-known solutions. As in the case of packing a moving van with assorted lamp shades, pianos, and armoires, the fact that you have come up with a best-known solution doesn't mean that someone else couldn't devise a better one.

Elsewhere we derived the lovely trigonometry resulting in an adjustment of $(1 - \cos(2\beta))/(1 - \cos(\beta))$ to convert from plane to sphere[7]; here, we merely summarize the conclusions. At the scale of the entire planet, going from one node to two nodes halves the worst-case latency. If one node is at the North Pole, whether a coffee shop or a content delivery node, the worst case is someone trying to access it from the South Pole. However, if we put service nodes at both the North Pole and the South Pole, the worst-case distance is halved: Anyone on the equator can be serviced equally well from either pole. At planetary—or spherical —scale, the worst-case distance is proportional to the inverse of the number of nodes. As we get down to continental or country scale, we get closer and closer to the result for the plane, which is the inverse square root law. For all intents and purposes, then, we can use the insight that the average or worst-case latency is proportional to the inverse square root of the number of nodes.

What does this all mean? There are early gains to be had in reducing latency through branch expansion. Given the importance of response time, it makes sense to either build out global, dispersed facilities yourself—if you are a Starbucks, a McDonald's, or a Google—or to leverage someone else's: If you are Procter & Gamble, distribute your goods via Walmart; if you are Procter & Gamble's Web site, pg.com, distribute your goods via, say, Akamai.

Of course, the cost to build a Starbucks or McDonald's is probably a million dollars or so, and the cost to build a data center is more like ten or one hundred million, so the breakeven points differ.

The bottom line in this analysis is that branch expansion is easy at first, driving revenues and customer experience higher, but there are diminishing returns. The high-value customers are served, marginal latency reduction approaches zero, and marginal revenue diminishes as new branches cannibalize old ones.

In the case of parallelization, we saw that speedup via the cloud could be free. In the case of latency reduction, the cost differential is application dependent. Some objects need to be copied into every location, regardless of user demand. These might be the image of the application that is running in each location or a data set. For example, if search queries are to be served out of every location, each location must maintain a copy of the entire Web, indexed. The cost to maintain this data in ten locations is ten times the cost to do it in one.

However, some costs—such as user data—are fixed *regardless* of the number of locations, in the same way that a bill for groceries is identical regardless of how many bags you pack them up in. Suppose an application maintains user profile information, of roughly, say, 1 megabyte. If there are a million users, that is 1 million megabytes, or 1 terabyte. If we divide this into ten locations, each serving 100,000 users, each location now only has to store one tenth of a terabyte, for an unchanged total storage requirement. Although a terabyte is no longer a lot of data, the day is not far off when users will "lifelog" their every waking—or sleeping—minute. At Blu-Ray

Disc quality, that works out to roughly 1 terabyte per day, or 1 petabyte every three years. Stored in the cloud, this will add up. Some might say that storage costs are plummeting, to which we would answer that video resolutions and frame rates are increasing. Your video camera probably shoots at 30 frames per second, but the state of the art in frame rates is 1 *trillion* frames per second.[8] Shooting in high definition is 2 megapixel resolution, but the state of the art in resolution is 150 *gigapixels*, almost 100,000 times finer.[9]

These trends suggest that there will be more data than we can comfortably store locally for a long time. There therefore will be a need for cloud storage, de-duplication, and dispersion for reduced latency in accessing that data and associated applications for a long time as well.

Summary

Because response time is important in an increasing number of applications, the distance between the user and the service is important. But, with a globally distributed base of users, if the cloud is to appear location independent, stringent response-time constraints can be met only with a distributed architecture.

The economics of building your own distributed service nodes or retail branches have rapidly diminishing returns: When the radius of a node is halved, the number of nodes required to cover a given area must be quadrupled. However, for many applications and scenarios, such as maintaining partitioned user data, the pay-per-use model of the cloud enables customers to enjoy latency reduction for free by exploiting dispersion, in the same way that, for many applications, the pay-per-use model of the cloud enables processing time acceleration for free.

> ### 💻 ONLINE
>
> "The Value of Dispersion in Latency Reduction," at http://complex-models.com/Latency.aspx, illustrates the benefits and diminishing returns of dispersion.

Notes

1. Tim Harford, *The Undercover Economist* (Random House, 2005).
2. Leonard Ciavattone, Alfred Morton, and Gomathi Ramachandran, "Standardized Active Measurements on a Tier 1 IP Backbone," *IEEE Communications Magazine* (June 2003).

3. Nimrod Megiddo and Kenneth J. Supowit, "On the Complexity of Some Common Geometric Location Problems," *SIAM Journal of Computing*, Vol. 13, No. 1, February, 1984, pp. 182-196. www.cs.uwaterloo.ca/~shai/cs886-F06/complexity_geometric.pdf

4. Pieter Merkus Lambertus Tammes, "On the Origin of Number and Arrangement of the Places of Exit on the Surface of Pollen-Grains" (Dissertation, Faculty of Mathematics and Natural Sciences, University of Groningen, the Netherlands, 1930), pp. 77-78 indexed at http://dissertations.ub.rug.nl/faculties/science/1930/p.m.l.tammes/?pLanguage=en&pFullItemRecord=ON with an abstract at http://dissertations.ub.rug.nl/FILES/faculties/science/1930/p.m.l.tammes/Tammes.pdf.

5. See "Figure 9: Baryon Density Isosurface for a B=97 Skyrmion with Icosahedral Symmetry," in Michael Atiyah and Paul Sutcliffe, "Polyhedra in Physics, Chemistry, and Geometry." http://arxiv.org/PS_cache/math-ph/pdf/0303/0303071v1.pdf.

6. Yoshinori Teshima and Tohru Ogawa "Dense Packing of Equal Circles on a Sphere by the Minimum-Zenith Method: Symmetrical Arrangement," *Forma* 15 (2000): 347–364. www.scipress.org/journals/forma/pdf/1504/15040347.pdf.

7. Joe Weinman, "As Time Goes By: The Law of Cloud Response Time," Working Paper, April 12, 2011.

8. http://web.mit.edu/press/2011/trillion-fps-camera.html.

9. http://rio.hk/projects/gigapixel_panoramas/urca/panoramas/sugarloaf_15tp/index.html.

CHAPTER 20

Dispersion Dilemma

Let's recap the logic of the last few chapters. We've argued that milliseconds and microseconds can mean millions of dollars. Whether trading equities or serving coffee shop customers, time is often of the essence. To reduce response time, we pointed out that you could leverage parallelism, where many hands make light work, and/or geodispersion, a sort of zone defense spread out over the planet.

In the case of response time reduction through parallelism, there are diminishing returns after early gains if you are attempting to achieve these gains yourself. However, the cloud can be a huge benefit, because, the pay-per-use model means that rather than suffering through a long elapsed time due to a small number of resources, a short elapsed time—leveraging many resources in parallel—can be achieved at no additional cost.

In the case of response time via dispersion, a *roughly* similar analysis holds. Increasing the number of delivery points can reduce time due to network latency by reducing the average or worst-case distance between a user and a service node. Again, using your own funds to pursue these gains rapidly becomes prohibitively expensive, because eking out smaller and smaller latency improvements requires rapidly growing investments. Again, the cloud can help by providing pay-per-use access to resources.

Generally, consolidation has benefits, such as aggregate demand smoothing, ability to leverage parallelism, and economies of scale, but dispersion has benefits in the way of a further reduction in response time for interactive applications. Which is better, or what should the relative proportion of these strategies be?

Strategies for Response Time Reduction

Parallelism and dispersion can be considered as specific tactics in a broad approach to response time reduction:

1. Eliminate the need for the transaction, if possible.
2. Tune (i.e., optimize) the application.
3. Use more resources to exploit any inherent parallelism in the service process.
4. Reduce the request-response latency by reducing the distance, either bringing the user to the service location or vice versa.
5. Reduce the number of round trips, for example, by sending more objects in each trip.

Many of these tactics can be used in conjunction with each other.

To understand these different approaches, let's consider how we might reduce the total time it takes to get a cup of coffee from the nearest coffee shop. The first approach, which cuts the effective response time to zero, is to eliminate the need for the transaction, by forgoing the cup of coffee entirely. Short of this, we could reduce the time spent getting coffee by cutting back on drinking it or buying a coffeemaker and placing it down the hall.

Suppose we *do* want a cup of coffee. We head down to the nearest coffee shop and realize that every time the barista makes a tasty concoction, he has to go to the back room to get an empty paper cup. We tune the application, suggesting a straightforward process improvement, namely that he keep a stack of empty cups up at the front. I'm using a simplified analogy here, but Starbucks' operations specialists tune processes all the time: They

> work obsessively to cut down the time it takes a barista to make any given drink; they call the coffee business "a game of seconds." [They use] automatic espresso machines that grind, tamp, and pull espresso shots at the push of a button, while steam wands equipped with temperature sensors stop foaming the milk at precisely the desired moment. This strips the luster from the "handcrafted beverage" idea, yet a latte-making process that once took a full minute now takes thirty-six seconds, which allows Starbucks to nearly double the amount of money it can make in that period of time.[1]

While we are helping the corner coffee shop with operations, we realize that there is only one barista and only one espresso machine. Without making any more process changes, we helpfully suggest hiring three more baristas and purchasing three more espresso machines. Sure enough, coffee arrives sooner. Rather than waiting for the three people ahead of us to be served sequentially, we immediately move to the front of the line.

In looking at the total time spent after performing these optimizations, we realize that we are still spending a lot of time walking to and from the coffee shop, so we suggest to the owners that they open another shop much closer—in fact, on the ground floor of the building in which we work. The owners of the coffee shop also might suggest that we move closer to them, but in any case, the distance and thus the transport latency would be reduced.

Finally, we realize that rather than going back and forth multiple times to get mocha frappuccinos for ourselves and our friends, we use a cup carrier. This reduces the number of round trips by transporting multiple objects simultaneously.

To review this example in the context of cloud computing, we can use several different approaches to speed up end-to-end, round-trip response time. The first approach, eliminating or reducing the need for the transaction, could leverage wide-area network acceleration gear to locally cache content, eliminating or reducing the need to fetch that content remotely from the cloud over a network.

The second tactic—application tuning—is the equivalent of process improvement at the coffee shop. Reengineering poorly written code, using best-in-class algorithms, and leveraging optimizing compilers eliminates wasted time and results in speedup.

The third principle is process parallelization. When the task may be parallelized, not only do many hands make light work, they make fast work.

The fourth approach is to reduce network latency by reducing the distance between the user and the service node: Doing this involves building out more geographically dispersed data centers or coffee shops.

Finally, parallelizing some or all of the network round-trips can result in a total response time reduction. Depending on the network protocol, browser settings, endpoint performance, and so forth, several objects can be fetched simultaneously.

All of these approaches can be useful, but a number of key Cloudonomics principles relate costs to these strategies. We noted earlier that building your own capacity for intermittent tasks would be cost prohibitive but that *in a cloud, speedup from parallelization can be free*. The fact that 100 cab rides costs the same whether we take them sequentially in one cab or simultaneously in 100 means that we can get free speedup, to the extent that the application can be parallelized.

Similarly, decreasing user or customer response times by building hundreds or thousands of data centers can be cost prohibitive, but *in a cloud, speedup for latency reduction can be free also*. But which approach should we leverage, consolidation to enhance parallelization and achieve other benefits such as scale economies or dispersion to reduce latency and achieve benefits such as enhanced user experience?

Consolidation versus Dispersion

Although there can be complicating factors, we will assume that a fully parallelizable process that takes time P takes only time P/p on p processors.[2] We've also noted that a network response time that takes time N takes only time $N/\sqrt{n}$ when exploiting n service nodes (excluding some details regarding spheres versus planes). When we add in a fixed time F for the serial portion of the application and any time spent in the endpoint, the total time is $F + N/\sqrt{n} + P/p$.

Both $1/p$ and $1/\sqrt{n}$ offer diminishing returns to scale in our pursuit of response time reduction. In other words, $1/p$ gets smaller as p gets larger, but does so less quickly, and $1/\sqrt{n}$ also gets smaller less quickly as n gets larger; therefore, the marginal benefit of one more processor or node—say, $(1/(p+1)) - 1/p$—gets smaller as well. We'd like to get rid of all response time, using either parallelism or dispersion, but we'll never get there. As Exhibit 20.1 shows, if we use ten processors, we can eliminate 90% of the time used for processing a parallel task. If we use ten nodes, we'll reduce just over two thirds of the time spent in traversing networks. The trick is to find an optimal balance between the two.

For example, if someone gave us budget for a quantity Q of 100 processors and told us to speed up a global application as best we could, we

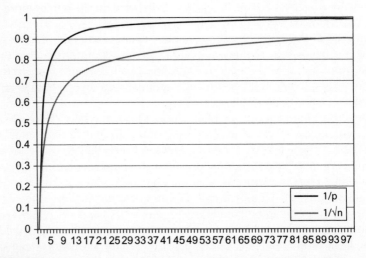

EXHIBIT 20.1 Relative Response Time Reduction from Increased Parallelism versus Increased Dispersion

could deploy 100 processors in 1 node, or 1 processor in each of 100 nodes, or 10 processors in each of 10 nodes. What's the best answer?

It turns out that for a given quantity $Q = n \times p$, the correct balance partly depends on the relative time spent in processing versus in network latency in the single-node, single-processor case. If latency is 1 second, say, then using all of our budget for dispersion will at most gain us 1 second in total response time. If the calculating portion takes a week, most of our investment is best spent on parallelism. Google understands this well: Initially, it focused on increasing the number of servers responding to search queries in parallel. Then, once it got in the range of network latencies, it began to focus on building out more data centers.

We derive the result elsewhere,[3] but briefly, given processing time P and network latency time N, the optimal number of dispersed nodes for the purposes of response time reduction is

$$n = \sqrt[3]{\frac{QN^2}{2P}}$$

Once we've determined the number of nodes, we set the number of processors p at each node to be Q/n.

Trade-offs between Consolidation and Dispersion

This equation brings us to what might be called the dispersion dilemma or perhaps the consolidation challenge. If we disperse our resources more and more, we improve response times by reducing network latency and network transport costs, but we *reduce* the benefit from parallelization and from statistical multiplexing. However, by consolidating, we improve our ability to parallel process. We also gain statistical multiplexing benefits. These benefits, interestingly, have an inverse square root effect, the same as for dispersion but for different reasons.

Unfortunately, we can't get both sets of benefits at once, so dispersion versus consolidation is one of life's trade-offs. However, customers of the cloud can leverage investments made by cloud providers to select an optimum balance, and, generally, they need not pay any more for the privilege.

Certain factors give consolidation an edge and others favor dispersion. Favoring consolidation, there are the statistics of scale, facility economies of scale, maximum manageable workloads given application coupling, and storage costs. However, user experience enhancements due to latency and response time reduction, business continuity, country compliance, customer (server hugger) comfort, favorable tax treatment, and network costs favor dispersion.

Benefits of Consolidation

The statistics of scale, as we saw in Chapter 15, can drive a $1/\sqrt{m}$ relative penalty cost effect when m independent workloads or customer demands are aggregated. In other words, as the volume of work grows in proportion to m, the expected absolute penalty only grows as $\sqrt{m}$, thus the relative penalty is $\sqrt{m}/m$ which is $1/\sqrt{m}$. To the extent that only "local" workloads are aggregated, dispersion causes problems due to "breakage." There is still a smoothing effect; demand just won't get as flat as with greater aggregation. Aggregating fewer workloads from within smaller regions, under an assumption that customers can't be serviced out of more distant nodes, means that the effective m is smaller and thus the relative penalty cost $1/\sqrt{m}$ is larger.

Suppose we have m customers, each with, say, normally distributed, independent demands, each with standard deviation σ. Let us partition these customers and thus their demands evenly among n nodes, so that each node has m/n customers. Since the sum of the variances is the variance of the sums, the standard deviation is the positive square root of the variance, and the mean absolute deviation for a normal distribution is $\sqrt{\frac{2}{\pi}}\sigma \cong .798\sigma$, we know that the expected absolute penalty at each node is $\sqrt{\frac{2}{\pi}}\sqrt{\frac{m}{n}}\sigma$, thus the total penalty across all nodes is $n \times \sqrt{\frac{2}{\pi}}\sqrt{\frac{m}{n}}\sigma$. This compares with an expected absolute penalty at a single consolidated node, i.e., where $n = 1$, of $1 \times \sqrt{\frac{2}{\pi}}\sqrt{\frac{m}{1}}\sigma$. The relative increase in the penalty function is then the ratio of the two, which is simply $\sqrt{n}$. As n gets very large, the $\sqrt{n}$ gets somewhat large, leading to increased penalties relative to a single node. It is for this reason that your local neighborhood bank branch either seems to be empty when you walk in, or you have to wait forever to do something complicated, such as open a checking account. Local branches are more convenient than a single main facility would be, reducing the latency to drive to the bank, but have more highly variable demand and thus either lower utilization or longer waits due to little statistical multiplexing given the number of "servers", i.e., bank clerks.

Facility economies of scale enable cost benefits due to size. As we have seen, while these benefits may be overstated, there certainly do tend to be such economies of scale in some areas, such as bandwidth pricing and facilities management. Firm economies of scale, such as branding and buyer power, don't vary based on consolidation versus dispersion. If you are buying a million servers from a vendor, you're going to get a pretty good discount regardless of whether you put them all in a single data center or distribute them to 100 data centers.

Some applications require a tight degree of coupling between elements running on different processors. Consequently, a minimum amount of capacity is required in a single location to be able to run such workloads.

Clearly, the extent to which resources are consolidated increases the maximum size of a tightly coupled workload that can be run by a provider. Given that there are other customers, a service provider won't necessarily want to block the other customers by allowing such an application to run, but even with a rule like "no more than 20% of capacity can be allocated to a given customer," the larger the facility, the larger the maximum workload of that type that can be run.

Finally, to the extent to which information must be replicated in each facility, building out more facilities implies more replication and thus greater cost, thus favoring consolidation.

Benefits of Dispersion

Other factors favor dispersion. We've already reviewed response time benefits, but there are other benefits as well.

There are serious business continuity issues with only having one location for services or information: What disaster recovery planners call a smoking-hole disaster can wipe out a business. A smoking-hole disaster might be due to a terrorist attack, hurricane, tornado, earthquake, flood, fire, or natural gas explosion but generally means something where the equipment is out of service and the data unrecoverable. The only mitigation or recovery solution is to replicate the hardware and software stack and data in the facility somewhere else. Doing this used to mean a disaster recovery facility, where equipment could be configured in a few days to replicate the lost processing capability and data could be recovered off of tape. Then it meant live distributed processing with synchronously mirrored data. Now it is returning back to the old strategy, in a way, with rapid provisioning of cloud resources being considered as a way of providing server disaster recovery without entailing the cost of a dedicated second site. A degree of partitioning reduces the cost of continuity. For example, if you have one facility and use a second site for recovery, the ratio of the cost of the continuity strategy to the cost of an unreliable architecture is two to one: 100% overhead. (This simple analysis ignores the costs of outages and the additional costs of network resources required to assure survivability and availability.) If you have two facilities, each with 50% of the "live" resources, it only takes a third facility sized to be the same as *one* of the facilities to recover from a single catastrophic disaster. Consequently, the ratio drops to $(2+1)/2$, or 50% overhead. As n increases, the ratio of $(n+1)/n$ approaches unity, so the marginal cost of continuity assurance approaches zero.

Yet another rationale for dispersion is country compliance. Some countries have very strict laws that data concerning their citizens or other information cannot leave the territorial boundaries.

Regardless of country compliance, some customers just like to have personal knowledge of the exact facility and location of their information and to be able to visit and even "touch" the resources. These customers are fondly known in the industry as "server huggers". A local presence can also enable favorable tax treatment (or, in some cases, what some view as unfavorable tax treatment, when sales tax must be collected if a company has a "physical point of presence" in the state).

Network costs may also be reduced via dispersion, since transactions need to travel less distance to be served. There is a belief in the industry that location doesn't matter, but of course it does. Aggregate transport capacity requirements are reduced when transaction distance is reduced. Trends in relative prices are likely to increasingly favor greater dispersion. A study conducted by storage-as-a-service provider Backblaze determined that, while storage costs per gigabyte have been dropping continuously at an average rate of 40% per year over the last quarter century, the cost of a megabit per second of bandwidth has been dropping only at 26% per year.[4]

Whether Moore's Law—which has had various restatements and interpretations—actually matches reality or not, price-performance for computing is certainly improving.[5] Performance for a given server is a challenge to estimate due to hedonic (quality-adjusted) price indexing and inflation adjustment, but the performance for a given cost has been estimated to double every 1.4 to 2 years.[6] There are other factors, including cost of power, operations, and so forth, but if we merely use the slower estimate of doubling every two years, it implies a 41% (since 1.41 is the square root of 2) improvement in performance every year for a given price, which may be restated as a 29% price drop (to .707 of the prior cost). This estimate matches at least one other study.[7] A doubling in performance/server cost in 1.4 years translates to a 64% improvement every year, which may be restated as a 39% annual price decrease in processing costs.

To put it another way, processing, storage, and network costs are all dropping. But if processing and storage costs drop faster than network costs do, which has been the trend for a long time, network costs over time asymptotically approach 100% of the cost of a given distributed computation.[8] As that becomes the case, dispersed resources become increasingly favored. Think of it this way: If the cost of gas keeps increasing, shopping at a remote wholesale club becomes increasingly less attractive.

The Network Is the Computer

In some of the preceding analysis, we've treated the nodes as independent, with the idea being that customers and their processing are partitioned. However, we can solve some problems by letting customers with demand that is too great for one node spill over to another one. This is the same as your local electric utility pulling in power over the grid from a distant one or your overbooked city hotel getting you a room at another one in the chain on the outskirts of town.

In this model, the resources are dispersed but rather than being a collection of pieces, they act as an intelligent whole. Customers are served by whichever node has capacity and the correct collection of data and services needed. Resources are physically dispersed but logically centralized and integrated.

John Gage, one of Sun Microsystems' first employees, has been credited with the phrase "The Network is the Computer."[9] More recently, Lew Tucker, formerly of Sun and now vice president and chief technology officer (CTO) of cloud computing at Cisco, observed that the network is the platform[10]; in other words, it becomes a programmable system. When I spoke with Lew on stage at Om Malik's Structure 2011 event, we shared a vision of the cloud as being not just a computing utility but as the next generation of intelligent, logically consolidated, physically distributed computing.[11] In this vision, the network is not the computer in the sense that the network replaces the computer; rather, the network and the computer become a single converged entity.

According to Matthew Finnie, group CTO of Interoute, a European network and IT services operator, computing resources are already converging into the network fabric.[12] Rather than the large monolithic data centers that have defined cloud over the past few years, processing nodes sized appropriately to demand, dispersed geographically and dissolved into the network fabric are likely to be the new architecture.

Dor Skuler, Alcatel-Lucent's vice president of cloud solutions, shares a similar view, believing that the cloud "should be a holistic part of the network itself. In his view, the cloud will leverage smaller data centers deployed in a highly distributed fashion, with "different points of presence that the cloud has access to by the way of exchanges."[13]

In such an architecture, an intelligent network becomes the necessary complement to intelligent endpoints and intelligent cloud resources and services. Such an intelligent network, besides being programmable, would offer bandwidth on demand, quality of service on demand, intelligent routing, and route control—the ability for a customer to determine a specific route—as well as the ability to predefine policies and have them execute programmatically.[14]

Beyond data center dispersion or content or application delivery network node dispersion, the processing power in smartphones, tablets, and other personal devices, not to mention dishwashers, digital watches, and greeting cards, is currently the ultimate in dispersion for individuals. Eventually, perhaps, we will see even finer dispersion, as multiple power-scavenging wireless nanobot sensors float through our bloodstream, perhaps zapping errant triglycerides or carcinogens as they do so, and someday, smart dust will float through the atmosphere, in what might be considered "true" cloud computing.

Summary

From an architectural point of view, there are fundamental benefits to consolidation, such as overhead reduction, ability to speed up tasks via parallel processing, de-duplication of some resources, and aggregate demand smoothing and thus better capacity utilization and lower delivered costs.

There are also benefits to dispersion, such as latency reduction leading to productivity and commercial benefits through an improved experience, and improved business continuity.

From an economic point of view, a do-it-yourself strategy for parallelization is costly, since for a given volume of work, acceleration implies greater resource expenditures and lower average utilization. A do-it-yourself strategy for dispersion is also costly, because quadrupling the number of nodes only halves the latency, and at some point adding billions of nodes, say, may reduce latency only by microseconds.

The cloud solves these dilemmas, offering free acceleration through pay-per-use parallel processing and, in some cases, free dispersion via partitionable resources.

Instead of treating each dispersed node as a stand-alone entity, weaving it into a global cloud fabric of processing and storage nodes integrated via an intelligent network can provide the best balance of consolidation and dispersion.

Notes

1. Taylor Clark, *Starbucked* (Back Bay Books/Little, Brown, 2007).
2. Joe Weinman, "As Time Goes By: The Law of Cloud Response Time," April 12, 2011. www.joeweinman.com/Resources/Joe_Weinman_As_Time_Goes_By.pdf.
3. Ibid.
4. Om Malik, "The Storage vs. Bandwidth Debate," *GigaOM.com*, June 24, 2011. http://gigaom.com/broadband/the-storage-vs-bandwidth-debate/.
5. Ilkka Tuomi, "The Lives and the Death of Moore's Law," *First Monday* (October 2002). www.firstmonday.org/issues/issue7_11/tuomi/#author.
6. William D. Nordhaus, "The Progress of Computing," Yale University and the National Bureau of Economic Research, March 4, 2002, version 5.2.2,

http://nordhaus.econ.yale.edu/prog_030402_all.pdf; Jonathan G. Koomey, Christian Belady, Michael Patterson, Anthony Santos, and Klaus-Dieter Lange, "Assessing Trends Over Time in Performance, Costs, and Energy Use for Servers," August 17, 2009, www.intel.com/assets/pdf/general/servertrendsreleasecomplete-v25.pdf.

7. M. Ekman, F. Warg, and J. Nilsson, "An In-Depth Look at Computer Performance Growth," *ACM SIGARCH Computer Architecture News* 33 (March 2005): 144–147.

8. Jim Gray, *Distributed Computing Economics*, Microsoft Research Technical Report MSR-TR-2003-24, March 2003. http://arxiv.org/ftp/cs/papers/0403/0403019.pdf.

9. Stefanie Olsen, "Sun's John Gage Joins Al Gore in Clean-Tech Investing," *CNET News*, June 9, 2008. http://news.cnet.com/8301-10784_3-9964131-7.html.

10. Ben Rooney, "The Network Is the Computer, Again," *Wall Street Journal Tech Europe*, February 1, 2011. http://blogs.wsj.com/tech-europe/2011/02/01/the-network-is-the-computer-again/.

11. Larry Dignan, "HP, Cisco: Entering a New Era in Cloud Computing," *ZDnet*, June 23, 2011. www.zdnet.com/blog/btl/hp-cisco-entering-a-new-era-in-cloud-computing/51291.

12. Matthew Finnie, conversation with the author, January 26, 2012.

13. Kavit Majithia, "Separating the Sky," *Capacity Magazine* (January 2012). http://www.capacitymagazine.com/Article/2959675/Search/Mobile-cloud-separating-the-sky.html

14. Joe Weinman, "Network Implications of Cloud Computing," presented at the Technical Symposium at ITU Telecom World, Geneva, October 24–27, 2011, pp. 75–81. www.joeweinman.com/Papers.htm.

CHAPTER 21

Platform and Software Services

We have focused heavily on infrastructure as a service (IaaS). However, there are two other major layers in the cloud: platform as a service (PaaS) and software as a service (SaaS), and dozens of other as-a-service offers which are usually considered variations or components of IaaS, PaaS, and SaaS: data as a service, compute as a service, integration as a service, business process as a service, etc. SaaS has changed the way organizations of all sizes acquire and utilize increasingly powerful business applications to perform their day-to-day functions and achieve their corporate objectives, according to Jeffrey M. Kaplan, managing director of THINKstrategies and founder of the Cloud Computing Showplace.[1] He argued that any organization that fails to capitalize on today's rapidly expanding array of SaaS solutions will be unable to keep pace with the escalating needs of its employees, customers, and business partners and therefore will be at a competitive disadvantage in the marketplace.

Generally speaking, IaaS offers are targeted at operations personnel: those whose job it is to *run* things; PaaS offers are targeted at developers: those who *build* things; and SaaS is targeted at end users: those who *use* things. One may think of the first as a U-Stor-It or warehouse space: Raw capacity can be rented. The second is Home Depot, with components of every shape and size ready for purchase, assembly, and customization—say, screws, knobs, and pine boards. The third is a dresser that can be bought at the furniture store rather than building your own with the Home Depot parts. PaaS blends into SaaS in the same way that an unfinished dresser that you paint or stain is midway between the two.

Correctly valuing SaaS or PaaS is somewhat trickier than might appear at first glance. There is little doubt that there are excellent applications, suites, and packages available from as-a-service cloud providers; their growing market share is proof enough. And, while we all have our pet peeves—I for one am irritated that Microsoft took away bicolor grid patterns from PowerPoint—there have been successes in traditional licensed software as well.

But rather than being cheerleaders for PaaS or SaaS, we need to be rigorous about how value is extracted from such services and take care not to confuse the software functionality per se with the delivery model, unless the two are irrevocably intertwined. If you receive a diamond ring in the mail, the value is in the ring, after all, not in the envelope. However, if the fact that the ring arrived at all is due to rigorous tracking and insurance, we can't discount that either. In other words, the fact that something of value is wrapped up in a particular delivery model means that we need to carefully distinguish how much value there is in the object versus how much is in the delivery approach.

The reason for this rigor is that the SaaS model is actually a bundle of arguably orthogonal options: specific software functionality, a deployment model that obviates installation, a managed runtime environment, Internet or other network access, and pay-per-use (say, per user per month or per transaction) charging.

Conceptually, any of these characteristics could be inverted: SaaS but with a one-time front-end lifetime fee; or software installed on a client's premises but remotely managed; or software installed and managed by the client but with usage-sensitive billing. To evaluate the likelihood of these various permutations requires a deeper analysis of the benefits and issues associated with PaaS and SaaS.

We also need to distinguish current but ephemeral advantages from sustainable or inherent ones. For example, one benefit that providers tout for SaaS is more frequent updates to the code base and thus more frequent bug fixes and feature updates than common from traditional software houses offering only perpetual licenses.

On one hand, is this truly a benefit of SaaS? Or is it merely a characteristic of the current crop of SaaS providers? If the latter is true, the "advantage" or "economic value" generated is essentially irrelevant and unsustainable. On the other hand, if it is inextricably linked to the essence of SaaS, it is relevant. The truth lies somewhere in between, actually: Developers in either delivery model can choose to make updates as frequently or infrequently as they choose to, but the centralized delivery model for SaaS means that it is easier to make updates to a SaaS code base. The updates need to be provided merely to a single global instance of the multitenant software or perhaps a single instance in each availability zone. We also need to be realistic: Although there is evidence that "elephants can dance," it would be prudent to carefully consider whether to bet on them in the tango competition.[2] SaaS may be as much a cultural orientation as a technology, operations, or delivery modality.

Finally, we need to keep in mind what we discussed in the preceding chapters: Although SaaS and PaaS may or may not be built on top of infrastructure service offers, they do need infrastructure to run, so many of the same benefits accrue: for example, being able to statistically multiplex independent demands requires fewer resources than building to peak in silos.

Infrastructure as a Service Benefit

A core set of benefits associated with SaaS ultimately is that associated with infrastructure as a service: Pay-per-use pricing is beneficial when there is variable usage; on-demand provisioning is beneficial when there is unpredictable demand; common infrastructure enables not just multiplexing, as with infrastructure, but the even more efficient multitenancy; and location independence, typically enabled by a SaaS cloud provider's distributed infrastructure, enables a responsive user experience.

However, we have to be careful to consider which models we are comparing. A distributed SaaS model may beat a single-instance enterprise data center software model thanks to a richer, more interactive experience due to geodispersion. But in the same way, a client app may beat a remote server-based one with an even richer and more interactive experience. And the client app will work even when the network is unavailable due to an outage or network coverage issues.

Applications with different profiles may have different breakeven points: A relatively low-powered device may benefit from the immense computational power that the cloud can bring: Running a search query on your smartphone is unlikely to be as fast as enlisting 1,000 state-of-the-art servers in parallel in the cloud. It is not unreasonable to assume that no matter how much data our smartphones can store, there will always be more data—whether personal or the world's information—that we will want to access. For many applications, there is no choice *but* the cloud.

When considering how SaaS benefits are partly inherited from cloud infrastructure benefits, it should be noted that SaaS platforms are not necessarily built on infrastructure as a service per se. A SaaS customer relationship management or human resources provider does not typically create a virtual server for each customer but rather uses a single instance for many customers. In this architecture, one row in a database may belong to a given customer, and the next one may belong to a different one. This approach achieves a high degree of efficiency, just as packing guests into a hotel ballroom takes less space than giving them each a private hotel room.

The point is that the key attributes of cloud—common infrastructure, pay-per-use, on-demand elasticity, and others—are foundational for SaaS. SaaS can provide additional benefits on top of those core ones.

Paying on Actuals versus Forecasts

One benefit of SaaS in its current formulation is that, typically, you pay based on the *actual* number of subscribers rather than a *projection*. Often projected use of a new application is lower than expected: Users can't seem to "get" the new system; they are too busy to attend scheduled training; other workarounds do the job just fine; access, security, language, or other implementation issues prevent certain functional groups, global regions, or groups with given devices or operating systems from being onboarded on schedule.

For all these reasons, paying as you go based on the number of users who actually are actively able to use the system or at least interested enough to acquire an account can cost less than an enterprise license sized to a higher number of users.

However, this benefit is not an insurmountable barrier for a legacy software vendor to overcome. There is no reason that licensed software couldn't be priced based on the actual number of users or even finer-grained metrics, such as CPU minutes via one-minute term licenses or percentage of CPU utilization. This is not hypothetical: I negotiated such a deal with a major software vendor a few years ago.

The challenge to existing software vendors is not that they can't do this, it's that they'd rather not: They have a track record of financials based on collecting revenues on a front-loaded basis. A package is sold at a given price, with maintenance of, say, 20% to 25% per year. This price holds until the next release. Switching models after a stream of quarters showing growing revenues could be a challenge, given publicly held companies' focus on quarterly results.

Installation

Installation is almost certainly a differentiator for SaaS. If enterprise software installation were as easy as on most tablets or smartphones—just click "Install" and wait a few seconds—it would not be much of a concern. However, in many cases, the process of enterprise software installation is more like installing a new kitchen. Everything is a mess for an interminable period, various random components function at unpredictable intervals as they are ripped out and replaced, nothing seems to fit the way it looked on the blueprint, and you eat off of paper plates for months. By comparison, SaaS is like going to a restaurant: As long as you have a means of access (transportation) and a credit card, you can eat all you want.

Investment

The profile of cash and capital changes with SaaS. Whether it is better or not depends on many factors. For a small number of users, the lack of up-front investment coupled with the nominal, low per-use prices can offer unbeatable savings versus traditional licensing models and ongoing maintenance fees.

However, as always, it is certainly possible that it is cheaper to agree to an enterprise license agreement for packaged software enabling unlimited users, or some number of anonymous users, than to pay by the user per month.

Updates

SaaS providers like to say that their ability to provide frequent updates is an advantage. This capability is *facilitated* by the SaaS model, but it's less clear that it is of necessity a sustainable difference. In the legacy model, software updates, patches, bug fixes, and so-called service packs are made available to thousands or even millions of customers, either "pushed" on an "Auto-Update" basis, where the update occurs automatically, or "pulled" when the user requests it. In the SaaS model, these changes are applied once (per cloud service node), and any users that subsequently access the service immediately begin using the new capability.

The advantage of this approach is application dependent. To take things to the extreme, if an application with 100 gigabytes of code were rewritten every hour in its entirety, thus requiring a complete download to each of hundreds of millions of users, the advantage of the SaaS software update model would be clear. However, if a 100-kilobyte applet is all that changes every few months and it must be distributed to a couple of hundred users, the SaaS advantage is less compelling.

Service-Level Agreements

Because SaaS is first and foremost a service, it can have the advantage of contractually bound service-level agreements regarding performance or availability, unlike a captive internal IT shop. No one wants the environment to fail, whether it's internally sourced or delivered externally as a service.

However, there can be advantages to the contractual guarantees inherent in commercial, arm's-length services.

Continuously Earned Trust

In the classic *The Evolution of Cooperation*, Professor Robert Axelrod, from the University of Michigan, explores the implications of a game-theoretic computer tournament where players receive a sequence of greater or lesser payoffs by playing the "Iterated Prisoners' Dilemma."[3] The simulation models sequences of iterations where a player can:

- Cooperate with the other and receive a good payoff
- Successfully take advantage of the other and receive a higher payoff
- Be taken advantage off and receive a zero payoff
- Achieve parity in noncooperation and receive a low payoff

Players used different strategies, such as random choice in each step, or "tit-for-tat," where a player matched the other's prior move. Axelrod showed that cooperation can spontaneously arise, but one key was repeated interactions. SaaS drives the evolution of cooperation, because each month another "iteration" of the relationship occurs.

With SaaS, the provider must continuously earn your trust and satisfaction. Sure, you can't always migrate between providers easily, so the switching costs must be lower than the pain is great, but SaaS providers have great incentive to deliver an excellent customer experience—there is not much runway to let quality issues fester.

Visibility and Transparency

With SaaS, customers have greater visibility into their costs; after all, receiving a bill every month that clearly indicates the direct costs: say, 473 users times $10. With owned software, it can be difficult to determine how many IT resources are actually used, including servers, storage, load balancers, accelerators, power, cooling, administrators, network, patching, security, and the like.

True, not all costs in using SaaS are represented by the bill from the SaaS provider. For example, there are will be network access costs. However, in most cases, network access must be provisioned for the endpoints anyway, so the *marginal* cost to a SaaS customer for network usage for SaaS may actually be zero. True, the provider must pay some network costs, but this is built into the price and is thus part of a charge with full visibility.

The difference is the same in eating a meal: It's easier to determine the total on your restaurant bill than to figure out the cost in your kitchen, including the allocated use of your stove, the gas that it uses, the power for your refrigerator, your time as cook, and so on.

In addition, the trust factor requires that SaaS providers offer a high degree of visibility into their operations and status. Although for some providers there is no one to call and unhelpful customer service communications, such as "We are down. Check our Twitter feed for updates," the leading providers offer a high degree of transparency into the state of their operations: trust.salesforce.com is a great example of detailed, real-time status.

As Peter Coffee, head of platform research at Salesforce.com, pointed out, service quality is not measured adequately by anything as simple as percentage uptime, because customers are far less forgiving of any imperfection when they feel that they're not in the loop, let alone not in control.[4] Closing that gap depends on how customers are treated during and after any departure from normal service. This treatment is known in the service quality field as "service recovery." Communications is a big help in eliminating feelings of helplessness.

Big Data and Computing Power

One key difference between the cloud and endpoints is certainly computing power. The amount of computing power and the size of the databases that a large cloud provider can bring to bear versus a smartphone or a desktop are clearly greater. For some applications—for example, word processing—this fact is hardly relevant. For others, such as Monte Carlo simulations, portfolio optimization, seismic analysis, particle collider data analysis, genomics, and search queries, there is a compelling advantage to the SaaS model, especially when complemented by scalable capacity.

Ubiquitous Access

The good news is that SaaS applications, since they are generally available over the Internet, are essentially accessible from anywhere and thus broadly usable. The bad news is that SaaS applications, since they are available over the Internet, are essentially accessible from anywhere. In an era of hackers and botnets, this accessibility may be a concern depending on what exactly it is that you're doing with the cloud. Some SaaS environments requiring highest security—such as the New York Stock Exchange Euronext community cloud—have no Internet connections.

Response Time and Availability

It took us six chapters to just skim the surface of response time and availability. To recap briefly, response time can be greatly improved by the cloud in two ways: a reduction in network latency via globally dispersed instances and a reduction in processing time via a high degree of parallel processing. Availability can also be enhanced by the cloud through maintenance of replicas of the data and the ability to call additional resources into service due to a demand spike or to recover from an outage on an emergency basis.

Although it is conceivable that, for some applications, these architectural benefits could be replicated via owned data centers or via infrastructure services, using a SaaS provider is likely to be easier. We expect a search engine or social networking site to work, hassle free.

Multitenancy, Shared Data

Sharing of servers, application instances, and storage among customers represents a true and dramatic gain for most applications. A small business, on average, might use 1/100th or less of the power of a server on average; consequently, many of such businesses can be resident on a single multi-tenant architecture instead of each buying its own and achieving terrible utilization.

John Keagy, chief executive officer of GoGrid, one of the largest infrastructure as a service providers, has calculated that on average, Salesforce.com uses .03 servers per customer or perhaps fewer. This is compared to a typical minimum configuration that a customer might deploy itself of two or three servers. This represents more than a 65-fold improvement. Moreover, as Keagy pointed out, "think of how much more efficiently SalesForce.com manages these 3,000 servers than 100,000 random companies could manage more than 200,000 servers."[5]

The same goes for storage: a small or medium business (SMB) with 1,000 customers, each needing a 1-kilobyte record—say, name, address, account balance—would use 1 megabyte—1 millionth of the capacity of the drive shipping with PCs today. And the space needed for other software components, rather than being replicated thousands of times for each of thousands of small businesses, can exist just once per location.

Cloud-Centric Applications

As reviewed in Chapter 7, a number of use cases inherently belong in the cloud, and some don't. The former cases create additional impetus for use of the cloud. For example, a repository—whether the Library of Congress, Wikipedia, or Google Books—is expensive to replicate thousands or millions of times. The economics of such scenarios are self-evident. Such a repository is almost certainly likely to be accessed via a SaaS interface.

Scalability

SaaS environments are designed and built to scale to serve as many customers as necessary facilitating ease of deployment, although in some cases at the cost of highest possible performance. For example, many NoSQL (Not only Structured Query Language) databases can easily scale: Data can be partitioned among multiple servers. On one hand, this partitioning does not always lead to optimal performance compared to indexed relational databases. On the other hand, even if such performance is theoretically not optimal, performance can remain stable even as the number of users or some other metric, such as number of transactions, grows by several orders of magnitude, leading to an advantage for SaaS. Sometimes performance and scale go hand in hand: Most search engines, which are a cloud SaaS solution after all, achieve incredible performance even while serving immense numbers of simultaneous users.

Communities and Markets

SaaS offers tend to be tied in with markets, service catalogs, and communities. These can be very rich: For example, an online SaaS market might permit you not only to sell one or more applications but also to enable others to act as retailers or distributors, under fairly complex policies: You might authorize distributors who in turn might authorize other distributors, but those distributors might not further authorize additional downstream entities to be distributors. These market constructs can enable richer capabilities in less time, greater sharing of best practices, more extensions to core functionality, and so forth.

Although licensed products also have communities associated with them, the public access inherent in the SaaS model and the ease of enabling try-before-you-buy—or what sales professionals call the puppy dog sale—provides SaaS with an edge.

Lock-in

A common issue that cloud skeptics like to raise is lock-in. One relevant dimension here is proprietary interfaces, processes, formats, and the like.

Another is data transfer costs to retrieve a body of data stored with a SaaS provider or migrate it to a competitor. Yet another is legal issues regarding ownership of content that has been submitted: If you submit a video, photograph, or restaurant or movie review to a site, who owns the rights to the intellectual property?

It can be argued that much alleged lock-in has nothing to do with the cloud. Lock-in—that is, familiarity with processes or interfaces—may happen with cloud software, or with desktop software, or with mainframe software, or with keyboard layouts, spoken language, where a stamp needs to be placed on an envelope, how to use cruise control, driving on the right or left side of the road, or any random cultural anomaly. Are there costs to migrate from one cloud provider to another? Sure, but there are also costs to move from one licensed software package to another. The quest for any software developer, whether licensed package or SaaS, to differentiate its product through the introduction of new features, may have lock-in as an intentional strategy or as a by-product of innovation.

Security and Compliance

Another issue that some raise is security. There are security challenges in private, public, and hybrid environments, and there are unique challenges entailed in the cloud. For example, Josh Corman, research director for enterprise security at The 451 Group, observed that "it's incredibly difficult to do court-admissible forensics without having logs at many levels that cross the . . . boundary between the cloud provider and the enterprise . . . making forensics a very ominous and difficult problem in any public cloud."[6] As well-known cloud blogger and researcher Krishnan Subramanian observed hybrid clouds create a larger IT perimeter to be defended and additional challenges in identity and access management, data transport, security policies, and security of the hybrid cloud management tools.[7]

However, chances are that leading SaaS providers can pay better attention to all dimensions of security—physical and logical—and compliance than an SMB, and even a well-run enterprise, just as a bank pays more attention to security than your mattress does. Are there potential security vulnerabilities by using a SaaS provider? Yes. But the question is: Are these vulnerabilities greater or lesser than do-it-yourself?

Today's world of compliance is an alphabet soup of standards, processes, certifications, laws, regulations, and bodies. Examples include the Statement on Auditing Standards (SAS) 70, the IT Governance Institute (ITGI) Control Objectives for Information and related Technology (COBIT), the Payment Card Industry (PCI) Data Security Standard (DSS), the Health Insurance Portability and Accountability Act (HIPAA), the Federal

Information Security Management Act (FISMA), and the Department of Defense Information Assurance Certification and Accreditation Process (DIACAP).[8] It is clearly easier to validate whether a trusted third-party software or infrastructure services provider is compliant and certified than to go through such a certification process yourself, in the same way that it is easier to peruse the diploma or board certification on your doctor's wall than to go to medical school, intern, start a practice, and get your own board certification.

PaaS: Assembly versus Fabrication

PaaS can be thought of as SaaS for developers. It is software delivered as a service that enables the construction of other software.

One key benefit of PaaS is inherent in the value of components and platforms. We might call this the *peanut butter sandwich principle*: It's easier to make a peanut butter sandwich if you don't have to grow and grind your own peanuts, grow your own wheat, and bake your own bread. Leveraging proven, tested, components that others have created can be faster than building them from scratch.

It is difficult to ascribe this benefit to the PaaS model alone, because it was the promise of service-oriented architectures (SOA) with reusable catalogs of components.

However, according to Peter Coffee, the biggest issue with SOA is the lack of a WIIFM—a "what's in it for me."[9] There is little to motivate an internal developer to create reusable components. In the platform world, however, the motivation is money: the creation of a component that will enter a publicly available library and be sold. It is like the difference, Coffee observed, between trying to get a teen to clean his or her room versus paying Merry Maids to do it. Profit is a strong motivator and unleashes the power of a competitive market.

Innovation and Democratization

We've covered a variety of cost-oriented benefits, but there is a broader context of relevance. As related earlier, John Dillon, chief executive of Engine Yard, pointed out that PaaS enables experimentation and "fast failure."[10] Although some think failure is bad, it is a necessary ingredient in learning and adaptation. The faster the failure, the sooner the success. Dillon further observed that "a progressive CIO [chief information officer] will allow experimentation; a reactionary one will be subject to end runs. The latter will create animosity instead of awareness and constructive engagement."

Such an approach is not restricted to just high-tech start-ups but also involves the entrepreneurially minded within established companies. Dillon drew parallels with the long-tail model of content enabled by e-tailers such as Amazon.com, pointing out that this democratization of IT *development* enables a long tail of IT.

Not that long ago, the creation of a professional graphics presentation required going to the graphics department and engaging professional artists to design and then print the results onto slides. Getting a document printed required a trip to the corporate print center. PCs, PowerPoint, and personal printers democratized graphics; PaaS is democratizing software *creation*.

Such innovation is not restricted to the boundaries of the firm. Barbara van Schewick, an associate professor of law at Stanford Law School, argued that technical architecture can either constrain or accelerate innovation.[11] Consider, for example, a closed system owned and directed by a single enterprise versus an open platform that defines interfaces but enables a boundless ecosystem to innovate on it. Whether it is smartphone platforms, the PC, a microblogging API, or even the rules of haiku poetry, van Schewick argued, the right balance of a framework defined by constraints or standards coupled with a group of self-interested actors drives an emergent system. Applying these insights to the cloud, the extensible foundation and framework offered by both infrastructure services and platform services creates a fertile environment for innovation.

Coffee has also argued that within the typical large corporation, operations work is not exciting and may not offer much of a career path.[12] By migrating personnel to a business unit that is focused on SaaS development and delivery, top talent can be rewarded appropriately. And in migrating the focus of work to empowered platform-enabled creativity, top talent can be retained.

Deconstructing the Pure SaaS Model

We started off this chapter by observing that the SaaS model bundles specific software functionality, a no-installation deployment model, a managed runtime, Internet access, and usage-sensitive charging. However, strategists and innovators will recognize that it is not inconceivable that various of these characteristics could be modified, eliminated, or inverted.

Rather than running in the cloud, the same software can run in the client or in an enterprise data center. If a customer has the resources to build a private implementation, if the usage levels are not that variable, or if the functionality offered by the software generates such value that the resource costs are relatively inconsequential, why not? Trade-offs exist in areas such as loss of SaaS multitenancy efficiency, but perhaps there are gains in performance if the application is tightly coupled to a legacy data center app. I believe that SaaS providers will realize that they are in the "S" business more than they are in the "aaS" business.

Consider Starbucks. It was originally a service provider, offering a satisfying beverage experience at thousands of globally dispersed service nodes (better known as coffee shops). Searching for growth, CEO Howard Schultz realized that there were customers who wanted Starbucks coffee but didn't want the experience or a service delivery model, just some ground coffee to brew in their own homes. In September 1998, Starbucks announced a relationship with Kraft Foods to sell Starbucks-branded coffee, leveraging Kraft's distribution muscle to reach 25,000 grocery stores.[13] In 2011, Starbucks transitioned the Kraft relationship in house, directly distributing to retail outlets. Company-owned stores still account for a majority of revenues, but consumer packaged goods and delivery of ground coffee to foodservice companies is now worth over $1 billion annually.[14]

In Pine and Gilmore's Experience Economy framework, Starbucks may have diluted high-value experiences with mere products, but it captured a substantial market opportunity.[15] You may argue that the benefits are greater via the service model—no capital expenditures for home or office coffeemakers, excellent scalability, quality management via professional operators (i.e., baristas) and economies of scale—but the fact is that the packaged coffee retailing business is steaming hot.

To abstractly state Starbucks' strategy, a service provider complemented its service business with a product business, enabling on-premises consumption. The as-a-service segment may be the largest fraction of the market, but it is hard to believe that enterprising SaaS providers will ignore the dollars from on-premises sales.

Somewhere between the choice of service provider and on-premises there is application streaming, where various modules comprising the software are streamed on demand to the endpoint as they are needed. This approach can provide some of the deployment benefits of SaaS with local response time characteristics.

Rackspace is an example of an innovator in the spirit of Starbucks. It recently introduced its Rackspace Cloud: Private Edition, which broadens its portfolio from pure services available at a Rackspace data center to both licensed implementations and customer-premises deployments.[16] For PaaS, there is the example of ActiveState, which offers its Stackato Private PaaS to run either in the cloud or in an enterprise data center.[17]

As for pay per use, it is not impossible to envision a fixed up-front fee offered with cloud delivery or a pay-per-use fee associated with on-premises delivery. TiVo—which is, after all, a cloud service that includes programming and recommendations—offers a "Product Lifetime Service" price for a one-time charge of $499.99, instead of a monthly fee of $19.99.

The breakeven point—excluding the discounting of cash flows and risk adjustment, is at 25 months, which is a reasonable deal. Conversely, although primarily focused on infrastructure, HP's "Local Burst" capability offers on-demand, pay-per-use resources *within* the corporate data center, leveraging HP Utility Ready Computing.[18]

Coffee has observed that such an approach for SaaS plays musical chairs with a traditional concern. It used to be that customers who were server huggers worried about being able to touch and manage infrastructure in the cloud. One concern of service providers about a private PaaS or SaaS model is being able to touch and manage services that are in the enterprise data center: When services are delivered in customer-owned and operated environments, "the water runs downhill in the direction of customizations" that weaken what should be fundamental SaaS and PaaS advantages of coherence and consistency, according to Coffee.[19]

One thing is clear: The cloud computing ecosystem has room for continued innovation.

Summary

From a high-level perspective, the benefits and value of PaaS and SaaS resemble those of infrastructure as a service. However, these two layers offer additional value in many dimensions.

PaaS has benefits in terms of accelerating the deployment of IT-based solutions, thus generating business benefits for those businesses that are IT enabled in some way—which includes virtually all firms these days. Beyond that, there are cultural dimensions to PaaS that are extending the reach of IT beyond the traditional IT organization, thus enhancing the agility and broadening the contribution of IT through its democratization.

Similarly, SaaS has unique characteristics that can't be defined in terms of mere cost savings. The ability to rapidly turn up service and updates, customize functionality, and enable management to focus on strategic areas can't be underestimated.

We have treated IaaS, PaaS and SaaS as separate entities, but they can be closely interwoven. Zynga uses a hybrid strategy for infrastructure (IaaS), which enables it to deliver some of the world's leading games (SaaS), but also has launched the Zynga Platform (PaaS) to create a new line of business for the company: generating revenue while enabling its ecosystem of game developers.

Notes

1. Jeff Kaplan, conversation with the author, January 12, 2012.
2. Louis V. Gerstner, Jr., *Who Says Elephants Can't Dance* (Collins, 2002).
3. Robert Axelrod, *The Evolution of Cooperation* (Basic Books, 1984).
4. Peter Coffee, conversation with the author, October 17, 2011.
5. John Keagy, "The Actual Truth About the Economics of Cloud Computing," *GoGrid.com*, May 26, 2011. http://blog.gogrid.com/2011/05/26/the-actual-truth-about-the-economics-of-cloud-computing/.
6. Angela Partington, "Cloud Control," *Capacity* (June 2011). www.capacitymagazine.com/Article/2846317/Search/Security-in-the-cloud-cloud-control.html.
7. Krishnan Subramanian, "Hybrid Clouds," www.trendmicro.com/cloud-content/us/pdfs/business/white-papers/wp_hybrid-clouds-analyst-ksubramanian.pdf.
8. Dennis McCafferty, "A Compliance Primer," *Web Host Industry Review* (October 2010).
9. Coffee, conversation with the author.
10. John Dillon, conversation with the author, January 29, 2012.
11. Barbara van Schewick, *Internet Architecture and Innovation* (MIT Press, 2010).
12. Coffee, conversation with the author.
13. Lee Moriwaki, "Starbucks Teams with Kraft for National Network," *The Seattle Times*, September 28, 1998.
14. Starbucks, *Annual Report for FY11*, January 21, 2011, Part II, p. 20. http://phx.corporate-ir.net/External.File?item=UGFyZW50SUQ9MTI0MzYyfENoaWxkSUQ9LTF8VHlwZT0z&t=1.
15. B. Joseph Pine II and James H. Gilmore, *The Experience Economy: Work Is Theatre and Every Business a Stage* (Harvard Business School Press, 1999).
16. www.rackspace.com/managed_hosting/private_cloud/.
17. Darryl K. Taft, "ActiveState Launches Stackato 1.0 Private PaaS Offering," *eWeek*, March 2, 2012. www.eweek.com/c/a/Application-Development/ActiveState-Launches-Stackato-10-Private-PaaS-Offering-685668/.
18. HP, "Bursting with HP CloudSystem," November 2011. http://h20195.www2.hp.com/V2/GetPDF.aspx/4AA3-6847ENW.pdf.
19. Coffee, conversation with the author.

CHAPTER 22

Availability

A maxim suggests that you shouldn't put all your eggs in one basket. Of course, whether this is sound advice depends on the cost of baskets, the value of the eggs, risk probabilities, threat vectors, and failure modes. Availability, performance, reliability, business continuity, and disaster recovery are all critical concerns for business operations and processes in general, and IT in particular. The cloud offers some unique advantages here.

"Availability" generally means the percentage of the time that the business is able to offer services. This is usually expressed as the percentage of uptime—that is, the ratio of uptime relative to total time, which is in turn uptime plus downtime. It can be impacted by scheduled downtime or unforeseen issues. There are two generic ways to maximize availability: (1) increase uptime—traditionally by using reliable components in a reliable architecture; and (2) reduce downtime, through accelerated processes for detecting, diagnosing, and repairing failures. However, the traditional architectural approach that builds on highly reliable architecture is succumbing to a new strategy that assumes that the foundation is inherently unreliable, in the same way that resilient buildings built on an unreliable tectonic foundation are now constructed to survive earthquakes.

"Performance" is a catchall term for a variety of factors, including response time—how quickly services are performed—and throughput—the volume of transactions. Availability, performance, and reliability are key factors in the overall user experience. Noriaki Kano, a professor at the Tokyo University of Science, created the Kano model of customer satisfaction, which divides product and service attributes into different types. Some attributes are *unexpected* and thus delight customers—say, Läderach Swiss Chocolate with roasted, caramelized hazelnuts on a hotel bed pillow[1]— others are *expected* and customers will *verbalize* their importance—for example, a comfortable bed and a good location—whereas others are *implicit* and unspoken—windows, a locking door, and breathable air. Availability, performance, and reliability are often in the implicit category. Customers won't necessarily tell you they want them, and they won't sing your praises if you do a great job, but they'll complain loudly and publicly if there is a service failure. Lack of availability means your customers can't buy or can't use what they've already bought, and that your employees have nothing to do. A system that is responsive but provides incorrect data is useless. Poor performance means loss of productivity or reduced revenues. If a Web site doesn't respond after a few seconds, most users won't wait around. It doesn't matter whether it's an availability issue or a performance issue.

One study showed that over half of online shoppers will abandon a site in less than three seconds.[2] That's the average; the younger demographic has even less patience. And a substantial fraction use their waiting time to visit a competitor.[3]

Generally, for availability, we are concerned with process or service availability—including work centers, people, and IT—and data availability. For example, a tax accounting firm needs to ensure that its buildings or data centers are operational, its personnel are able to work, and its tax preparation systems are functioning; *and* it needs to make sure that both paper and computer files are accessible and that the data are not corrupted. There are a variety of approaches for enhancing availability, ranging from "cold" disaster recovery—where the assets supporting processes need to be *rebuilt* from scratch; "warm" disaster recovery—where processes need to be *reconfigured* using existing assets; and true business continuity—where there is no loss of functionality or data, even in the event of one or more significant operational issues or events. Such issues may include floods, earthquakes, tornadoes, hurricanes, acts of terrorism, acts of God, acts of human error, fires, power outages, and explosions. Service availability and continuity of operations usually require spare processing resources: If one coffeemaker is broken, use the other one. Data availability generally requires making a copy of the data, whether it is photocopying a document and putting it in the safety deposit box, making a backup copy of a CD, or backing up a song or other file to the cloud.

Availability may be enhanced in a variety of ways: technology diversity, service provider diversity, location diversity, and route diversity. The idea is that if something goes wrong somewhere, maybe it will continue to work somewhere else. Replicating resources is a cornerstone of this approach: Having two data centers helps if something happens to one. There is good news and bad news here: We can always increase availability by additional replication. For example, if two data centers are more survivable than one, then three are better than two, four are better than three, and so on.

However, the returns diminish rapidly, and we will never get all the way to perfect 100% availability anyway.

It turns out that the cloud can help.

Uptime versus Downtime

Generally, if high availability is desired, both uptime and downtime should be addressed. Uptime is a function of components and architecture, whereas downtime is a function of a process that includes monitoring, fault and failure detection, diagnosis, repair preparation, repair processes, testing, and service restoration. To understand these individual terms, consider a variety of things that need to happen when a service goes down.

- *Monitoring*. If you don't monitor status and performance, there will delays in recognizing that there has been an outage.
- *Detection*. Just because you monitor, it does not mean that you will realize that there is an actual problem.
- *Diagnosis*. Realizing that there is a problem does not mean that the root cause will be immediately obvious. Often an issue in one area—say, network congestion—will cause a problem in another—say, service unavailability due to an application time-out.
- *Repair preparation*. The fact that a root cause has been identified does not mean that a repair will occur immediately. For hardware problems, spare parts may need to be ordered or correctly retrieved from spares inventory; for software problems, a patch may need to be written.
- *Repair*. The repair process may require time: disassembling components, shutting down zones, and so forth.
- *Testing*. Ensuring that the repair was conducted properly and that the component, subsystem, or system is ready for use requires time as well.
- *Restoration*. Finally, a cutover of the offline components to return them to service is required.

There are those who will argue that this is the old-school approach and is no longer relevant. Not necessarily. A recent limited duration power outage from a leading cloud provider became an extended service outage, due to incorrectly documented configuration data, staff insufficiently trained in correct procedures, faulty analysis regarding the actual state of the data center, and decisions that were made and reversed on this faulty analysis in the middle of the crisis.[4] This end-to-end process can have a lengthy cycle time. If the entire service went down every time the slightest problem occurred, customer satisfaction would be low, revenues would decrease, and the entire business could fail.

Many techniques impact various steps in this cycle. For example, advanced correlation algorithms can speed diagnosis, and onsite spares can speed repairs. But an even better approach is to take the downtime cycle completely out of the equation where possible by leveraging the statistics of redundancy.

Availability and Probability

In the game of Russian roulette, one bullet is loaded into a six-chamber revolver. Then the chamber is spun and the revolver fired repeatedly. The gun may not fire on the first round, or the second, or even the 143rd, but it will, sooner or later.

The probability that the gun *fires* on the first round is 1/6, and the probability that it *doesn't* is 5/6, or roughly 83%. These are decent odds, or so it would seem. However, the probability that it doesn't happen *either* in the first round *or* in the second round is 5/6 times 5/6, which is 25/36, or 69%. The probability that it doesn't happen in the first round *or* in the second round *or* in the third round is 5/6 times 5/6 times 5/6, or $\left(\frac{5}{6}\right)^3$, which is 125/216, or 58%. By the fourth round, the probability is $\left(\frac{5}{6}\right)^4$, or 625/1296, or only 48%. In other words, the probability has now shifted in favor of a catastrophic event if you're on the wrong side of the Russian roulette "wheel." If, instead of a revolver selecting a chamber, we are rolling a die, the same math applies.

This logic is inescapable no matter how many chambers the revolver has or sides the die has. The eventual outcome is never in doubt, only the timing: Bad things are guaranteed to happen sooner or later. The likelihood that an event such as this happens either on the first round or on the second round or on the third round or on *some* round is near certainty.

If we are rolling a die repeatedly, we know that sooner or later we'll roll, say, a six. If we roll multiple dice, we know that the more dice we roll, the more likely it is that at least one will show a six.

But conversely, if we roll 100 dice and ask what the chances are that *all* of them land on six, the answer is that it's practically impossible. It's not *completely* impossible, but close to it: $\left(\frac{1}{6}\right)^{100}$ In other words, it's highly *likely* that sooner or later *one* die will land on six; it's highly *unlikely* that *all* rolls will land on six.

This principle can work against or in favor of the cloud.

Availability of Networked Resources

The cloud does *not inherently* increase availability; in fact, if used unwisely, it can *reduce* availability.

If, as we've discussed, clouds provide services or resources over a network, presumably accessed by some sort of local endpoint, such as enterprise data center resources or a smartphone, tablet, or sensor, instead of one point of failure, there can be many.

For a desktop application to function, your PC must be working, and the app must be working. But for a cloud-based application accessed by your PC to work, your PC must be working, the browser must be working, your Internet access must be working, the cloud must be working, and the cloud-based app must be working. And, in turn, for your Internet access to work, your wireless card must work, your Wi-Fi router must work, it must be configured properly, your Internet service provider must be up, the cloud data center's network access must be functioning, and so forth.

Unfortunately, all components are imperfect. As a rule, the more imperfect resources we try to string together, the less likely the whole thing is to work. So, merely moving a portion of work to the cloud may have lots of benefits in terms of elasticity and total cost reduction but, in and of itself, could hinder availability. Used correctly, however, the cloud can enhance availability.

Availability via Redundancy and Diversity

As argued, while sooner or later a rolled die will come up with a six or any other number we select, the chances that *all* rolled dice land on a given number become lower as the number of rolls increases. It is relatively unlikely (1 chance out of 216) that the first die lands on six and that the second die lands on six and that the third die lands on six. If, instead of dice, we are considering data center outages, it means that the chance that the first data center is down *and* that the second data center is down *and* that the third data center is down is extremely unlikely, assuming that outages are independent.

The chance that the original instance of the data is lost in a disaster *and* that a remote copy of the data is lost in a disaster *and* that another copy of the data in a third location is lost in a disaster is also extremely unlikely, again, assuming independent events, such as hurricanes and fires.

Merely increasing the number of components, as we argued, can reduce availability. But if those components are appropriately replicated, with cross connections between parts of the system to ensure functionality even in the event of a single point of failure, the overall availability can *increase*.

Availability tends to increase with redundancy. If a single component has an inherent availability or reliability of 90%, then two of them have 99%, three have 99.9%, and four have 99.99%. If the single component has an inherent reliability of 99%, then two have 99.99%, three have 99.9999%, and four have an outstanding 99.999999% (again, assuming independent failures).

Traditionally, systems required for high-availability environments were designed and built for high availability from the ground up, by duplicating every component and providing a mechanism for failing over from a damaged component to the working one. Examples include everything from duplex electronic switching systems such as AT&T Network Systems' 5ESS Electronic Switching System for telecommunications, Tandem (now a division of HP) NonStop computers, redundant load balancers with stateful failover, and the like. Such $n \times 2$ reliability is still used today for many systems.

The other approach is to assume that components will fail but to ensure that there are extras around. If n components are needed at any given time, having $n + 1$ or $n + 2$ can work under failure conditions. $n + 1$ enables one component to fail and still to have enough components to meet the required load. $n + 2$ either can survive two simultaneous failures or enables preventive maintenance on a given component while still operating in fail-safe mode. $n + 100$, or $n + 1000$, enables lots of individual components to fail and permits a laissez-faire approach to the replacement of those components.

Google fellow Jeff Dean said that it's "better to have twice as much hardware that's not reliable than half as much that's more reliable."[5] Google expects thousands of machines and thousands of hard drives to fail every year in a data center, with additional components overheating or otherwise acting strangely.

In the cloud, there is redundancy through many mechanisms: among data centers, within data centers, and between data centers and endpoints. At the macroscopic level, there are multiple data centers spread out over multiple geographic locations. Even if, say, an earthquake or tornado impacts a single data center, one or more other locations are available to pick up the load. For a given quantity of resources, there are benefits to partitioning across more locations. Backing up nine data centers with a tenth requires proportionally fewer additional resources than backing up two data centers with a third.

Consequently, although consolidation can result in a decrease in overhead costs and economies of scale, it must be traded off against system reliability challenges. The other challenge is that although it is unlikely that multiple tornados will simultaneously take out multiple data centers, because the events are largely *independent*, it is not at all unlikely that some sort of software bug or other human error will take everything down simultaneously. Moreover, cascades of problems can occur, where one thing leads to another and then another. Perversely, mechanisms set up to aid in disaster can cause further issues, like fire engines racing to put out a fire that collide with each other.[6]

Within the data center, there are many avenues for redundancy, including network connections and individual resources. The fundamental structure of virtualization and the cloud implies that various individual components, such as servers can go down, and it won't make a difference. In a hotel, if the air conditioning doesn't work in a room, it's either fixed or the guest is moved; no sweat. In a cloud, if a server doesn't work, the app is moved; no problem. Moreover, today's software is built and tested to ensure that it functions reliably *even when* there are component outages. Netflix uses a "Rambo Architecture" and "Chaos Monkey" to ensure availability. Rambo is the mythical Sly Stallone character who single-handedly could fight his way out of the jungle. The Rambo Architecture approach is to ensure that each component of the architecture can survive on its own as well. The Chaos Monkey is built on the idea of toughening Rambo by constantly trying to break components. As John Cianciutti of Netflix commented, "If we aren't constantly testing our ability to succeed despite failure, then it isn't likely to work when it matters most—in the event of an unexpected outage."[7] Jesse Robbins, self-described "master of disaster" and the cofounder of Opscode, a cloud infrastructure automation firm, used the term "GameDay" to describe such an approach to "large-scale fault injection."[8]

In such a world of software-based reliability, a different set of trade-offs occurs. Technology blogging, research, and events firm GigaOM.com founder and senior writer Om Malik observed that in this new approach, minimizing outages ultimately requires minimizing software changes.[9] Doing this creates a new set of trade-offs; as Urs Hölzle, Google senior vice president, mused, "[I]n our apps, we're not actually shooting for five nines because that would lower the feature velocity."[10]

Sam Johnston, president of the Open Cloud Initiative, has argued that there is a critical difference in the economics of this new approach: As applications scale out to larger implementations, the *marginal cost of reliable software is zero*, whereas the marginal cost of reliable hardware is *linear*.[11] In other words, it may cost a little bit more up front to get the software correct and fault tolerant, but running on low-cost, commodity hardware can lead to immense savings as demand grows.

Between data centers, or between data centers and user endpoints, network availability is critically important to basic cloud functionality. Generally core networks tend to function with four nines (99.99%) or five nines (99.999%) availability, or even higher. However, sometimes, as in the hours after 9/11 or floods or earthquakes, networks may be unavailable within a region. Sometimes certain coverage areas are down. Rarely, but not so rarely that they shouldn't be planned for, entire networks go down, such as when AT&T's 4ESS-based long-distance network suffered a chain reaction outage in 1990, or when Research In Motion's network went down for several days in 2011, impacting messaging and browsing.[12] Network provider diversity can help protect against the last scenario. However, there are also failure modes where provider diversity is useless: For example, so-called backhoe attenuation, where a construction worker digs up fiber optic cables, can lead to many or all providers being cut, since many of them may use the same routing or right-of-way, such as a bridge, a particular conduit, or path adjacent to a railroad line.

To protect against these issues, technology diversity can help: The chance that a wireline connection is down is not zero, so backing it up via a cellular wireless connection can help. It is less likely that a virus will attack both PCs and Macs, or Apple's iPhone's IOS and Google's Android.

Ultimately, a variety of application- and strategy-dependent trade-offs must be made between factors such as availability, continuity, dispersion, fault tolerance, performance, response time, and cost.

On-Demand, Pay-per-Use Redundancy

In addition to redundancy *within* a data center or across multiple data centers in the cloud, there can be redundancy *between* an enterprise data center and the cloud. For data, this is achieved by keeping one or more replicas in the cloud, the way you might protect an important document at home by keeping one copy at your office and another copy in the safe deposit box at the bank. Even if your house burns down the same day that your office building does, you still have a copy safely stored.

For resource availability, the cloud can't be beat. Traditional disaster recovery and business continuity architectures used a sister site approach, which was very costly. In effect, it was as if, to protect against the possibility of your house burning to the ground, you had a complete replica of it, down to the picture of Grandpa and Grandma on the wall over the fireplace. Having such a replica makes the total cost of the solution double, or worse.

Of course, most people can't afford a spare residence in the event of a housing catastrophe or an extra car just in case theirs doesn't start. Instead, they would stay in a hotel or rent a car. The fully on-demand business continuity architecture is a particularly beneficial use case for the cloud. It provides all of the protection of a full spare with none of the cost. If a disaster never happens, the cost of the spare capacity is exactly zero.

This approach to continuity refers to the servers; data replicas cost something. But even there the cloud can be more cost effective. Although a safe deposit box costs more than the allocated cost of your desk drawer, it costs a lot less than it would to build an entire replica of your house or home office. In the same way, copies of data can be kept in the cloud for substantially less than building a sister site just to house mirrored data.

Summary

Availability is a complex mixture of components, including architecture, processes, partner selection, and technology diversity. Just moving some architectural elements from on premises to the cloud could reduce availability by increasing the number of components that all must work together for the end-to-end system or application to function.

However, when done right, redundancy in various parts of the system, including servers within a cloud data center, data centers in multiple locations, and services such as distributed object storage that leverage this inherently reliable infrastructure can enhance availability, leading to more satisfied customers, more productive employees, and better business results.

Various attributes of the cloud, such as geographical dispersion and on-demand, pay-per-use resources, make the economics of cloud availability compelling.

Notes

1. Reason alone to stay at the InterContinental Geneva.
2. PhoCusWright and Akamai, "New Study Reveals the Impact of Travel Site Performance on Consumers," June 14, 2010. www.akamai.com/html/about/press/releases/2010/press_061410.html.
3. Ibid.
4. Rich Miller, "When the Power Goes Out at Google," *Data Center Knowledge*, March 8, 2010. www.datacenterknowledge.com/archives/2010/03/08/when-the-power-goes-out-at-google/.
5. Stephen Shankland, "Google Spotlights Data Center Inner Workings," *CNET News*, May 30, 2008. http://news.cnet.com/8301-10784_3-9955184-7.html?part=rss&tag=feed&subj=NewsBlog.
6. Rich Miller, "Amazon: Networking Error Caused Cloud Outage," *Data Center Knowledge*, April 29, 2011. www.datacenterknowledge.com/archives/2011/04/29/amazon-networking-error-caused-cloud-outage/.
7. John Ciancutti, "5 Lessons We've Learned Using AWS," *Netflix Tech Blog*, December 16, 2010. http://techblog.netflix.com/2010/12/5-lessons-weve-learned-using-aws.html.
8. Jesse Robbins, "Creating Resiliency Through Destruction—LISA11," December 7, 2011. www.slideshare.net/jesserobbins/ameday-creating-resiliency-through-destruction.
9. Om Malik, "Google Infrastructure Czar: Cloud Gets It Done," *GigaOM.com*, April 12, 2011. http://gigaom.com/2011/04/12/google-infrastructure-czar-cloud-is-about-getting-it-done/.
10. Ibid.

11. Sam Johnston, conversation with the author, January 25, 2012.

12. Simson Garfinkel, "History's Worst Software Bugs," *Wired*, August 5, 2011, www.wired.com/software/coolapps/news/2005/11/69355?currentPage=all; David Meyer, "RIM Explains BlackBerry Downtime as Outage Spreads," ZDNet UK, October 12, 2011. www.zdnet.co.uk/news/business-of-it/2011/10/12/rim-explains-blackberry-downtime-as-outage-spreads-40094166/.

CHAPTER 23

Lazy, Hazy, Crazy

The foundation of economics for much of the twentieth century was the notion that humans are rational economic decision makers. Given a choice between buying an apple for 53 cents or one for 54 cents, a rational consumer would choose the former. Moreover, if the price were stochastic, a person would use probability to determine the expected price, perhaps adjusted by a utility function representing personal value, and select accordingly.

Unfortunately, as an avalanche of elegantly designed experiments over the last several decades has shown, such cool, calculating rationality rarely matches actual human behavior. Instead, it might be said—more colloquially than behavioral economists would probably prefer—that we are *lazy, hazy,* and *crazy*.[1]

Human behavioral anomalies are important to the cloud, because they impact everything from value propositions to customer decision-making processes, in some cases favoring cloud characteristics, such as the lack of up-front commitment and on demand, but in some cases acting as obstacles to adoption.

Behavioral Economics

People are often *lazy*, in that they tend to minimize the cognitive, emotional, physical, and financial costs of activities and decisions where possible. As Gregory Berns, the distinguished chair of neuroeconomics at Emory University, has quipped, "The brain is fundamentally a lazy piece of meat."[2] We tend to equate laziness with moral turpitude but could also use the term "efficient." Evolutionary forces presumably did not encourage inefficiency in a world where today's feast of fresh antelope might be followed by a weeklong famine.

303

People are often *hazy*, in that rather than determining a mathematically correct answer to a problem, they use heuristics—rules of thumb—to quickly arrive at an answer. Instead of hazy, we could also use the term "computationally efficient." The late Nobel laureate Herbert Simon proposed "bounded rationality," based on risk, uncertainty, the lack of information as to the statistical distribution of outcomes, incomplete information about alternatives, and the complexity of calculation relative to the cost of such calculations, in time or hard dollars.[3] In other words, rather than attempting to arrive at perfect decisions using information and stochastic models that we don't have using complex algorithms requiring unlimited processing time, we just make do. In computation, a heuristic is an algorithm that can arrive at a good-enough mathematical answer in a relatively short time. In behavioral economics, though, heuristics include nonmathematical mechanisms, such as the affect heuristic, where you might evaluate a financial deal offered by a friendly salesperson more favorably than the same one offered by one you disliked.

And people are *crazy*—or what Duke professor and author Dan Ariely referred to as "predictably irrational."[4] In other words, we often make decisions that are not rational but also not necessarily random. Scores of cognitive biases are prevalent across our species and beyond. Human behavioral attributes might be viewed as representing an optimal synthesis of rational cognitive processes with emotional ones. Sometimes, though, the "brain is like a computer operating system that was rushed to market."[5]

Herbert Simon might have been among the first to question the assumption of humans as rational actors, but the giants in the field are longtime collaborators Daniel Kahneman and the late Amos Tversky. Kahneman was awarded the Nobel Prize in economics, a notable feat for a psychologist.

Kahneman and Tversky conducted numerous elegant experiments to determine how people actually behave.[6] Today, these approaches are augmented by neuroeconomics, which uses functional magnetic resonance imaging to see what the brain is actually doing. Other testing methodologies—such as galvanic skin response, which measures stress—have also been applied in the pursuit of assessing exactly what happens when our rational mental processes collide with our emotional, intuitive, irrational behaviors.

Loss and Risk Aversion

One of the core insights Kahneman and Tversky derived is that for most people, the pain associated with a loss is typically perceived as greater than the joy associated with a commensurate gain.[7] This asymmetry often affects our behavior, causing individuals to make economically suboptimal decisions. For example, investors tend to hold on to stocks that have declined in value rather than selling them, because selling entails making the loss tangible.[8]

Chief information officers (CIOs) must exercise due diligence regarding proposed cloud initiatives but need to coolly evaluate options. For example, most surveys show that cloud security is a top concern of CIOs. However, how many have conducted a comprehensive comparative analysis of their company's own vulnerabilities versus those of a cloud provider? Awareness of this bias is the first step in countering it.

Partly due to loss aversion, many—but not all—people tend to be risk averse. They generally would rather take a sure benefit, say, $10,000, than an uncertain one, say, a 1% shot at $1 million. They would rather risk an uncertain loss than accept a certain one.[9] There are some people who are considered risk seekers: helicopter-skiing bungee jumpers, for example. It has been hypothesized that there is a genetic, "neurocomputational" basis for such risk-seeking behavior that impacts the way such individuals process information regarding risky options.[10]

Risk aversion can lead to sticking with the devil you know—legacy IT practices and architectures—over the devil you don't—this new cloud thing.

Flat-Rate Bias

One of the defining aspects of a cloud service is that it is pay per use: When usage varies, so does the incurred charge. In Chapter 11 we saw that such a payment scheme can enable economically optimal solutions, yet customers often prefer flat rates.

According to Anja Lambrecht of the London Business School and Bernd Skiera of Goethe University of Frankfurt, there are several reasons for the "flat-rate bias."[11] The "insurance effect" is one: Customers want to smooth monthly bills and appease their aversion to loss. The "taxi meter effect" is another: Watching the taxi meter running up a bill reduces the pleasure associated with an activity. Even without an actual meter, "mental accounting" can have the same impact.[12] The "convenience effect" is related to the ease of selecting the default option, which is often flat rate. Finally, the "overestimation effect" occurs when customers believe that their usage levels will be higher than they actually are. Consumers are likely to overestimate their ability to forecast future usage, leading them to overpay by selecting the wrong plan.[13]

The flat-rate bias may not be that irrational: Celina Aarons had a T-Mobile phone service family plan with a normal monthly bill of less than $200. Her brother sent some text messages and downloaded some videos while in

Canada for two weeks and rang up a bill for the month of over *$200,000*.[14] Lack of policy-based control, a pricey rate plan, and lack of real-time visibility regarding charges are among the culprits in such scenarios.

Today's tablets offer convenient access to information, such as videos, music, and even "print" magazines, such as *Wired*. However, the tablet edition of *Wired* issue 19.12 was 648 megabytes. Not enormous; it could fit on a CD. However, although there are currently data plans priced at roughly $10 per gigabyte, there are still cellular roaming rates reaching up to $25 per *megabyte*. Under such a plan, downloading an issue would cost over *$16,000*, clearly more than the dollar or so per-issue price via subscription.[15]

This bias is not restricted to consumers. A CIO doesn't want to get called into the boardroom to explain rogue expenses any more than a spouse or teen wants to get called into the kitchen to explain them.

However, although customers love flat rates, they can be bad for just about everyone, including the customers themselves. In their desire to save money, they may end up spending more. One study purportedly showed that consumers were paying an average of over $3 per minute for wireless calls.[16] Although there were no doubt quite a few getting their money's worth, plenty on $60- or $80-a-month plans just weren't gabbing enough. As author William Poundstone has wryly noted, "Not knowing the break-even point is becoming the postmodern condition."[17]

Organizations are made up of people, and so the flat-rate bias plays a role in business decisions as well. In addition, businesses typically have rigid planning and budgeting cycles that variability can disrupt. Even if everything balances out in the end, periodic results reporting can create variances and thus stress.

In any situation involving usage-based fees, there can be issues due to lack of concern over consumption, concern over consumption levels but lack of visibility, visibility into consumption without awareness of price impact, awareness without control, or awareness and control but with information lags.

Mat Ellis, the founder and chief executive officer of Cloudability, has seen all of these issues.[18] Cloudability is a monitoring and alerting service that manages customers' bills across multiple service providers. One customer was autoscaling new virtual servers and not shutting them down. Every few days the customer hit a service provider charging limit. Assuming that there was some inexplicable constraint placed by the service provider, the customer bypassed the service provider's controls and opened up a new account under a different credit card. The customer finally realized the problem, but not before being hit with over $100,000 in charges. In another example, quality assurance testers were launching test machines, but at the end of the day—like kids coming upstairs from the basement for dinner but leaving the stereo, video games, and lights on—they went home, forgetting to terminate them. Ellis also told the story of a developer who left a company, but software he had left running in the cloud continued to rack up bills.

Framing and Context

The way propositions are framed can impact how well they are received.[19] Asking the kids "Would you like to go to Disneyworld?" may get a different reception than "Would you like to sit in the car for eight hours?" even though both queries may be semantically equivalent. Anchoring is another bias, where a random starting point, such as the number on a card drawn from a deck, influences unconnected behavior, such as how much to bid for an item.

Framing and transparency can impact cloud satisfaction. Cloudability's Ellis explained that a bill that indicates "500 hours of use—$500" is preferable to one merely showing an amount.

Framing and the anchoring bias, where certain factors are given more weight than they deserve, are also relevant to cloud decision making. Having a discussion on security vulnerabilities in the cloud may impact cloud adoption decisions negatively; having one regarding the IT application backlog may impact decisions positively.

One of the causes of flat-rate bias—loss aversion—is based on fear of unplanned variability in usage leading to high bills. However, this cognitive bias can—and has been—reframed successfully in other industries. Rather than the variability leading to an increase in charges above a base rate, the variability can be expressed as a refund to a higher rate. Such variability, rather than being a source of angst, then becomes a source of pleasure—a so-called intermittent variable reward (or reinforcement), causing addictive behavior, even in animals. This is what makes exchanging currency at the airport utilitarian but casino gaming hedonic; the brain gets more stimulated by the occasional win, even though the expected return from each transaction in both cases may be a few percent negative.

Companies do this with payrolls: Rather than framing variable pay as "You will need to return part of your pay if the business doesn't do well," they frame it as "profit sharing." Some insurance companies also do this, returning extra money collected from premiums but not paid out in claims as "policyholder dividends." Opportunities for creative pricing in the cloud can leverage such behavioral anomalies.

Need for Control and Autonomy

The need for control is a basic human requirement that can literally mean the difference between life and death. The absence of control is helplessness, which can cause stress and depression. This need is so basic that it isn't restricted to humans: In a classic psychological experiment, dogs exhibited "learned helplessness" and refused to jump over a low wall to avoid pain because they didn't think that they could.[20]

The loss of control impacts us at a fundamental emotional and physiological level. As Amy Arnsten, a professor of neurobiology at Yale, said, "The loss of prefrontal function only occurs when we feel out of control. . . . Even if we have the illusion that we are in control, our cognitive functions are preserved."[21] But without at least the illusion of control, we become seriously unable to function.

Engaging your employees may provide a greater perception—and perhaps reality—of control and autonomy than the use of a service provider. Use of cloud services, however, may provide a greater degree of control than use of your own IT organization. After all, cloud providers will allow you to instantly provision and deprovision resources, build applications, and utilize services—all without those pesky corporate approval processes and IT budgeting.

A variety of characteristics can enhance the perception and reality of control. Control begins with visibility and transparency. Leading providers offer a high degree of transparency, with real-time stats on performance and availability. Examples include trust.salesforce.com, which provides real-time information on performance issues, availability in terms of service disruptions and planned downtime, and progress toward issue resolution, among others. As Peter Coffee, head of platform research at Salesforce.com, explained, people are willing to take risks when the risk is voluntarily assumed, but not when it is imposed externally and the degree of risk is opaque. Coffee asserted that Salesforce.com, and by extension SaaS providers in general, need to be "that much better to be perceived as equal."[22]

Fear of Change

There are hard-dollar costs associated with change. Determining relevant options drives up information costs: bringing in the vendors for technical reviews; clarifying requirements through innumerable business unit meetings; writing requests for information, requests for proposals, and requests for quotes; legal review; evaluating responses; repairing relationships with the vendors who were not selected. Making the change incurs switching costs: contract termination or renovation, training in new processes, computing environment migration, and application rewrites. And, given that all these activities require resources, there are not only the hard costs of engaging in them but the opportunity costs of diminished or delayed progress in other activities on which these resources could be working.

In addition to a rational assessment of the costs of change, a host of complementary psychological, behavioral, and neuroeconomic factors dissuade people from change: Generally, change entails uncertainty, and humans are hardwired to dislike uncertainty. As Paul Strebel, a professor at the International Institute for Management Development said, top managers see change as way to improve the business and for personal development, but for "many employees . . . change is neither sought after nor welcomed. It is disruptive and intrusive. It upsets the balance."[23]

Fear of change is intimately tied in with the need for control and the need for certainty. It is not necessarily change that we don't like; it is the fact that the change is out of our control.

Herding and Conformity

In stressful times, such as change, humans and other animals tend to herd, i.e., follow what others seem to be doing. We are, after all, first and foremost social primates. As neuroeconomist Gregory Berns puts it, "the fear of social isolation is deeply woven into the human brain. We readily discount our own perceptions for fear of being the odd one out."[24]

Such behavior may confer evolutionary fitness, as speed of reaction is not limited to one's own ability to perceive or deduce danger, but the collective intelligence of the group. If everyone is running through the jungle like crazy, it may be beneficial to run too, rather than waiting to see if there really is a lion. And, as James Surowiecki argues in *The Wisdom of Crowds*, the average answer of a group is often closer to the truth than virtually all of the individuals in the group.[25]

However, author and financial analyst Robert Prechter argues that herding, "while appropriate in some primitive life-threatening situations, is inappropriate and counterproductive to success in financial situations," and presumably many other contexts.[26] If herding always predominated over rational independent nonconformist analysis, we'd still believe that the sun revolved around the earth, which would still be flat.

Solomon Asch, the founder of social psychology, conducted a series of experiments over half a century ago, demonstrating the impact of conformity. A subject, surrounded by confederates, was asked a simple question, such as which of three lines was the same length as a reference line. Most subjects would agree with incorrect answers provided in unison by the confederates at least a third of the time, rather than provide answers that they otherwise could easily determine but would depart from the group view. Using functional magnetic resonance imaging, Berns showed that when others in the group gave answers, the decision-making regions of the brain shut down and the perceptual processing portions of the visual cortex were activated, in effect, generating false perceptions of the visual stimuli based on inputs from the others. Moreover, when a subject gave an answer that disagreed with the others, the fight-or-flight regions of the brain lit up.[27]

In a time of technological transformation such as the shift to the cloud, chief information officers, who are only human, will be swayed by what other CIOs are doing. Early cloud adopters have helped pave the way for others. As more move to the cloud, using the cloud for a broader variety of applications will become easier for more people to accept psychologically, as one generally finds in any technology adoption lifecycle.[28]

Endowment Effect

In a classic experiment by author and professor Dan Ariely, formerly at the Massachusetts Institute of Technology and now at Duke, and Ziv Carmon of international business school INSEAD , conducted while both were at Duke, behavior in valuing Duke University basketball tickets was assessed.[29] Because tickets to games are hard to get, there is a tortuous process involving camping out in sometimes muddy fields and responding to random bullhorn announcements to be eligible to participate in a lottery for them.

For students who *didn't* receive tickets at the end of this process, the most that they were willing to *pay* for a ticket was, on average, just under $170. For those who *had won* tickets, the average amount that they were willing to *sell* a ticket for was just over $2,400. In other words, the same good did not have a fixed value, even among a select population, but was worth more once it was "owned."

This asymmetry of valuation has been called the *endowment effect* and arises in a number of situations, such as the difference between the value an owner places on her home versus what a prospective buyer may offer. A related effect is the *choice-supportive bias*, in which people rationalize selections that they have made or, perhaps even selections that have been made for them.

Not only do individuals overly value things the way they are—the status quo bias—they are willing to dig themselves in ever deeper—as with traders unwilling to take a loss—to protect the illusion that they made the right choice. This particular facet of human irrationality is sometimes referred to as escalation of commitment and is related to the *sunk-cost fallacy*, which involves considering prior investments and attempting to extract at least a minimum return from them rather than looking only at current choices and their relative impact on payoffs.[30]

These biases can apply to a chief information officer or executive team that made certain decisions years ago with respect to enterprise data center siting or application architecture. The traditional environment benefits not only from the fear of uncertainty and dislike of change reviewed earlier but the endowment effect, the choice-supportive bias, escalation of commitment, and sunk-cost fallacy.

Need for Status

David Rock, author and co-founder of the NeuroLeadership Institute, has argued that humans have extremely fine-tuned status detectors, presumably deriving from our descent from social primates and other social animals.[31] Since such status typically enables one to eat and mate first, and attempted violation can result in death, it makes sense that we would be deeply aware of status and concerned about maintaining it.

Throughout the existence of societies—animal or human—social rank and alpha status was based largely on physical prowess and perhaps also on age and thus experience and wisdom or royal and noble birth. In the corporate world, title and the size of the organization confer status. This fact is more than a behavioral anomaly; whether fair or not, job evaluation criteria, compensation, and bonuses are often correlated with direct and indirect span of control.[32]

Unfortunately, although it is easy to count the number of people in an organization, it is much harder to directly correlate an individual with the business results of an organization. The payback for changes and initiatives instituted today may not be felt for years, and those impacts may be masked.

This issue can be a challenge for widespread adoption of the cloud—or use of any service for that matter—overmaintaining a large organization. After all, if status, power, and pay are dependent on organization size, it is a natural for a self-interested executive to maintain a large organization. We really can't blame him or her—incentive structures often foster such behavior.

The challenge for customer organizations is to move beyond such incentives, to ensure that individual rewards—both explicit and behavioral—are aligned with organizational goals: revenue growth, earnings growth, market share, customer satisfaction, and emerging technology and business model innovation.

Paralysis by Analysis of Choice

You would think that freedom and choice are important in maximizing sales and customer satisfaction, but experiments show that too many options can cause mental confusion, and result in no choice.[33] In a now-classic experiment conducted by Sheena Iyengar of Columbia University and Mark Lepper of Stanford, some shoppers were presented with the option of sampling 6 varieties of jam, others with 24.[34] You might suppose that more varieties would increase the likelihood of a match between consumer and topping, thus increasing sales in the high-option case. However, while 30% of the prospects exposed to a smaller assortment bought jams, only 3% of those exposed to the larger collection did so. In effect, their brains were paralyzed by too many choices.

Moreover, an assessment of the happiness that we believe we will have due to being able to choose and enjoy variety turns out, in retrospect, to be illusory. Daniel Gilbert, a professor of psychology at Harvard University, has claimed that we make "a systematic set of errors when we try to imagine 'what it would feel like if'" and presented experimental evidence that variety over time is less pleasurable than a recurring favorite choice.[35]

The impact for cloud service providers is that a proliferation of options can actually *delay* and *reduce* purchasing. Small, medium, large, or extra-large instance? Windows or Linux? On-demand or reserved instance? Although such choices appear to provide the customer greater flexibility, they may jam up the purchase process.

Hyperbolic Discounts and Instant Gratification

Many of the issues just discussed are behavioral issues that may hinder rational adoption of the cloud; there also are several biases that benefit the cloud.

In classic financial analysis, there is a time value of money: A dollar today is worth more than $1 a year from now, because the $1 today can be invested or gather interest and therefore be worth, say, $1.10 in a year. Beyond the rational analysis based on financial rates of return, there is another effect at work.

Hyperbolic discounting is the irrational bias that exists beyond the rational calculation of the time value of money. In effect, a dollar today is perceived as not just worth 1.1 times as much as the one in a year but twice as much or ten times as much, and not just in one year but in one hour.

In a famous experiment conducted at Stanford, children four to six years old were given the choice of eating one marshmallow or Oreo cookie immediately or delaying consumption by 15 minutes and receiving a second one as a reward. Follow-up analyses years later showed that those who had demonstrated the ability to defer gratification were rated as more competent.[36]

But who wouldn't prefer benefits sooner, especially in today's hyper-competitive world? Rare is the leader who would say "Let's wait and see" rather than immediately taking advantage of a business opportunity.

These biases are favorable for both private and public cloud implementations: Instant access to resources is preferred to any delay. The ability for a developer or even end user to gain instant gratification and solve a problem—coupled with the competitive importance of time—favor the cloud.

Zero-Price Effect

Kristina Shampanier of the Massachusetts Institute of Technology, Nina Mazar of the University of Toronto, and Dan Ariely of Duke conducted an interesting experiment.[37] They offered subjects the opportunity to receive a free $10 gift card or pay $7 for a $20 gift card. Which would you take? Most subjects picked the free one. However, a moment's thought shows that the net economic gain from a free $10 gift card is $10, whereas the net gain from a $20 gift card for which you pay $7 is higher: $13.

Shampanier, Mazar, and Ariely called this finding the "zero-price effect." There is an analog in risk reduction: Consumers will pay more for an infinitesimal reduction to zero risk than a much larger reduction in risk to a small quantity. Zero, in other words, has a special appeal.

This bias is favorable for the cloud: Free trials, no commitment, no subscription fees, no implementation costs, no nonrecurring installation fees eliminate barriers to purchase and accelerate adoption.

Summary

The last few decades have seen the demise of the view that we humans are rational decision makers, always perfectly assessing options and their probabilities, determining a mathematically optimal course of action, and pursuing it based on correct economic valuation of sunk costs and appropriate discounts for the time value of money. Instead, we are a mix of bounded rationality; predictable irrationality; cognitive, emotional, and financial decision-making anomalies; and other various biases.

Some of these biases may hinder cloud adoption whereas others, such as the special appeal of "free," work in favor of the cloud.

Prospects considering cloud services should become aware of their own biases and incorporate that knowledge into their decision-making processes. Service providers marketing to those prospects or existing customers should be aware that there is more to decision making than return-on-investment calculations.

Notes

1. Joe Weinman, "Lazy, Hazy, Crazy: The 10 Laws of Behavioral Cloudonomics," GigaOM.com, June 6, 2010. gigaom.com/2010/06/06/lazy-hazy-crazy-the-10-laws-of-behavioral-cloudonomics/.

2. Gregory Berns, *Iconoclast: A Neuroscientist Reveals How to Think Differently* (Harvard Business Press, 2008).

3. Herbert A. Simon, "Theories of Bounded Rationality," in C. B. McGuire and Roy Radner, eds., *Decision and Organization* (North-Holland, 1972) p. 36.

4. Dan Ariely, *Predictably Irrational: The Hidden Forces that Shape Our Experiences* (HarperCollins, 2008).

5. Jonah Lehrer, *How We Decide* (Houghton Mifflin Harcourt, 2009) p. 24.

6. Daniel Kahneman, "Maps of Bounded Rationality: A Perspective on Intuitive Judgment and Choice," Prize Lecture, December 8, 2002. www.nobelprize.org/nobel_prizes/economics/laureates/2002/kahnemann-lecture.pdf.

7. Ori Frafman and Rom Brafman, *Sway: The Irresistible Pull of Irrational Behavior* (Doubleday, 2008).

8. Jonah Lehrer, scienceblogs.com/cortex/2008/09/loss_aversion_and_the_stock_ma.php.

9. Daniel Kahneman and Amos Tversky, "Prospect Theory: An Analysis of Decision Under Risk," *Econometrica* 47, No. 2 (March 1979), pp. 263–292.

10. Cary Frydman, Colin Camerer, Peter Bossaerts, and Antonio Rangel, "MAOA-L Carriers Are Better At Making Optimal Financial Decisions Under Risk," *Proceedings of the Royal Society B* 278 (2011): 2053–2059.

11. Anja Lambrecht and Bernd Skiera, "Paying Too Much and Being Happy About It: Existence, Causes and Consequences of Tariff-Choice Biases," *Journal of Marketing Research* 43 (May 2006): 212–223.

12. Richard H. Thaler, "Mental Accounting and Consumer Choice," *Marketing Science* 4, No. 3 (1985): 199–214.

13. Michael D. Grubb, "Selling to Overconfident Consumers," *American Economic Review* 99, No. 5 (2009): 1770–1807.

14. Patrick Fraser, "Help Me Howard: $201,000 Cell Phone Bill," WSVN Channel 7 News, October 17, 2011. www.wsvn.com/features/articles/helpmehoward/MI93365/.

15. Kevin O'Brien, "Bill Shock Without Leaving Home," *New York Times*, December 11, 2011. www.nytimes.com/2011/12/12/technology/12iht-rawdata12.html.

16. David Lazarus, "Talk Isn't Cheap? For Cellphone Users, Not Talking Is Costly Too," *Los Angeles Times*, March 8, 2009. articles.latimes.com/2009/mar/08/business/fi-lazarus8.

17. William Poundstone, *Priceless: The Myth of Fair Value (and How to Take Advantage of It)* (Hill & Wang, 2010), p. 173.

18. Mat Ellis, conversation with the author, October 21, 2011.

19. Amos Tversky and Daniel Kahneman, "The Framing of Decisions and the Psychology of Choice," *Science* 211 (January 1981), pp. 453–458.

20. Martin E. P. Seligman, "Learned Helplessness," *Annual Review of Medicine* 23 (February 1972): 407–412.

21. Amy Arnsten, quoted in David Rock, *Your Brain at Work* (HarperBusiness, 2009), p. 124.

22. Peter Coffee, conversation with the author, October 17, 2011.

23. Paul Strebel, "Why Do Employees Resist Change?" *Harvard Business Review* (May–June 1996). hbr.org/1996/05/why-do-employees-resist-change/ar/1.

24. Gregory Berns, *Iconoclast*, p. 87.

25. James Surowiecki, *The Wisdom of Crowds: Why the Many Are Smarter Than the Few and How Collective Wisdom Shapes Business, Economics, Societies, and Nations* (Doubleday, 2004).

26. Robert R. Prechter, Jr., "Unconscious Herding Behavior as the Psychological Basis of Financial Market Trends and Patterns," *The Journal of Psychology and Financial Markets*, Vol. 2, No. 3, 2001, p. 120. www.journalofbehavioralfinance .org/research/pdf/unconsious_herding.pdf.

27. Gregory Berns, *Iconoclast*, pp. 92–97.

28. Everett Rogers, *Diffusion of Innovations* (Free Press, 1962).

29. Ziv Carmon and Dan Ariely, "Focusing on the Forgone: How Value Can Appear So Different to Buyers and Sellers," *Journal of Consumer Research* 27 (December 2000), pp. 360–370. duke.edu/~dandan/Papers/PI/bb.pdf.

30. Barry M. Staw, "Knee Deep in the Big Muddy: A Study of Escalating Commitment to a Chosen Course of Action," *Organizational Behavior and Human Performance* 16 (1976), pp. 27–44.

31. David Rock, "Managing with the Brain in Mind," *Strategy + Business*, August 27, 2009. www.strategy-business.com/article/09306.

32. Valerie Smeets and Frederic Warzynski, "Testing Models of Hierarchy: Span of Control, Compensation and Career Dynamics," Working Paper 06-10, Universidad Carlos III de Madrid and CCP, Aarhus School of Business, November, 2006, http://www.hha.dk/nat/wper/06-10_vasfwa.pdf.

33. Barry Schwartz, *The Paradox of Choice: Why More Is Less* (Harper Perennial, 2004).

34. Sheena Iyengar and Mark Lepper, "When Choice Is Demotivating: Can One Desire Too Much of a Good Thing?" *Journal of Personality and Social Psychology* 79, No. 6 (2000): 995–1006.

35. Daniel Gilbert, *Stumbling on Happiness* (Vintage Books, 2005), p. 82.

36. B. J. Casey, Leah H. Somerville, Ian H. Gotlib, Ozlem Ayduk, Nicholas T. Franklin, Mary K. Askren, John Jonides, Marc G. Berman, Nicole L. Wilson, Theresa Teslovich, Gary Glover, Vivian Zayas, Walter Mischel, and Yuichi Shoda, "Behavioral and Neural Correlates of Delay of Gratification 40 Years Later," *Proceedings of the National Academy of Sciences of the United States of America* 108, No. 36 (2011): 14998–15003. www.pnas.org/content/108/36/ 14998.long.

37. Kristina Shampanier, Nina Mazar, and Dan Ariely, "Zero as a Special Price: The True Value of Free Products," *Marketing Science* 26, No. 6 (November–December 2007), pp. 742–757.

CHAPTER 24

Cloud Patterns

A variety of cloud patterns—architectures and usage scenarios—have economic characteristics well beyond trading off unit costs and pricing strategies or balancing distribution against consolidation. We looked at some of these use cases in Chapter 7. Here we analyze some in more depth, touching on abstract characteristics that translate directly into business benefits. For example, hub-and-spoke networks require fewer physical connections than fully connected point-to-point networks and benefit from statistical multiplexing. However, these benefits come at the expense of longer average distance and thus latency, hub investments, and potential congestion.

Patterns such as markets, i.e., buyers connected to sellers, offer not only connection savings, as in a hub-and-spoke network, but the potential to get a better price or find a more perfect match. Here the benefit depends on the distribution and dispersion of values among buyers or sellers. If most prospects are buyers and there is limited price dispersion, it only takes a few buyers to get close to a best price.

This chapter illustrates that cloud-native applications can be evaluated using a variety of mechanisms well beyond the cases considered earlier.

Communications Patterns

Today we take for granted that we can use a wireline or mobile phone to call anywhere in the world or a tablet or smartphone to call up any Web site on the Internet, but it wasn't always so. During the mid-1870s, inventors such as Alexander Graham Bell, Elisha Gray, and even Thomas Edison ushered in "acoustic telegraphy" (i.e., telephony). Initially, though, phone connections were point to point. If you wanted the ability to call, say, your office, the police, your brother, and the hospital, you needed four telephones. Each one was hardwired to the other location. If you went off-hook (i.e., picked up the handset) on the first telephone, the phone at your office would ring. Pick up the second one, and the phone at the police station would ring. And so forth.

On January 28, 1878, what may well be the first cloud service of the modern era—the telephone exchange—went live in New Haven, Connecticut.[1] This predated the first electric cloud service, introduced in 1881.[2]Although this first exchange could only handle two simultaneous calls, it was the forerunner of operator services, analog and digital electronic switching systems, and today's core routers that enable the mother of all cloud services: communications. Gaming, collaboration, social networking, and markets all have communications at their core. Even peer-to-peer applications often use a cloud server to maintain user metadata and rarely use point-to-point physical connections.

Exhibit 24.1 illustrates a few generic approaches for connecting n nodes. Exhibit 24.1(a) shows a point-to-point architecture, which requires $n(n-1)/2$ connections. Exhibit 24.1(b) shows the use of a hub-and-spoke or star topology, which only requires n connections. Exhibit 24.1(c) illustrates a broadcast architecture, which might be one way, as is typically the case in electricity generation, television or radio or satellite broadcasting,

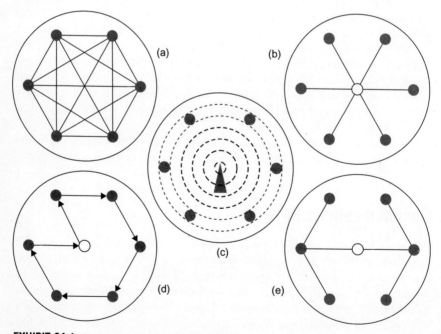

EXHIBIT 24.1 Communications Architectures

or two way, as in satellite communications. The cost can be invariant in the number of connections (subject to aggregate traffic, in the two-way case). Exhibit 24.1(d) shows a multipoint ring, Hamiltonian circuit, or delivery route approach or multipoint bus or traveling salesman path if the return to the center is not required. The cost in terms of link length of such an approach in a bounded area grows as $\sqrt{n}$, so the expected latency can grow similarly. However, if latency is based on the number of stops—as anyone who has ridden a bus knows—it is proportional to n. Finally, Exhibit 24.1(e) illustrates a tree or hierarchical network, whose cost and latency depend on the degree of fan-out at each node: When the fan-out is only 1, the "hierarchy" is trivially a line, as in Exhibit 24.1(d). When the fan-out is n, the hierarchy is the hub-and-spoke shown in Exhibit 24.1(b).

As Exhibit 24.2 shows, the different approaches have different relative costs as n scales, based on assumptions such as the size of any costs associated with hubs and connections.

However, additional nuances are worth considering. Although traveling hundreds of extra miles to and from a hub because there are no direct flights available may be efficient for the service provider, it is not necessarily efficient for the end user in terms of routing complexity or transit time and distance. To get a better handle on these trade-offs, we consider a simple problem.

Suppose that we pick two customers at random within a geographic region. What is the expected increase in distance, if any, by using a central hub rather than a direct point-to-point connection?

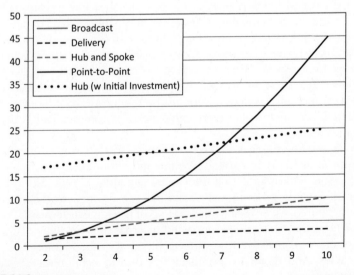

EXHIBIT 24.2 Cost Comparison

We can model this as two points selected at random within the area of a circle with unit radius. A point-to-point connection can never be longer than transiting via the hub. It can be the same, if the hub lies on the straight line connecting the two points. Or the point-to-point connection can be nearly infinitely better: Two points on the perimeter of a unit circle can be a distance apart arbitrarily close to 0 yet would need to traverse a distance of 2 via the hub.

The expected value of the Euclidean distance (as the crow flies rather than, say, Manhattan blocks) on an s-dimensional ball (a sphere plus its interior) of diameter d, when s is even, is[3]:

$$\frac{s}{2s+1} \times \frac{2^{3s+1}\left(\left(\frac{s}{2}\right)!\right)^2 s!}{(s+1)(2s)!\pi} \times d$$

When $s = 2$, that is, the multidimensional ball is just a disk (a circle plus its interior), and the radius is 1 (i.e., the diameter is 2), this formula then evaluates to $128/45\pi = .9054$.

If we use a hub-and-spoke architecture, we can make use of the fact that for a point selected at random on a circle (or disk), the expected value of the distance from that point to the center is 2/3. Therefore, the expected value of the distance via the hub is twice that—4/3, or 1.3333. This math is supported by the simulation referenced at the end of this chapter.

Therefore, the distance penalty that we expect to pay by using the hub is 1.333/.9054, which is 1.472, or nearly 50%. This distance penalty can mean substantially longer latencies. This analysis is not just theoretical: So-called hairpinning is an important concern in engineering and site location for highly interactive services. A 50% penalty in and of itself can render a perfectly usable service unusable by crossing a response time threshold. Perhaps more important, the 50% penalty is an average. In the worst case, as mentioned, two nearly adjacent points must travel a long distance relative to their actual separation, as if you traveled from New York to Philadelphia via Singapore.

Other issues can arise as well, when congestion at the hub causes further delays. Such effects depend not just on the locations of random points relative to the center but also aggregate patterns of communication between pairs of points.

So far our analysis has looked at latency, another way of viewing the difference is in terms of capital investments. Although a significant oversimplification, let's assume that the capital expenditure required to build a network is linearly proportional to distance. In the real world, of course, there are differences: Subsea cables don't cost the same as terrestrial ones to lay, and terrestrial ones can be impacted by costs such as rights-of-way and rights of entry. Microwave towers have different cost structures from fiber optic cables. And there are nonlinearities due to economies of scale as capacity increases.

Accepting—and excepting—all that, however, we'll assume there is a linear cost per unit distance of c_m. Let's assume that there is a cost of the hub of c_b (although, in practice, costs of one or more hubs and core connections will scale as the number of endpoints does). To oversimplify even further, we'll ignore whether these are capital expenditures, operating costs per unit distance—say, mile—or a mix.

Then the expected value of the cost of the point-to-point connections in a network with n nodes is $c_m \times \frac{n(n-1)}{2} \times \frac{128}{45\pi}$, which is just the cost per unit distance times the number of (full duplex) connections in a point-to-point network times the expected distance. Conversely, in a hub-and-spoke architecture on those nodes, the expected value of the cost is $c_b + c_m \times (2/3)n$. The difference between the 4/3 earlier and the 2/3 here is that each node adds an expected cost of $(2/3)c_m$ for the link from it to the hub, whereas in terms of latency, a message must go from an endpoint to the hub to the other endpoint (i.e., using two links).

The hub-and-spoke network's cost is linear in the number of nodes, whereas the point-to-point network's is quadratic (i.e., order(n^2)). Adding in a hub shifts the cost line upward, as shown in Exhibit 24.2, but sooner or later the cost of the point-to-point network will exceed it. In this analysis, we assume complete connectivity. If we want to connect only, say, a few pairs of endpoints, the point-to-point network can be more efficient.

We've looked at costs, but it is worth touching on the *value* of such networks as well. There is a common belief that the value of a network on n nodes is order n^2 (Metcalfe's Law) or is perhaps proportional to the number of unique subgroups and is thus 2^n (Reed's Law). Unfortunately, such laws assume that all connections or subgroups are equally valuable. Under different assumptions, we can mathematically show a value of order ($n \log(n)$), or, in the real-world case where there are convergent value distributions or intrinsic limits of consumption, the network may generate value merely proportional to n.[4]

Hierarchies

The organization of a hierarchy can vary. At one extreme, it has many levels, with less span of control; at the other extreme, it is flattened, with larger span of control. In the limit, this is a central hub with only one layer of "reports." All layers may have similar fan-out, but research into actual networks, such as the Internet or real-world friendships, illustrates a range of structures, ranging from "small-world" networks, which have a mix of local and long-distance connections, and "aristrocratic" networks, which illustrate "power law" distributions: a few nodes with many connections, and many nodes with few connections.[5]

Hierarchical networks can be very efficient. Consider a hierarchical k-ary—for example, binary or ternary—tree (see Exhibit 24.3).

The structure in Exhibit 24.3 is that used by one of the oldest cloud services in existence—the plain-old telephony system (POTS)—which had five such layers. The fan-out—the number of connections to a lower level in the hierarchy—in Exhibit 24.3 is 3 but can be any integer greater than zero. In general, however, if the fan-out at any node is k and the number of levels is m, there are some straightforward calculations to determine the benefits—and trade-offs—of a cloud service.

In such a network, it is easy to see that if n is the number of endpoints, $n = k^m$. To do so requires not just one hub node, as in a hub-and-spoke network, but $\sum_{i=0}^{m-1} k^i$. For example, the number of endpoints or "leaf nodes" in Exhibit 24.3, where each hub node is of degree 3, is $3^3 = 27$, and the number of internal nodes is $\sum_{i=0}^{3-1} 3^i = 3^0 + 3^1 + 3^2 = 13$. The number of links is clearly the number of leaf nodes plus the number of internal nodes less 1 (since each node except the topmost one has exactly one upwardly bound link.

Determining the expected number of links that will be traversed is a little more challenging. If the leftmost node in Exhibit 24.3 wants to communicate with either of the 2 next leftmost endpoints, it merely needs to traverse one link up and one link down. For the next 6 endpoints, it needs traverse two links up and two links down; for the remaining 18 endpoints,

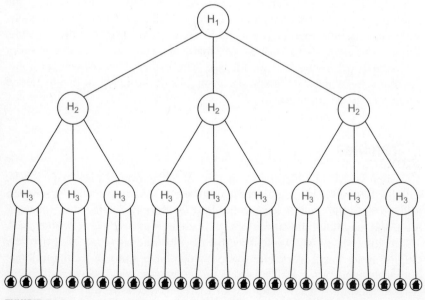

EXHIBIT 24.3 Hierarchical Tree

three links up and three links down. Generalizing this approach, the expected value of the distance (assuming all links are of unit distance) is:

$$\frac{1}{(k^m - 1)} \sum_{i=1}^{m} 2i \times \left(k^i - k^{i-1}\right)$$

This approach, then, lies somewhere between the point-to-point and hub-and-spoke networks: It requires more connections than the hub but less than point to point. The number of links (and thus "hops") can be greater, but the length of each link is shorter. Although the length of the link depends on the exact network topology, as a simplifying assumption, we can assume that the internal nodes are somehow optimally and evenly packed into the unit circle, in which case each hub covers an area of $\pi(1)^2/(\sum_{i=0}^{m-1} k^i)$. In the example given, each node would cover $\pi/13$. The radius of such a circle satisfies $\pi r^2 = \pi(1)^2/(\sum_{i=0}^{m-1} k^i)$, so therefore $r = \sqrt{\frac{1}{(\sum_{i=0}^{m-1} k^i)}}$. To complicate things further, for all links except the topmost one, the distance traversed for an "up link" is $2r$ and for a "down link" is $2r$, but for the topmost hub, which must be traversed to enable any pairwise connection, the distance traversed is r up and then down. Given all this, we end up with the somewhat unwieldy expansion of the formula into an approximate expected distance in a unit circle, assuming that all points are on the circumference of the circle defined by the lowest-level hub:

$$\frac{1}{(k^m - 1)} \sum_{i=1}^{m} (2(i-1)+1) \times \left(k^i - k^{i-1}\right) \times \sqrt{\frac{1}{(\sum_{i=0}^{m-1} k^i)}}$$

In such a network, even two endpoints that are "nearby" can have a worst-case routing through the top of the hierarchy with a maximum separation distance, in this case $10 \times r$.

Markets

If the patterns just discussed are exemplified by communications networks, a different pattern is perhaps exemplified by eBay or Amazon. Rather than all endpoints communicating with each other, a cloud-based marketplace can be divided into buyers and sellers that interact only between groups, not within.

This situation occurs not only when people are engaging in commercial transactions involving goods and services but in other contexts: those seeking romance at Match.com, recruiters and job seekers at

Monster.com, or content providers and customers. Traditional bilateral structures are giving way to peer-based "prosumer" ones (where participants can be both producers and consumers), but even there participants often can be categorized: Although anyone *can* upload content to YouTube, most just view it.

As we saw earlier, when there are n communicators, the number of point-to-point connections is $n(n-1)/2$, but the number of connections to a hub is just n. When there are m buyers and n sellers, the number of direct connections is $m \times n$, whereas a market requires only $m + n$ connections.

When there are quite a few buyers and sellers, there is a dramatic difference between the two functions. Suppose the number of buyers equals the number of sellers. Then $m = n$ and the number of direct connections would be n^2 whereas the number of connections to a market would only be $2n$. The larger n gets, the larger the advantage that a market confers. This inherent advantage is worth paying for, hence the cut that the intermediary receives of each transaction.

It is easy to see that if each connection costs exactly the same, after a certain point it costs less to use a hub-and-spoke architecture—a centralized cloud service—than many private connections. This point occurs when $m \times n > m + n$ or, if there is a fixed cost, c_b, to run the hub, when $m \times n > m + n + c_b$. If we consider the additional cost of the longer physical distance, on a two-dimensional disc. We would have something like $m \times n > 1.472(m + n) + c_b$, using the ratio identified earlier. We can keep making this more complex—for example, instead of a single hub, consider multiple interconnected hubs. United Airlines currently has hubs in Newark, Houston, and Chicago. Network service providers have core routers in major cities as well. We could also consider inequalities where the cost of the hub is a function of the number of connections—that is, $c_b = f(m,n)$, for example, the case where $c_b = k(m + n)$.

Suppose, though, that instead of considering the difference in the cost of the number of connections, we consider the difference in the value generated for a given cost. In other words, rather than the hub-and-spoke pattern providing a cheaper way to connect market participants, suppose that we consider the value of connecting more participants for a given cost.

Consider the simplest case, where there are m buyers and one seller. You have put a "For Sale" sign up in front of your house. That done, you are pondering how much to sell it for, when someone knocks on your door and says, "I love it. I'll give you $500,000 for it. Call me at this number if you are willing to sell it." As he drives off, another person knocks on the door and offers you $510,000. As she drives off, another person knocks on the door and offers you $505,000.

What should you do? To put it another way, what is the marginal value to you as a seller of receiving bids from additional buyers?

This scenario is equivalent to a sealed bid auction where bidders don't know each other's bids and the highest bidder wins. It contrasts with the so-called English auction where bidders try to outdo each other and bidding wars can occur. The question is, what is the expected value to the seller of an additional buyer, or, conversely, what is the expected value of one more seller to a buyer? The answer partly depends, as Nobel laureate in economics George Stigler has observed, on the magnitude of search costs relative to price dispersion.[6] Generally, it is useful to get more than one quote, but not too many are needed: According to Stigler, there are rapidly diminishing returns to search. This is because the costs of search typically are linear in the number of options assessed, whereas the expected price improvement for each additional option—even scaled by the quantity purchased—generally declines exponentially.[7] The cloud changes the math somewhat, because search costs can drop to near zero.

Let's consider a simple case, where each prospective buyer (bidder) values the house somewhere in the range of 0 to 1 (say, $1 million), and these bids are uniformly distributed between 0 and 1. The expected value of the bid from the first buyer is .5 (million). With an infinite number of buyers, we could get arbitrarily close to 1 (million—we'll stop mentioning this). But even with a small number of buyers, we can expect to get quite close to 1. With five prospects with bids b_1, b_2, b_3, b_4, b_5, for example, the likelihood that the highest bid won't beat .9 can be calculated as:

$$p(\max(b_1, b_2, b_3, b_4, b_5) \leq .9) = p(b_1 \leq .9) \times p(b_2 \leq .9) \times p(b_3 \leq .9)$$

$$\times p(b_4 \leq .9) \times p(b_5 \leq .9)$$

$$= .9 \times .9 \times .9 \times .9 \times .9 = .9^5 = .59049$$

Therefore, the likelihood that the highest bid is at least .9 is 1 minus that value, or .40951.

To generalize this logic, if we have m bidders, where each bid is drawn from a uniform distribution ranging from 0 to 1, the likelihood that the maximum bid from this group will be less than or equal to k (where k is between 0 and 1) is k^m. Conversely, the probability that the maximum bid will be greater than k is $1 - k^m$.

As the size of the set grows, the expected value of the maximum of a set of samples taken from a bounded underlying distribution, such as a uniform distribution, exhibits diminishing returns. What this means is that we shouldn't necessarily sell the house to the first bidder, but it doesn't take too many visitors to our front door to find someone who is willing to pay close to top dollar.

This good news for the house seller puts an interesting spin on the value of the cloud when used to enable a market. It suggests that if there are many buyers (or sellers) with limited dispersion of bids (or prices), a market can be small and localized. If, among many prospects, there are few *active* participants, and they exhibit substantial price dispersion, the market may need to be large and require a global reach, as in finding a buyer willing to pay \$28,000 for a grilled cheese sandwich.[8]

It is worth noting that there are computability benefits to aggregating resources in a single market (a topic beyond the scope of this book). Briefly, it turns out that when there are many buyers with needs for a varying quantity of resources where the resource purchases can't be partitioned, it can be very difficult, i.e., computationally intractable, to match buyers with sellers.[9] However, if all of the resources are consolidated in a single location, the problem becomes easy to solve.[10] To the extent that a market hub performs this function, it not only enables more cost-effective relationships between buyers and sellers but also eliminates computational complexity issues.

This discussion is generally relevant to physical markets and software as a service or Web sites that enable markets, whether Match.com or eBay. They use efficient physical layer networks to enable efficient markets by offering buyers more sellers and sellers more buyers.

Repository

The cloud can also act as a repository of information. Consider the Library of Congress, Google Books, or the index of all the accessible Web sites on the planet that each major search provider maintains.

The benefit of a single repository versus multiple copies is a function of the cost of storage relative to the cost of networking and the pattern of access. When storage is cheap and networking is expensive, it's better to maintain a local copy of the information. Conversely, when storage is expensive and networking is cheap, it's better to access a remote copy.

When both storage and networking are attractively priced, but nonzero, there is a breakeven point based on the pattern of access. Frequently accessed items should be stored locally, and infrequently accessed items should be accessed remotely.

If we exclude network costs, the benefit of a single repository is clear: It is less expensive to maintain one copy than n copies. If the cost to store a copy is s, the cost to access a copy is a, and the number of accesses is k, then the break-even point between strategies occurs when the cost to store n copies locally—$n \times s$—is equal to the cost to remotely access a single copy k times, which is $s + k \times a$.

Perimeters and Checkpoints

Another place where the cloud comes in handy is in establishing a perimeter. Let's consider a fence that is cordoning off a square plot of land. Assuming that the plot is s feet (meters, miles, parsecs) on a side, it takes $4s$

length of fencing to enclose s^2 square feet (square meters, square miles, square parsecs) of area. This equation provides a nice nonlinearity: When we double the quantity of fencing, we don't merely double the area fenced in but quadruple it.

This principle turns out to be very relevant to the cloud. Consider a network service provider that offers services to millions or tens of millions of customers. To provide cyberattack protection to those customers may not necessarily be a function of the number of customers as much as it is the size of the interface between those customers and the outside world.

In the same way, various agencies secure only the *perimeter* to the country rather than patrolling every square foot of the interior of the country. Customs and Border Patrol secures primarily the land perimeter, the Coast Guard secures the water perimeter, and NORAD—the North American Aerospace Defense Command—secures the air and space perimeter, leaving it to others (state police, FBI, local sheriffs) to provide defense in depth. Both approaches have their value and optimum configuration.

The benefit of perimeter protection in contrast to defense in depth is application and domain dependent. For a planar area, it is on the order of the difference between a value and the square of that value. For a square, it is $4s$ versus s^2. For a circle, it is the difference between a circumference of $2\pi r$ and the area enclosed, namely πr^2. For cyberdefense or spam prevention, it is the relative cost of licenses and equipment at the network perimeter versus that for individual endpoints, with the added benefit that nipping unwanted traffic in the bud, namely at the first detection by the network, eliminates network bandwidth used to carry such traffic, creating economic value through better resource utilization.

Summary

The point behind exploring a variety of patterns—perimeter, repository, hub and spoke, market—is to point out that a variety of cloud architectures can exhibit complex benefits: not only cost reduction but expected value enhancement. Some application patterns—what might be called compelling cases for the cloud[11] —do more than just leverage economies of scale or on-demand pricing.

🖥 **ONLINE**

"Hub and Spoke vs. Point-to-Point," at http://complexmodels.com/ HubOrDirect.aspx, illustrates the trade-offs between direct, point-to-point links and traversal of a centralized hub.

Notes

1. www.nps.gov/nhl/DOE_dedesignations/Telephone.htm.
2. "A Brief History of Con Edison: Electricity," conEdison, www.coned.com/history/electricity.asp.
3. Bernhard Burgstaller and Friedrich Pillichshammer, "The Average Distance Between Two Points," www.math.uni-muenster.de/reine/u/burgstal/d18.pdf.
4. Bob Briscoe, Andrew Odlyzko, and Benjamin Tilly, "Metcalfe's Law Is Wrong," *IEEE Spectrum* (July 2006), http://spectrum.ieee.org/computing/networks/metcalfes-law-is-wrong; Joe Weinman, "Is Metcalfe's Law Way Too Optimistic," *Business Communications Review* (August 2007), pp. 18–27. www.joeweinman.com/Resources/WeinmanMetcalfe.pdf.
5. Duncan Watts and Steven Strogatz, "Collective Dynamics of 'Small-World' Networks," *Nature* 393, No. 6684 (1998): 440–442; Albert-László Barabási, *Linked: How Everything Is Connected to Everything Else and What It Means* (Plume, 2003).
6. George J. Stigler, "The Economics of Information," *Journal of Political Economy* 69, No. 3 (June 1961), pp. 213–225.
7. The actual rate of decline depends on the distribution of prices—a uniform distribution is assumed here.
8. "'Virgin Mary' Toast Fetches $28,000," *BBC*, November 23, 2004. http://news.bbc.co.uk/2/hi/4034787.stm.
9. Joe Weinman, "Cloud Computing Is NP-Complete," February 1, 2011. www.joeweinman.com/Resources/Joe_Weinman_Cloud_Computing_Is_NP-Complete.pdf.
10. Note that if there are even just two locations, the problem is at least weakly NP-complete due to a straightforward transformation to PARTITION, as proven in the prior reference.
11. Joe Weinman, "Compelling Cases for Clouds," *GigaOM.com*, November 15, 2009. http://gigaom.com/2009/11/15/compelling-cases-for-clouds/.

CHAPTER 25

What's Next for Cloud?

We've spent most of this book discussing the underlying forces that impact the economics of the cloud. These have included quantitative factors, such as economies and statistics of scale, and qualitative factors, such as the psychology of cloud customers: behavioral Cloudonomics. How might these factors impact the evolution of the cloud market, pricing for cloud services, and the roles of participants in the cloud ecosystem? Although nothing is certain, we can make some educated guesses.

Pricing

Many cloud services are characterized by pay-per-use pricing, but such a pricing model is far from the only possible model, even in today's cloud. Many cloud services are advertiser supported, and Wikipedia is "pay-what-you-like," which may include nothing. One lesson that can be drawn from other industries is that innovation applies not only to products and services but to how they are priced: Both the product and its pricing are key elements of the marketing mix. And today, we've moved beyond competition just on *price* to competition on *pricing*.

America Online caused Internet usage to triple by eliminating per-minute dial-up rates in favor of unlimited usage in 1996.[1] Similarly, AT&T Wireless Services introduced Digital One Rate in 1998—moving from pay-per-use to essentially flat rate—and then in 2011 migrated from unlimited usage to usage-sensitive plans.[2]

There are dozens of pricing strategies, each with its own business model and customer acceptance implications. "Free" causes a unique human behavioral response, where consumers will select free goods even when they are a worse value.[3] Moreover, "free" and "profitable" are not mutually exclusive terms. As Harvard Law School professor Yochai Benkler observed in describing the economics of commons-based peer production, even though IBM has tens of thousands of patents, its Linux-related services revenues grew from zero to over $1 billion in less than two years, surpassing income from their intellectual property.[4] Google prints money by offering users "free search," monetized of course by third-party advertisers. Chris Anderson, serial deep thinker, PhD physicist, and editor in chief of *Wired*, outlined several types of "freeconomic" approaches: the cross-subsidy, where the razor is free but blades are pricey, or selling an ebook reader below cost but making it up on zero-marginal-cost ebooks; the freemium model, where a few paying users subsidize freeloaders; advertising-supported; zero or low pricing on zero- or low-marginal-cost goods; and nonmonetary exchanges, such as exchanging labor for reputation rather than money.[5]

Free services may be monetized outside the technology domain: Rovio's Angry Birds game is not just a for-free or for-fee app; it is now also a full-fledged brand, selling angry—but cute—birds as plush toys offered by Build-A-Bear Workshop, key chains, flip-flops, and recipe books. At least for consumer brands, such licensing may be where the business opportunity lies: Licensing fees for the California Raisins—animated, fictional raisins—were larger than for the actual raisin industry.[6] If this seems like a stretch, cloud purists should realize that the Walt Disney Company—currently worth over $60 billion—began in the cloud content medium of its day—animation—with a cat named Julius and a lucky rabbit named Oswald, well before a Mickey Mouse. Who's to argue that Rovio can't emulate that success?

Other ways to monetize free services exist, such as selling consumer preference and analytics data to third parties. Of course, cloud providers can also directly monetize services: There is a plethora of nonzero charging schemes[7]:

- Lifetime subscriptions
- Nonlinear pricing
- Multipart tariffs
- Nonuniform pricing
- Tiered pricing
- Block tariffs
- Spot pricing
- Pay what you like[8]
- Pay for quality or priority
- English, Dutch, Vickrey, and other auctions
- Wright tariffs and Shapley pricing[9]
- A variety of congestion pricing schemes

One congestion pricing scheme has been proposed by Jeffrey MacKie-Mason, a dean and professor at the University of Michigan, and Hal Varian, emeritus professor at the University of California at Berkeley, and Google Chief Economist. They proposed auctioning off Internet capacity each moment through a Vickrey auction, where the price paid by the winner(s) is that bid by the highest nonwinning bidder.[10] University of Minnesota professor Andrew Odlyzko has proposed Paris Metro pricing, where similar resource pools are sold at differing prices.[11] Because fewer people want to pay the higher price, there are fewer users for a given quantity of resource and thus lower congestion. To all these may be added dozens of variations in offers, charging, and billing: prepaid, postpaid, installment paid, or progress payments; reserved versus on demand; rollover resources; commitments, fees; bundles.

Different customers may be offered different prices or plans for the same or similar goods. Such price discrimination comes in various forms, but in self-targeting, different customers are charged different amounts based on what each is willing to pay, revealing such preferences by opting for "platinum" instead of "standard" service levels, for example.

One of the most likely trends that we will see is the adoption of dynamic pricing and nonuniform (differential) pricing, where different resources are priced differently based on location or time of day, and the price of a given computing time slot varies based on the level of demand. There are four types of workloads: immediate, schedule based, deferrable, and discretionary. In airlines, some travelers will pay a premium to travel immediately; some have long-term advance notice but little time flexibility; some adjust travel dates to minimize fares; others jump at special deals to destinations they didn't know they wanted to visit. Online, a vast majority of users want searches or financial trades executed instantaneously; businesses with predictable variation want to reserve capacity for future spikes; testing can be deferred to off-peak times; and a new category of discretionary processing will emerge, where additional compute cycles can create value at a low enough price.

Different types of customers—time buyers and time sellers—are willing to make different trade-offs between immediacy and parsimony. This is good, because the complementary combination is a win-win-win: Time buyers meet their need for instant gratification; time sellers meet their need for expense reduction; service providers increase utilization and profitability by serving both together.

Given all of the options that we have outlined, which is to be preferred? As a rule, customers—both consumers and enterprises—often prefer flat rates, due to simplicity and loss aversion, as explored in Chapter 23. However, pay per use is a more rational model: It correctly aligns usage with investment and economically and correctly allocates resources, without the anomalies found in flat-rate models such as moral hazard, adverse selection, and excess consumption.[12] Companies offering flat-rate plans are conflicted: Once the sale is made, they perversely, as profit-seeking businesses, want customers to consume as little as possible of their product or service. And because no company can afford unbounded investment with finite revenues but potentially unlimited consumption, service will inevitably suffer in what essentially is a tragedy of the commons.

Generally, pay per use will dominate over flat rates when there are:

- Broad dispersion of consumption levels
- Nonzero marginal cost of goods sold, making such consumption differences profitability impacting
- Perfect competition, driving prices down to those marginal costs
- Low metering costs relative to the cost of goods sold
- Active, rational users
- Predictable usage levels
- Low information and switching costs[13]

In such a world, there are interesting dynamics: Even if users are randomly divided between flat-rate and pay-per-use service providers, the light users migrate to pay per use and the heavy ones migrate to flat rates. Over time, the flat-rate price rises, driving more shifts to pay per use. In the end, only some of the heaviest users are left using the flat-rate plan. Somewhat counterintuitively, the total customer spending and therefore provider revenues don't change due to such customer defections. This theoretical result is matched in practice: AT&T's average revenue per user barely budged after it replaced "unlimited" plans with usage-sensitive ones.[14]

In a universe of pricing options, there typically are alternating epochs of convergence and differentiation. One vendor breaks from the pack to differentiate via unique pricing. If unsuccessful, it returns to the fold; if successful, it generates imitators and a new standard practice, at which point the cycle restarts.

In summary, many variations are conceivable, and cloud providers are well advised to spend as much time thinking about pricing as about technology.

Ecosystems, Intermediaries, and the Intercloud

One recent assessment of the emerging cloud computing ecosystem identified six major roles: infrastructure, such as physical equipment but also identity and billing; platforms, such as development environments, open source projects, and standards organizations; software, from SaaS vendors but also SaaS marketplaces, cloud resellers, and cloud distributors; services, such as certification, audit and compliance, and certification; partners, such as consulting, integration, and outsourcing, and communities, such as development and test.[15] In such a world, partners, third parties, and intermediaries—some of which are sometimes called cloud service brokers—play a key role. If all pricing from all vendors were a flat 10 cents per server hour, choices might be made based on differentiators such as brand, location, and relationships. But if one provider is charging 10 cents now and 8 cents in two hours, and another one is charging 9 cents now but requires a commitment for future purchase, there is not just room but a dire need for intermediaries and instruments.

Intermediaries can help increase the efficiency and liquidity of cloud markets, selling off unused perishable resources while helping customers to save money. When there are multiple providers with roughly equivalent services, different types of intermediaries can arise: such as buyer's agents who, for a fee, help customers select among multiple providers, and seller's agents, such as manufacturer's representatives, who help extend the reach of distribution. The complexity inherent in multiple cloud providers will drive business to consultants and integrators.

In a world of complex and dynamic resources and prices, markets and market makers tend to arise. Ecological niches in the cloud jungle are being filled by established and emerging companies such as RightScale, which helps customers use multiple clouds; Enomaly's SpotCloud, a capacity exchange; Cloudability, which helps monitor and manage billing; Strategic Blue, which acts as a broker-dealer; and additional new entrants.

In the case of networking, Arbinet's Marketplace Services is an example of how an intermediary can support trading of technology services, in this case bandwidth, from over 1,000 customers.[16] In the cloud, one early trial of such an approach is Enomaly's SpotCloud. Reuven Cohen is the founder and chief executive officer (CEO) of Enomaly, now a division of Virtustream, which sells software to enable cloud service providers and offers SpotCloud, one of the earliest cloud capacity exchanges. He disclosed that there has been progress but there also remain challenges, such as the fact that computing resources from the different providers are not a commodity.[17] West Texas Intermediate Crude has defined density and sulfur content. But if you buy a "virtual server," or a "large instance," what exactly are you getting? Is the physical server you're running on state of the art? Or a few years old? And the same way that your experience of a center airline seat partly depends on who's sitting near you and whether they are kicking or screaming, the actual performance you experience in the cloud may vary based on who else is computing in "adjacent" resources. Rather than oil, the cloud may be more like wine—with differences not only between Two Buck Chuck and Château Latour but also between vintages, from bottle to bottle, and even from sip to sip.

Cohen pointed out that even advertised service-level agreements don't necessarily provide clarity, because while customers view them as some sort of guarantee, service providers may view them more as a target and an indicator of how much they may need to refund or credit.

According to Dr. James Mitchell, CEO of Strategic Blue, the differing preferences of cloud providers and cloud consumers provide an opportunity for cloud broker-dealers.[18] Strategic Blue acts as a financial intermediary between cloud provider and cloud consumer without interfering with the technical access to the cloud, similar to the way a bank will finance your car without helping to drive or maintain it. Strategic Blue can buy on cloud providers' terms, often up front at a discount, and sell on cloud consumers' terms, which can include extended payment, change of currency, flat-rate pricing, or a fixed-price deal.

Although it may be a while before servers and storage are traded on commodities exchanges, "reserved instances" are partly a financial instrument. Amazon Web Services reserved instances, for example, have different flavors but are a combination of a volume discount, prepayment discount, capacity reservation mechanism, and hedge.[19] By prepaying, fees for services may be discounted but also may be locked in for a period of one to three years, which may not be beneficial to the user if on-demand prices decrease more than the discount, but conceptually can at least act as hedges against price increases, in the unlikely event that any might occur.

Markets need not exist solely between service providers and customers. In the same way that participants in the eBay marketplace may act as either buyers or sellers, businesses with spare computing capacity may be able to offload it to others on a peer-to-peer basis or mediated by trusted markets with reputation management (e.g., "this seller is rated 97% positive"). Technologies exist to enable secure processing on untrusted resources, so a customer may not think about the location he is running in any more than a bank customer wonders where the interest on her account comes from.

In the last century, the canonical corporate architecture was arguably the vertically integrated firm. Ford's River Rouge plant had its own docks, made its own steel, and generated its own electricity, and so—in effect, it turned dirt into cars. Today, weight loss is in, and in the era of networked virtual corporations, business webs, and open innovation, a focus on core rather than context has become increasingly prevalent. Individual cloud providers would surely love to capture all of customers' IT spend, but it is more realistic to expect that various firms will carve out unique positions and customer franchises.

When the world is fragmented, opportunities lie in the glue that holds it all together. Loosely coupled mashups, standards for interoperability, commercial arrangements, and robust, reliable connections to build a network of clouds—the Intercloud—will be where much of the value migrates.

Every firm must find a balance between running today's business and experimenting with innovation to create the products that will drive tomorrow's revenue stream. Occasionally, a company shifts from cost reduction to renewed investment in its future. Sometimes a company that has been in exploratory mode tightens its focus, as when Google CEO Larry Page decided to put "more wood behind fewer arrows" resulting in the discontinuation or deprecation of Google Buzz, Code Search, Jaiku, and other services.[20] The lesson is that even when a business is highly profitable, it needs to ensure that the products in its portfolio pull their own weight, unless there is an overall portfolio plan that lets mature products feed others in their infancy. Such actions lead to a broader set of players that each can excel, in turn feeding the rise of the Intercloud.

Most real ecosystems are rich and diverse. Various niches and roles arise such as predators and scavengers. The cloud ecosystem is no different. In addition to the roles just described, there will be boutiques and specialists to complement the big-box retailers. There will be virtual operators, wholesaling capacity from other providers and retailing it to others. Some cloud services are built on other cloud offers: Netflix famously uses cloud infrastructure for transcoding and content delivery clouds for streaming.

We can also predict a variety of federations and alliances, where companies complement each other's resources to fill coverage gaps. This is happening in some areas already: Spain's communications carrier Telefonica, for example, is fostering a content distribution federation, where various entities will build out regional infrastructure that other partners will be able to leverage.[21] Some federations and alliances—like dating before marriage—likely will turn into joint ventures, mergers, acquisitions, and roll-ups.

Even without alliances, hotels and airlines sometimes refer a customer who is the victim of overbooking to a competitor. And insurance companies rely on reinsurance to further mitigate risk beyond the risk reduction derived from statistical multiplexing. It would be prudent, then, for one cloud service provider to offer, either for an up-front premium or just for the opportunity to gain new revenue, capacity reinsurance to another provider, possibly on a reciprocal basis.

Beyond operational federations, there are and will continue to be innovation federations. The OpenStack community leverages software initially from both Rackspace and NASA, released on an open source basis.[22] Currently comprising over 140 players, including rivals such as Cisco, Dell, and HP, this is a strategy of co-opetition, shifting the basis of competition among themselves as well as to counter other market players. Participants in OpenStack, who leverage and also enhance the code base, have decided to compete on their brand, operational capabilities, customer service, and footprint rather than on the core software that they run. This is not that different from what occurs in other industries: Major airlines fly the same planes; rental car services offer the same makes and models.

To counter the asymmetric power of large providers, smaller customers sometimes band together in buyers' cooperatives to wield greater influence and negotiate volume discounts. TM Forum's Enterprise Cloud Leadership Council, first chaired by ServiceMesh founder and CEO Eric Pulier, is an early example.[23]

Regulators, quasi-governmental entities, and nongovernmental entities ranging from the United Nations International Telecommunications Union to the World Economic Forum are becoming more involved in the cloud.

Products versus Services

Starbucks was originally a service provider but augmented its service business by moving into products: selling ground coffee and whole beans in tens of thousands of grocery stores via a distribution and licensing agreement with Kraft. Microsoft was originally in the product business, selling software such as Windows and Office and hardware such as Xbox. Software became "software + services," and game consoles moved from stand-alone devices to online, multiplayer games. The lesson: Service providers can encapsulate their capabilities as products; product companies can expand into services.

There are clearly numerous benefits to cloud services, as we've delineated. That said, cloud companies today have developed innovations in features and functions as well as delivery models. In some cases, the delivery model is orthogonal to the capability, the way coffee bean selection, roasting, and grinding is insensitive to delivery via a barista or a bag. It is therefore likely that some service providers will extract and productize their intellectual property, as stand-alone appliances, software capabilities intended for private installation, remotely managed systems, or integrated product-service system hybrids.

In other words, rather than being beholden to a specific architecture or delivery model, it makes sense to solve a customer problem—strategically exploiting IT in the pursuit of competitive advantage—with a solution that may have multiple product and service embodiments. By solving customer problems with compelling solutions, the revenue will follow.

Consolidation and Concentration

Some believe that within a few years, only a handful of cloud providers will exist. Ultimately, this argument is based on an assumption of significant economies of scale and related factors, such as innovation and branding. If two providers can merge and drive their costs lower, they can undercut the

competition and gain market share. Eventually, the industry would end
with a few players or only one mega-corporation (if not for antitrust reg
lation and countries' desires to nurture their own domestic participants).

But, as I've argued, although there are economies of scale and network
effects, I believe that the industry is likely to have a diverse ecosystem
of players. There will be Walmart and Target but also 7-Eleven, Neiman
Marcus, Nordstrom, Barneys, mom-and-pop shops, and malls, competing
respectively on operational excellence but also convenience, premium
services, customer service, niche focus, local customer relationships, and
breadth of portfolio as an aggregator.

The concentration of firms in an industry can be measured by a concentration ratio (e.g., the share held by the four largest firms in that industry)
or the Herfindahl-Hirschman (HH) Index.[24] The economies-of-scale argument, blindly applied, suggests that *every* industry would have a concentration ratio of 100%—say, among the four or eight largest firms—or a high
HH index, or a single monopolistic competitor, yet that is not what we find.

Consider hotels, a real-world example of pay-per-use, on-demand
capacity. Hotels fall under North American Industry Classification System
(NAICS) code 721. As of the most recent U.S. economic census (2007), the 4
largest firms accounted for 19% of industry revenues, the 20 largest ones
accounted for 36%, and even the 50 largest service providers didn't break the
50% mark.[25] And that is just in the United States.

At the other extreme, where there may be not only economies of scale
but also unique characteristics, such as spectrum auctions that require deep
pockets and also, literally, network effects, consider telecom (NAICS 517).
As of 2007, the four largest U.S. firms had 56.2% of the market, and the 20
largest ones had 82.2% of the market.[26] Still, there are over 1,000 network
operators in the world.

There will likely be a mix of concentrations as we consider the different
layers and services in the cloud. On one hand, there will be companies like
Facebook that leverage network effects to achieve a high degree of concentration, or ones like Amazon, Google, Microsoft, and Apple that continue
to enhance unique algorithms and services that closely link to endpoints.
Companies with unique expertise and competencies in specific verticals—
say, tax preparation or protein folding—or horizontals and functions—say,
customer relationship management or analytics—will dominate their segment of the cloud business.

On the other hand, much lower industry concentration may be
expected if:

- A medium-size customer base provides a reasonably good cost structure, as we saw in Chapter 15.
- Enabling technologies diffuse broadly, as is happening now.

> nsolidation of facilities are opposed by latency
> in Chapter 20.
>
> cost-effectively enabled by technologies such as
> a centers.
>
> macy or vertical expertise remain important.

rs are currently pursuing cloud strategies; that will add roughly
ayers to the global count.

According to McKinsey principal Will Forrest, the firm's research suggests that in cloud services, "size is not destiny."[27] Cloud services are at the eye of a perfect storm of demand-side diversity, regulation, and continued customer preference for local presence. Forrest argued that these forces will counterbalance the well-documented economies of scale possible with the cloud. McKinsey's conclusion: The market for cloud providers is likely to remain relatively fragmented for at least the next five years.

City in the Clouds

Allegedly, on May 23, 2007, a milestone was reached.[28] For the first time, half the world's population lived in cities.[29] Why the shift? The answer has to do with the magnetic attraction of cities.

According to Brendan O'Flaherty, a professor of economics at Columbia University: "Urban agglomerations are a great idea. Concentrating a lot of activity in a small area saves on transportation; allows all sorts of convenience, sharing, and economies of scale; encourages the spread of new ideas; and simply satisfies the human desire to be social."[30] This concentration is similar to network effects such as at Facebook: People go there because that's where the people are. But besides interpersonal network effects, there is another feedback loop at work. As O'Flaherty quipped, "The motels and garages are in [the city] because people who crash go [there], and people who crash go to [the city] because that's where the motels and garages are."[31]

Cities offer services and resources: libraries, parks, restaurants, theaters, museums, clubs and raves, specialists in chronic obstructive pulmonary disorder, antique shops specializing in the Han Dynasty, comic book shops specializing in Han Solo. The breadth of this collection of services and resources attracts those interested in the richness of city-dwelling. In other words, in a virtuous cycle, the availability of resources and services attracts customers, and the existence of customers attracts businesses offering these services. These customers could live in the suburbs or rural environments, as a decreasing percentage of humanity does, but the attraction of the city is proximity (i.e., *latency reduction*).

The same thing is happening in the cloud. Rich data sets in the cloud—so-called big data—drive more applications in the cloud. Cisco vice president and chief technology officer (CTO) for cloud computing Lew Tucker has claimed that the future of the cloud will be "dominated by data," since it's easier to move an application to a large data set than to move a large data set to the application.[32] In data mining, as in gold mining, it's easier to move the processing equipment to where the resources are. More applications in the cloud drive additional data to be acquired, organized, and delivered. And the size of big data is exploding: Perhaps the ultimate example of big data is the stream coming out of the Large Hadron Collider at the European Organization for Nuclear Research (CERN). It currently produces 15 petabytes[33] (over a million million million bits) of information *each year*, which it shares with over 100 research facilities around the globe. As if that weren't enough, this deluge from CERN—part of what Bret Swanson, president of Entropy Economics, a strategy and economics consultancy, has called the "global exaflood"—is expected to grow by several orders of magnitude in the next year.[34]

The general system dynamics of such evolution have been explored by Albert-László Barabási, now of Northeastern University, who described the process as preferential attachment.[35] The rich get richer, and the connected get more connected. For cities, O'Flaherty observed that history matters: In the case of New York and Chicago, the construction of the Erie Canal between Albany and Buffalo in the early 1800s was the final link that utilized the Hudson River and the Great Lakes to connect the agricultural bounty of the Midwest with the markets of the East Coast and Europe. A different decision regarding the construction of the canal might have made Philadelphia or Baltimore the largest city in the United States. Such dynamics are normally referred to in chaos theory as "sensitive dependence on initial conditions."[36] One implication of preferential attachment and sensitive dependence: Arbitrary choices made now, such as where certain data sets are located, may dramatically impact the future equilibrium states of the cloud—the countries, universities, or cloud providers that are the centers for physics research, financial transactions, genetics, and the like.

Spending More while Paying Less

If there truly are dramatic economies of scale via the cloud that in turn drive the lowest possible unit costs, then the cloud will no doubt save money, as measured in the cost per unit of computation or storage, after accounting for search costs, switching costs, worker retraining, and the like.

Moreover, in Chapter 11, we argued that you could save money even while paying *more* for a unit of computing delivered via cloud, if there was sufficient resource demand variability. After all, the total value proposition of the cloud is not just that you pay a given amount for a particular set of resources or services but that you *don't* pay anything when you aren't using them.

By definition, then, the cloud—whether used singly or in a hybrid—can't help but reduce the average cost of a *unit* of IT. But if the cost comes down, doesn't that mean that IT departments will spend less? This question is best answered by analogy.

The reduction in cost from the original cell phones to today's smartphones, by a factor 100 or so—more if normalized for increased functionality and performance—was accompanied by an increase in mobile services from an original market size of zero to today's $1 trillion-plus market. The same has happened with energy: As its cost has dropped and ubiquity grown, its usage has increased. This effect is called Jevons' Paradox, but it doesn't seem to be much of a paradox.[37] Many goods exhibit price elasticity of demand: Demand increases as price decreases—typically in conjunction with product and process innovation and with economies of scale tied to the technology adoption life cycle. If, as a result, the percentage increase in the quantity sold is greater than the percentage decrease in price, industry revenues expand. In the case of mobile telephony, the price decrease by a factor of 100 corresponded to market growth from zero customers to over 5 billion and revenue growth from zero dollars to $1 trillion.

There is price elasticity of demand for computing as well, and it is a general-purpose technology. If the cloud—either itself or in combination with existing approaches—lowers the average cost per unit of computation, it will make sense for computing to be used in more cases, such as in replacing travel via video conferencing; in replacing actors via increasingly realistic animation; and in automating tasks currently performed by manual labor. And, as we've argued, more and more products are becoming computerized and informationalized, such as singing greeting cards and intelligent light bulbs. It can't be that long before a $5 paper greeting card includes video recording and playback together with live HD video communications via the cloud. In short, the reduction in average unit cost will drive more computing: both for cost reduction of tasks formerly not done via IT and by the increasing ability to differentiate products and services by making them smart.

Enabling Vendor Strategies

What are the implications for enabling vendors? Excluding macroeconomic cycle anomalies, price elasticity and the Jevons argument suggest more IT. More IT means more systems and more components built into those systems. That's the good news. However, more product does not necessarily mean more profit: The business is already highly competitive. The challenge in any business that has a continuing trend of technology innovation driving continued cost reduction is to grow or maintain revenue and profitability in the face of endless price-performance improvements. The structure of the industry is thus likely to favor scale on the supply side. On the demand side, for these systems vendors, enabling software vendors, and network service providers, an increasing percentage of their business will shift away from individual enterprises, systems integrators, and perhaps even business process outsourcers and toward cloud service providers and buyer cooperatives. This shift may lead to further margin compression. Continued growth in IT-enabled solutions may lead, however, to relatively stable returns on invested capital, as volume growth compensates for margin declines.

How much IT systems spend will migrate out of the enterprise and into the cloud? This is an important question for software and hardware vendor sales leaders and strategists. If there *is* a big switch to the cloud, to use Nicholas Carr's term, many IT vendors would need to dismantle their enterprise sales forces, would see their margins shrink due to the increased purchasing power of concentrated buyers, and would see greater business volatility as large clients were won or lost.[38] The IT equipment and software industry would resemble the jumbo jet or nuclear reactor construction industry: no retail outlets in malls, no sales calls on enterprises, just a laser focus on a small number of service providers.

Conversely, cloud computing might be just one of an eclectic set of tools to meet a diverse set of business requirements. Chief information officers (CIOs) might, for a very long time, use a mix of in-house development, licensed software, and software as a service (SaaS), as well as a mix of legacy, private cloud, and public cloud resources.

Then, rather than the service provider segment being the only customer segment, as for nuclear power plants, it would be one among many, as with automobiles. According to Jesse Snyder, a senior editor at *Automotive News*, unit sales of light vehicles—passenger cars, SUVs, pickups, and vans—are typically 80% retail, with the other 20% "fleet": 6% daily car rental services, 5% government, and 9% corporate.[39] To put it another way, enterprises fulfill a *minority* of their requirements for ground transportation via on demand, pay per use.

Neither nuclear reactors nor automobiles are perfect analogies for IT hardware and software. The main point is to illustrate that many segments can remain viable, and that relative segment size is not a foregone conclusion. One way to attempt to ascertain the future balance is to refer to our earlier analysis regarding the cost optimality of hybrids.

Nicolas Berggruen is an unusual "homeless" person: He is a billionaire retail and media magnate, who travels around the world living out of hotels, having sold off his residences years ago.[40] But he is the exception that proves the rule: Hotels are popular, but there is still room for people to own homes and companies to own buildings. Taxicabs and rental cars are moving forward, yet people still own cars and enterprises still own fleets. The restaurant business is cooking, but kitchens are still ubiquitous.

In Chapter 11, we saw that hybrid solutions are likely to be the answer for a long time based on optimizing operational costs but also due to a variety of other factors, such as the prohibitive costs to migrate legacy applications. There are many complicating factors, such as whether cloud providers have and can maintain scale economies; virtuous cycles where data moving into the cloud drives applications into the cloud drives data into the cloud; the proportion of applications that are highly interactive and thus latency sensitive; and so on. If hybrids are the best solution, the implication is that baseline resources—and purchasing decisions for them—will stay in an enterprise data center, and the spike—and its supporting resources and purchasing—will move into the cloud. If so, what are the implications for the proportion of IT spend from the enterprise versus service provider segments?

It clearly depends on the application profiles that shape the hybrids, which vary by industry and customer, as we saw in Chapter 9. However, let's consider an example of a workload such as we might find in retail, as shown in Exhibit 25.1. The peak-to-average ratio looks to be about four to one, from which we might conclude that 25% of IT spending will come from the enterprise and 75% from the cloud.

However, as Exhibit 25.2 shows, it's not the peak-to-average ratio that is important in this type of analysis but the actual IT resources used (e.g., server hours)—that is, the area under the curve. Assuming that the enterprise

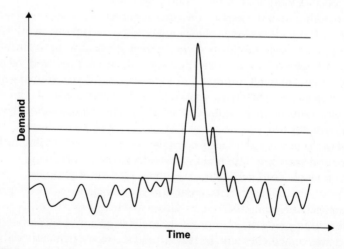

EXHIBIT 25.1 Illustrative Variable Demand over Time

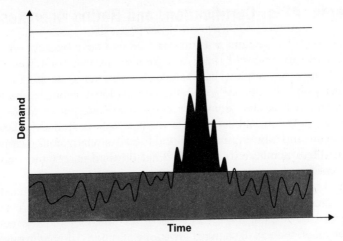

EXHIBIT 25.2 Relative Proportion of Resource Requirements

is buying resources at a fixed level to safely handle the baseline, its purchasing is as shown in the area shaded in gray; the portion of purchasing intermediated and controlled by the cloud provider is shown in black.

As can be seen, the efficiencies that the cloud generates through resource pooling mean that less IT resource investment is required: This is good for value generation but counterintuitive in terms of which segments will drive spend. Rather than three parts cloud to one part enterprise based on the peak-to-average ratio, the relative proportions of gray and black areas roughly show three parts enterprise to one part cloud, based on the relative proportion of compute cycles.

This logic applies to storage as well. Vanessa Alvarez, an analyst with Forrester Research focusing primarily on storage architectures and strategy, has argued that CIOs must consider a hybrid storage strategy, in which on-premise storage and cloud service provider storage will be one and the same. She said: "It won't matter where your capacity is coming from or how much you need . . . you'll just have it, always on, always available."[41]

Clearly, numerous other factors will influence uptake: A SaaS provider may have some new functionality that drives more use to the cloud, but conversely, someone may sell some innovative capability that is available only in an on-premises appliance or configuration.

The bottom line: An increasing amount of spending on enabling physical and operations infrastructure is likely to migrate to the cloud, both in percentage and in absolute terms. However, it is likely to be balanced by continued consumer and enterprise spending, with network service providers helping connect the players. Hardware and software companies selling into this environment will see their proportion of sales shift.

Standards, APIs, Certification, and Rating Agencies

Commodities exchanges and government agencies have rigorous standards defining what can be called U.S. No. 2 Yellow Corn or West Texas Intermediate Crude. Accounting has standards such as generally accepted accounting principles (GAAP) and the International Financial Reporting Standards (IFRS). Appliances have bodies such as Underwriters Laboratories and Consumers Union, publishers of *Consumer Reports*. Robert Parker gives scores to wine and Morningstar to mutual funds. Similarly, in the cloud, the evolution of both standards bodies and objective third-party ratings agencies can be expected.

According to Steve Diamond, chair of the Cloud Computing Initiative of the Institute of Electrical and Electronics Engineers (IEEE), the evolution of the cloud—including the emergence of the Intercloud—will require a variety of roles, such as exchanges to handle commercial relationships and gateways to translate data, and thus a variety of standards in areas such as protocols, formats, processes, practices, and governance. Diamond counted dozens of active cloud standards programs in organizations such as the IEEE, the U.S. National Institute of Standards and Technology, and others.[42]

Technical performance benchmarks are nothing new: The Transaction Processing Performance Council (TPC) is a body whose mission is to "disseminate objective, verifiable . . . performance data."[43] It is likely that either an industry-funded entity, such as TPC, or a completely independent group, equivalent to Consumers Union, will arise. In any event, sharing of experiences, either verbally or through forums similar to Epinions.com, will help customers assess price–quality trade-offs. Agents that audit and certify compliance inhabit a space somewhere in between standards bodies and rating organizations.

One area of some standardization is the application programming interface (API). Marten Mickos is CEO of Eucalyptus, a company offering an open source version of software that is compatible with Amazon Web Services APIs, enabling companies to build private clouds with similar functionality. This position corresponds to his former one as CEO of MySQL, which offered an open source database. He cautioned, however, that as much as the cost structure of the open source model would theoretically cause it to become a market share leader, computing industry history suggests that the most likely scenario, given enterprise buying behavior, is for open source to coexist with legacy and proprietary software.[44]

Lew Moorman, president of Rackspace's cloud business, observed that an API is more than just an interface but a "window into underlying technology."[45] In other words, a car steering wheel is not just a rotary interface for controlling direction but requires some physical embodiment—tires, rack and pinion, and so forth. Although a different mechanism may implement the API, there must be *some* embodiment of the functionality, and it must behave the same way. Therefore, a cloud service provider must consider the API, its implementation, and the performance characteristics of the technology behind it: availability, response time, scalability. The implication is that API standardization will not commoditize the market, any more than standard placement and use of the brake pedal, accelerator, and steering wheel cause all cars to be priced the same.

Price competition for compute cycles, storage, and networking ultimately will put pressure on price points for a nontrivial percentage of cloud services, particularly at the infrastructure layer, but even at the application layer. This competition in turn is likely to drive adoption of a variety of open source elements, from Web servers such as Apache, to infrastructure stacks such as OpenStack, CloudStack, and Eucalyptus to open source applications. Thus, an ecosystem niche will be created for consulting, design, implementation, and support, representing not just a single open source stack but offering a portfolio of open source options, such as in Cloudscaling's business model.[46]

If APIs are uniform across providers, the basis of competition shifts to the performance and reliability of the underlying systems implementing those APIs, which in turn *might* drive commoditization.

Commoditization or Innovation?

There are divergent views concerning the extent to which there is and will be commoditization in the cloud.

Leading Edge Forum's Simon Wardley is perhaps the best-known proponent of the view that the cloud is the result of the inevitable commoditization of discrete IT activities. According to Wardley, this process is inexorably driven by customer demand which drives ubiquity in conjunction with provider competition which causes convergence. In a counterpoint to the Pine and Gilmore view that the world begins with commodities and successively evolves to products, services, and experiences, in Wardley's view, the life cycle begins with a one-off innovation, followed by custom-built and then increasingly standardized products. After this, products become commoditized and ultimately may be provided as a utility service. Wardley drew an analogy with electricity, where the original innovation has evolved to a ubiquitous, undifferentiated, commodity service. Similarly, he argued, since the early innovations in computing, we have now moved into the era of commodity computing services.[47] A cadence of price cuts among leading providers, some of which are operating with thin margins, lends credence to Wardley's view.[48]

Wardley may be correct, although such an outcome would be disappointing for cloud service providers hoping to maintain margins. However, there are alternate lenses with which to see through the haze of the cloud. Paul Strebel, of the International Institute for Management Development, a business school in Lausanne, has argued that most industries progress in an alternating cycle of competing through differentiation and competing on cost: Michael Porter's classic competitive strategies. Over time, greater and greater value gets delivered at lower and lower cost. Strebel recounted the evolution of the PC industry: a period of innovation and development leading to early devices, such as the Apple II, followed by a period of standardization and cost reduction, the IBM PC and clones. Then a new period of "rejuvenation" led to differentiation in the second-generation PCs, followed by standardization and cost reduction via the PC clones. Then another period of rejuvenation—with the development of laptops and workstations—was followed by a period of standardization and cost reduction, also known as commoditization.[49] Although Strebel's book was written years ago, it correctly characterizes recent developments, where the laptop was impacted by the netbook, and both were in turn disrupted by the smartphone and the tablet.

Strebel argued that all markets do not necessarily follow a perfect, alternating path: Some—such as the fashion business—have multiple waves of rejuvenation; others have multiple waves of cost reduction as sequential process technology innovations occur.

Moreover, it can be argued that commoditization is often a failure of the imagination rather than an inexorable characteristic of the market. For example, consider water. There could be no bigger commodity than water: It covers two thirds of the earth's surface, falls for free from the sky, and is available as a utility everywhere that you, as a reader of this book, are likely to be, even in mundane locations such as, say, Dandridge, Tennessee.

But Dandridge, Tennessee, happens to be the source of Bling H2O, regularly priced at $40 per bottle, thanks to its nine-step filtration process.[50] However, in a Swarovski encrusted bottle, it costs $2,600.[51] If that's too cheap, you can always spring for a bottle of Acqua di Cristallo Tributo a Modigliani for $60,000. It includes Icelandic glacier water in a 24-karat gold bottle.[52]

The other third of the earth's surface is covered with rocks. Yet Gary Dahl became a millionaire in a few months by selling rocks costing pennies, packaged as "Pet Rocks," for almost $4 each.[53]

Turning to service providers, in the hotel business, we find Motel 6 and Holiday Inn, but there are also high-end chains, such as the Four Seasons, the Mandarin Oriental, and the Ritz-Carlton. In transportation, there is Yellow Cab but also Boston Coach. Just as Porter posited, there is competition on price and competition on features, in a broad range of service provider industries.

In the cloud computing business, some—maybe even a lot—of the industry will resemble Motel 6, which claims "the lowest price of any national chain." There will always be a segment that wants a decent room—or virtual machine—at a good price. But I believe that there are plenty of opportunities for differentiated offers to co-exist in the business. Restaurants offer tap water and Perrier, General Motors offers Chevy and Cadillac, and InterContinental Hotels Group owns both the Holiday Inn Express in Paris, Texas, and the InterContinental Paris–Le Grand, in Paris, France. The cloud market is large enough to usefully segment, and there is room for different offers at different price points—as part of a portfolio or for price discrimination—from the same company.

The Marriott Marquis offers an unparalleled location, only seconds away from New York's Times Square. The New York Stock Exchange's Capital Markets Community Cloud offers a similarly excellent location, only 70 microseconds away from the trading systems of the NYSE. Other locations can offer reduced latency for increased performance and user experience related to interactive applications. Being on high-bandwidth metro rings will enable customers to cloudburst—leverage temporary cloud capacity when needed—cost effectively and companies, such as those in media and entertainment, to move or access enormous data sets associated with the production of today's movies. Different brands already own positions in customers' minds around performance, cost, carrier neutrality, innovation, business orientation, or billing relationships.

And while there is no doubt that cutthroat price competition is here to stay for many classes of cloud services offers, it is also likely that established players will continue to innovate, new entrants will continue to disrupt, and all will attempt to differentiate, not necessarily by lowest cost. In Sweden, data centers are being cooled by water, thus heating the water which then may be used to heat buildings; other data centers are innovating new cooling systems; still others are doing without cooling. New breakthroughs seem to arrive every day, such as HP's memristor, Intel's Tri-Gate 3-D transistor, Infinera's photonic integrated circuits, Calient's micro-electro-mechanical adaptive photonic switching, and coherent fiber transmission technology that will raise top speeds from today's 40-gigabit-per-second systems to speeds of 100 gig, 400 gig, and even 1 terabit per second.[54]

Unusual phenomena, such as quantum entanglement, and inexplicable observations—perhaps but not definitively due to experimental error—such as faster-than-light neutrinos could drive unprecedented paradigm shifts and enable new technologies.[55]

Potential disruptions such as cloud mainframes, clouds based on graphics processing units, low-power architectures, innovative water-cooling technologies, quantum computing, or unique encryption approaches, such as homomorphic encryption, quantum encryption, and random thermal encryption, and even a quantum Internet, will create new markets for those best able to leverage them.[56]

These technologies, in turn, will enable new solutions. To Russ Daniels, former HP Cloud Services and Enterprise Services CTO, the cloud is not just a delivery model but a means of tackling problems—leveraging geolocation, big data analytics, elastic capacity, distributed intelligence, and real-time feedback loops—beyond the limits of traditional technical and economic approaches.[57]

Mark Thiele, executive vice president of data center firm Switch and president and cofounder of Data Center Pulse, has argued that there are boundless opportunities for innovation and thus decommoditization whether in the physical facility itself, the computing infrastructure, or up through the application layer. He sees new technologies every day—better ways to streamline the input/output path for storage, flatter networks, OpenFlow,[58] virtualized switching, security and firewalls, automated deployment of machines—with no end in sight. Farther up the stack, Thiele observed that IT is like a painter's palette: Every new painting is different, even when it is the same painter with the same palette.[59]

James Urquhart is vice president of product strategy at fast-growing enterprise cloud management firm enStratus and author of popular cloud blogs for CNET and GigaOM.com. For Urquhart, the cloud is a complex adaptive system, exhibiting unpredictable, emergent behavior as its components interact and evolve. Random mutations and fitness determine success and survivorship to the next generation. And he pointed out that in the world of IT, the agent of learning or change is the engineer, software developer, or systems administrator. The most successful cloud computing technologists make systems stronger over time; they are constantly assessing the health, efficiency, and effectiveness of the elements in their control and making adjustments to the code, data, configuration, policy, and automation of those systems to protect against what they can't control.[60]

This view could be expanded to encompass all the interacting agents that are contributing to this maelstrom of innovation and adaptation: pure and applied research scientists, engineers, software developers, operations personnel, strategists, marketers, and users, all collaborating—intentionally or not—at an accelerating pace.

IT is a general-purpose technology and thus can be used for mundane tasks, such as calculating tax withholding on paychecks or collecting statistics on the number of vehicles using a section of highway. At the other extreme, IT can be used to differentiate and informationalize products and services, accelerate innovation, strategically optimize core processes, and enhance customer relationships: in short, as a means of gaining competitive advantage. The subset of IT that is cloud computing can be used for mundane benefits, such as reducing the cost of IT spend. At its best, however, it is more than merely an operations or deployment strategy for IT. It is, rather, an inseparable element of a number of strategic

IT-enabled scenarios: communications, collaboration, open innovation, accelerated development of new products. Cloud computing will increasingly be a means for cost-effectively delivering unforgettable customer experiences and flattening our world to increase opportunities available to those with talent and the willingness to apply it. The cloud is increasingly the basis of social transformation and greater accountability from governments to the governed.

As much as the cloud has evolved over the past few years, it is likely to keep picking up steam. As Werner Vogels, CTO for Amazon Web Services, has reported: "Almost on a yearly basis we see 'cloud' evolving more. We definitely see customers building more and more sophisticated applications. As such it is still day one. There is a lot of work to be done."[61]

Just as real clouds continuously form, re-form, and storm, driven by forces unleashed by solar, thermal, and kinetic energy, this flood of innovation—engaged in a virtuous cycle with emerging applications solving problems in a world of accelerating complexity—is the energy source preventing the cloud computing system from descending into a static, commoditized equilibrium. The chaotic, stochastic, complex adaptive characteristics of this industry and its ambient environment suggest that we are still at the beginning of a Cambrian explosion in information technologies generally and in the cloud in particular.

The future of the cloud is sunny indeed.

💻 ONLINE

"The Market for Melons," at http://complexmodels.com/Melons.aspx, illustrates system dynamics and constant total revenue in a duopoly with one flat rate and one pay-per-use provider.

"Network Evolution," at http://complexmodels.com/Aristoframe.htm, illustrates evolution to a power-law distribution as new entrants preferentially attach to prior ones.

"Yard-Sale Simulation," at http://complexmodels.com/Trading.aspx, shows winner-take-all effects and wealth concentration after sequences of random trades.

Notes

1. Hilary Poole, *The Internet: A Historical Encyclopedia* (MTM Publishing, 2005), p. 140.
2. http://findarticles.com/p/articles/mi_m3457/is_n19_v16/ai_20766102/.

3. Kristina Shampanier, Nina Mazar, and Dan Ariely, "Zero as a Special Price: The True Value of Free Products," *Marketing Science* 26, No. 6 (2007): 742–757.
4. Yochai Benkler, *The Wealth of Networks: How Social Production Transforms Markets and Freedom* (Yale University Press, 2006).
5. Chris Anderson, "Free: Why $0.00 Is the Future of Business," *Wired* 16, No. 3 (February 2008). www.wired.com/techbiz/it/magazine/16-03/ff_free.
6. Clifford Nass, *The Man Who Lied to His Laptop* (Current, 2010).
7. Joe Weinman, "The Market for Melons: Quantity Uncertainty and the Market Mechanism," September 6, 2010. www.joeweinman.com/Resources/Joe_Weinman_The_Market_For_Melons.pdf.
8. José Fernandez and Babu Nahata, "Pay What You Like," April 2009. http://mpra.ub.uni-muenchen.de/16265/.
9. Costas Courcoubetis and Richard Weber, *Pricing Communication Networks: Economics, Technology, and Modeling* (Wiley, 2003).
10. Jeffrey K. MacKie-Mason, and Hal R. Varian, "Economic FAQs about the Internet," *Journal of Economic Perspectives* 8, No. 3 (Summer 1994): 75–96. quod.lib.umich.edu/j/jep/3336451.0001.110/1:8?rgn=div1;view=fulltext.
11. Andrew M. Odlyzko, "Paris Metro Pricing for the Internet," *Proceedings of the First ACM Conference on Electronic Commerce* (ACM Press, 1999), pp. 140–147.
12. Joe Weinman, "The Market for Melons: Quantity Uncertainty and the Market Mechanism," September 6, 2010. www.joeweinman.com/Resources/Joe_Weinman_The_Market_For_Melons.pdf.
13. Ibid.
14. Kevin C. Tofel, "AT&T: Killing Unlimited Data Doesn't Hurt Our Earnings," *GigaOM.com*, July 22, 2010. http://gigaom.com/2010/07/22/att-killing-unlimited-data-doesnt-hurt-our-earnings/.
15. Stéphane Gagnon, Véronique Nabelsi, Katia Passerini, and Kemal Cakici, "The Next Web Apps Architecture: Challenges for SaaS Vendors," *IT Pro*, September/October 2011, pp. 44–50.
16. www.arbinet.com/page.php?cid=1.
17. Reuven Cohen, conversation with the author, December 12, 2011.
18. James Mitchell, conversation with the author, January 28 2012.
19. http://aws.amazon.com/ec2/reserved-instances/.
20. Thomas Claburn, "Google Kills Buzz in Friday Product Purge," *InformationWeek*, October 14, 201, www.informationweek.com/news/development/web/231900856; Official Google Blog, "A Fall Spring Clean," September 2, 2011, http://googleblog.blogspot.com/2011/09/fall-spring-clean.html.
21. "New Services: Innovation and Future in The [*sic*] Telecommunications," www.telefonica-wholesale.com/en/pdf/datasheet_nuevos_servicios_EN.pdf.
22. http://openstack.org/.
23. www.tmforum.org/EnterpriseCloudLeadership/8009/home.html.
24. Stephen A. Roades, "The Herfindahl-Hirschman Index," *Federal Reserve Bulletin*, March 1993, 188–189.
25. U.S. Census Bureau, "American FactFinder," factfinder2.census.gov/faces/tableservices/jsf/pages/productview.xhtml?pid=ECN_2007_US_72SSSZ6&prodType=table.

26. Ibid, factfinder2.census.gov/faces/tableservices/jsf/pages/productview.xhtml?pid=
    ECN_2007_US_51SSSZ6&prodType=table.
27. Will Forrest, conversation with the author, November 3, 2011.
28. Mike Hanlon, "World Population Becomes More Urban than Rural," May 28,
    2007. www.gizmag.com/go/7334/.
29. World Bank, "More than Half the World's Population is Urban, UN Report
    Says," July 11, 2007. http://web.worldbank.org/WBSITE/EXTERNAL/TOPICS/
    EXTPOVERTY/EXTMIGDEV/0,,contentMDK:21405637~pagePK:210058~piPK:
    210062~the SitePK:2838223,00.html.
30. Brendan O'Flaherty, *City Economics* (Harvard University Press, 2005), p. 2.
31. Ibid., p. 4.
32. Katie Fehrenbacher, "The Future of the Cloud, as Seen by Cisco," *GigaOM.com*,
    June 22, 2011. http://gigaom.com/cloud/the-future-of-the-cloud-as-seen-by-cisco/.
33. "Worldwide LHC Computing Grid," http://press.web.cern.ch/public/en/LHC/
    Computing-en.html.
34. Bret Swanson, "The Coming Exaflood," *Wall Street Journal*, January 20, 2007,
    www.discovery.org/a/3869; Richard Irving, "Light at the End of the Tunnel,"
    Capacity (January 2012), online as "Fast Just Got Faster," www.capacitymagazine
    .com/Article/2936530/Fast-just-got-faster.html.
35. Albert-László Barabási, *Linked: How Everything Is Connected to Everything Else
    and What It Means* (Plume, 2003).
36. James Gleick, *Chaos: The Making of a New Science* (Viking, 1987), p. 23.
37. http://andrewmcafee.org/2011/01/jevons-computation-efficicency-hardware-
    investmen/.
38. Nicholas Carr, *The Big Switch: Rewiring the World, From Edison to Google*
    (Norton, 2008).
39. Jesse Snyder, conversation with the author, January 31, 2012.
40. Stacy Meichtry, "Man Without a Country," *WSJ Magazine*, October 2011, online
    as September 29, 2011, online.wsj.com/article/SB1000142405311190483610457 6
    556982258399652.html.
41. Vanessa Alvarez, conversation with the author, January 31, 2012.
42. Steve Diamond, conversation with the author, January 12, 2012.
43. www.tpc.org/information/about/abouttpc.asp.
44. Marten Mickos, conversation with the author, January 26, 2012.
45. Lew Moorman, conversation with the author, January 2, 2012.
46. Randy Bias, conversation with the author, December 14, 2011.
47. Simon Wardley, conversation with the author, January 26, 2012.
48. Dina Bass, "Amazon Sees Further Price Drops in Cloud, Pressuring Microsoft,"
    March 16, 2012, *Bloomberg*, www.bloomberg.com/news/2012-03-16/amazon-
    sees-further-price-drops-in-cloud-pressuring-microsoft.html.
49. Paul Strebel, *Breakpoints: How Managers Exploit Radical Business Change*
    (Harvard Business School Press, 1992).
50. http://most-expensive.net/bottled-water.
51. www.blingh2o.com/store/product_info.php?products_id=95&osCsid=ntjja4h119
    rjstn2qg1dmo8su2.
52. http://most-expensive.net/bottled-water.

53. www.time.com/time/specials/packages/article/0,28804,1947621_1947626_1947 687,00.html.

54. Irving, "Light at the End of the Tunnel."

55. Dennis Overbye, "Scientists Report Second Sighting of Faster-Than-Light Neutrinos," *New York Times*, November 18, 2011. www.nytimes.com/2011/11/ 19/science/space/neutrino-finding-is-confirmed-in-second-experiment-opera-scientists-say.html; Associated Press, "In Retest of Neutrinos' Speed, Another Challenge to Einstein Falls," *New York Times*, March 16, 2012. http://www .nytimes.com/2012/03/17/science/einstein-challenge-falls-in-retest-of-neutrinos-speed.html.

56. John Markoff, "China Has Homemade Supercomputer Gain, With Own Chips," *New York Times*, October 29, 2011. www.nytimes.com/2011/10/29/world/asia/ china-unveils-supercomputer-based-on-its-own-microprocessor-chips.html; Alex Knapp, "Lockheed Martin Installs Quantum Computer," *Forbes*, October 31, 2011. www.forbes.com/sites/alexknapp/2011/10/31/lockheed-martin-installs-quantum-computer/; Greg Taylor and George Cox, "Behind Intel's New Random-Number Generator," *IEEE Spectrum* (September 2011). spectrum.ieee.org/computing/ hardware/behind-intels-new-randomnumber-generator/0; Saswato R. Das, "Path Clears Toward a Quantum Internet," *IEEE Spectrum*, April 11, 2012. http:// spectrum.ieee.org/telecom/internet/path-clears-toward-a-quantum-internet.

57. Russ Daniels, conversation with the author, February 1, 2012.

58. www.openflow.org/.

59. Mark Thiele, conversation with the author, February 20, 2012.

60. James Urquhart, conversation with the author, January 11, 2012.

61. Janko Roettgers and Nicole Solis, "OH: Trends, Tweets and Food for Thought at Structure 2011," *GigaOM.com*, June 23, 2011. gigaom.com/cloud/structure-2011-twitter-recap/.

About the Author

Joe Weinman is currently Senior Vice President, Cloud Services and Strategy, Telx, a leading carrier-neutral colocation, data center, and cloud computing service provider. Prior to joining Telx, Weinman held executive leadership positions at Hewlett-Packard, AT&T, and Bell Laboratories.

TechTarget has named him a "Top 10 Cloud Computing Leader," GigaOM.com says he is a "deep thinker on the economics of cloud computing," George Gilder has called him a "brilliant strategist," IDG claims he is "one of the nation's leading cloud computing strategists," Search Cloud Computing has called him a "serial deep thinker" and "cloud brainiac," Light Reading says he is "undoubtedly one of the keenest cloud evangelists," and Yankee Group declares that he "has long been at the forefront of cloud computing thought leadership."

Weinman is a frequent global keynote speaker, industry and academic conference presenter, blogger, and the founder of the Cloudonomics® blog and Cloudonomics—a rigorous, multidisciplinary approach to valuing the cloud incorporating statistics, computational complexity, system dynamics, calculus, economics, and behavioral economics.

Weinman brings a wealth of experience in corporate strategy and business development, partnerships, alliances, product management and marketing, emerging technologies, and research and development.

He has been awarded 14 U.S. and international patents in diverse fields such as pseudoternary data communications, cloud services, consumer products, intelligent networks, and distributed storage architectures. His market insights have been showcased in numerous global television broadcasts and print and online publications.

Weinman received a bachelor of science in computer science from Cornell University, a master of science in computer science from the University of Wisconsin-Madison, and has completed executive education at the International Institute of Management Development in Lausanne, Switzerland.

He may be reached at joe@cloudonomics.com or on Twitter as @joeweinman.

About the Web Site

ComplexModels.com is an easy-to-use Web site accessible from any laptop, tablet, or smartphone, illustrating and quantifying the Laws of Cloudonomics. Graphical animations and Monte Carlo simulations help analyze and illustrate statistics and system dynamics of cost optimization via the cloud; the value of resource pooling; investment requirements for latency reduction; the value of demand aggregation in reduction of the coefficient of variation and utilization enhancement; network evolution through preferential attachment; translation distance for random walks; ecosystem wealth evolution to power-law and winner-take-all end-states through random trades; point-to-point distance characteristics of random graphs; and pricing model competition between pay-per-use and flat rates.

The simulation models and their results can be viewed with nothing more than a click, or with varying degrees of parameterization. For example, the utility pricing simulation allows selection of a variety of application demand profiles, including uniform demand, 9-5 workers, late night gamers, aperiodic events, cyclical and seasonal demand, and monotonic growth. A variety of metrics and cost assumptions in turn enable examination of tradeoffs among build-to-peak, fixed capacity, pure cloud, and hybrid architectures. The geographic dispersion simulation allows selection of node placement based on regular lattices, uniform, or normal distributions. Other models enable other customizations.

These models will be useful for customers considering the relevance of cloud computing from an economic and financial perspective; cloud strategists; and students and academics in a variety of fields spanning cloud computing, theoretical computer science, statistics, mathematics, business, management, and economics.

In addition, by going to www.wiley.com/go/cloudonomics (the password is weinman), you will find a bonus chapter—"The Cloud for non-IT Executives," the author demystifies the cloud for executives from other functional areas of the corporation, drawing parallels, insights, and best practices from manufacturing, distribution, finance, strategy, and human resources. For example, computing is a type of production where the raw material is data and the "information factory" uses processors instead of presses. In the same way that manufacturing has evolved from dedicated production lines to flexible manufacturing, computing has evolved from physical hardware dedicated to a single application to the flexible cloud. In both domains resources are acquired on a just-in-time basis and cross-functional, collaborative teams are erasing the boundaries between design and production operations. Finance determines the optimal balance of debt and equity; human resources structures a mix of employees, contractors, and temps; and strategy focuses on core competencies and differentiators. Similarly, IT needs to determine the correct proportion of dedicated, internal IT resources and externally sourced on-demand resources. Numerous other parallels exist, for example, the use of third parties for transport logistics—whether goods or data—and for delivery to the customer—whether retail or content delivery.

Index